The Rise and Decline
of Fidel Castro

The Rise and Decline of
FIDEL CASTRO
An Essay in Contemporary History

by Maurice Halperin

University of California Press
Berkeley / Los Angeles / London

University of California Press; Berkeley and Los Angeles, California.
University of California Press, Ltd., London, England.
Copyright © 1972, by The Regents of the University of California.
ISBN: 0-520-02182-7. Library of Congress Catalog Card Number: 77-182794.
Printed in the United States of America. Designed by Dave Comstock.

For Edith, Judith, and David

Contents

Preface

THE MAIN NARRATIVE of the present volume is concerned with the first five years (1959–1964) of Fidel Castro's regime and its external relations. This is primarily the period of the rise of Fidel Castro, although it was also the time when the seeds of decline were sown. The symbiotic relationship between rise and decline is illustrated by means of disgressions into events of the following years, when the seeds have sprouted and reveal the shape and measure of the decline.

Hopefully, this scheme offers the reader a substantial grounding in the earlier history of the Cuban Revolution and, at the same time, permits him to be abreast of developments until mid-1971, when the book was completed. A second volume, of similar design, is contemplated for the period 1964–1969, thereby completing an account of the first decade of Castro's rule.

Although the reader will become aware of the fact that the book reflects my personal experience in Cuba, as well as in the Soviet Union, it may be helpful for him to learn at the outset that I spent close to six years in Cuba (1962–1968), following a period of more than three years in the USSR.

Aside from these remarks, the book needs no further explanation. It should "explain" itself, and if it fails to do so, no extended commentary on my part concerning my aims, methods, biases, and so on will be of much value. In the writing of history, as in the exploits of gastronomy, "the proof of the pudding is in the eating."

In connection with the writing of this book, I wish to express my appreciation for the many facilities provided by Simon Fraser

University, including the outstanding services of its library and financial assistance by the President's Research Grants Committee. I am especially grateful to Dr. Robert J. C. Harper who, as head of the Department of Behavioural Sciences, not only offered indispensable shelter but also an intellectual environment thoroughly conducive to research and scholarship.

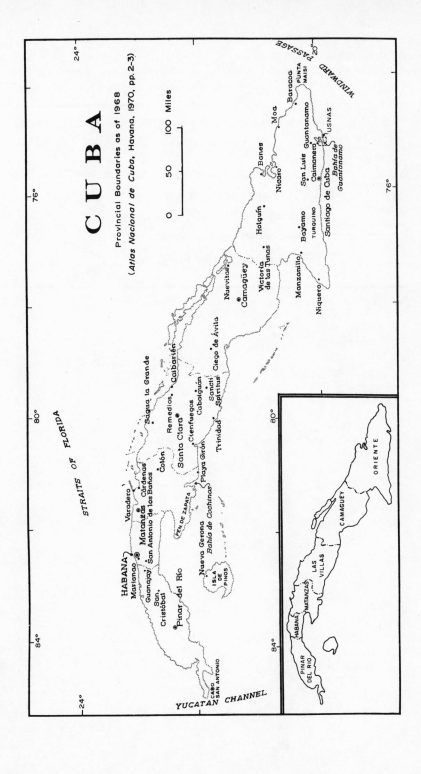

C U B A

Provincial Boundaries as of 1968

(*Atlas Nacional de Cuba*, Havana, 1970, pp. 2-3)

0   50   100 Miles

There is nothing more difficult to carry
out, nor more doubtful of success, nor
more dangerous to handle, than to initiate
a new order of things.

MACHIAVELLI, *The Prince,* 1513

1

■

The Real Revolution
and Its Roots

Fidel's Prophesy

FOR MANY MONTHS after the triumph of the Revolution on January 1, 1959, the following kind of performance would take place in Havana two, three, or even four times a week:

It was past two o'clock in the morning of April 3, 1959. Fidel Castro had been talking on television and radio for four hours and was still going strong. A half million Cubans—perhaps a million—glued to their sets would get little sleep before beginning their daily chores. Words tumbled out in an earnest, high-pitched voice as he moved back and forth over a score of topics. He spoke extemporaneously, the rambling and verbosity amply compensated by the impact that the free play of a nimble mind and ebullient personality could produce. The informality of the bearded young guerrilla leader turned statesman-in-shirt-sleeves was contagious.

Now he was winding up. Relations with the United States and charges of communism were the two most troublesome topics of the moment, and he was back on their trail. Why is *Time* magazine in a rage? he asks. Because we execute Batista's war criminals instead of shooting Communists. "But communism is only a pretext. . . . What they fear is our program for agrarian reform, . . . for economic development, . . . for economic independence." Communism? "In our cabinet we have ministers like Felipe Pazos [National Bank], López Fresquet [Finance], Regino Boti [Economy], and

Manuel Ray [Public Works]. No one can accuse them of being ultraradical." In the United States "they compare us with Guatemala [in 1954], but they are mistaken. We won't run away. If we are attacked it won't be a picnic for them." Some fainthearts warn that Cubans must respect the cold war policies of the United States, that "we exist only because the United States allows us to. . . . Well, our attitude is that we defend our own right to live and our own princi- ples. . . . This is a *real* revolution. . . . This revolution will take its place as one of the greatest political events in history!" [1]

Much of what Fidel said in these early days did not stand the test of time. Thus, in a matter of months three of the four cabinet officers held up as examples of moderation had defected; and two years later, when Fidel officially proclaimed the Revolution to be socialist and, shortly thereafter, Marxist-Leninist, there was no longer any point in refuting the charges of communism. Yet on the key issues of the Revolution—the radical transformation of Cuba's social and economic structure and the assertion of national self-determina- tion—Fidel revealed over the years a fundamental consistency of purpose. The conditions under which the implementation would take place, which in turn would affect its velocity and form, could only be matters of speculation.

One condition, however, was already clearly taking shape: a con- frontation with the United States. Fidel's acceptance of this chal- lenge was unequivocal, unwavering—and reckless. It lent credibility to the claim that he was heading Cuba into a "real revolution." Neither Fidel nor anyone else at the time could suspect that in the womb of the "real revolution" the seeds of other confrontations lay dormant, those with China and the Soviet Union.

It has been said that Fidel promised one kind of revolution and delivered another. Perhaps it would be more accurate to say that he promised two kinds of revolution, probably in good faith, but they proved to be incompatible. What he presented as a humanist design for a fundamental restructuring of Cuban society, "revolution . . . with all the freedoms," [2] broke down under the impact of pressures

1. *El Mundo*, April 3, 1959.
2. From a speech to the Shell oil workers in Havana, February 6, 1959. In that same speech: "In other revolutions throughout the course of history, revolutionary minorities, in order to manage to govern with substantial changes in the social order, have had to apply force, have

that his inexperience was unable to foresee and that his temperament in some degree provoked. The ideal revolution was destined to give way, for better or for worse, to the "real" revolution.

In the early morning hours of April 3, 1959, Fidel Castro made a remarkable prediction that any sober listener undoubtedly dismissed as the product of an overheated imagination. Yet the Cuban Revolution, generator and center of the world-shaking missile crisis, did not fall very far short of being "one of the greatest political events in history." But perhaps of more enduring significance for Cuba, a small nation submerged in the backwash of history, the Revolution lifted it into the limelight and gave it a place in the sun.

Cuba in the Context of Latin American History

Viewed against the background of Cuban history, the only thing unique about Fidel Castro's insurrection was that it succeeded. Not only the aims but also the method and, we might even go so far as to say, the style and temperament of the Fidelista uprising to a large degree were shaped by the traditions of nearly a century of frustrated struggle for national independence. In this respect, the experience of Cuba differs substantially from that of continental Latin America, a fact that helps explain why the Fidelista phenomenon appeared in Cuba rather than elsewhere.

In continental Latin America, Spanish and Portuguese colonial rule was eliminated shortly after 1820, long before a significant middle class and urban proletariat had made their appearance and long before foreign economic penetration had begun to exert pressures affecting the independence of the newly created republics. This

---

had to use terror against vested interests, have had to impose their revolutionary laws by force. We have not. . . . Regardless of how revolutionary the laws we propose to enact may be, they will be enacted without violating one single right, without suppressing even one public liberty, without beating anyone, and without even insulting anyone." (English translation of text taken from Maurice Zeitlin and Robert Scheer, *Cuba: Tragedy in Our Hemisphere* [New York: Grove, 1963], p. 78.) All of this today seems wildly implausible. No doubt political expediency was one of the motivating factors at the time, but it is safe to say not the only one. In addition to being a shrewd political practitioner, Fidel has always had sufficiently strong and genuine messianic convictions to which he could attribute, in his own mind, his political behavior.

meant that, on the one hand, notwithstanding the influence of the French and American revolutions, the dominant trend of the independence movements would be military-aristocratic rather than civil-democratic; and on the other hand, the sovereignty of the new nations would be relatively secure once they were severed from Spain and Portugal. Thus, in effect, power was transferred from Madrid and Lisbon to the native oligarchies ruling over genuinely independent states. Later, the long-established institutions of national sovereignty helped conceal the weakening of effective sovereignty as the entire region drifted into the orbit of expanding European and United States economic interests.

In Cuba, however, armed struggle against Spanish rule did not get under way until 1868. It ended thirty years later with the Spanish-American War and the occupation of Cuba by American troops. Moreover, by this time Cuba was no longer the typical Spanish colony of the early nineteenth century. In addition to the large plantations, Cuba was also a country of small farmers, urban workers, and a noteworthy intelligentsia of lawyers, doctors, scientists, writers, teachers, and students in touch with the main cultural, social, and political currents in the advanced societies of the time. Anarchist and socialist ideas, including those of Karl Marx, were not unknown,[3] which resulted in the radicalization of the Cuban independence movement. The goal was not only separation from Spain but modernization of Cuban society. Hence, in its final stage the independence struggle was also a revolutionary struggle.[4]

During the greater part of the nineteenth century, the annexa-

3. In 1892 the first workers' congress held in Cuba approved the following resolution: "The working class will not be emancipated until it embraces the ideas of revolutionary socialism . . . which cannot be an obstacle for the triumph of the independence of our country since it would be absurd if those who aspire to obtain individual liberty would oppose the collective freedom of a people." Cited by Blas Roca (pseudonym of Francisco Calderia), *Los fundamentos del socialismo en Cuba* (Havana: Ediciones Populares, 1960), p. 92. The Spanish colonial government broke up the congress and imprisoned its leaders.

4. Class conflicts were sharpened during the protracted war by the great destruction of rural property resulting in the impoverishment of small farmers, many of whom left their land and migrated to the cities. At the same time, the gradual substitution of slave labor by wage earners on the sugar plantations further dislocated the traditional social and economic structure of the island and gave rise to a rural proletariat, which added a new dimension to the turmoil of the period. See Foreign Policy

tion of Cuba either by purchase from Spain or by outright seizure had been openly discussed by responsible political leaders in the United States. Then, toward the end of the century new patterns of American economic expansion in Latin America increased the apprehension of independence-minded Cubans that freedom from Spain could be converted into one form or another of United States domination. Thus, anti-imperialism was also built into the Cuban independence movement.

Cuba, unlike Puerto Rico, escaped outright territorial annexation by the United States but obtained less than full sovereignty. The Platt Amendment, which granted the United States the right to intervene in the internal affairs of the new republic, was made a part of the Cuban Constitution of 1901 and incorporated in a permanent treaty between the United States and Cuba. At the same time, Cuba was obliged to cede a piece of its territory on a ninety-nine year lease at Guantánamo Bay, where a United States naval base was installed.

Under provisions of the Platt Amendment, American intervention took place in 1906, 1912, 1917, and 1920. In 1934, following the overthrow of the Machado dictatorship and a violent upsurge of Cuban nationalism, the United States agreed to revoke the Platt Amendment. The Guantánamo naval base, however, remained, although with the advance of military technology its strategic significance gradually disappeared. Twenty-five years later its continued presence helped Fidel Castro to mobilize Cuban patriotism behind his regime.

President Franklin Roosevelt's "good neighbor" gesture in annulling the Platt Amendment only partially relieved the sources of friction between the two countries, because by this time great American investments and a trade treaty binding Cuba to the American market, although by no means wholly disadvantageous to Cuba, had substantially reduced the substance of Cuban sovereignty. Leland Jenks, writing in 1928, with some justice entitled his now classical study of Cuban-American relations *Our Cuban Colony*.

Although among the Spanish-speaking republics Cuba had achieved a higher level of economic development and per capita income than most, nowhere in contemporary Latin America was a

---

Association, Commission on Cuban Affairs, *Problems of the New Cuba* (New York: Foreign Policy Association, 1935) and Julio Le Riverend, *Historia económica de Cuba* (Havana: Escuela de Comercio Exterior, 1963).

better breeding ground for nationalism, radicalism, and anti-imperialism created than in Cuba.

José Martí and Fidel Castro

The great leader of Cuban independence, the "Apostle of Liberty," was José Martí (1853–1895), an extraordinary individual whose role in Cuban history combined those of Washington, Jefferson, Lincoln, and Walt Whitman in American history. Poet, philosopher, soldier, patriot, and martyr—his voluminious writings, his selfless dedication to a great cause, and the hint of folly that ennobled his genius nourished the minds and hearts of succeeding generations of Cuban rebels.

Martí was a rare phenomenon, an explosion of the accumulated frustration of a nationalism that had come to envisage more than freedom from Spain. "Cuba must be free from Spain and the United States" is the message Martí constantly repeated, in prose and in verse. His strictures on the pitfalls of a sugar-based economy and the domination of trade by a single country were prophetic: "The day when a people entrusts its livelihood to a single product, it commits suicide. . . . The excessive influence exerted on a nation when it trades with a single country is converted into political dependency. . . . A people that wants to die sells to a single country." [5]

Many years later Fidel Castro had to face these problems in unexpected ways. Sugar, the single product, remained the pillar and the bane of the new socialist economy. When trade with one "single country"—the United States—ended, Fidel discovered that he had to cope with the problem of political dependency on another single country—the Soviet Union—which took its place.

Martí's social views were equally provocative. Since slavery had recently been abolished in Cuba,[6] he leveled his attack against racial discrimination, which he called "a sin against humanity." The working class had his full support: "We live in a period of struggle between capitalists and workers. . . . In our country of workers, a militant alliance of workers will be a tremendous event. They are

5. The quotations of Martí in this section are from Oscar Pino-Santos, *Historia de Cuba* (Havana: Editora Universitaria, 1964), pp. 218–222.

6. The emancipation law was enacted in 1880 ending slavery six years later.

even now creating it. Their struggle will stir up and shake the universe." For Martí, capitalism already meant monopoly "seated like an implacable giant at the doorstep of the poor. . . . As for me, I wish to cast my lot with the poor of our land." Concerning Karl Marx, with whose works he had only a nodding acquaintance, Martí said when informed of his death, "Since he placed himself on the side of the poor, he deserves to be honored."

Martí, the father of his country, was a poet of genuine distinction and one of the great prose stylists writing in the Spanish language. This rare circumstance undoubtedly explains something of his impact on succeeding generations. The phrasing of his ideas stirred not only the intellect but also the imagination. The passion of his conviction glowed with the boldness of his metaphors. With the deeds of a patriot Martí transmitted the dream of a poet.

As for his deeds, Martí was a sixteen-year-old student when he began his revolutionary career. He spent many years in exile, the last of them in the United States, where with the funds collected among tobacco workers and other Cuban sympathizers he purchased small boats and arms for an invasion of the island. He landed on the southern coast of Oriente Province, near the eastern extremity of Cuba. Five weeks later he was killed in battle, at the age of forty-two.

The tradition of youthful rebellion culminating in an invasion-insurrection was older than Martí, who in turn transmitted it to future Cuban revolutionaries, among them Fidel Castro. Fidel was also a student when he began his career as a political agitator. He prepared an armed invasion while in exile, part of which he spent in the United States raising funds among resident Cubans. His expedition landed on the southern coast of Oriente Province. That he did not become a martyr was a miracle. Fidel did not fall into this pattern by accident; he was directly influenced by Martí. Thus, on November 1, 1955, speaking to eight hundred Cubans at a fund-raising meeting in New York, Fidel reminded his listeners that in asking for financial support "we are doing what the apostle taught us to do when he was in a similar situation." Again recalling Martí, he declared in a dramatic flourish, "I can inform you in all sincerity that in 1956 we shall be free or we shall be martyrs." [7]

7. From an eyewitness account of the meeting in *Bohemia*, Havana, November 6, 1955.

Antonio Guiteras, Precursor of Fidel Castro

The immediate precursor of Fidel Castro was Antonio Guiteras (1906–1935), who was a spiritual descendant of José Martí. An uncle of Guiteras had also attempted an armed invasion of the island during the independence war, but was caught by the Spaniards before he landed and immediately executed. Guiteras, like Martí before him and Castro after him, was not a Cuban of pure old stock. Both of Martí's parents had emigrated from Spain. Guiteras was born in Philadelphia of an Irish-American mother. Castro is the son of a Spanish immigrant father. One is tempted to find significance in this demographic coincidence. As a matter of fact, excepting Argentina, Uruguay, and Chile, Cuba is the only Spanish-American country in which an important European immigration occurred in the nineteenth and twentieth centuries. Since the great bulk of Cuban immigration was Spanish, assimilation was rapid.[8]

The children of Spanish immigrants were not only Cuban born, they were completely absorbed in the mainstream of Cuban culture. At the same time, it would appear they injected into this stream a tendency toward mobility, enterprise, and nonconformity inherited from their immigrant origins. Of the persons who played—and are still playing—a leading role in Fidel Castro's Revolution, a surprising number are wholly or in part first generation Cubans.

Antonio Guiteras, whose Cuban father returned to the island with his family in 1912, was a high school student when he began his revolutionary activities. These were intensified after 1925, when Gerardo Machado y Morales, an uncommonly brutal despot with good connections in Washington, took power. During the early 1930s, when the world depression sent sugar prices to their lowest levels in history, Cuba began to move toward a great social and political upheaval that came close to accomplishing what Fidel Castro succeeded in doing more than a score of years later.

In 1933 Antonio Guiteras, by now an experienced activist with a prison record, responded to the mounting crisis in the old-fashioned Cuban manner—armed struggle. Leading a small group of young rebels, on April 29 he assaulted and captured the army barracks at San Luis, a town situated at the edge of the Sierra Maestra moun-

8. There was also a sizable inflow of Haitians, Jamaicans, and Chinese and to a lesser extent, after World War I, of East European Jews.

tains close to Santiago, Cuba's second largest city. San Luis was less than twenty miles away from the spot where José Martí was killed in battle thirty-seven years earlier. Guiteras held the town for several hours, then retreated to the hills where for several weeks he fought off Machado's troops in a series of guerrilla engagements before he was captured and sent to prison in Santiago.

A similar exploit took place some twenty years later when Fidel Castro, on July 26, 1953, headed an attack on the Moncada barracks in the center of Santiago. The coincidence was even closer: Guiteras had planned a simultaneous attack on Moncada, which did not occur. Fidel failed to take Moncada. Imprisoned and then exiled, he returned at the end of 1956 with a boatload of armed rebels to continue the struggle in the same general area where Guiteras fought his short war against the Machado regime.

Early in August 1933, after United States Ambassador Sumner Welles, in the face of imminent chaos, persuaded Machado to turn power over to a reliable dummy and flee the country, Guiteras emerged as the head of a strong revolutionary movement in Oriente Province and a vociferous critic of the Welles intervention. On September 4, 1933, a sergeants' revolt headed by the later malodorous Fulgencio Batista toppled Mr. Welles' government. Ten days later, with the militant support of Havana's radical student movement, Grau San Martín, a liberal professor at the university's medical school, was installed as provisional president of Cuba.

With this turn of events, Guiteras was summoned from Oriente to become minister of the interior, war, and navy, the key post in the new government. On taking office, in the shadow of American warships deployed just outside Havana harbor, Guiteras declared what no Cuban cabinet member had ever said aloud before and none would say after him until Fidel was in power: "No movement in Cuba can be revolutionary unless it is anti-imperialist. One can serve either imperialism or the people; their interests are incompatible." [9] In the five months that the Grau San Martín government existed (it was not recognized by Washington), Guiteras pushed through a series of radical reforms and made history by placing the American-owned electric power company under government control and drastically lowering consumer rates. On August 6, 1960,

9. Cited by Pedro Luis Padrón, "Guiteras," *Granma Weekly Review*, May 19, 1968.

twenty-five years after the death of Guiteras, the Castro government nationalized the company and renamed it after Antonio Guiteras.

On January 15, 1934, the now Colonel Batista, who after the sergeants' revolt had remained in control of the army, overthrew the Grau San Martín government with the connivance of the United States State Department.[10] Guiteras, with a price on his head, went into hiding and organized an underground paramilitary force which at the height of its strength had over six hundred members. Among their exploits was the spectacular kidnapping of a leading Havana tycoon, by which they succeeded in obtaining a cash ransom of $600,000. This was the war chest that was to finance a coordinated invasion and insurrection, an event that because of a number of accidents never took place.

Severely injured during a chase by the police, Guiteras was persuaded to seek asylum in Mexico, where he would complete the preparations for an invasion of the island. On May 8, 1935, as he was waiting for a small skiff that was to take him to safety, he was shot down in an exchange of gunfire with Batista's police, the victim of an informer. He had not yet reached his twenty-ninth birthday.

The Program of Antonio Guiteras in 1934

A comparison between the revolutionary programs of Guiteras' movement in 1934 and of Castro's in 1953 reveals a striking resemblance in purpose and motivation despite differences in detail and style. The former was published as a pamphlet entitled *Joven Cuba*,[11] the name taken by the organization Guiteras set up when he went underground. Fidel Castro made his pronouncement orally at his trial on October 16, 1953, following the Moncada defeat. Soon after, he

10. There was considerable pressure in Washington for direct U.S. military intervention, still legally permissible under the provisions of the Platt Amendment. However, with the recent inauguration of the "good neighbor" policy and with strong counterpressure coming from the governments of Argentina, Brazil, Chile, and especially Mexico, President Franklin Roosevelt ruled against it, wisely as it turned out; for the same objective was achieved by other means. Twenty-seven years later, President Kennedy's management of a similar problem was far less skillfull.

11. [Young Cuba] Havana, 1934, 30 pages. The text was drafted by a committee headed by José Miguel Irissari, a lawyer who played an important part in setting up the Grau San Martín government in the fall of 1933.

prepared a written version that was circulated under the title of *La historia me absolverá* [History will absolve me].

As a movement, Young Cuba disintegrated after the death of Guiteras, but the fame of the young martyr was very much alive among the restless youth of Fidel's generation, and particularly in Fidel's native province of Oriente where the capture of the San Luis barracks had become part of regional folklore. Thus, in a brief manifesto that was to be released in the event of success in the attack on Moncada, Fidel included the Young Cuba program along with the ideas of Martí as the source of his inspiration.[12] Evidently, Fidel's *La historia me absolverá* was directly influenced by his knowledge of the Guiteras pamphlet. Nevertheless, each document reflects a different period in Cuban history, as well as the particular circumstances under which they were produced.

Guiteras was operating as an underground leader when Cuba was in the midst of a revolutionary crisis. His program was formulated in sharp, concise terms. Nationalism, anti-imperialism, and socialism were its explicit objectives:

> Cuba contains all the elements that are indispensable for nationhood: physical unity, demographic unity, unity in its traditions and history. . . . Yet Cuba has still not become a nation. . . . It is still a *colonial territory* whose economic structure is controlled by foreign capital.
>
> We subscribe to anti-imperialism as an essential part of our credo since we propose to establish a genuinely Cuban foreign and domestic policy.
>
> For a Cuban nation to achieve a stable existence, the Cuban state must adopt a structure that conforms to the postulates of socialism.

The model, however, was not Marxist-Leninist socialism.

From these general principles a whole series of specific measures to be taken was proposed, including the abolition of the "current prostitution of foreign policy"; "confiscation of properties obtained by the use of illegal political influence"; recognition that "property is

12. According to K. S. Karol (*Les guérilleros au pouvoir* [Paris: Robert Laffont, 1970], p. 163), who was shown the manifesto in the Havana revolutionary archives. It is entitled "Manifiesto a la nación de los asaltantes al cuartel Moncada."

not an absolute right but a social function as a result of which the orientation of the economy will be frankly national." This in turn leads to the "nationalization of subsoil rights" and of "public services"; "agrarian reform," which includes "expropriation of large estates when the public interest or social necessity so requires"; "the creation of agricultural cooperatives" supplied with adequate credit; and the setting up of an agrarian institute with jurisdiction over these matters.

Many other proposals dealing with questions of industrialization, labor, housing, and public health were included. Nevertheless, these samples are sufficient to give the tenor of the Guiteras program and to show how closely it foreshadows Fidel Castro's 1953 pronouncement and, even more faithfully, what took place after the first of January 1959; for in 1953 Fidel did not spell out the specifics of many measures he was to take when he assumed power.

There is another point in Antonio Guiteras' program that needs to be mentioned. In the section on foreign policy, he proposed "the immediate convocation of the 'Parliament of [Latin] America' to be made up of the representatives of producers', employees', workers', and professional organizations of all the countries of [Latin] America." This plank in the program was based on a long historical tradition. Ever since the early nineteenth century, when the struggle for independence got under way, the radicals of Spanish America developed a cultural and spiritual kinship that frequently took the form of joint political and military involvement in the unending battle against local tyrants and intervention by European powers and the United States.

Thus, much in the spirit that moved Lafayette and Pulaski to fight in the American Revolution, dozens of volunteers from various Latin American countries fought alongside the Cubans over the long years of the island's struggle against Spain. And many radicals, José Martí among them, actively espoused the idea that Latin America in its culture and traditions was a single nation and should therefore become a single political unit. For Martí, as for Guiteras and later Castro, this was not only idealism but also a practical means of resisting encroachment by the United States. When Fidel Castro, after taking power, gave prime importance to Cuba's relations with Latin America, there was already a long tradition behind him, rooted in political realism although largely phrased in idealistic terms.

The Program of Fidel Castro 1953

Fidel Castro's *History Will Absolve Me* [13]—appropriate selections of which in time every Cuban schoolchild would read much as American schoolchildren read Lincoln's Gettysburg Address—appeared at a low point in Cuban revolutionary activity. Early in 1952 an electoral campaign was under way that raised some hope that an honest government, responsive to popular pressures for social and economic reform, would be voted into power. These hopes were laid to rest on March 10, 1952, shortly before the elections were to take place, by one of the presidential candidates, the one-time sergeant and later colonel and president, Fulgencio Batista, who seized the government in a military coup d'etat.

It was an easy, bloodless affair. The Prío Socorrás regime, which he overthrew, was too corrupt to rally any support. The new Batista government was quickly recognized by Washington. The economic situation by Cuban standards was tolerably fair. A general apathy set in among most of the Cuban population, only moderately stirred in late July 1953 by Fidel's attack on Moncada and the torture and slaughter of scores of prisoners taken after the defeat.

Fidel by the merest chance was not killed after his capture. He was tried, convicted, and given a long prison sentence which was later commuted. In his cell on the Isle of Pines, he prepared a written version of the defense argument he presented to the court during his trial. In due time the text was smuggled out of prison. Already planning the next phase of his revolutionary career—if and when he would be released—he took the long and broad view. Thus, *History Will Absolve Me* avoids terminology that would restrict its appeal since, with the exception of those with vested interests in the Batista dictatorship, it was aimed at arousing the great majority of the population from its mood of pessimism.

"When we speak of the people," the document declares, "we do not mean the conservative elements . . . who welcome any regime of oppression, any dictatorship. . . . The people we counted on in our struggle were these: 700,000 Cubans without work, . . . 500,000 farm laborers, . . . 400,000 industrial workers, . . . 100,000 small farmers, . . . 30,000 teachers and professors, . . . 20,000 small busi-

13. Quotations below are taken from the English edition published in Havana in 1967; 161 pages.

ness men, . . . 10,000 young professionals. . . . These are the people, the ones who know misfortune and are therefore capable of fighting courageously." Five "revolutionary laws" were offered as immediate reforms:

1. Restoration of the Constitution of 1940 (a confused liberal-radical document more honored in the breach than the observance and never reinstated by Fidel or replaced by another constitution) "until such time as the people should decide to modify or change it."

2. Full ownership of small farms worked by tenants, share-croppers, and squatters.

3. The right of workers and employees "to share 30 percent of the profits of all large industrial, mercantile, and mining enterprises, as well as sugar mills."

4. The right of agricultural workers on sugar plantations "to share 55 percent of the value of sugarcane produced."

5. Confiscation of "all property and wealth secured through politically protected fraud and graft during previous regimes."

Then would come "another series of . . . fundamental measures" such as agrarian reform, educational reform, and nationalization of public utilities (American owned). Also, there are references to housing and public health deficiencies and the need for industrialization and technical progress in order to overcome "the ruinous competition" by imports from Europe and the United States.

At the same time, the document rejected the "absolute freedom of enterprise, guarantees to investment capital and the law of supply and demand" as guiding principles for the solution of Cuba's economic problems; it pointedly noted that "more than half of the most productive land belongs to foreigners," specifically singling out the United Fruit Company in this connection.

Finally, there was the promise that "Cuba's policy in the Americas [Latin America] would be one of close solidarity with the democratic peoples of this continent, and that those politically persecuted by bloody tyrants oppressing our sister nations would find generous asylum, brotherhood and bread in the land of Martí; not the persecution, hunger, and treason they find today. Cuba should be the bulwark of liberty and not a shameful link in the chain of despotism."

It is evident that there are highly significant areas of general agreement in the Castro and Guiteras pronouncements, as well as a similarity in many concrete proposals. At the same time, unlike the *Joven Cuba* program, Castro does not present his aims as stemming from any identified ideological conceptions; in fact, the words "nationalism," "anti-imperialism," and "socialism" are nowhere to be found in *History Will Absolve Me*. Nevertheless, Fidel's nationalist, anti-imperialist, and "socialistic" frame of mind is not concealed. Anyone who could have remembered the text of *Joven Cuba* would have had no difficulty in concluding that, if Fidel Castro ever got loose, the ghost of Antonio Guiteras would walk beside him.

Nationalism and Communism

A final matter of historical interest requiring an explanation concerns the relations between Antonio Guiteras and Cuba's Communist party, since in some important respects the relations between Fidel Castro and the party fell into similar patterns.

The Communist party of Cuba was organized in 1925 and in the following decade developed considerable strength among urban and rural wage earners, students, and intellectuals. In the then prevailing revolutionary climate, Marxist ideas could be sown in fertile soil. In fact, few radicals outside the party were not affected by some of the views it propagated. At the same time, the party's tactics conformed closely to the prevailing inflexible norms of the Comintern in this pre–Popular-Front era. This prevented any effective cooperation with independent radicals like Guiteras or with the heterogeneous Grau San Martín government despite the fact that it was the first Cuban government that was set up without permission from Washington.

For the party, the collapse of Guiteras' military uprising in Oriente Province confirmed (as did later the early reverses of Castro) its firmly held theoretical conviction that this type of insurrection was useless. At the same time, it failed to take into account that the insurrection had transformed Guiteras from an obscure conspirator into a popular hero.

Later, when Guiteras joined the Grau San Martín cabinet, there was considerably more friction than harmony in his relations with the party. In general terms, what appeared to separate Guiteras and the Communist party, despite a similarity of views on a number of important issues of the day, might be expressed as follows: Guiteras was ideologically and temperamentally rooted in Cuba's national revolutionary tradition; the Communist party was primarily oriented by an international revolutionary theory and practice, as interpreted by Stalin's Comintern. At one point during his period as minister of the interior, war, and navy, Guiteras approached the party, as the only important organization he felt could be relied on to remain firmly anti-imperialist, to obtain help in organizing a workers' militia to meet the inevitable counterrevolutionary challenge of Batista's army and the American embassy. The Communists turned him down.[14]

Not long after taking power, Fidel Castro also sought the help of Communists at home and abroad. They appeared to be among the few reliable and available allies on whom he could depend. In due time, the same kind of issues that had earlier separated Guiteras and the Communists came to the surface. Fidel dismantled the old Communist party, created his own Communist party, and declared his political and ideological independence from foreign Communists. It was, however, more difficult to maintain his independence than he imagined, as he later discovered.

14. The biography of Antonio Guiteras and a serious analysis of his role in Cuban history remains to be written. The brief sketch presented here is based on scattered and scanty printed material, supplemented by interviews in early 1968 in Havana with his sister Calixta Guiteras (who made available her copy of *Joven Cuba*) and with José Miguel Irissari, who collaborated with him in 1933–1934. After 1960, when the writing and rewriting of Cuban history largely fell into the hands of the "old" Communists and their disciples, Guiteras was relegated to the role of a minor martyr in the revolutionary hagiography. However, with the advent of the new Fidelista Communist party, the memory of Antonio Guiteras has been in the process of being fully restored.

2

■

The Opening Challenge

"Cuba's Good Fortune"

IN LATE FEBRUARY 1957 Fidel Castro was interviewed by Herbert Matthews of the *New York Times* at a remarkable meeting in the wilderness of the Sierra Maestra. It was Matthews who first provided Cuba and the world with solid evidence that Fidel was alive and kicking after the catastrophic invasion landing of the *Granma* on December 2, 1956, which only a handful of the eighty-two men aboard survived.[1] Matthews wrote, "The 26th of July Movement talks of nationalism, anti-colonialism, anti-imperialism. I asked Señor Castro about that. He answered: 'You can be sure we have no animosity toward the United States and the American people.'"[2] This was his first foreign policy statement after taking up arms. It was a prudent statement and less than candid, which was revealed the day after he came to power.

Batista flew off before dawn on January 1, 1959. Camilo Cienfuegos and Che Guevara, with a few hundred bedraggled and bearded fighters, marched into Havana on January 3 in the midst of a pande-

1. The number of survivors most often cited is twelve, but it seems to be a mythical figure, perhaps adopted because it corresponds to the number of apostles of Jesus Christ, a coincidence that would impress many Cubans. The figure has never been authenticated, and Fidel from time to time uses other figures. In a speech on April 19, 1971, for example, he said that the struggle was begun "by the insignificant figure of seven armed men who had become reunited at the end of December, following the set-backs suffered at the beginning of the month." *Granma Weekly Review*, May 2, 1971.

2. *New York Times*, February 24, 1957.

monium of joy and celebration of practically the entire population of the capital.

Meanwhile, Fidel came down from the mountains and made a triumphal entry into nearby Santiago, some 500 miles to the east of Havana. Here, on January 2, he made his first postrevolutionary pronouncement and inaugurated his system of "direct government." From then on, he would converse with the masses in an incessant flow of extemporaneous and voluminous discourses. It was a system admirably suited to his temperament and his virtuosity, as well as to Cuba's splendid outdoor climate, the versatile syntax of the Spanish language, and the traditional Latin esteem for spoken rhetoric. With a national hookup of radio and television, he would soon be able to project his words and personality to the far corners of the island.

On this momentous day in Santiago, his speech contained what was in effect a foreign policy declaration and, in the context of the occasion, a significant statement. "This time," he declared, "it is Cuba's good fortune that the Revolution will really, take power. It will not be as in '98 when the Americans arrived, took control of the situation, intervened at the last moment, and then would not even permit Calixto García, who had been fighting [for Cuban independence] for thirty years, to enter Santiago." [3]

This was, in fact, what happened in 1898. General García had bottled up Santiago and protected the landing of the Americans. When the Spaniards surrendered the city, the Americans marched in and prevented the Cubans from entering. For the Cubans it was an act of betrayal compounded with insult, and the memory of it had not faded, especially in Santiago.

Here was Fidel with his soldiers, the descendants of Calixto, in Santiago, and he gave it effective symbolic meaning. The presence of Camilo and Che in Havana would mark the transfer of power to the Revolution; but he, Fidel, the supreme commander, would first declare the independence of Cuba in the city where it would have been proclaimed by Calixto but for the American intervention.

If not a challenge, it was at least a warning to the United States and by ordinary standards would appear to be premature. True, any satellite, of any great power, that aspires to assert its sovereignty sooner or later runs the almost certain risk of colliding with the great power; but the circumstances and the costs of the collision are not

3. *Noticias de Hoy*, January 6, 1959; generally known as *Hoy*.

predetermined. Hence, why the haste? Why look for trouble before there was any? Prudence alone would dictate verbal restraint on so dangerous an issue.

The explanation lies in the singular character of the Cuban Revolution, which is another way of saying the character of Fidel Castro; for it must be clearly understood that his personality, style, and leadership have dominated the Cuban Revolution as profoundly as Louis XIV molded the destiny of seventeenth-century France. In this sense he is Fidel I, and his Cuba can as well be described as a socialist monarchy as by any other nomenclature. Here the analogy with Louis XIV largely ends. The Fidelista style is the product of shrewd calculation and reckless plunging, of a disarming informality and a compulsive idealism, of an impish sense of humor and a great reservoir of personal courage, of an intense patriotism and an irrepressible urge to make history, and above all of a supreme confidence in one's own judgment.

Thus, to untangle the moods and motives that shaped Fidel's behavior on any given occasion can be an enormously complicated matter. In Santiago on January 2, 1959, Fidel Castro had indulged in a self-gratifying gesture with an eye on history; but there was undoubtedly more to it than that. He was banking on the appeal of nationalism to rally the widest sort of popular support, a matter of prime importance. In this respect his judgment was sound, for the response to his appeal was enthusiastic.

An Emerging Confrontation

Before the Revolution was a month old the theme of sovereignty and independence had become one of the important staples of the new political diet, and frequently it was seasoned with vinegar and red hot pepper. Thus on January 10, in a panel discussion on television, "Dr. Castro" (in Cuba all lawyers were called "doctor") was asked about a report from Washington that the State Department was prepared to withdraw the United States military mission from Cuba if the Cuban government would send a formal note requesting such action. Fidel's reply was not calculated to reduce tensions: "I don't think we need this mission. It trained Batista's soldiers how to lose the war, so we don't want them to teach us anything. [Laughter in the studio.] We don't need to send them any note. It is the sole prerogative of the Cuban government to decide on the presence of the

North American Military Mission." [4] The next day Fidel got word to the mission to pack up and go home.

While Castro was sometimes capable of generating international friction out of sheer delight in tweaking Uncle Sam's nose, it must be said that across the Florida Straits there was sufficient provocation to spur him on. Although there were cool heads in Washington, less impressed by Fidel's antics than by the need to move carefully in a delicate situation (one of them, Philip Bonsal, replaced Ambassador Earl Smith, who was compromised by his cordial relations with Batista), there was an instinctive and violent reaction among the influential die-hard conservatives, in and out of Congress, to the effect that any regime standing to the left of Batista was an enemy of mankind.

This was reflected in the media. A stream of wire-service dispatches, many of which were printed in the Havana press, harped on two themes: communism and the execution of "war criminals." In retrospect, it can be seen that these dispatches to a certain extent distorted the climate of opinion in the United States, including that of the establishment, a part of which, at least for the first five or six months, had maintained an open, if skeptical, mind on the Castro regime. The reports, however, were eagerly printed by the arch-conservative *Diario de la Marina*, in the hope they would stimulate counterrevolution, and by *Revolución*, the official organ of Fidel's 26th of July Movement, as proof of congenital Yankee hostility. In any event, they ended up as grist in Fidel's mill.

On the charge that he was a Communist, Castro could at the time truthfully say, as he did speaking at a Rotary Club luncheon on January 15, "I am not a Communist." Yet he did not stop with the denial, but used it as a springboard to counterattack: "Anyone who doesn't sell out or knuckle under is smeared as a Communist. As for me, I am not selling out to the Americans nor will I take orders from the Americans." Then, developing the theme further, he repeated an old adage of José Martí: "Without economic independence there can be no political independence." [5]

This was strong stuff only two weeks after taking power—and to the Rotarians, among whom were American businessmen, it was not very comforting. But again, Fidel was not only venting his feelings, which were genuine enough; he knew his words would carry to the Cuban people and reinforce his image as a fearless and dedicated

4. *Hoy*, January 11, 1959.   5. *Hoy*, January 16, 1959.

champion of national dignity. It was, moreover, a true image of the man, and over the years the knowledge by the Cuban people that this was so helped him immeasurably in maintaining his sway over them.

The issue of the "war criminals" generated more heat because feelings in Cuba about the atrocities committed by Batista's police ran high. "The world has read about the assassination of prisoners," wrote the *New York Times* on November 8, 1957, "the torture and mutilation of political adversaries regardless of sex or age, the merciless bombing of the civilian population." On January 2, 1959, the day after Batista fled, the *Christian Science Monitor* reported that a "black-book file has been kept of all Batista police and officers who persecuted and tortured their fellow Cubans. . . . Many of these officers face the ultimate penalty for the cruelties they have inflicted. As a consequence, dozens of Batista Cabinet members and government officers have fled to Miami, New Orleans, Jacksonville and New York by plane and boat."

The Temperature Rises

In a matter of a few weeks, charges of a wild bloodbath in Cuba and countercharges of American complicity in the Batista terror mounted to the point where they touched off Fidel's first major broadside against the United States. On January 21, addressing several hundred thousand Cubans gathered in the plaza facing the Presidential Palace (*Revolución* in its exuberance estimated one million, that is, the equivalent of the entire population of Havana and its environs), Castro minced no words: "At Hiroshima and Nagasaki, with the pretext of hastening the end of the war and avoiding useless deaths, they killed 400,000 Japanese with their atomic bombs. Well, in Cuba we'll execute some 400 war criminals; one for every 1,000 assassinated in Hiroshima and Nagasaki." Why this campaign abroad? he asked. "They want to discredit the Cuban Revolution. They don't want the Cuban Revolution to be able to hold up its head," and at this point he added a new and significant dimension to the argument, "so that the rest of the peoples of [Latin] America will not raise their heads. . . . Ours is a people's revolution which must be a beacon of hope for [Latin] America," he exclaimed. "How badly the peoples of [Latin] America need a revolution like ours. . . . Because Cuba wants to be free . . . politically and economically, Cuba has become a dangerous example for all of [Latin] America. . . . We must defend our Revolution not only for the sake of Cuba but also for [Latin] America." [6]

As a matter of fact, the pot was already boiling. *Revolución* was carrying extensive and provocative coverage of the intolerable state of affairs in Latin America. Within four months, the Dominican Republic, Nicaragua, and Panama were to become targets of invasion (all unsuccessful) by expeditions mounted in Cuba. There was even a farfetched plan to "liberate" Spain, which was scotched by Fidel when he learned of it. On April 9, the first hijacked plane, proceeding from Port-au-Prince with six Haitian revolutionaries aboard, landed in Santiago.

For the sake of the record we must note that it was also at this meeting that Fidel named his younger brother Raúl, then twenty-seven years old (Fidel was thirty-two), as number two in the leadership of the movement and his successor if he were killed, with the warning that the enemies of the Revolution would have nothing to gain because "he's more radical than I am." Fidel was unquestionably wrong about "nothing to gain," for if Fidel were eliminated, neither Raúl, an intelligent enough and hard-working lad, nor anybody else at the time or for some years to come, could possibly have kept the Revolution afloat. As for Raúl being "more radical than I," this was conceivable at the time, since it was pretty much of an open secret that he had been a member of the Communist Youth for a brief period. Raúl, who like his brother had miraculously survived the *Granma* disaster, had in all likelihood been number two during the insurrection; and he remained heir apparent during the six-year process that metamorphasized the 26th of July Movement into the new Communist party of Cuba, of which he was second secretary in 1971.

6. *Revolución*, January 22, 1959. In the following pages, the source of Castro's speeches and lesser pronouncements, unless otherwise indicated, is the version published on the day after the event in *Revolución* and, following its demise at the end of September 1965, in *Granma*. If the source is the English weekly edition of *Granma*, it will be so noted. Since the start of the regime, Castro's speeches have been reproduced in the form of verbatim stenographic transcripts, with no editing to speak of. In addition to the newspapers, most of Castro's major speeches have been published in the official quarterly of the Cuban Ministry of Foreign Relations, entitled *Política Internacional*. The first number is dated January–March 1963 and carries Castro material going back to October 1962.

Raúl's special responsibility in the Castro regime was the armed forces, of which in due time he officially became minister. Though brothers have been known to betray each other, Raúl has been singularly loyal. With Fidel as the creator and uncontested military and political leader of the Revolution and his brother entrusted with the role of alter ego, the free-wheeling and hence normally vulnerable Fidel has been immune from the fate that befell the somewhat similarly disorganized and careless Ben Bella in Algeria. There could be no Cuban Boumediène, though there must have been times when sober members of the government, not to mention the Russians, regretted that the possibility did not exist.

The Venezuela Gambit

During the first decade of the Revolution, the extraordinarily mobile Fidel, who was constantly charging from one end of the island to the other unhindered by a fixed office or domicile, left Cuba only on the rarest of occasions. The first was a trip to Caracas, Venezuela, where he received a tumultuous welcome on his arrival on January 22, 1959. It was estimated that more than 100,000 people gathered in the vast Silencio Plaza to listen to his speech.

Almost a year before to the day, an uprising by part of the Venezuelan army with mass support supplied by leftist groups, including the Communist party, had swept away a much hated military regime. Fugitives from other Latin American dictatorships, including that of Batista, streamed into Caracas. Here, considerable amounts of money and arms were collected for the Cuban Revolution and made their way across the Caribbean to the Sierra Maestra.

Castro came to give his thanks, but also to have a strategic platform from which to speak to Latin America—and to size up the situation. Venezuela, more than Cuba, could be the key to the continental revolution that was already in the back of his mind. The masses in Caracas, the seat of power in Venezuela, had been radicalized, and nationalism was rampant. It was here that Richard Nixon, then vice-president of the United States, had been subjected to the greatest indignities during his ill-fated goodwill tour of South America in May 1958. Hooted, jostled, spat upon, and stoned, Nixon barely escaped serious injury. President Eisenhower had been on the verge of sending a task force to rescue him.

Venezuela is strategically located on the southern rim of the Caribbean Sea. Its western frontier adjoins strife-ridden Colombia, and directly to the south lies the increasingly unstable Brazil. Venezuela is one of the world's major producers of petroleum and a significant exporter of iron ore. Some 60 percent of all American direct investments in Latin America are located in Venezuela. Clearly, this country could play a role in a continental upheaval of far greater significance than could Cuba. Or at the very least, it could become a "second front" of sufficient magnitude to distract the attention of Washington from its Cuban problem.

All of this might well have crossed Fidel's mind, for he spent five days in Caracas, most of it in private conversations probing Venezuela's political complexities and potentialities. It was already clear that the Venezuelan revolutionary pattern differed in important respects from that of the Cuban. In Cuba Fidel Castro had, so to speak, thrust himself into a power vacuum. The collapse of Batista's army had also wiped out his entire police and administrative apparatus. Such political parties as existed were extraordinarily weak and could offer no competition, let alone resistance.

In Venezuela the armed forces and the administrative apparatus were intact. Political parties were well organized and had roots in the population. An election had taken place that had been won by Acción Democrática, a moderately leftist party. The president-elect, Rómulo Betancourt, an ex-Marxist who for years had engaged in a running battle with the Communist party, was to take office a few days after Castro's departure.

Fidel's First Pronouncement on Revolutionary Theory

The highlight of Fidel's visit to Caracas was the great mass meeting in the Silencio Plaza, where the Cuban spellbinder put on a performance long remembered in the city. One statement in his speech was particularly provocative: "It was commonly said and repeated that nowadays a revolution against the army was impossible, and that only when the revolution took place within the army itself could the revolution succeed, . . . that if there were no economic crisis and no hunger there would be no revolution. . . . All these concepts the Cuban Revolution has smashed to smithereens." [7]

This was a scarcely veiled reference to Venezuela's "unfinished" revolution. More important, as it turned out, it was the opening of the debate in a polemic that was to grow in intensity and geographic scope over the years—in fact, until October 1967, when the failure of

7. *El Mundo,* January 24, 1959.

Cuban armed intervention in several countries, and particularly in Bolivia, provided sufficient empirical evidence to place the dispute in a new perspective. The debate concerned the assessment of the Cuban experience as a model for revolution in Latin America. From the theoretical point of view, it involved a challenge to established criteria and principles, including those professed by the exponents of Soviet Marxism. From the practical point of view, it was related to the pressures that could be exerted in Latin America in support of the Cuban Revolution, that is to say, the national interests of the new Cuban state. On this last point Fidel in later years was silent, preferring the image of Cuba as a self-sacrificing champion of all downtrodden humanity. However, during this period, as for example in a television appearance on March 6, 1959, he was explicit about what was involved when he invoked the community of interests between Cuba and Latin America: We ask for the support of the peoples of Latin America, he declared, because "we are fully aware that in order to consolidate its victory, the Cuban Revolution needs the power of public opinion of these peoples." Che Guevara and the young French philosophy teacher Régis Debray [8] were to join Fidel Castro in greatly expanding and embellishing the new theory of revolution announced in Caracas. However, that part of Fidel's thesis concerning the lack of economic crisis and hunger in Batista's Cuba had to be dropped when scarcities and production failures required the revolutionary regime to stress quite a different theme, what it claimed to be the appalling underdevelopment [9] and privations that afflicted the people of prerevolutionary Cuba.

8. Debray was sentenced in mid-1967 to a thirty-year prison term in Bolivia for complicity in Che's unhappy guerrilla adventure, but was released in late December 1970 by the new leftist military government.

9. The connotations of the term "underdevelopment" applied to Cuba in 1958 can be misleading, suggesting that the country was in some meaningful way comparable to Burma or Zambia. Some have preferred to use "semideveloped" or "intermediate stage of development" as more appropriate for Cuba. One student of the Cuban economy wrote that Cuba "was not an underdeveloped peasant society but rather a misdeveloped proletarian one" (Dennis W. Wood, "The Long Revolution," *Science and Society* 34, no. 1 [spring, 1970]: 39). For an extended discussion of this question, see Theodore Draper, *Castroism: Theory and Practice* (New York: Praeger, 1965), p. 97ff., and Richard R. Fagen, "Revolution—For Internal Consumption Only," in *Cuban Communism*, ed. Irving Louis Horowitz (New York: Aldine, 1970), pp. 37–43.

3

■

Complexities and Perplexities

The Moderates

WITH THE BENEFIT OF HINDSIGHT, it is not difficult to see that from the outset the Cuban Revolution had embarked on a consistently bold and aggressive foreign policy. At the time, however, a number of factors tended to becloud the view. With respect to Fidel, his close associates like Raúl and Che, and the leading spokesmen of the 26th of July Movement, one could not be sure that their bite would equal their bark. These were colorful, erratic, inexperienced young men, flushed with victory and power; but they had not yet had to face up to the realities of Cuba's dependent economy and its geographic proximity to the United States.

In addition there was the fact that, although he dominated the government, Fidel had, prudently enough, appointed moderates to important posts in the cabinet who, along with other influential supporters of the Revolution, spoke a more temperate language. These were men of an older generation, usually of professional distinction, who had honorable records of political opposition to Batista, had in one way or another cooperated with Fidel's movement before the fall of Batista, and were by and large intellectually committed to the social, political, and economic reforms Fidel had advocated during the struggle against Batista.

Men of this type Fidel had appointed to key posts, such as provisional president of the Republic, prime minister, secretary of state for foreign affairs, president of the Bank of Cuba, and secretary of the treasury. Either out of conviction or tactical considerations that normally motivate responsible statesmen, they expressed friendship with the United States. Hence, they tried to minimize and delay the friction over questions that would inevitably arise between the two countries, such as agrarian reform, regulation of foreign investment, upward revision of the Cuban sugar quota in the United States, and import duties on American products sold in Cuba— questions that almost from the beginning were on the agenda of debate between the Revolution and the United States.

True, these men were in many respects the nominal government, but they might become the real government. Even after Castro took over the office of prime minister in mid-February 1959 (until then he was commander in chief of the armed forces and head of the 26th of July Movement) and after changes in June and July when militants such as Raúl Roa and Oswaldo Dorticós became secretary of state for foreign affairs and president of the Republic, respectively, spokesmen for the Revolution continued to speak in many tongues.

It was not until the end of November, when Ernesto Guevara was appointed president of the Bank of Cuba (banknotes printed during his term in office which he signed "Che" have become collectors items), that a good deal of verbal confusion was removed. By that time, other dismissals from office and important defections from the movement had occurred, counterrevolutionary activities had broken out, and whatever grounds for negotiation that had existed between Cuba and the United States had pretty much disappeared.

The Communists

There were other incongruities that made it difficult to evaluate the political scene in Cuba during the first year of the Revolution. In June 1958 Carlos Rafael Rodríguez, a leading figure of the Partido Socialista Popular (PSP), the nomenclature of the Cuban Communist party at the time, was sent as a representative of his organization to Fidel's headquarters in the Sierra Maestra, where by his own account a decade later, he grew a beard but did not take part in combat and remained until the fall of Batista.[1]

1. *Bohemia*, May 2, 1969, p. 15 (supplement). Carlos Rafael, as he is invariably called in Cuba, had been a minister in Batista's cabinet in 1944 before he became a minister under Castro, and he remained a

The record shows that the PSP had rallied late to Fidel's insurrection. In its publications it had been consistently skeptical of Fidel's chances of success, disdainful of what it believed to be his political naiveté, and had dismissed him as an adventurer, albeit a well-meaning one. By one of those strange quirks of fate that are the despair of the historian who looks for a rational explanation of the course of human events, the Communists' erroneous assessment of Fidel's insurrection was an indispensable prerequisite for its success, since Communist hostility provided Fidel with immunity from an early and very likely decisive American intervention.

The party had alternately opposed, supported, or been indifferent to Batista over a period of twenty-five years. A force to reckon with during its heyday in the 1930s and early 1940s, its influence sharply declined in the 1950s. When Batista took power for the last time in 1952, with an eye on Washington he broke diplomatic relations with the Soviet Union and illegalized the PSP. Relatively unmolested by Batista's police, it led a comfortable underground existence.

Why the party and Fidel decided to enter into a working relationship in June 1958 can be surmised. To begin with, despite the ideological and tactical differences separating them, there were areas in which their views were not incompatible. Looking ahead, Fidel could reasonably expect the Communists to support his radical domestic program and to back him completely in a confrontation with the United States. Also looking ahead, for the Communists Fidel's petty bourgeois radicalism—as they defined his ideological position—could create the conditions that would permit the PSP once more to participate freely and fruitfully in the political life of the country.

In the second place, by June 1958 it was not inconceivable that Fidel might win, though it was by no means certain. Perhaps the decision of the party, probably hotly debated, amounted to the purchase of an insurance policy to be paid for by sending money and supplies to the Sierra. No more than a handful of Communists

---

minister while Castro blew hot and cold and hot again toward the Soviet Union and engaged in several purges of unrepentant old-time Communists.

participated in combat. Che Guevara at one time said he knew of only three.

As for Fidel Castro, the main engagements with Batista's forces were yet to come. To win the war he would have to send his guerrillas into the plains where he could scarcely anticipate an easy victory. In addition, in April he had suffered a serious political defeat when the nationwide general strike he had called for fizzled out ignominiously, in part because the PSP had failed to support it. Thus, on the eve of his pact with the Communists, Fidel's prospects were still in doubt. On the other hand, the risk of accepting Communist aid was small, since the agreement was to be secret. In addition it could in no way present a threat to the total control he exercised over the military and political operations of the insurrection.

With the fall of Batista, the PSP was again a legal party and immediately resumed publication of *Noticias de Hoy*, a daily newspaper that joined *Revolución* in giving full backing to Fidel. This development, which the new regime explained as the natural result of restoring political and press freedom after the overthrow of the tyranny, was, of course, more than that. In Washington, it was an early sign, among others, that Fidel would probably be a tough customer to handle. In Cuba, where anticommunism was the normal attitude of most of the population, whether through habit, conviction, or the belief it was necessary in view of the proximity of the United States, *Hoy* circulating freely in the streets and its support of the Revolution created mixed feelings, to say the least.

Although the PSP was much weaker than the 26th of July Movement, it was better organized and had an optimistic view of its potentialities. It apparently maintained discreet lines of communication with Fidel, whose pragmatism outweighed whatever personal feelings he had about the party's past behavior, and with Raúl and Che who, though critical of its shortcomings, were from the beginning ideologically closer to the Communists than Fidel.

As a result, the party looked for opportunities to improve its position and extend its influence, which brought it both into open conflict with the bureaucracy of Fidel's movement and to a strange rapprochement with a former enemy, the anticommunist Directorio Revolucionario Estudiantil, a militant student revolutionary organization.

National Communism in Embryo

It is scarcely surprising that, for the observer at the time, unusual and bewildering complexities made political diagnosis and prediction uncommonly difficult. During almost the entire year of 1959, the PSP and the movement were engaged in a sharp dispute that was fully reflected in their respective daily newspapers. This, in turn, distracted attention from the fact that on most of the important issues of the day the two groups were basically in agreement. "To distinguish nationalists from Communists is difficult," wrote a more than ordinarily perceptive Associated Press correspondent from Havana,[2] although here again a puzzling element existed because *Revolución* was more aggressively, more impatiently, more flamboyantly revolutionary—hence more radical—than *Hoy*.

In its aggressive polemic against the Communists, *Revolución* constantly belabored the PSP for its one-time collaboration with Batista, for having climbed on Fidel's bandwagon very late, for its dogmatism and imported ideology, and for being power hungry. As the weaker party, the PSP had little choice on most issues but to remain politely on the defensive. The last blast, of limited scope, appeared in *Revolución* on December 15, 1959.

One of the sharpest and in retrospect most meaningful attacks on the "disreputable oligarchy of the PSP" appeared in an editorial in *Revolución* on September 14, 1959. How strange, it said, that Carlos Rafael Rodríguez, who once was a minister in Batista's cabinet and who was scarcely more than a tourist during the fighting in the Sierra, is still a leading figure in the PSP. "The Catholic Church was more sensible, removing from positions of leadership those who were too compromised with the recent past to be expected to go along with the current revolutionary process."

As for being a Communist, the article continued, there is no objection if one is a Communist "pure and simple," since it is one of the many ways of understanding reality; but "to be a Communist in a party that belongs to the Cominform is something else again, for it undoubtedly means adopting a type of Marxism compromised by the interests and needs of a metropolis that one blindly believes will bring about the establishment of socialism over the entire globe." What at the time could appear to be a subtle distinction in the argu-

2. *El Mundo*, April 26, 1959.

ment on communism was in fact something more significant. It was the embryonic expression of a point of view that eventually gave birth to Fidel's national communism.

Conflict in the Labor Movement

One of the most important areas of friction between the two groups was the labor front. Here the PSP, with some strength and a good deal of experience, hoped to make its greatest gains. The result was a series of bitter conflicts punctuated by charges and countercharges of fraud, as the two organizations ran rival candidates in trade-union elections.

The climax in this running battle occurred toward the end of November 1959 at the first postrevolutionary national congress of the Cuban Confederation of Labor (CTC), whose leadership down to the level of union locals had by that time been purged of Batista appointees and their collaborators. Here the internal struggle reached the point where Fidel himself intervened to "suggest," as *Hoy* put it (November 22), that David Salvador, a stalwart of the 26th of July Movement since before the fall of Batista, be elected secretary-general to preserve unity. This ended the debate.

However, in less than six month, Salvador ran into trouble with the minister of labor over jurisdictional matters and was forthwith purged. Some time later he was caught trying to make his way from Cuba and sent to jail. In another six months the PSP was fairly well in control of the labor movement.

The Locus of Power

One of the issues that came up at the labor congress and that generated considerable heat on many levels was that of unity. Whenever "unity" was invoked, the opinion was unanimous that it was indispensable for safeguarding the Revolution. However, the term did not have the same meaning for Fidel's movement, which held power, and the PSP, which aspired to share the power. Whenever the Communists spoke of achieving unity through a "coalition" of revolutionary forces, the movement rejected this concept in no uncertain terms.

As Marcelo Fernández, at the time top executive of the movement, repeatedly argued, we need a "civic" (political) organization to guarantee the permanence of the Revolution. It must be composed of the most revolutionary, most honest and self-sacrificing elements, hence it can only be the Movement of July 26th. "Let all good and loyal revolutionaries join us. We welcome them. Unity under our leadership is the only way to achieve the solidarity of the Revolution." [3]

Castro himself rarely took part in the public debates on these matters. While *Revolución* fought the ideological battle, he assumed the position of the bearded patriarch, respected by all members of the revolutionary family whose quarrels he observed with patience until an issue arose that seemed sufficiently serious for him to intervene and provide "orientation."

It was thus significant that at one point Fidel felt compelled to express himself on the question of unity. Under the heading of "Why the Government Cannot Be Shared," he was quoted as having declared, "All revolutionary sectors must support the Revolution. To take part in the government, however, is another matter. We need to keep control in our hands or the Revolution will fall apart, as in 1933. *And nobody presented us with power as a gift.*" [4]

This may be the only time that Castro publicly expressed himself with such complete candor on this vital subject. With the exception of nationalism (and its paradoxical twin, internationalism), the locus of power has been the only permanent political feature of the Cuban Revolution since its inception. From humanism to orthodox Marxist-Leninism to national Marxism and back to neo-orthodoxy, from the first "integration" of the revolutionary organizations [5] to

3. *Revolución*, April 15, 1959.

4. *Revolución*, July 6, 1959; emphasis added. In his public utterances, Fidel almost never refers to himself in the first person singular but as "we," "us," and "our." Roger Brown, discussing the "pronouns of power and solidarity" (*pluralis maiestatis* or *dignitatis*), states that "plurality is a very old and ubiquitous metaphor for power. . . . An emperor . . . is the summation of his people and can speak as their representative. Royal persons sometimes say *we* where an ordinary man would say *I*." *Psycholinguistics: Selected Papers* (New York: Free Press, 1970), p. 305. According to J. B. Hofmann and Anton Szantyr, the use of the first person plural in official addresses and decrees by the Roman emperors dates from the reign of Gordianus III (238–244). See *Lateinisch Syntax und Stilistik* (Munich: C. H. Beck'sche Verlagsbuchhandlung, 1965), 2:20.

5. In mid-1961, the Movement of July 26th, the PSP, and the Directorio Revolucionario were formally disbanded, its members becom-

the 1965 version of the Communist party of Cuba and beyond—through ideological and organizational thick and thin—"control in our hands" has not diminished. Thus, it later turned out that the new Communist party of Cuba was not the progeny of the PSP or even an amalgamation of revolutionary sectors, but a reincarnation of the Movement of July 26th, purged, toughened, polished, and streamlined, with Fidel Castro at the head and practically all positions of strategic importance occupied by veterans of the old movement.

The Directorio Revolucionario Estudiantil

A third revolutionary group in the early jockeying for power was the Directorio, as it was called in short. This was a student organization led by José Antonio Echevarría, who lost his life in a daring attack on the Presidential Palace on March 13, 1957. The assailants came within an ace of killing Batista. Had they succeeded, the history of Cuba would have been different; for Fidel Castro was still struggling to survive in the mountain wilderness of Oriente, far from the center of power, and Echevarría was an able leader not lacking in charismatic appeal.

In February 1958 some fifteen members of the Directorio led by Faure Chomón, who had been badly wounded in the attack on the palace and miraculously escaped with his life, opened their own guerrilla front in the Escambray hills of central Cuba. In December 1958 a number of this group joined Che Guevara's advancing column and fought in the last and decisive engagement against Batista's troops in Santa Clara. According to contemporary newspaper accounts, one of their number, Rolando Cubela, played an important role in the victory, although the official history of the event, written by the Movement of July 26th, leaves Cubela and the Directorio out of the picture.

Prior to Batista's fall, an alliance between the Directorio and the PSP would have been considered an even more unlikely combination than that of Fidel's movement and the PSP. Although the students in the Directorio were ardent nationalists, they had been even more hostile to the Communists than the movement, not only on ideological but also practical grounds; for the two groups had long

---

ing part of the Integrated Revolutionay Organizations (ORI), which in turn became the United Party of the Socialist Revolution (PURS) and finally the new Communist party of Cuba.

been rivals in the student political battles at the University of Havana.

Nevertheless, the unthinkable again took place, precipitated by friction between the movement and the Directorio. Some members of the latter had emerged from the underground and others had rushed in from exile in Miami a few hours after Batista fled, and seized and fortified the Presidential Palace. A tense moment occurred when Camilo Cienfuegos' and Che's columns arrived on January 3, but the Directorio wisely capitulated.

When Fidel arrived in Havana, he publicly criticized Chomón, but since the latter was a hero of the attack on the Palace and the acknowledged head of the Directorio, Havana's largest revolutionary student organization, he had sufficient bargaining power to survive. As a result, like the PSP, the Directorio became a junior partner in the Revolution, a situation that created common interests between them, until later events revived old animosities, as I shall presently explain.

For a long time the Directorio and the PSP carefully refrained from referring to their past quarrels and expressed common views on many issues, and in particular on those that concerned the larger role for the junior partners in the power structure of the Revolution. More surprising—and disconcerting for the observer at the time— was the fact that the formerly outspoken anti-Communist Directorio was almost from the beginning outspoken in expressing sympathy toward the Soviet Union and China at a time when the movement's lambasting of the PSP would occasionally spill over and include international communism in general and the Soviet Union in particular.

It can be suspected that tactics more than conviction motivated the attitude of the Directorio. However that may be, in mid-July 1960 Faure Chomón became Fidel's first ambassador to the Soviet Union. Chomón staffed the embassy with his own people, including the exceptionally able Orlando Pérez Rodríguez (who in due time was to zigzag his way to the top as president of the National Bank). In this manner, Fidel astutely threw a fair-sized bone to the Directorio while removing its leadership from the seething political cauldron in Havana and, at the same time, pleasing the Russians without sending a Communist who might be too easily swayed by the Kremlin to be a reliable envoy.

A short time later the wheel turned. Chomón was recalled early in 1962 when Fidel needed support in his first purge of the PSP, then technically nonexistent, which was caught flagrante delicto building itself into a position of independent power. Chomón became minister of communications (subsequently minister of transport) and an effective speaker throughout the island against the perils of "sectarianism," a euphemism for PSP ambitions.

Another Turn of the Wheel

Later, old suspicions and animosities were again revived. In 1964 the informer who, shortly after the event, had betrayed the hiding place of four survivors of the Directorio attack on the Palace was discovered. The unfortunate youths had been killed on the spot by the police, and after the fall of Batista their names had been placed on the official rolls of revolutionary martyr-heroes.

The informer, Marcos Rodríguez, confessed and was tried and executed. He turned out to have been a member of the Communist youth organization at the University of Havana who had infiltrated the Directorio. More significant, although suspicion had been cast on him much earlier, he had been protected by leading members of the PSP, in particular by Joaquín Ordoqui, a Communist party veteran of more than thirty years' standing and serving in 1964 as quartermaster general of the armed forces.

The scandal rocked the country, and it took all of Fidel's skill and authority to mend the rifts it created. Chomón, understandably deeply affected by the revelations, reopened the campaign against "sectarianism," whereupon Castro publicly reprimanded Chomón for pouring salt in old wounds, thereby doing a disservice to revolutionary unity. He also reprimanded Ordoqui and his wife (the ex-wife of Carlos Rafael Rodríguez and in 1964 head of Cuba's official cultural organization) for carelessness and bad judgment; and finally he papered over the mess by giving a clean bill of health to the old PSP.

A few months later, Ordoqui and his wife were fired from their jobs and placed under house arrest. According to a persistent rumor at the time, they were under suspicion of having cooperated with American intelligence agencies. Years have passed and no word has been released concerning their fate.

Chomón, however, kept his job, henceforth carefully toeing Fidel's line, and in 1965 was appointed to the secretariat of the Central Committee of the new Communist party, a position that like all others in this "ruling" body is mainly honorary.

Faure Chomón had more bad luck the following year when Rolando Cubela—prominent Directorio veteran of the fighting at Santa Clara and later student body president of the University of Havana (and as such the leading representative of revolutionary Cuba at international student conferences)—was discovered plotting the assassination of Fidel Castro. Cubela was tried, confessed, and was sentenced to prison for twenty-five years after Fidel "asked" the court not to impose the death sentence.

The Cubela affair, in which no other member of the old Directorio was implicated, nevertheless did not help the reputation or fortunes of these once aspiring junior partners. No more than two or three, including the durable Chomón, were able to survive in the upper levels of the bureaucracy. (At the end of 1970, however, Chomón was dropped from the cabinet for undisclosed reasons, but retained his membership in the secretariat of the Central Committee.)

Every year since 1959, the anniversary of the aborted attack on the Palace is marked by fitting tributes to the martyrs and the Cuban dedication to revolution by armed struggle, and by a mass meeting at the university, broadcast and televised throughout the country. Faure Chomón is always among the notables on the platform, but it is years since he has been among the speakers, even those in the preliminary warm-up performances. The main event is the speech by Fidel.

4

■

The Cuban Anomaly
and the World Situation

An Intact Economy

A PROPER PERSPECTIVE on the great anomaly that is the Cuban Revolution requires some further explanation of the domestic and international environment in which Fidel Castro sailed his ship of state. As Castro himself stated, there was neither economic crisis nor hunger when the Revolution took power, although one could add that the economy was not flourishing and there was poverty in the countryside. One could also add that there had been no destruction of property to speak of and scarcely any war—certainly nothing remotely comparable to the devastation and loss of life during the unsuccessful first phase (1868–1878) of the struggle for independence from Spain.

Fidel has frequently spoken of 20,000 casualties suffered during the struggle against Batista, although no further details concerning the source of the data or the nature of the casualties have been given (in 1958 the population of Cuba was approximately six million). However that may be, an overwhelming proportion of the casualties must have been civilian victims living in mountain villages bombed by Batista's airforce and victims of police repression in urban centers, for the scale of military operations was extremely limited. As Fidel himself explained on January 18, 1960, as late as June 1958 his "army" consisted of 300 men; and when he began his final offensive in August he had 800 men. As for Batista's army of 50,000, with one notable exception in mid-1958 probably fewer than 5 percent were at any given time in action against the rebels.

In fact, what are termed "battles" in the reminiscences of the rebel leaders were skirmishes, with rarely more than a score or two guerrillas involved and frequently fewer. This does not detract from the fighting skill or the heroism displayed by the men in combat, but it does provide perspective on the magnitude of involvement and damage in the fighting.

Thus, Castro took over an economy that was intact and functioning almost as if nothing had happened. There was the added advantage that January marked the beginning of the sugarcane harvest and hence the season of peak employment. It was to be a good harvest; the price of sugar and the market were steady, which meant that the capacity to import and the level of economic activity would be normal. There was money in the bank and the usual amount of inventories in shops, factories, and warehouses.

This situation helped maintain the popularity, indeed the enthusiasm, of the great majority of the population for the Revolution. Not only had it swept away a venal, corrupt, and increasingly brutal military dictatorship, but there was no price to pay. On the contrary, a large public works program, reduction of rents and household utility rates, and similar early benefits for the mass of the population visibly increased purchasing power, which in turn stimulated business. A kind of prosperity ensued for about two years, fed by the fat accumulated before the Revolution and by an inflation caused by the rise in purchasing power that was not matched by an increase in production.

Hence, an extraordinary course of events took place. Instead of being confronted with the arduous material and political task of reviving production in a shattered economy, instead of being immediately faced with the urgent need of a hard-headed economic program and of clearly defined political objectives, the Cuban Revolution on taking power could at once be generous in matters of social welfare, permissive in matters of political and intellectual debate, and irrational in matters of economic policy. And all of this, by an odd coincidence, precisely suited the temperament of a leadership stirred by idealistic visions and naive optimism, reinforced by the astounding achievement of taking power in the face of seemingly overwhelming odds.

By the end of 1961 the dissipation of Cuba's reserves and the American trade embargo, by threatening to asphyxiate the new socialist utopia, might have shocked the leadership into sobriety. However, the providential intervention of the Soviet Union not only kept the Revolution afloat but made it immune to the laws of bankruptcy. As a result, it took nearly a decade of steadily declining production, mainly the result of incredible planning failures and gross mismanagement, for the Cuban Revolution to reach the point where drastic social revolutions generally begin: with austerity, discipline, and the complete regimentation of all social, political, and intellectual activity by the central authority.

Latin America

While Fidel Castro in 1959 was an illiterate in economics and an amateur in philosophy, he was by comparison a highly sophisticated practitioner of politics, an art whose application he was able to extend from the domestic to the international scene. Here again, the world picture at the time provided a number of favorable conditions for his enterprise which he recognized and was able to exploit.

In 1954, while Fidel was in prison on the Isle of Pines, the CIA-engineered overthrow of the Guatemalan government marked the high point of right-wing ascendency in one of the alternating cycles of radical upsurge and collapse that have long characterized the fluctuating Latin American scene. In the case of Guatemala, an agrarian reform that affected land held in reserve by the United Fruit Company, and that looked as if it might drastically alter the whole system of land tenure in the country, triggered the crisis. When the leftist government of Colonel Jacobo Arbenz, which was denied arms in the United States, imported a boatload of weapons from Czechoslovakia, it was swept away by an invasion staged in a neighboring country.

Five years later the fate of Guatemala still cast a shadow over Cuba. Che Guevara, who had been in Guatemala when Arbenz fell and who was deeply moved by the experience, in his first public address in Cuba on January 19, 1959, warned that "aggression was being prepared by foreign imperialism against us, like in Guatemala." [1]

The prophesy, purely a product of Che's fatalistic views since it was far too early for the United States to anticipate the need for such an aggression, was nevertheless fulfilled in April 1961 at the Bay

1. *Hoy*, January 20, 1959.

of Pigs. However, the political climate in Latin America and other parts of the world had changed since 1954, a fact that President Kennedy understood and that inhibited his use of United States armed forces to give sufficient support to the invasion to ensure its success.

In synthesis, the turn in Latin America came when the economic upswing brought about by World War II and its aftermath began to taper off after 1955 and in a short time was converted in most countries into a deep recession. As reported in the *New York Times* on January 14, 1959, "1958 was one of the worst economic years in decades for Latin America. Inflation was rampant, currencies depreciated, domestic budgets ran staggering deficits, foreign earnings were pathetically inadequate to pay for essential imports." As a matter of fact, as the record of the sixties shows, Latin America appeared to have entered into a period of prolonged economic, social, and political crisis.

Under these conditions, the political pendulum began to swing toward the left in a number of important countries, while Fidel was still bottled up in the mountains, and continued to swing in that direction for some time after 1959, partly as a result of the example set by the Cuban Revolution. In Argentina and Brazil, the trend led to the election of left-of-center Arturo Frondizi and Jânio Quadros as presidents of their respective countries. In Chile the Communist party, after spending a decade underground, was legalized and again got its representatives elected to both houses of Congress. In Mexico, President López Mateos moved away from the conservativism of his stodgy predecessor. In Venezuela one of Latin America's most firmly entrenched military dictatorships was overthrown. In Colombia, also, a military dictatorship fell. And so on. In all cases these changes were to one degree or another responses to radical and nationalist pressures from below.

In Latin America, nationalism is always first and foremost, if not exclusively, directed against the United States, that is, "el imperialismo yanqui." As the Peruvian Eudocio Ravines wrote after he was expelled from the Peruvian Communist party and while Batista still ruled Cuba: "One can discuss the existence or non-existence of imperialism [in Latin America], but what one cannot deny is the existence of a militant anti-imperialism directed against the United

States." [2] An additional comment by Boris Goldenburg, that "anti-imperialism is the deepest political sentiment in Latin America," is still relevant.[3] One need only recall Governor Nelson Rockefeller's mission for President Nixon in mid-1969, eleven years and two swings of the Latin American political pendulum after Vice-President Nixon's disastrous tour of South America. Greeted by serious rioting in Honduras, Colombia, and Ecuador, Rockefeller was not permitted by the Bolivian government to leave the airport at La Paz; while Peru, Chile, and Venezuela, in an unprecedented departure from normal diplomatic conduct, canceled his visit outright.

To return to Fidel Castro, it is clear that his rise to power coincided with a change of climate in Latin America that was distinctly in his favor. In the beginning it provided him with important leverage in his confrontation with the United States although, as it turned out, he exaggerated its potentialities. Today the situation in Latin America still remains a consolation for him; for although conditions in Cuba could hardly excite the envy of most knowledgeable Latin Americans, neither can it be said that conditions in Latin America could excite the envy of many Cubans, even those with access to information other than that supplied by Castro's regime.

Asia, Africa, and the West

In 1955 the Bandung Conference in Indonesia, in which twenty-nine Afro-Asian governments participated, gave formal expression for the first time to a set of principles reflecting the common interests of the nations of the Third World. Essentially, the stress was on the defense of their sovereignty and independence against the encroachment of the great powers and on their noninvolvement in the cold war. Bandung amounted to a rejection of NATO, the Warsaw Pact, SEATO, CENTO, and the Monroe Doctrine.

During the following year Egypt nationalized the Suez Canal, and soon after Nasserite radicalism and nationalism spread to Syria and Iraq, creating a zone of militant Arab anti-imperialism, to which Algeria would be added on winning independence from France in 1962.

2. Cited by Boris Goldenburg, *The Cuban Revolution and Latin America* (New York: Praeger, 1965), p. 316.
3. *Ibid.*

Between the Bandung Conference and its successor, the Belgrade Conference of 1961, in which Cuba participated and obtained significant support, twenty-two new independent states were carved out of British and French colonial possessions in Africa. Some leaned far to the left at one time or another in the years following their independence: the Sudan (1956), Ghana (1957), Guinea (1958), the Congo (Brazzaville, 1960), Mali (1960), and Tanganyika (1961, later incorporating Zanzibar and becoming Tanzania). In all circumstances, and similarly in the newly independent states of Asia such as India, Indonesia, and Ceylon, sovereignty was a word to take seriously. Thus, when Fidel Castro's Cuba appeared on the scene in the United Nations, there were scores of Afro-Asian countries prepared to give it a sympathetic hearing.

Meanwhile, Western Europe had completed its postwar reconstruction. By the late fifties the Marshall Plan lay in the past, the capitalist system was secure, and the European Common Market had come into being, marking the beginning of the decline of the Atlantic alliance. Concurrently, the cold war was abating and trade with eastern Europe and China was picking up. In other words, the United States had lost a perceptible amount of its influence outside the western hemisphere, including Japan. No country outside the western hemisphere, not even Spain (or for that matter the Vatican), broke diplomatic or commercial relations with Cuba, with the exception of West Germany, which did so only when Cuba established diplomatic relations with East Germany. When the United States cut off trade with Cuba, among other capitalist countries England, France, Spain, Italy, and Japan—and Canada in the western hemisphere—increased their trade with Cuba and in most cases far above the pre-1959 level. In due time Cuba was able to purchase transport and industrial equipment on credit in Engand, France, and Spain.

To be sure, this trade was quantitatively insignificant compared with the flow of goods and credit from eastern Europe and China. However, it permitted Cuba to alleviate critical shortages of consumer and capital goods unavailable in the Communist countries and, in some instances, to benefit from the more advanced technology of the capitalist countries. In addition, good commercial relations usually went hand in hand with good political relations, a matter of obvious importance for Castro's regime.

The Soviet Union

The most extraordinary chronological coincidence affecting the Cuban Revolution was the fact that Fidel Castro came to power at almost the precise moment when the Soviet Union acquired both the capability and willingness to underwrite the survival of a revolution 6,000 miles from its border and 90 miles from the United States.

Capability and willingness were interlocking phenomena directly related to the thaw that followed the death of Stalin in 1953 and, more particularly, the emergence of Nikita Khrushchev as the uncontested leader in 1957. In expanding Russian power and influence, Stalin never ventured beyond territory accessible to the Red Army, nor did he abandon an austere self-sufficiency as one of the guiding principles of economic policy.

Khrushchev broke out of this hermitic world into the postsputnik era, expanding international trade and seeking to promote the political and economic ambitions of the Soviet state far beyond the confines of Stalin's continental bastion, even as far as Latin America.[4] Thus, Russia was buying sizable quantities of Cuban sugar

4. Russian interest in the southern part of the western hemisphere goes back to Peter the Great, who gave serious thought to the conquest of Spanish America but abandoned the idea. The next two centuries saw little Russian concern or contact with the area. Thus, when interest was revived immediately following the October Revolution, Latin America was virtually *terra incognita* to the Bolsheviks. In addition, what little guidance Russian leaders derived from Marx and Engels was not helpful. Marx's unflattering evaluation of Bolívar was perpetuated in Soviet historiography until 1956. They were also influenced by Marx's low opinion of Spaniards and still lower opinion of Latin Americans, and by Engels' attitude toward the Mexicans. Engels considered them incapable of self-development and applauded the seizure of half their territory by the United States in 1847. Lenin was too busy with more urgent matters to pay much attention to Latin America. This task fell mainly to the Comintern which, to its other infirmities, added ignorance in building an impressive record of political ineptitude in Latin America, with only a few exceptions. Prior to World War II, diplomatic relations were established and then broken with Mexico and Uruguay. During World War II and the Soviet-American alliance, the more important countries (except Argentina), and even some of the small right-wing dictatorships, either established or reestablished diplomatic relations with the Soviet

(approximately three-quarters of a million tons in 1956–1958), while Fidel was still an outlaw guerrilla leader in the Sierra Maestra. In 1958 Argentina negotiated a large credit for the purchase of Soviet machinery. In 1959 Brazilian and Chilean trade missions visited Moscow for the first time. At the end of the same year, an impressive Soviet exposition took place in Mexico. As a matter of fact, the exhibits that appeared in a similar display in Havana in February 1960 were transported directly from Mexico City.

A fortuitous development of decisive importance for the Cuban Revolution was the sudden spurt in Soviet petroleum production. Somewhere between 1950 and 1955, Russia changed from being a net oil importer to a net exporter. In 1955 it exported a total of some 3 million tons of crude petroleum. The entire amount would have barely met Cuba's needs at that time.[5] In 1960, the year Russia began to supply Cuba, exports had jumped to nearly 18 million tons. The next year the figure went up to more than 23 million tons; and by 1965, when Cuban consumption was more than 4 million tons, Soviet exports were more than 43 million tons.[6]

Petroleum is practically the only source of energy for the Cuban economy and over 99 percent must be imported. Without Russian oil, the "real" revolution that Fidel had promised would have been throttled in its infancy. It is one of the many ironies in the history of the Cuban Revolution that for Fidel Castro it was a great stroke of luck to have failed to capture the Moncada barracks on July 26, 1953. For although, like the proverbial leader favored by destiny, he might have been the right man in the right place, he most certainly would have been at the wrong time.

Union. In 1946 Argentina followed suit. However, by 1953 the cold war had reduced the countries continuing to maintain relations to Argentina, Uruguay, and Mexico. Then, in the post-Cuba breakthrough, Brazil, Chile, Colombia, Venezuela, Ecuador, Peru, and Bolivia were added to the list. Trade turnover with all Latin America rose from a mere trickle in 1950 to 28 million rubles in 1956 and 178 million (excluding Cuba) in 1966. See Stephen Clissold, ed., *Soviet Relations with Latin America, 1918–1968: A Documentary Survey* (London: Oxford University Press, 1970).

5. Consumption in 1958 was 3,012,000 tons. In 1967 it rose to 4,867,000 tons. *Bohemia*, November 15, 1968, p. 92.

6. Robert W. Campbell, *The Economics of Soviet Oil and Gas* (Baltimore: Johns Hopkins University Press, 1968), p. 228.

5

■

A Thorny Olive Branch

Fidel Castro Goes to Washington

FIDEL'S VISIT to the United States, to which he added a brief appearance in Montreal in April 1959, followed by his performance at the Inter-American Economic Conference in Buenos Aires on May 2 added puzzling new elements to the question of what he was really up to. Although he was not an official guest of the United States government—he had asked for and received an invitation to address the Washington Press Club before he had assumed the premiership in mid-February—he was doing what was traditionally expected of any new head of government in Latin America.

Had all his tough talk about the United States been a bluff? Or was the trip itself a bluff designed to hoodwink the American government and Cuban conservatives at home to gain a little time? The first possibility, at the time, could not be entirely ruled out. That every Latin American ruler had his price was a common and not unreal assumption in Washington. Had this young bearded upstart been building up pressure in order to raise the ante? But Fidel broke with tradition by asking for nothing explicitly, either publicly or in his private conversations with Secretary of State Herter and Vice-President Nixon (President Eisenhower, by what many believed was more than a coincidence, had left town to play golf).

Castro apparently went so far as to instruct his economic advisers to avoid all discussion of financial assistance with American officials, bankers, and investors. As one of his experts, Treasury Minister López Fresquet, reported in a book he wrote after he went into exile, when he asked Fidel what he had in mind, Fidel replied, "the

Americans will be surprised. And when we go back to Cuba, they will offer us aid without our asking for it. Consequently, we will be in a better bargaining position." [1] Maybe Castro believed or at least half-believed this. He was still an amateur at this game, very much aware that the year was 1959 and not 1954, flushed with success and, as always, a congenital optimist. In any case, he certainly overestimated his bargaining position, although in so doing he was no more inept than Herter and Nixon who considerably underestimated his bargaining position, as later events proved.

Castro Outlines His Position

Much of what Fidel said in his speeches and in press and television interviews during his ten days in the United States (April 15–25) could not be printed or even whispered in Havana today, although with the exception of *Hoy*—the Communist daily, which maintained a virtual blackout on the trip—all Cuban newspapers at the time published extensive reports.

Fidel, in short, had unexpectedly become a paragon of moderation and good behavior, even to the extent of being punctual at his appointments (for which the herculean efforts of his staff must be given due credit), although not to the point of restricting himself to the time allotted for his speeches. Thus, on April 17 at the National Press Club in Washington, instead of the thirty minutes assigned him, he spoke for two hours (in creditable English) before an audience of 1,000. In essence, what he said here and elsewhere during his trip—New York, Princeton, Harvard—boils down to the following:

1. Cuba is not looking for favors or money in the United States but a better commercial treaty; that is, it wants to sell more sugar and to raise tariffs on imports from the United States. With respect to the latter issue, this would mean that American exporters, instead of having a protected market in Cuba, would have to compete with other countries for Cuban sales and, at the same time, that Cuban enterprise would be encouraged to develop by the protection afforded against more efficient American producers. To the argument that the preferential treatment of American goods in Cuba was part of a deal by which Cuba was guaranteed a handsome quota of American sugar consumption at considerably higher prices than

1. Rufo López Fresquet, *My Fourteen Months with Castro* (Cleveland: World Publishing Co., 1966), p. 106.

those prevailing in the open world market, he replied that since 1948 Cuba has had an accumulated deficit of $1.5 billion in its trade with the United States.

2. Foreign investments in Cuban industry, but not in agriculture, are welcome when they fit Cuba's needs. With respect to agrarian reform, there are no plans for expropriation of foreign property.

3. The Cuban economic program has three basic planks: agrarian reform, industrial development, and the expansion of the purchasing power of the domestic market.

4. There are three ways in which economic development can be financed: by national savings, by promoting foreign private investment, and "by having a friend give us a billion dollars every year." This remark was intended to be taken as a joke but turned out to be prophetic. "We prefer doing it by our own efforts," that is, through national savings.

5. "I can tell you clearly we are not Communists" (at the National Press Club). "We are not Communists or capitalists. We are Cubanists" (at an impromptu gathering on a Washington street corner).

6. "We have received no aid from Russia or any other state, nor have we asked for any aid."

7. As a self-professed enemy of dictators, he was asked about Khrushchev: "We are against all dictatorships, personal or class. That's why we don't agree with communism."

8. "We shall continue our membership in the Rio Treaty," referring to the 1947 inter-American pact pledging mutual assistance in case of an attack coming from outside the western hemisphere. "We shall respect existing treaties but we will not sacrifice our independence. . . . Every country, including Cuba, should speak with absolute independence at the United Nations."

9. Cuba will provide a haven and full moral support for Latin American exiles opposed to dictatorships in their countries (in context meaning the Dominican Republic, Haiti, Nicaragua, and Paraguay). But Cuban policy is nonintervention in the internal affairs of Latin American governments.

10. Concerning Puerto Rico, "I did not authorize the Movement of July 26th to support the Independence party [the consistent line of *Revolución*]. Only the people of Puerto Rico can decide

what they want. I am grateful to Governor Muñoz Marín [bête noire
of the Independence party and all Communist parties in Latin
America] for defending our right to execute our war criminals."

An Unlikely Explanation

I have gone to some length in attempting to summarize what Castro
said during his visit to the United States because, at the time and
later, much importance was attached to this visit. Some have maintained that by ostentatiously rejecting any suggestion that he would
accept financial assistance from the United States (although Fidel's
plea for a revision of the commercial treaty could be viewed as implying such a request), he was deliberately closing the door at this early
date to any accommodation with the United States and was already
contemplating a deal with Russia. His trip was, thus, purely and
simply a barnstorming stunt designed to influence public opinion in
the United States.

This explanation is unlikely. Fidel has made political miscalculations during his career, but he has never been politically simple-
minded. Like all successful political leaders, whether they profess a
belief in God or Karl Marx, he has been a disciple of Machiavelli,
capable of inconsistency, opportunism, and deceit but not for their
own sake and always weighing anticipated profits against costs in any
political operation.

There were costs to contemplate in his performance in the
United States. In Cuba the dominant left wing of his movement was
clearly embarrassed. *Revolución* was hard put to "edit" Fidel's re-
marks as they juggled, scrambled, and slanted reports of his speeches.
Hoy simply imposed a virtual blackout on news about his trip. And
among Cuba's valuable nationalist and anti-imperialist supporters in
Latin America, one can imagine the doubts raised about Fidel
Castro, the firebrand orator of Caracas less than three months before.

The costs were high if Fidel's objective was to gain time by dis-
orienting public opinion in the United States and Cuban conservatives at home. Did he need the time, and how much time would he
gain, when he already knew that his agrarian reform law would be
on the books three weeks after his departure from the United States?
But the costs were acceptable, indeed inevitable, if Castro was in
fact seriously and hopefully seeking a deal, a "new deal" and in his
own inimitable way to be sure, but nonetheless a deal.

The Russian Reaction

There is evidence to indicate that the Russians were disturbed about Castro's trip, and understandably so. Here, for the first time in Latin America since the Mexican Revolution of 1910, there were genuinely troubled waters to fish in. Although at this early date and for some time to come the Soviet attitude about involvement in the Caribbean Sea—the mare nostrum of the United States—was one of caution and restraint, Castro's nationalism and radicalism offered exciting possibilities, no doubt amply discussed by a stream of high-ranking PSP commuters between Havana and Moscow. There must even have been speculation, grounded in the theory of the "national democracy," a definition applied to the new Cuban regime, that Castro represented a transitional stage of development to be followed in due time by a PSP take over. However, Castro's presence in Washington could put an end to this promising outlook. In any event, if his trip was indeed an elaborate exercise in dissimulation, the Russians seemed to be unaware of it. Carlos Lechuga, a feature writer for *El Mundo*, which was at the time a sober middle-of-the-road Havana daily (Lechuga was to replace a pro-Soviet ambassador to the United Nations following the October 1962 missile crisis), sent an amusing dispatch (April 19) about Soviet Ambassador Menshikov's appearance at a reception for the Washington diplomatic corps which Castro gave at the Cuban embassy. There was the customary brief handshake, after which Fidel turned to greet other incoming guests. Later, according to Lechuga, Menshikov, followed by photographers, kept trying to get close to Fidel but somehow failed. The implication was that Fidel was consciously dodging, although Lechuga did not say so specifically. He did mention, not without malice, that Cuba had no diplomatic relations with Russia, as if to say, What was Menshikov doing there in the first place?

Perhaps this episode merely adds a bit of local color to the story of Castro's trip (there was a good deal of local color to report, such as the picket promenading in front of Fidel's hotel in Washington with a placard reading "We don't like beards! BARBERS OF AMERICA"). A TASS release picked up and circulated by the Associated Press on April 15, the day Castro reached Washington, was more significant. TASS quoted *Volkstimme*, organ of the Austrian Communist party, as making the following comment concerning Castro's visit: "It is expected that Castro will be a tough negotiator with the American monopolies. He has often said that Cuba was prepared to ask for aid from the socialist countries if the United States continues its economic pressure against his country."

Thus far, Fidel had never stated that he had asked or would ask for any kind of aid from the socialist countries, at least not publicly. Hence, this obvious bit of provocation, the responsibility for which could technically be attributed to an obscure Communist paper, can only be explained by an uneasiness concerning Fidel's intentions. For TASS, a sophisticated agency of the Soviet government, the effect of this maneuver could be anticipated: it would confirm the worst suspicions about Castro already loudly voiced in Congress and elsewhere by the hard-line opponents of the Cuban Revolution.

A Genuine but Unacceptable Offer

The most reasonable assumption about Castro's visit to the United States is that he came bearing an olive branch. Moreover, it is consistent with his thinking at the time. Fidel was first and foremost a nationalist. Here his ideas were clear. He knew exactly what he wanted—sovereignty and independence—and he also knew this meant a confrontation with the United States.

Fidel was also a radical, but here his ideas were not clear. They reflected Martí and later Cuban rebels like Guiteras. He might even have considered himself a socialist after the manner of Guiteras, which was a far cry from "scientific" socialism. In no sense was he a Marxist or Leninist about whose doctrines he knew next to nothing. His philosophical views about social justice could more easily have come from Cervantes and Victor Hugo than from Lenin or Stalin. When he and his spokesmen repeated time and again that they were "neither capitalists nor Communists but humanists," that they were equally opposed to "capitalist freedom without bread" and "Communist bread without freedom," that their ideology was as "Cuban as the palm trees on our island," they were not perpetrating a hoax.

In this context, his statements on economic matters in mid-April were genuine expressions of his ideas at the time. This becomes clear if we examine the keystone and most radical innovation of his economic program, the agrarian reform law, which was promulgated

on May 17, 1959, soon after Castro's return to Cuba. Many writers have erroneously considered this event as the point of no return in Castro's leap into socialism and the showdown between the United States and Cuba.

The fact is, however, that the Cuban law in most respects resembled the texts of agrarian reform laws adopted in Mexico in 1911 and Bolivia in 1952. Foreigners were forbidden to acquire new landholdings, but otherwise they were treated on equal terms with Cuban nationals. Efficient producers (which would include practically all American sugar planters) were permitted to retain up to approximately 3,000 acres, that is, three times the normal maximum of 1,000 acres, with indemnification provided for all land expropriated. In addition, the law did not affect ownership of sugar mills, the most important of which belonged to American corporations and accounted for about 50 percent of sugar production, thus occupying a strategic position in the sugar economy.

As the French economist Michel Gutelman points out in his book *L'agriculture socialisée à Cuba*—the most competent treatment of the subject so far—the law of May 17, 1959, was primarily designed to "create and firmly establish a lower-middle-class peasantry," organized in cooperatives where sugarcane land was concerned since it could not be exploited efficiently in small individual units. "There was no question of eliminating private property on the land or of setting up state farms." [2] Gutelman in addition notes that the pace of land distribution was surprisingly slow at the beginning. During the first ten months—that is, well into 1960—only 6,000 families received land. "At this rate it would have taken twenty years to satisfy the needs of some 150,000 potential beneficiaries." [3]

The sudden spurt of wholesale expropriations, which led before the end of 1960 to the de facto conversion of cooperatives into state farms, to the nationalization of all important industrial enterprise including the sugar mills, to the wiping out of close to a billion dollars worth of American investments—in short, to a socialist economy—was the result of Fidel Castro's exuberant response to a combination of unplanned circumstances, a subject I shall deal with at a later point in this narrative.

Gutelman makes a good case when he explains that, quite apart from other factors, the technical characteristics of sugar production

2. Paris, 1967, p. 55.   3. *Ibid.*, p. 54.

and the fundamental role of sugar in the economy and social structure of Cuba would have made it difficult to implement a bourgeois
democratic revolution of the Mexican or Bolivian type. But he also
points out that this does not mean that a socialist state was inevitable.
In fact, he goes on to say, "state appropriation of the means of
production in the dominant sectors does not *ipso facto* mean a socialist economy. It is entirely conceivable that the Cuban Revolution
could have moved into some form of state capitalism, of the Egyptian
or Malian type, for example." [4]

Thus, again, it is not at all improbable that Castro came to
Washington waving an olive branch. But it is altogether improbable that, even assuming Washington's ability to recognize the
signal, it would have been willing or able to respond. There were
large, prickly thorns on the olive branch, both economic and political;
and besides, how could one conduct businesslike negotiations with
this arrogant, eccentric, and unpredictable young Cuban? For the
United States all of this turned out to be unfortunate and, weighing
the pros and cons of what occurred in the following decade, for the
Cuban people as well. But for Fidel it was another one of those
providential mishaps, like the Moncada defeat, that paved the way
for his meteoric rise to fame, and with him a place in the sun for
Cuba.

The Buenos Aires Epilogue

A brief epilogue to Castro's North American tour was enacted in
Buenos Aires on May 2, 1959, where he delivered a speech at an
inter-American economic conference. Herbert Matthews wrote that,
if the speech was taken literally, it "offered the last chance for
the United States . . . to keep Castro within a more or less democratic, certainly non-Communist, hemispheric framework." [5]

The speech was notable for three things, a declaration of principles and two economic proposals: "We have declared that the
democratic ideal is the ideal of this hemisphere . . . ; however, economic and social conditions in Latin America make the realization
of the democratic ideal impossible. . . . Whether power is held by a
dictatorship of the left or of the right, what counts is that they are

4. *Ibid.*, p. 50.
5. Matthews, *Fidel Castro* (New York: Simon and Schuster, 1969),
p. 166.

dictatorships and thus completely deny the principles which are the aspiration of the peoples of Latin America." [6]

The two proposals he made—and indeed the entire economic program of the Cuban Revolution at this time—came directly from the studies and recommendations of the United Nations Commission for Latin America, headed by the prestigious Argentine economist, Raúl Prebisch. One of Castro's leading economic advisers, who was with him in Washington and Buenos Aires, was Regino Boti, a former member of Prebisch's staff (he later headed Fidel's socialist Central Planning Board for four years and then passed into obscurity). Both proposals were politically premature, to say the least. One was to create a Latin American common market. It was only in 1967 that such a project (excluding Cuba) was officially approved by the Latin American republics. The other amounted to a request that the United States make available a $30-billion credit for the economic development of Latin America over a period of ten years. In a sense, he did what he refused to do a week earlier in Washington, that is, ask for American financial assistance; but this time his "dignity" was unimpaired since he was in Buenos Aires and speaking in behalf of all of Latin America.

Matthews wrote that a "figurative roar of laughter went up in all communications media from the Canadian border southward. The American delegation dismissed the idea with amused contempt. But less than two years later President Kennedy put forward the proposal for his Alliance for Progress, pledging $10 billion for the first ten years. Later President Johnson promised another $10 billion to continue the program." [7]

Concerning Castro's appearance in Buenos Aires, Javier Pazos, a young economist who left Cuba in September 1960, had some interesting things to say in an article published in the *New Republic* on January 12, 1963. He was a member of Fidel's staff both in Washington and at the Buenos Aires conference, where he had a number of opportunities to speak with him and observe him closely. "During his stay in Argentina at the Inter-American Conference," Pazos wrote, "Fidel was very enthusiastic about his private Alliance for Progress scheme for $30 billion. . . . My impression then was that he was contemplating the possibility of staying on the American side of the fence as a sponsor of this $30 billion scheme and as the

6. Cited on the editorial page of *El Mundo*, March 1, 1960.
7. Matthews, p. 167.

leader of a Nasser-type revolution in Cuba and Latin America. In any case, I repeat, Fidel considered himself to be in a strong position vis-à-vis the United States." Later in the article he stated that the "Americans *did* want to negotiate [in Washington] but we don't know what they were willing to negotiate. . . . If the United States had . . . been disposed to lend money to Cuba, it should have said so publicly, stating its conditions in an unambiguous way."

Castro's performance in Buenos Aires had long been consigned to the dustbin of history when Benjamin Welles wrote in 1969 apropos the vanishing esteem for the Alliance for Progress in Latin America: "Foreign investment in Latin America now runs close to $1.4 billion [per annum]. . . . Latin economists believe that at least $3 billion in investment is needed yearly." [8] This sounds remarkably like the proposition Fidel made almost exactly ten years before.[9]

After Buenos Aires, the prospects for a modus vivendi between the United States and Cuba rapidly diminished. In August 1961, four months after the Bay of Pigs invasion, Cuban proposals for "peaceful coexistence" were turned down at an Organization of American States (OAS) meeting in Uruguay. In late 1963, the start of a "dialogue" between John Kennedy and Fidel Castro was cut short by the president's assassination. In a speech on July 26, 1964, Fidel offered to abandon the Latin American (and world) revolution in return for the normalization of relations with the United States, but the offer fell on deaf ears. In 1971, when President Nixon hinted at a possible reconciliation, Fidel indignantly rejected the overture because, as he said, "Normal relations with the imperialists would mean renouncing our elementary duties of solidarity with the revolutionary peoples . . . of Latin America." [10]

8. *New York Times*, May 12, 1969.

9. Let it be said, as a consolation for presidents Kennedy and Johnson, that if the Alliance for Progress failed to solve the economic problems of Latin America, so has Marxism-Leninism, or at least its Fidelista version, in Cuba.

10. Speech on April 19, 1971, the tenth anniversary of the Bay of Pigs victory. *Granma Weekly Review*, May 2, 1971. See also the *New York Times* editorial, "No Ping-Pong for Castro," April 21, 1971. The only Latin American "revolutionary peoples" with whom he was actively promoting "solidarity" at the time were those of Chile, Peru, and Bolivia and their governments, all three of which maintained normal relations with the United States.

6

∎

A Developing Conflict

Debate in the United States

IT IS NOW COMMON KNOWLEDGE that President Eisenhower gave his consent on March 17, 1960, for what was to become the Bay of Pigs invasion a little more than a year later. Although it was not an irreversible decision—as President Kennedy to his sorrow later realized—it is fair to say that it marked a crystallization of American policy, at least in a formal sense. Actually, however, sustained paramilitary hostilities against Cuba can be said to have begun on January 12, 1960, when a small plane proceeding from a base in Florida dropped a few incendiary bombs on the Hershey Company cane fields on the north coast of Havana Province.

According to credible data compiled by José A. Benítez in *David Goliat Siglo XX*,[1] until the end of the sugar harvest in May similar raids on close to a score of cane fields in various parts of the island destroyed an estimated half-million tons of sugarcane, damaged other property, and caused a few human casualties. In the case of four planes that crashed, the pilots were discovered to be Americans and documents aboard showed that the planes had flown from Florida airports.

In a sense it can be said that the decision of the Eisenhower administration was a natural one. There was the immediate precedent of the intervention in Guatemala and before that scores of major or minor military incursions in Latin America going back to the Mexican War of 1848. Or one could say it all began in 1823, when the Monroe Doctrine first set forth the principles that were to serve as justification of American hegemony in the western hemisphere.

1. Havana: Ediciones Granma, 1967, pp. 118–119.

And in the specific case of Cuba, there had been a particularly active tradition of American interference since 1898.

However, these explanations oversimplify the complexities of Cuban-American relations in the fateful year of 1959. While the historical response of American policy finally prevailed, it was by no means an automatic response. What is also interesting is that this was reflected in the Cuban press at the time.

In examining the record, it comes as a surprise years later to come across this statement in mid-1959 by Barry Goldwater: "every country has a right to make its own reforms. Cuba's agrarian law is an internal matter. . . . The United States has no reason to interfere in Cuba's agrarian reform." [2] A few weeks later Nelson Rockefeller, then in Puerto Rico and possibly influenced by the local political climate which was favorable to the Cuban Revolution, nevertheless went on record as saying, "I think Fidel Castro has done a magnificent job." [3]

At the end of October, Senator Mike Mansfield was still friendly toward Castro, suggesting that if he would be "practical" in his relations with the United States, he could "go a long way." [4] At the end of the following month, George Aiken, Republican member of the Senate Foreign Relations Committee, on returning from a tour of Latin America, including Cuba, was asked to comment on the economic sanctions that the hawks in and out of Congress had for many months been pushing as a way of bringing down the Castro regime. He said, "I wouldn't vote for the lowering of the Cuban sugar quota"; he went on to say, "Castro is not a Communist. . . . I believe this is a nationalist movement." [5]

At about the same time, Harold Cooly, Democratic chairman of the powerful House Agriculture Committee was quoted as saying that he, too, was opposed to cutting the sugar quota. His reason, less than altruistic but nonetheless showing political insight, was that "it would make a martyr of Fidel Castro." [6] Clearly there was no unanimity of opinion on the Cuban problem in the important American media. Suffice it to mention the contrast between the hostility of the *Journal of Commerce* and the Luce publications, on

2. United Press dispatch in *Revolución*, July 22, 1959.
3. *Revolución*, August 7, 1959.   4. *El Mundo*, October 28, 1959.
5. *El Mundo*, November 22, 1969.
6. *El Mundo*, November 21, 1959.

the one hand, and the moderation of the *New York Times, Saturday Evening Post,* and *Look,* on the other.[7]

A curious item in the ultra-hawkish New York *Journal American* is also revealing. First, it pulled together and printed some of the canards then circulating, such as, there were Russian military advisers in Cuba, the Russians were sending arms to Cuba via submarine, the Russians had begun to construct missile sites in Cuba (how weird it all seems now after pure fiction was converted into the real thing). Then it went on to say that the United States had a powerful weapon with which to bring down the Cuban economy, "but there is a strong current of opinion in the State Department that we must continue to live with Cuba, with or without Castro, and that such economic reprisal will never be forgotten by the Cuban people." [8]

This criticism was, of course, aimed at the State Department, and it is true that there was some reason for complaint. In March 1959 Philip Bonsal had arrived in Havana as the new United States ambassador. Unlike his two predecessors, who got along famously with Batista, Bonsal was a sophisticated professional diplomat, with many years of experience in Latin American affairs and an understanding of the process of change under way south of the Rio Grande. Bonsal's appointment could well be interpreted as an indication that the State Department wished to explore the possibilities of negotiation.

7. Maurice Zeitlin and Robert Scheer, *Cuba: Tragedy in Our Hemisphere* (New York, 1969) conclude that, on the basis of their analysis of nine magazines and three daily newspapers, U.S. press coverage of the Cuban Revolution (January 1, 1959–October 19, 1960) was overwhelmingly hostile (pp. 283–302). Michael J. Francis ("The U.S. Press and Castro: A Study in Declining Relations," *Journalism Quarterly* [Urbana, Ill.], summer 1967, pp. 257–266), after studying seventeen daily newspapers, found that for the year 1959 the attitude of ten of these papers toward the Castro regime ranged from "cautious" to "quite hopeful." Two mimeographed documents tend to support the diversity of approach found by Francis: "A Press Digest on United States–Cuba Relations, 1957–1961," compiled by a group of Harvard graduate students, with a foreword by Joyce Kolko (Cambridge, Mass., 1961); and "The American Press and Cuba, 1958–1959: Editorial Attitudes of Four Newspapers," a master's thesis by Thomas H. Brose (University of Missouri, 1960).

8. Reproduced in *Revolución,* November 13, 1959.

Much later, in a rare mood of contrition, Fidel Castro admitted that "we" shared some of the responsibility for the breakdown of relations with the United States, but he gave no details.[9] Thus with better luck in Havana and Washington, something might have come of Bonsal's appointment.

Domestic Pressures in Cuba

Fidel's problems began to mount in the second half of 1959, and they were not all subjective. In a sense the Revolution was acquiring a momentum of its own. Confusion reigned and at times turned into chaos, as youthful, enthusiastic, and inexperienced officials of all ranks began to administer government decrees and improvise policy on the working level "por la libre," a Cuban expression that translates literally as "in a free manner" but with connotations of the Cuban's natural disposition toward anarchy (it took years for Fidel, himself a practitioner of "por la libre," to bring it more or less under control in the lower ranks of the bureaucracy).

Thus, agrarian reform to a certain extent became a process of helter-skelter expropriation of properties with no regard to legal procedures, while in the new cooperatives the members were frequently reduced to the status of employees by the government-appointed technical supervisors.

There was also haste and confusion in embarking on other economic reforms. Various kinds of no-profit enterprises were set up. Decrees were enacted slashing urban rents, the price of drugs and medicines, and telephone tolls. New legislation on mineral rights and mining operations was introduced. The reforms and irregularities at this stage were still marginal in relation to the economy as a whole, which was booming along; but they affected enough people—including American property holders—to be a noticeable source of irritation and apprehension concerning the future.

There were also trigger-happy squads of the rebel army patrolling the streets of Havana. People became accustomed to the sound of gunfire at night. The following incident gives some idea of the problems on this level. One of the largest beach clubs in the fashionable Miramar suburb of Havana, which was expropriated and turned over for use by primary and secondary schoolchildren, now bears the

9. Stenographic report of interview with sixty-seven foreign correspondents in Santiago; *Revolución*, July 29, 1964.

name of "Comandante Cristino Naranjo Social Club" (*coman-dante*, or major, is the highest rank in the Cuban army), in honor of a fallen revolutionary hero. Few today remember how Cristino Naranjo met his end. On the night of November 13, 1959, the comandante and two soldiers, all in civilian clothes, were driving rapidly on a dark street when they were intercepted by an army patrol car on the lookout for suspicious characters. Asked to produce his identification papers, Comandante Naranjo reached in his pocket, whereupon the patrol, apparently assuming he was going to draw a pistol, opened fire. The two companions of the comandante at once returned fire. When the fracas was over, one person was wounded and three lay dead including the comandante.[10]

In this setting, counterrevolutionary activities, which were bound to come sooner or later, came sooner. Early in July 1959, the government decreed that the death penalty, hitherto restricted to "war criminals," would apply to espionage, counterrevolution, and specified types of political and economic subversion.

Two important defections from the higher revolutionary ranks took place, one in June and the other in October 1959. The first defector, Major Pedro Díaz Lanz, appeared as a witness before the United States Senate Internal Security Subcommittee, an event that Castro wrathfully denounced as American intervention in Cuban affairs. The second, Major Huber Matos, went to prison. In both cases they declared that communism was the issue over which they broke with Fidel.

This may have been so, or it may have been personal rivalries, thwarted ambitions, or a combination of any number of grievances. The motives of human beings can be complex and difficult to un-ravel, and not infrequently an individual may have only a dim per-ception of what really moves him. Or putting it another way, who can say how many of those who have climbed the ladder of oppor-tunity in Fidel's regime have remained loyal to the Revolution out of pure conviction or because they have reached the upper strata of the bureaucracy, where the exercise of authority, prestige, and some of the amenities denied the rest of the population are preferable to the dangers of defection or the hardships of exile?

However it may be, the defections and associated ideological polemics became a source of mounting psychological warfare between

10. *El Mundo*, November 14, 1959.

Cuba and the United States which, in turn, exacerbated the already strident nationalism of Castro's following and reinforced Castro's intransigence. Paradoxically, American-generated anti-Communist propaganda designed to discredit the Castro regime had the opposite effect in Cuba. Fidel in his speeches could make a convincing distinction between noncommunism and anticommunism, the latter being equated with treason and counterrevolution.

Thus, there were extenuating circumstances to explain Fidel's growing irritation and impatience with the United States. At the same time, his response to the conflicting signals emanating from the north was not only a matter of judgment but, perhaps even more, of temperament. As he would say from time to time in his speeches, "We are not afraid of danger. As a matter of fact, we thrive on it. And besides, everyone has to die sooner or later." Coming from the leader of suicidal exploits, his remarks were entirely credible.

A Revealing Episode

The question of trade relations with the United States meant first and foremost sugar. Here the indications were increasingly that there was no prospect for a significantly higher Cuban quota. On the contrary it might be lowered if Castro did not behave. Early in June 1959, further confirmation came from a spokesman of the United States Department of Agriculture to the effect that it was impractical to think of raising Cuba's quota since agrarian reform would likely cut down sugar production.

Reacting impulsively to the shadow cast on his agrarian reform, Fidel, on June 4, 1959, sent a cable over his signature to the secretary of agriculture in Washington offering to sell 8 million tons of sugar in 1961 at 4 cents a pound. He also requested a reply by June 15.

This was a startling departure from the norms of intergovernmental communication and, coming from any other source, would have been dismissed as a practical joke. The quota in 1959 was 3 million tons at 5.4 cents a pound. Fidel was offering a bargain at 4 cents, take it or leave it by June 15. To export 8 million tons to the United States would have meant that Cuba would have had to produce 9 million tons to meet domestic needs and other commitments, and only once in its history had Cuba produced as much as 7 million tons; these facts, however, did not deter Fidel in the least. He undoubtedly believed that he was making a serious proposition.

His 8-million-ton figure was not a sudden improvisation. Great visions of massive sugar production had been stirring in his fertile imagination. A month earlier he had told a group of small sugarcane farmers that "we should be producing 8, 9, 10, 12 million tons" [11] without the slightest notion of how it could be done or where such quantities would be sold.

Later, as we shall see, the vision changed. Sugarcane monoculture, the curse of Cuba's underdevelopment, was to be eradicated through crop diversification and industrialization. Disaster followed, bringing back the old vision, this time with a specific goal of 10 million tons in 1970. The task of producing this magic quantity—for which in the end the entire population had to be mobilized and sent to the cane fields, while many essential activities were brought to a virtual standstill—became the economic and social nightmare that ushered in the second decade of the Revolution.

The United States Department of Agriculture sent a courteous reply to Castro before his offer expired. The gist of the message was that the United States would be unable to absorb 8 million tons of Cuban sugar, since total consumption in 1961 was estimated at 9.2 million tons, of which 4.8 million had been allocated to producers in the United States and its possessions and nearly one million tons to the Philippines.[12]

Here, then, is one example—more colorful than others but essentially not untypical—of the obstacles that lay in the path of meaningful Cuban-American negotiations. Somebody in the Department of Agriculture made a politically provocative (though otherwise sober) prognosis concerning Cuba's agrarian reform. Castro eagerly swallowed the bait, abandoned normal channels, and in a spectacular gesture made a wild offer, which the department turned down on technically unimpeachable grounds, thereby casting doubt on Fidel's intentions or competence, or both.

In a strange way, both sides were now happy. Each side believed it had scored some good points in the debate, and each side had confirmed its darkest suspicions of the other. Washington was more convinced than ever that it was dealing with a dangerous eccentric. Havana was more than ever convinced of Washington's implacable hostility toward the Cuban Revolution.

To conclude this particular story, the record shows that the

11. *El Mundo*, April 5, 1959.   12. *El Mundo*, June 11, 1959.

Department of Agriculture was wrong about the immediate prospects of Cuba's agrarian reform but right in the longer run. In 1961, by harvesting uncut cane left over from previous years, Cuba produced close to 7 million metric tons of sugar, the second largest crop in its history. Production, however, fell sharply in the following eight years, averaging well below the yields in the decade preceding the Revolution.

7

A Global Foreign Policy

A New Foreign Minister

ON JUNE 12, 1959, IT WAS ANNOUNCED that Roberto Agramonte, a proponent of conciliation with the United States, was replaced as secretary of state for foreign affairs (a title soon to be changed to minister of foreign affairs) by Raúl Roa. Washington understood this appointment, at least in part, because Roa, a leading intellectual of the previous revolutionary generation, was a radical and fervent nationalist. However, other implications of this appointment were more difficult to evaluate at the time. Roa had been closely associated with and perhaps a member of the Communist party in the late 1920s but then moved away from the party and became a severe critic of its policies. After Batista seized the government in 1952, he went into exile in Mexico, where in due time he formed close ties with the Movement of July 26th.

In Mexico, Roa continued to write extensively on political, literary, and philosophical topics. Among his publications during this period was an article containing a scathing attack on the Soviet Union for its suppression of the Hungarian uprising in 1956. Interrestingly enough, this article was reprinted in a collection of Roa's essays published in Cuba in November 1959 entitled *En Pie, 1953–1958* ("Standing firm"), a book that later disappeared from Cuban bookstores and libraries.

It is worth sampling the flavor of this article not only because Raúl Roa is Cuba's foremost master of invective but because he is still Castro's minister of foreign affairs: "the brutal methods used by the Soviet army to suppress the patriotic uprising of the Hungarian people" have created the "deepest repugnance in the free conscience of the world." Not content with this, he went on to heap scorn on western Communist intellectuals, calling them "the trained seals and chatterbox lackeys of Moscow, . . . the brainwashed trumpeters and stableboys of Caesaristic-Papist Marxism." [1]

A New Roving Ambassador

It was also in mid-June 1959 that Comandante Ernesto "Che" Guevara—who by now had become a leading public exponent of militant anti-Yankeeism—left on a three-month tour of Africa, Asia, and Europe, which greatly disturbed Washington.

There was speculation about why Fidel sent Che on this long journey. It was suggested that his hard-hitting speeches and known Communist sympathies were an embarrassment to Fidel at this time, and therefore his absence from Cuba would relieve tensions. If this were so, then Fidel miscalculated, for Che stirred up more embarrassment abroad than he did at home. However, the explanation for the trip is much more simple. Castro, as a matter of principle that went back to José Martí, considered that the exercise of Cuban sovereignty required the development of independent political and commercial relations on a global scale. At the same time—and this was a matter of some urgency—such relations would strengthen Cuba's position vis-à-vis the United States. In this connection, particular emphasis was given to securing the support of the nonaligned nations of the Third World. This policy was to be pursued even after the Soviet Union had become the chief underwriter of the Cuban Revolution, a seeming anachronism but not entirely so in view of the fact that Cuba never became a member of the Warsaw Pact and that Cuban foreign policy in due time clashed with Soviet policy on a number of important issues.

To head this path-breaking mission Fidel could have found no one better qualified than Che. The then thirty-one-year-old Argentine physician turned guerrilla leader was already a colorful figure in the world press. Among Fidel's reliable but inexperienced associates, he was certainly the one with the keenest mind and most arresting personality. Thus it was that, accompanied by three aides, Che reached Cairo on June 16, 1959, on the first leg of a journey that was then to take him in succession to India, Japan, Indonesia, Cey-

1. Roa, En Pie, p. 217.

lon, Burma, Pakistan, Yugloslavia, Morocco, and back to Havana via Madrid on September 8. He had expected to visit Ghana and Iraq, but for some unexplained reason failed to do so. When asked why he left out Israel, he simply replied that it was not on his itinerary.

Commercially, the mission turned out to be no great success, although it was hailed as a great step toward economic independence. Che straightened out a sugar problem in Tokyo and made a few stabs at barter agreements in his other stops in Asia, while his stay in Cairo resulted in Nasser sending a commercial delegation to Havana in early August. What apparently took Che, Fidel, and their companions some time to grasp was that trading with the underdeveloped countries of the Third World, like Cuba exporters of raw materials and importers of manufactured goods, was in no sense an alternative to trading with the United States. It was the equivalent of taking in each other's washing.

From the political point of view, there was evidence that the barnstorming trip was useful in several countries, notably in Egypt, Japan, India, and Yugoslavia. It also contributed to the tension between the United States and Cuba, principally because of Che's outspoken remarks at news conferences, which were picked up by the wire services and given wide distribution.

Among these remarks was a virtual declaration of Cuban neutrality in the cold war, an attack on the United Fruit Company which he accused of organizing counterrevolution in Cuba as it had in Guatemala, and, concerning the establishment of diplomatic relations with the USSR, a flat statement that "we are planning to do so soon"—this in Cairo on June 28, 1959. It was also in Cairo that Che, as he stated on his return to Havana,[2] met with embassy officials of one or more Communist countries. In the context of his remarks, they almost certainly included military personnel, and probably Czechs, since Cuba's first source of weapons from East Europe was Czechoslovakia.

There is still another aspect of Che's travels that deserves mention. For his travels throw light on his ideological development and, to the extent that Che influenced the Cuban Revolution, on the early stages of the odd process that culminated in Fidel's announcement at the end of 1961 that the Cuban Revolution was a Marxist-Leninist revolution.

2. *Revolución*, September 9, 1959.

The country that most impressed Castro's roving ambassador was Yugoslavia, where he was very warmly greeted by Tito. In an interview in Belgrade on August 16, Che recalled that Tito, like Fidel, led a guerrilla army to victory. "There is a great similarity between the kind of struggle that gave Yugoslavia its freedom and independence and that which brought about the triumph of the Cuban Revolution," he stated; "We must follow the same road on which Yugoslavia embarked fifteen years ago." [3] And on August 20, in a second interview unmistakably underscoring Tito's resistance to Stalin, he declared, "We have seen how the Yugoslavs are building their country according to their own free determination." [4]

On his return to Havana, Che was even more explicit: "The country where we have seen the most interesting things, and in all sincerity as a revolutionary I must say so, whether some people like it or not, is Yugoslavia." [5] The "some people" were not hard to identify. They were the Soviet Union—where Tito, briefly "rehabilitated" by Khrushchev, was again in the doghouse—ipso facto the local PSP Communists, and of course China, which had not yet openly attacked the Russians but which was fiercely belaboring Yugoslav "revisionism" as a surrogate for the main object of its wrath.

What particularly impressed Che, as he explained, was the "great freedom of discussion" and the system by which workers "own and manage the factories in which they are employed," while the state regulated wages and exercised a broad supervision over the economy. "The system is complicated," Che reported, "and somewhat difficult to understand, but very interesting." [6]

That it was the Yugoslav brand of socialism which initially attracted Che does not seem surprising. It was not only the first with which he had direct contact but was, relatively speaking, independent and libertarian; and as he also noted, it had succeeded in industrializing an agrarian society, the great dream at the time of the Cuban Revolution. However, it is ironic that once socialism got under way in Cuba, Che became the chief exponent of the antithesis of the Yugoslav socialist model, a view in due time shared by Fidel. When Cuba began to export revolution to Latin America and both the

3. *Revolución*, August 18, 1959.
4. *Revolución*, August 22, 1959.
5. *Revolución*, September 9, 1959.   6. *Ibid.*

Soviet Union and Yugoslavia stepped up trade and aid to the governments Castro was trying to overthrow, then once more, as in the early stage of the Sino-Soviet conflict, Yugoslavia was given the role of surrogate and roundly denounced by Castro as "revisionist" and "capitalist."

After Che's death, several collections of his writings, speeches, and other remarks were published in Havana and by his admirers abroad. What he said about Yugloslavia in mid-1959 is nowhere included.[7] In all fairness to Che, if he were alive he would protest this omission. Though he became more and more dogmatic and fanatical in his beliefs as time went on, he never completely lost his candor and attachment to the free discussion he so admired in Yugloslavia on his first and only visit to that country.

More Reshuffling at the Top

While Che was on tour, two important changes took place in the government, both of which pointed in the direction of a hard line in Cuban foreign policy. On July 17, in something of a comic opera performance, Castro forced Manuel Urrutia, a gentleman lawyer of the old school and his first appointee as president of the Republic, to resign and replaced him with Osvaldo Dorticós, also a lawyer of an older generation and reputed to have been at one time a member of the PSP. In any event, he had joined Castro's underground movement in the late 1950s. On becoming president (a post he still held in 1971), he also became one of the prime minister's most trusted assistants, frequently heading missions abroad and eventually adding the directorship of the Central Planning Board to his functions.

On August 3, 1959, Marcelo Fernández, twenty-seven-year-old national director of the Movement of July 26th and a one-time student of engineering at the Massachusetts Institute of Technology who became a principal underground organizer for Fidel during the insurrection, was named undersecretary of state for foreign affairs. His main task was that of transforming a somnolent, largely decorative institution into a modern global network of political and commercial offices. Marcelo, an ardent and zealous Fidelista, was also

7. Also omitted in the most complete scholarly collection published in the United States, Rolando Bonachea and Nelson Valdes, eds., *Che: Selected Works of Ernesto Guevara* (Cambridge, Mass.; M.I.T. Press, 1969).

in the front ranks of the movement's anti-PSP polemicists and had to be purged, along with others, less than a year later to appease the PSP and the Russians. Eventually, when Fidel's honeymoon with the PSP-Russian complex ended, Marcelo got back in the good graces of Fidel, becoming president of the National Bank, then minister of foreign trade (where he remained in 1971), and finally a member of the Central Committee of the Communist party of Cuba.

An Easing of Tensions

Meanwhile, in mid-August, while Che was on the road and the foreign ministry was being reorganized, a special meeting of the foreign ministers of the Organization of American States was convened in Santiago, Chile. It was the beginning of a series of such meetings in which the United States first set about to counter Castro's offensive in Latin America and then to mobilize the governments of the region against him. It ended with the expulsion of Cuba from the OAS in January 1962.

Cuba, however, won the first round in Santiago. Although there was no lack of evidence of Cuban incitation of revolutionary activity against a number of Caribbean governments and of direct participation in armed intervention against three of them, the climate of public opinion in most of Latin America favored Castro over the disreputable military dictatorships which had lodged charges against him and which, in any case, had no serious trouble in repelling the invasions. As a result, the United States could not muster sufficient support against Cuba and had to be content with a few innocuous resolutions.

It was under the spell of Cuba's easy success in Santiago that Fidel, on September 5, 1959, received Ambassador Philip Bonsal, "after a number of implausible postponements," as Bonsal later explained.[8] The meeting lasted five hours, and according to Bonsal the "atmosphere was relaxed and friendly. . . . I had the impression that Castro had given a polite and appreciative hearing to my views. . . . The interview left me in a moderately hopeful mood." [9] Apparently, Fidel was less hopeful, although more forbearing than

8. Bonsal, "Cuba, Castro, and the United States," *Foreign Affairs*, January 1967, p. 269.
9. *Ibid.*

usual; for in a television interview on September 17, after acknowledging the ambassador's "goodwill," he said that it was undermined by anti-Cuban propaganda and hostile activities in the United States. "Policy does not entirely depend on him," he said. "They have created obstacles for his work in Cuba."

The next day, *Revolución* highlighted one of the recent "obstacles" and at the same time reflected Fidel's subdued pessimism and mildly conciliatory mood. Noting that Admiral Arleigh Burke, chief of United States naval operations, was constantly attacking the Cuban Revolution, and taking particular exception to his latest statement that Russian submarines were operating in Cuban waters with the complicity of Cuban authorities, *Revolución* declared with unaccustomed restraint, "We believe Admiral Burke is acting on his own. But how long will the White House remain silent while the admiral shoots his mouth off?"

On the very next day, September 19, *El Mundo* reported that in response to an official protest by the Cuban embassy in Washington, a navy spokesman had declared that Admiral Burke had been "misquoted." All in all, it appeared that while relations between the two countries were still far from cordial, tensions had eased somewhat.

The First Performance at the United Nations

At this critical moment, Raúl Roa, heading the Cuban delegation, appeared at the Fourteenth General Assembly of the United Nations where he made the first formal presentation of the new Cuban foreign policy. Roa's speech on September 24, 1959, was notable for a number of reasons: it was a forthright "declaration of independence"; it proclaimed Cuban neutrality in the cold war; it linked Cuba with the Third World, specifically the underdeveloped nations of Africa, Asia, and Latin America; and it placed Cuba in a position without precedence among the Latin American governments.[10]

It was a speech that undoubtedly reflected the real position of the Cuban government at the time, not only with respect to the United States but also to the Soviet Union, because much of it could only have been extremely irritating to the Russians and could not have been given had there been any anticipation of the kind of

10. *Revolución*, September 25, 1959.

relations that were soon to develop between Cuba and the Soviet Union.

Thus, there could have been small comfort for the Russians listening to Roa when he said that Cuba (quoting Castro) rejects both world systems because it refuses to "choose between capitalism under which people starve to death, and communism, which solves economic problems but suppresses the liberties that are so dear to mankind"; or when Roa, giving his own and more cogent version of the unacceptable choice declared, "We favor neither capitalism as it has functioned throughout history nor communism as in reality it is practiced today."

Roa also touched on a topic concerning which the Russians were particularly sensitive. Referring to the abuse inflicted on small nations by the great powers, he said, "Aggression of the type committed against Guatemala, [British] Guiana, Hungary, Algeria, and Tibet must not be repeated." The mention of Hungary—and the Chinese annexation of Tibet—in the same breath with Guatemala was, of course, shocking to any Communist, including the Cuban Communists who expressed "surprise" at Roa's "confusion." [11]

It all makes strange reading today. So much of what was said was soon destined to be repudiated. Explanations had to be given. Fact and fiction were intermingled and myths were created. When Roa was confronted on the Hungarian question at a later meeting of the United Nations, he simply said that he was mistaken, that at the time he did not know the facts. What else could he say and remain operative? It was the kind of problem that Fidel, champion of the sovereignty of small nations, had to face from time to time in the years that followed. Thus, in August 1968 he gave his support to the Soviet violation of the sovereignty of Czechoslovakia. He had his reasons, though he invented others. For the admirers of Fidel Castro, it was painfully embarrassing.

The Hard Core of Cuban Foreign Policy

There was, however, an element of stubbornness in Cuban foreign policy under Castro that remained constant through all the ideological confusions and contradictions that befuddled the Cuban Revolution, as well as its friends and enemies. In this respect, Roa's speech had prophetic implications. Precisely in connection with his

11. *Hoy*, September 25, 1959.

strictures concerning Guatemala and Hungary, Roa declared, "In the chess game of power politics, you will never find us playing the part of a docile pawn." It is in the nature of things that a small nation, once it falls into the sphere of influence of a great power, cannot easily escape the role of pawn when it suits the purpose of the great power. Castro made this discovery to his consternation during the missile crisis in October 1962. Nevertheless, the fact remains that Cuba under Castro has by and large not been a "docile" pawn. Thus, Roa could make the statement today without raising much objection in the United States, the Soviet Union, or China.

A significant example of Cuban indocility at the meeting of the General Assembly deserves mention. It will be recalled that the "spirit of Camp David" brightened the atmosphere at United Nations headquarters in the fall of 1959. Hence, delegation after delegation of the great and not so great powers spoke cheerfully and hopefully of the promise held forth by the recently concluded conversations between President Eisenhower and Chairman Khrushchev.

The Cuban representative could do no less than the others in calling attention to this event, which he found to be "encouraging." However, Roa must have startled the Assembly when he got down to what seemed to matter most to Cuba. "Nevertheless," he declared, "we are not at all favorably impressed by the fact that these conversations were planned and took place without taking into account the opinion of the small nations and particularly, in our case, of those which constitute the Latin American community. This regional community has the right . . . to expect that it be informed and consulted in matters which affect it directly." [12]

The burden of the criticism this time was meant to fall mainly on Eisenhower, and there was, to be sure, a play for Latin American sympathy. But it was the same principle that Fidel invoked three years later, when Kennedy and Khrushchev settled the missile crisis without consulting Cuba, only that time the burden fell on Khrushchev.

For the United States, Roa's performance must have been even more disagreeable than it was for the Soviet Union. Despite the slurs Roa cast on the latter, Cuba was not then a Soviet satellite, hence the Russians lost nothing and had something to gain by the mere fact that a Caribbean satellite was slipping out of the American

12. *Revolución*, September 25, 1959.

orbit. On the other hand, there was nothing to compensate the United States for the loss, and it was a real loss. Cuba was indeed slipping out of orbit.

"Cuba today," Roa announced to the Assembly, "for the first time in its history, is in fact free, independent, and sovereign; and as a consequence its foreign policy has been emancipated from every kind of shackle, subordination, and servitude. Formerly Cuba always voted as it was instructed to by another party. Today, Cuba votes as it alone sees fit." [13]

This Cuba did, but not rashly. On several African issues, its position differed from that of the United States. Notably, in the case of the war in Algeria then in progress, Cuba strongly supported Algerian independence, in keeping with its anticolonialist and pro–Third World position. The only cold war issue on which it reversed the previous Cuban position was on the perennial question of China's admission to the United Nations. Here Cuba registered an abstention in the voting, a gesture of independence to be sure, but a relatively prudent one consistent with its neither-capitalist-nor-Communist posture.

The Meaning of the Cuban Performance

The Cuban performance at this meeting of the United Nations undoubtedly further complicated whatever possibilities still existed for a negotiated settlement of Cuban-American differences. Yet it is difficult to see how the Castro regime could have avoided raising provocative issues on this occasion. On other questions, such as those involving property and trade, there was at least in theory some room to maneuver. Fidel at this time was by no means committed to setting up a socialist economy or risking the severing of economic relations with the United States.

However, the matter of sovereignty was a fundamental one for the Cuban Revolution, perhaps *the* fundamental one, a constant and invariable aim to which Castro and his generation of Cuban nationalists were committed from the very beginning. In addition, given the immensely important symbolic value that would be attached to its first statement of principles before the General Assembly of the United Nations, the new Cuban government could do no less than assert its sovereignty in the strongest terms.

13. *Ibid.*

We are not privileged to know the weight attached to this Cuban performance by the American policy makers. However, one can appreciate their difficulties. Cuban "neutralism" not only meant the loss of a sure vote in the United Nations—not in itself a catastrophe, but it opened up a Pandora's box of disconcerting problems: A "neutral" Cuba in a stictly committed inter-American system? The future of the United States naval base at Guantánamo? The Russian KGB competing on equal terms with the American CIA ninety miles from Florida? As Stalin felt when Tito passed out of his control, as Brezhnev would later feel when he suspected that Dubcek was going to do likewise, so in Washington the men engaged in *Realpolitik* must have contemplated the situation with the most serious misgivings.

8

■

Escalation and Denouement

A Final Effort at Dialogue

THERE WERE SO MANY STRAWS piling up so rapidly that it is difficult, and perhaps pointless, to identify the one that broke the camel's back. In any event, Bonsal reported that in "late November [1959], the cabinet was reorganized in a manner precluding any further possibility of rational dialogue between our two governments." [1] The most significant change was the appointment of Che Guevara as president of the National Bank.

Nevertheless, according to Bonsal, another and final effort at dialogue was made by Washington early in 1960. It took the form of a statement in part drafted by Bonsal and issued by the White House on January 26. Its salient points as described by Bonsal can be summed up as follows: a pledge of nonintervention by the United States and of "doing all in its power to prevent the use of its territory" as a base for hostile raids against Cuba; and respect for Cuba's "sovereign right" to undertake domestic reforms "with due regard" for its "obligations under international law," in which connection the United States will "defend the rights of its citizens in Cuba as provided under international law."

There was another point, which Bonsal did not mention in his article, directed against the "intrigues of international communism"

1. Bonsal, "Cuba, Castro, and the United States," *Foreign Affairs*, January 1967, p. 270.

which it was hoped the Cuban people would recognize and destroy. This point, whatever it was meant to accomplish, did not improve the prospects of dialogue with the Cuban government. In his reply to the White House, President Dorticós was particularly resentful about it. Bonsal's views concerning this statement, although not those of a completely disinterested evaluator since it embodied his own recommendations at this time, are nonetheless extremely interesting. They deserve to be quoted *in extenso:*

> This policy implied continued moderation and restraint on our part, denying Castro the chance to make political capital out of alleged American economic aggression. It could have slowed down the Soviet involvement in the Cuban economy, an involvement, in my judgment, more ardently desired at that time by Castro and Guevara than by Moscow. It would have given the Soviets the opportunity to counsel moderation instead of being forced to act or to let Castro fall. And even if the policy had failed to prevent Castro's move into the Soviet orbit, it would have gained sympathy and support for our Cuban policy in inter-American and international public opinion by relieving us of responsibility for precipitating events or destroying existing ties. Further it would have created more favorable conditions for local opposition to crystallize. And considering the state of disorganization and confusion then existing in the Cuban government, it was not Micawberish to hope that if events were not precipitated something might well turn up to alter the situation before Castro consolidated his security controls.[2]

Possibly Bonsal, writing in 1967 and with the benefit of hindsight, was reading things into the policy that were not there at the time it was formulated. However that may be, Bonsal further explains, "This policy lasted but a few weeks," to which one may add that during this time there was not the slightest indication that Castro would pick up the option or swallow the bait, whichever it was intended to be.

It was late in the game of confrontation. By mid-December 1959—that is, a full three months before Eisenhower's secret directive and sixteen months before it gave birth to the landing in the Bay of Pigs—Fidel was predicting an invasion of Cuba and organizing a student and workers' militia to meet it. "I am sure," said Fidel on

2. *Ibid.,* p. 271.

December 16 at a convention of sugar workers, "that we shall have to defend the Revolution with arms in 1960. . . . We must become psychologically prepared to fight against great odds. . . . We shall fight to the last man."

Given the Cuban temperament, this was not bad news. As a perceptive Spanish Communist in Cuba explained to me shortly after my arrival in Havana, "El cubano es muy luchador pero poco trabajador," which can be translated as "Cubans are great fighters but not much as workers." Accordingly, patriotic fervor ran high and continued to mount as the weeks and months passed. "The most significant political fact about Cuba today," the Boston *Daily Globe* reported on February 25, 1960, "is not communism but the wave of nationalism which has swept up almost every Cuban man, woman and child."

Thus it would seem that by the end of 1959, Fidel's position had hardened to such a point—cheerfully, we might add—that it would have taken a lot more than the Bonsal–White House gambit at the end of January 1960 to turn him around.

From Mikoyan's Visit to the Point of No Return

The confrontation between the two countries moved rapidly to what was now to be its inevitable denouement. In February 1960 Mikoyan opened the Soviet exposition in Havana and before he left signed a trade and loan agreement with the Cuban government.

On March 4 the French ship *Le Coubre*, carrying seventy-six tons of ammunition purchased in Belgium, exploded at the dock in Havana. Some 350 casualties were reported (weeks later the figure was cut in half). It was assumed to be a case of sabotage (later verified as such), and a banner headline in *Revolución* promptly blamed the United States. This was an unsubstantiated accusation, which Fidel later toned down to a "logical deduction," and which succeeded in causing a great amount of recrimination in Washington and Havana.

It was on this occasion that Fidel ended a fiery speech with the phrase "patria o muerte" ("fatherland or death"). Then on June 9, 1960, precisely at 3:40 A.M., Fidel signed off a speech to the Barbers' Union with "patria o muerte, venceremos" ("fatherland or death, we shall overcome"). Thus was born, in two installments, the most sacred slogan of the Cuban Revolution, the binding closing benediction of every speech made in Cuba since that day.

On March 18 in Havana, Yugoslavia signed a commercial agreement with Cuba. It was the second socialist state to do so. On the same day, Castro, who was having difficulty purchasing a helicopter in the United States, was presented with one as a gift from the USSR. The package also included surgical equipment for the benefit of the victims of the *Le Coubre* explosion.

On March 25 *El Mundo* announced that a total of 130,000 tons of sugar were sold to China, thereby in effect inaugurating trade relations with Peking. On April 1 the signing of a commercial agreement with Poland was announced. On April 3 the *New York Times* reported that the United States might cut off economic aid to Poland because of the agreement.

On April 6 the Havana press revealed that 155,000 acres belonging to the United Fruit Company had been expropriated, with an offer of compensation of $3.8 million in "agrarian reform" government bonds. This was the first significant chunk of American property to be affected by the agrarian reform of May 17 of the previous year. The amount offered never reached the bargaining stage, and there is no record that any agrarian reform bonds were ever printed.

On April 22 the secretary-general of the Chinese trade unions and a sizable delegation arrived in Havana from China. On the same day a commercial agreement was signed with Japan, an old customer, calling for the sale of 500,000 tons of Cuban sugar over a three-year period and, for the first time, the purchase of a sizable quantity of Japanese textiles among other items. American textile exporters were reportedly alarmed. The next day Castro announced that Cuba's foreign exchange reserves had risen from $78 million in January 1959 to $142 million. He was in a state of unabashed euphoria as he lashed out once more against American plans for aggression.

On May 7, 1960, diplomatic relations between Cuba and the USSR were reestablished. Roa, according to *El Mundo* on May 8, explained that "in fact they were tacitly established in January and ratified during Mikoyan's visit."

On May 12 headlines and front-page stories in Havana revealed that the United States embassy had in its possession stickers bearing the American flag and the following legend (in Spanish): "This property is owned or occupied by U.S. citizens, hence under the protection of the U.S. embassy. Please cooperate in the protection of this property. Philip Bonsal, U.S. Ambassador."

A scorching manifesto drawn up by the Federation of University Students declared that since this request for protection was not directed to the Cuban authorities, the stickers could only be explained as preparation for invasion. Bonsal replied that the printing of such stickers was routine procedure by American embassies all over the world for use in case of emergencies. There was no plan, he said, to distribute the stickers in Cuba. Fidel had the last word. If this were so, he replied on television on May 13, "Anybody with the most elementary notion of what the sovereignty of a country is must agree that this is a colonialist concept."

On June 8 *El Mundo* reported a statement made by Núñez Jiménez, at the time executive director of the National Institute of Agrarian Reform. He was in Moscow on a trade mission. In a conversation with Khrushchev, the latter told him that the Soviet Union did not need missile bases in Cuba because "by pressing a button we can hit any spot on earth." This was followed, on July 9, by Khrushchev's first and often repeated public statement that, "figuratively speaking," the Soviet Union would flatten the United States with atomic missiles if Cuba were attacked.

The Cuban press, by now more or less politically "coordinated," paid no attention at this time or later to the subtle ambiguity of "figuratively speaking," so that for the Cuban people the chairman was "literally speaking," thereby enormously boosting their confidence in the wisdom of Fidel's foreign policy.

On June 29 the Cuban authorities took over the Texaco oil refinery and on July 1 they completed the job by seizing the Esso and Shell installations. The companies, faced with an ultimatum to refine a certain amount of Russian crude oil (about a third of Cuba's annual consumption), apparently had some doubt about complying but decided not to do so after consulting Washington.

The only reason for this decision that makes sense is that Washington and the companies calculated that, should Castro retaliate by expropriating the refineries, the companies would be able to cut off Cuba's supply of petroleum. In this they were counting on a number of factors, principally on their ability to put pressure on the owners of independent tanker fleets not to charter their vessels to the

Russians. With not enough tankers of their own, the Russians would not be able to transport sufficient oil to meet Cuba's requirements. As a result, the Cuban economy would be paralyzed and the Castro regime would collapse.

This calculation turned out to be a fatal error of judgment, less ostentatious but comparable in magnitude to the Bay of Pigs miscalculation. Since the tanker business was depressed at the time and there were enough operators interested in making money, the Russians were able to overcome the difficulty of supplementing their own fleet which, at the same time, was in the process of being greatly expanded.[3] By 1968, according to Castro, the rate of delivery of Russian petroleum to Cuba was on the average of one tanker every fifty-four hours.

However one looks at it, the refinery crisis was certainly the point of no return in the process by which in a very few months Cuban sugar was cut off from the American market and all American property, with a book value of some $850 million, was nationalized.

Two Declarations

On August 29, 1960, the United States scored a point against Cuba at an OAS meeting in Costa Rica. With only Cuba voting against it, there was unanimous approval of the "Declaration of San José" which condemned "intervention and threat of intervention, even when conditional, from an extra-continental power" in the affairs of the western hemisphere.

It was not a resounding success for Washington. Cuba was not mentioned by name. While the Soviet presence in Cuba was under-

3. Khrushchev explains what took place, as follows: "Life on the island was in danger of coming to a standstill. It was urgent that we organize an oil delivery to Cuba on a massive scale. But that was easier said than done. We didn't have enough oceangoing vessels in our own tanker fleet. . . . When Italy agreed to sell us the necessary tankers, it caused a sharp conflict between Italy and America. . . . The lesson of the whole incident was that if a capitalist country sees a chance to make some extra money . . . it couldn't care less about economic solidarity." *Khrushchev Remembers*, with an Introduction by Edward Crankshaw (Boston: Little, Brown, 1970), p. 490. To one familiar with Cuban-Soviet relations, Crankshaw's firm belief in the authenticity of the reminiscences—"[with] all its limitations, its evasions, concealments, deceptions, omissions (some deliberate, some due clearly to the forgetfulness of the old)" (p. viii)—appears to be justified.

standably a matter of real concern for the United States, most Latin American governments were indifferent. Besides, many foreign ministers had to keep in mind public opinion at home, important sections of which were well disposed toward the Cuban Revolution. Hence, it took a bit of arm twisting by Secretary of State Herter to put the declaration through. But it was enough for Castro, who rose to the occasion.

On September 2, at a huge mass meeting which he declared to be the "Plenary Assembly of the Cuban People," Fidel excoriated the San José document, announced the opening of diplomatic relations with China forthwith (it would be a decade before Canada became the second western hemisphere country to make a similar move), and presented the first Declaration of Havana (there was to be a second declaration later on) for the approval of the masses.

The declaration, a long statement, included everything that could arouse the people of Cuba—and of all Latin America, for it was broadcast throughout the continent and published in many of the southern republics—against the United States and the Latin American governments that supported it. It was a frank declaration of political warfare, with no holds barred. Appended to the document was a resolution specifically approving Cuba's close ties with the Soviet Union and China. Put to a "vote" in a demonstration of "direct democracy," it was in fact enthusiastically endorsed by more than a half million sweating, shouting Cubans in an outburst of national pride and patriotic fervor. Fidel clearly won this round.

Fidel Castro at the United Nations

From September 19 to 28, 1960, Fidel attended the Fifteenth General Assembly of the United Nations in New York. Even though Nikita Khrushchev was also there, as well as numerous other heads of state, Castro the master showman stole the show. Running into a minor difficulty about accommodations at the Shelburne Hotel, his temper flared and he announced that he would pitch camp on the United Nations grounds. Finally, however, he had another inspiration and he and his retinue moved into the Theresa Hotel in Harlem. Hundreds of spectators blocked traffic at 125th Street and Seventh Avenue. In Havana a mass meeting was assembled to protest the discrimination against Fidel, attributed to the machinations of the United States State Department.

Nikita, not a slouch at showmanship, called on Fidel in his Harlem hotel accompanied by scores of reporters and photographers, and a few days later Nasser and Nehru followed suit. At the United Nations, Tito and Nkrumah, among others, made a great display of cordiality toward Fidel, who was also the guest of honor at an official reception given by the Uruguayan delegation. In Washington, where plans for the Bay of Pigs invasion were moving ahead, all of these events were unwelcome news.

Castro's speech before the General Assembly on September 26 was largely a rehash, skilfully done, of the Cuban position vis-à-vis the United States, including the now familiar appeal for support from the Third World. "The situation confronting Cuba," he declared, "is the same as that of the Congo, Egypt and Algeria." [4] He also gave notice that Cuba intended, by "legal means," to end the American occupation of Guantánamo Bay, a hopeless task that he prudently abandoned.

Like all of Fidel's speeches, his discourse at the United Nations was studded with pungent remarks, as when he referred to John F. Kennedy, whose threats against Cuba were outdoing those of Richard Nixon in the election campaign then under way, as an "illiterate and ignorant millionaire" [5] (after President Kennedy's assassination, Fidel spoke of him as an "enemy" for whom he had acquired a much higher opinion).

In retrospect, it is also interesting to recall a point made by Fidel that at the time seemed to many to be a rational rejoinder to an irresponsible "brass hat." It concerned Admiral Burke, the same one previously mentioned in our narrative, and Khrushchev's threat to defend Cuba with Soviet rockets. Fidel first quoted the admiral as saying in an interview that the threat was meaningless because Khrushchev "won't fire his rockets" since "he knows he'll be destroyed if he does." Then Fidel, obviously casting doubt on the admiral's sanity, continued, "This is indeed a dangerous calculation, because this gentleman actually reckons that in case of an attack against us we are going to be all alone. . . . But suppose that Mr.

4. *Claman los Pueblos por Justicia y Paz* (Havana: Imprenta Nacional de Cuba, 1960), p. 81. The pamphlet contains the speeches at the General Assembly by Kwamee Nkruma, Nikita Khrushchev, Fidel Castro, and Gamal Abdel Nasser, in that order.

5. *Ibid.*, p. 80.

Burke, even though he is an admiral, is mistaken?" [6] At this point the record shows that the whole Soviet delegation, with Khrushchev in the lead, broke out into loud applause.[7]

After the missile crisis of October 1962, a legend reading "Cuba Is Not Alone," which had been pasted on walls and windows throughout the island, disappeared. In 1966 and 1967, when relations between Cuba and the USSR reached their lowest point, Fidel would remind the Cuban people time and again, "We are all alone."

Point and Counterpoint

Meanwhile, the economic battle between the United States and Cuba had been gathering speed and amplitude. On July 6 President Eisenhower had ordered the reduction of sugar imports from Cuba by 700,000 tons, the remainder of Cuba's 3.1 million ton quota for 1960. Precisely one month later, Cuba, in a great leap forward, expropriated American property valued at $500 million. Then, on September 17 the American banks on the island were taken over with assets of about $250 million. On October 24 Castro nationalized all remaining American property. On December 16 Washington announced that no Cuban sugar would be imported during the first quarter of 1961, in effect marking the end of a Cuban sugar quota in the American market.

While these blows were being traded, dozens of official notes passed back and forth between the two governments, protests and counterprotests, propositions and counterpropositions, which each side knew in advance would be unacceptable to the other. They were notes in which each side was scoring debating points for the record. It was, as the French say, "un dialogue de sourds." Effective communication had broken down early and was replaced by the self-fulfilling prophesy: each side predicted that the confrontation would end in a total and irreconcilable clash and then proceeded to make its prophesy come true.

The Break in Relations

On January 2, 1961, at a huge rally commemorating the second anniversary of the Revolution, Castro again put on one of his unique performances. It began to drizzle and Fidel said, "I hope the rain won't spoil our celebration." The crowd shouted back, "We'll stay

6. *Ibid.*, p. 79.   7. *El Mundo*, September 27, 1960.

and get wet." Fidel: "In that case I'll get wet too." He removed his rain cape and tried to get on with his speech but a tremendous roar drowned out his words: "Put it back on, put it back on!" He continued for a sentence or two but the roar did not abate. He shrugged his shoulders and swung the cape over his back. A great applause and then silence. The drizzle had turned to rain as Fidel, his beard dripping, got to the main business of the day. "The revolutionary government has decided," he exclaimed, "that within forty-eight hours the embassy of the United States must reduce its personnel to the exact number in our embassy in Washington, which is eleven." Wild applause broke out, shouts of "Get them out of here, throw them out!" Fidel struggled to continue but had to wait until the noise subsided. "Let me explain," he went on. "There are more than three hundred of them here and 80 percent are spies. If they want to leave we won't stop them."

Under the circumstances Washington had no choice but to accept the invitation. This was how Castro managed to have the record show that it was the United States that severed diplomatic relations with Cuba on January 3, 1961.

A Drastic Improvisation

The break in relations came as an anticlimax to what William Appleman Williams aptly described as something out of "a script for a crude burlesque on the action-reaction, vicious-circle type of diplomacy" or game of "tit-for-tat . . . infused with the mounting anger and small-boy behavior" guided by a "spirit of dare and double-dare." [8] Nevertheless, in the last analysis, the larger responsibility for the failure to find a rational solution to the crisis must lie with the United States. The difficulties inherent in untangling and reordering a whole series of complex, interlocking economic and political bonds were enormous, and there were also prickly psychological barriers to surmount; but incomparably greater resources and skills presumably existed in the United States than in Cuba.

Of Professor Williams' two "small boys," it may be confidently said that only one thoroughly enjoyed acting out his part of the script and going far beyond it. In the course of the performance, Fidel had not only taken over all American property but with a few strokes of

8. Williams, *United States, Cuba, and Castro* (New York: Monthly Review, 1962), pp. 143–144.

the pen merrily wiped out the most important part of Cuban non-agricultural private enterprise, including both industrial and large retail establishments.

This drastic measure was not part of the script. It was an improvisation due to a convergence of motivations, none of which was strictly speaking ideological. It sprang in part from the rapid linkup with the planned economies of the Soviet bloc and China. There was also the design of securing acknowledgment by the Soviet Union that Cuba had been accepted as a member of the "socialist club," thereby hopefully strengthening the Russian commitment to defend Cuba against the United States. There was, in addition, a strong impulse to destroy the economic base of potential political opposition. Finally, there was Fidel's reckless optimism combined with his insatiable thirst for performing new and great deeds, for his own glory and that of Cuba, which in his mind were and remain inseparable.

And there was yet another factor: Fidel, Raúl, Che, and all their overheated young followers had not the faintest notion of what it would take to create and run a state-owned economy, not the remotest idea of what they were getting into. Paradoxically, among Fidel's collaborators only the Communists of the PSP, as the record shows, had some inkling of what was involved and counseled prudence.

Nearly a decade later, with much of the Cuban economy reeling under the impact of unending mismanagement and irrational policy, Fidel, undaunted, was still "moving forward," with gigantic, never-before-seen, world-shattering feats of economic derring-do, promising that the golden era of a new, egalitarian, money-free, and prosperous Cuba was just around the corner. Yet so unprecedented is the Fidelista phenomenon that it would be a bold skeptic who would preclude the possibility of some modest recovery of material well-being in Cuba. Cuba is so rich in natural resources that given time, and provided that the Russian subsidy and the patience of the Cuban people hold out, Fidel may eventually stumble into something that works. On the other hand, if he does, he may just as easily stumble out of it.

However that may be, by the end of October 1960, for all practical purposes, Cuba was a socialist state. The "commanding heights" of the economy had become state property, and a great deal of small enterprise as well. In one respect, Cuba in 1960 had jumped ahead of many of the socialist countries: about 70 percent of agricultural production was nationalized, as compared to 10 to 30 percent in Poland, Yugoslavia, Bulgaria, and Hungary. Parenthetically, it may be noted that in 1968, Fidel eliminated every last bit of private enterprise right down to street vendors and bootblacks, with the exception of small farmers who from the beginning produced the bulk of the domestic food supply; and, to be sure, excepting the ever-increasing number of black marketeers and thieves, an inevitable consequence of aggravated shortages of goods and services.

However, there were other, more spectacular aspects of Cuban socialism. It was a unique socialism in a setting Christopher Columbus described as "the fairest island human eyes have yet beheld" and which, four and a half centuries later, Lowry Nelson, an American sociologist, truthfully declared to be "one of the most favorable spots for human existence on the earth's surface." [9] It was a sun-drenched socialism, slashed with the brilliant colors of tropical vegetation and the deep blue of the surrounding waters. It pulsated with the rhythmic and erotic traditions of its African heritage. It spoke Spanish, a new and fresh idiom that for a long time would remain largely free of stereotyped Slavic-Marxist jargon. *Revolución*, its leading daily, with its lusty cheesecake and flamboyant makeup, was until its demise in 1965 the antithesis of *Pravda*. And by and large, it was a prosperous and generous socialism, still living off the fat accumulated by capitalism. Except for a small minority for whom any socialism was anathema, it can truly be said that at this time, as Columbus might have described the scene, "it was the most joyous socialism human eyes have beheld."

Alas, it was destined to change.

The Hub of the Universe

Paradoxically, the vast majority of Cubans at the end of 1960 were not concerned with socialism. They were not told that the new system was socialistic, and when later they were told they remained indifferent so long as it seemed to work. And in some respects it never failed to work, such as in the vast expansion of educational and health services—largely subsidized by the Soviet Union, it is true,

9. Nelson, *Rural Cuba* (Minneapolis: University of Minnesota Press, 1950), p. 47.

but nonetheless motivated by the values of the new system—and the elimination of the most sordid and venal features of life in Cuba under Batista.

And in other respects, its failures were endured, not only—and perhaps not principally—because of the extraordinary charisma of Fidel Castro and the increasing efficiency of the state's machinery for indoctrination and repression, but by virtue of an aroused nationalism, promoted and manipulated, to be sure, but deeply imbedded in the Cuban consciousness.

Thus, it could be said that it was Castro's foreign policy, responding to the impact of the accidents of history on his quixotic temperament and assisted by American diplomacy, which created the conditions leading to the kind of rapid and total restructuring of Cuban society which he himself had not anticipated and which simultaneously unleashed the national pride binding the people to the Revolution.

A remark by Foreign Minister Roa gained currency in Havana in the early days. Commenting in a television interview on his little time for sleep and never a day off he quipped, " In the old days it was the easiest job in the government. The only work the foreign minister ever had to do was pick up the telephone and get instructions, in English."

For Cubans, what Roa's dry humor had underscored was no doubt the great miracle that Fidel had brought about. Cuba had fearlessly taken on the Colossus of the North, trading blow for blow. Cuba had a powerful new ally equipped with intercontinental ballistic missiles. Six hundred million Chinese pledged "undying support for the heroic Cuban people." Arms were arriving from Czechoslovakia, telephone equipment from Hungary, and butter from Poland.

Cuban missions were roaming over the globe promoting diplomatic and trade relations not only among the familiar nations of western and eastern Europe, but in such distant lands as Indonesia, Ceylon, Cambodia, North Korea, North Vietnam, Iraq, Ethiopia, Ghana, Liberia, and Guinea. In the United Nations, the voice of Cuba had stirred the conscience and imagination of the whole world. And in Latin America, Cuba's Fidel was already being compared with the towering figure of Simon Bolívar, the great continental leader in the war for independence from Spain.

"We represent the first great revolution in a small country,"

Fidel had told his enthralled fellow countrymen as he wound up a speech at two in the morning on June 5, 1960, "which makes us a privileged generation of Cubans, not only in terms of our own history but in the history of all the peoples in the world." [10] All eyes were on Cuba, so it seemed. As Nineveh was to the ancient Assyrians, as Cuzco to the fifteenth-century Incas, and as Boston to the nineteenth-century New Englanders, so Havana at the end of 1960 appeared to the Cubans to be the hub of the universe.

10. *El Mundo*, June 5, 1960.

9

∎

Prelude to the Bay of Pigs

The "Year of Education"

AFTER THE ESTABLISHMENT of the Castro government, it became customary at the beginning of each year to dedicate the following twelve months to a major purpose or goal of the Revolution. Thus, 1959 was designated as the "Year of the Revolution," and 1960 became the "Year of Agrarian Reform." And in his speech on January 2, 1961, Fidel announced that the new year would be the "Year of Education."

The main task was the elimination of illiteracy. Without going into the question of costs and economic priorities at this stage of the Revolution, matters about which a cool appraisal could raise some doubts, in other respects the campaign turned out to be a brilliant success. Some 300,000 "alphabetizers" were mobilized, including 100,000 secondary school pupils, and dispatched to every nook and corner of the island. A few were killed by counterrevolutionary bands roaming the hills and joined the ranks of revolutionary martyrs; but by the end of the year, according to government figures, some 700,000 adults had been taught the rudiments of reading and writing.

As a result, the adult illiteracy rate was reduced in one fell swoop from some 24 percent to approximately 4 percent. This was the lowest rate in Latin America, and Cuba could claim that it had accomplished in a one-year crash program what countries like Mexico and Brazil had been unable to do in decades of difficult planning and plodding. Thus, the year was aptly named, although in a broader sense than anticipated it was also the "Year of Education" for John F. Kennedy. This brings us to the events that culminated in the battle of the Bay of Pigs.

The Twenty-Day Alert

Beginning in late October 1960,[1] credible information began to appear in the Latin American and United States press that Washington had armed and was secretly training a group of Cuban exiles in the hills of Guatemala for an invasion of Cuba. More information began to pour in during November and December, and Castro ordered a mobilization of the army and militia in the first days of January 1961. He declared that the danger of an invasion would last until January 20, the day that Eisenhower would relinquish the presidency to Kennedy. Eisenhower, he explained, was committed to his plan and could very well execute it before leaving office. If not, then Kennedy, despite his election campaign against Cuba, might take a fresh look and hopefully abandon "this insane" project. He, Castro, on January 20, would give him the benefit of the doubt and demobilize. Meanwhile, at the United Nations and using every other available channel, the Cuban government warned about the impending invasion.

1. Six months earlier there had been a flurry of excitement when Guatemala and Cuba each claimed it was to be the target of an aggression mounted on the territory of the other (later events proved that both were correct). On April 28 Guatemala withdrew its ambassador and his entire staff from Havana. Referring to this situation Fidel said in his May Day speech in the Plaza de la Revolución: "One day the President of Guatemala . . . breaks relations with Cuba and declares that in the Sierra Maestra . . . troops were being prepared to invade Guatemala. It was such a flimsy, such an absurd, accusation that it would have lacked logical explanation if it were not for the fact that we had reports that the Foreign Office [*Cancillería*] of the United States was preparing an aggression against Cuba through [*a través de*] the government of Guatemala" (*Revolución*, May 2, 1960). Whether Fidel Castro actually had firm knowledge of Eisenhower's top-secret decision less than two months after it was made has not been confirmed. Possibly he merely "smelled a rat" or invented the "explanation." From other statements it would appear that he had no conclusive evidence of the forthcoming invasion until several months later. Thus, for example, in a speech delivered in Havana on July 26, 1963, he said, "we remember back there *at the end of 1960* when news of training camps in Nicaragua and Guatemala began to reach us" (emphasis added).

More Backing from Moscow

At the same time, the Soviet Union seconded the Cuban warnings and, significantly, in coordination with Fidel's position. Thus on January 12, 1961, the Russian mission at the United Nations issued a statement which said, "The *present* administration of the United States continues preparations for direct aggression against Cuba." [2] Ten days earlier, on the occasion of the second anniversary of the Cuban Revolution, Khrushchev had sent a congratulatory message to Fidel in which he declared, "The Cuban people can always count on the solidarity and support of the Soviet people in their struggle for independence, freedom, and economic progress." [3] The statement avoided provocation, and earlier references to atomic missiles had disappeared. Nevertheless, the impression conveyed was that the Soviet Union was taking more than a formal interest in the situation.

The impression was reinforced by Che Guevara's two-month visit to eastern Europe, China, and North Korea. On January 6, 1961, immediately after his return, he gave a glowing television and radio report of his trip. He stood next to Khrushchev on Lenin's tomb in Red Square during the parade on November 7 marking the anniversary of the Bolshevik Revolution. In Peking he sat beside Mao at a banquet at which he was the guest of honor. The socialist camp, Che explained, had agreed to purchase four million tons of Cuban sugar, which would normally have been sold in the American market. "There was no real commercial reason" for this deal, he added; "they did so on a political basis, on a direct request by our government signed by Fidel." [4]

Then there were other agreements, including copious credits for Cuba's industrial development and an arrangement by which 2,400 Cuban students at different levels would enroll in universities and technical schools in various countries, of which one-third would be assigned to the Soviet Union. All of this had been negotiated in Moscow, to which every country in the socialist camp, including China, had sent representatives.

Che understandably gave no details of military aid, but no one could doubt that here, too, substantial investments were made. In any event, the picture presented was that of a monolithic bloc, under

2. *El Mundo*, January 13, 1961, emphasis added.
3. *El Mundo*, January 3, 1961.   4. *El Mundo*, January 7, 1961.

the leadership of the Soviet Union, now fully committed to the support of the new Cuba.

Fidel Accentuates the Positive

On January 20, 1961, John F. Kennedy made his inaugural address, the complete text of which was carried by the Havana press the next day. One sentence in particular attracted attention: "to those nations who would make themselves our adversary, we offer not a pledge but a request: that both sides begin anew the quest for peace, before the dark powers of destruction . . . engulf all humanity in planned or accidental self-destruction." [5]

It was a new note in Washington and Fidel gave his reply. That very night, at a huge mass meeting including 40,000 armed members of the Havana citizens' militia (in itself an impressive demonstration of Fidel's confidence in their loyalty and apparently overlooked by CIA intelligence experts), Fidel exclaimed, "Militia men and women, the moment of greatest tension has passed. . . . We are going back to work but we remain alert. With the Fatherland and the Revolution intact, we have won another battle."

This statement turned out to be true, although the battle had not yet taken place. The mobilization had been an invaluable rehearsal for the one that proved so effective in mid-April at the Bay of Pigs. "It was a great experience," Fidel said, "and we had to make extraordinary efforts. . . . We had to mobilize all our weapons, including those for which we had no trained personnel. We had to train artillery men in twenty-four hours." Later, he recalled the great dearth of instructors (presumably Czechs since the weapons were recent Czech importations). Consequently, a system was improvised by which men who trained in the daytime taught others at night by lantern light what they learned, and then continued training and teaching around the clock.[6] These improvised artillery soldiers played a decisive role in defeating the invaders.

Mainly, however, Fidel talked about other things at the mass meeting on the night of January 20; and coming from one who for some time back had warned that an invasion was inevitable, what he

5. *El Mundo*, January 21, 1961. The English text cited here is from the official version of the speech.
6. Speech on the second anniversary of the battle April 19, 1963. *Política Internacional* 1, no. 2 (April–June 1963): 135.

now was saying was unexpected: "Today the new president spoke. His speech had some positive aspects which we welcome, especially when he tries to make a new approach. . . . It is a difficult task. . . . He will have to choose between yielding to great pressures . . . or decide bravely to face up to them. We Cubans don't want to prejudge. We can wait calmly. We have no hatred or hysteria."

An Optimistic Outlook

That the calm was real was confirmed by an astonishing statement made by Che Guevara in a speech on January 23 in Pinar del Río: "There is almost no reason now to say *patria o muerte*, because the great threat which hung over our *patria* is gone. . . . We can't be sure, but it is so. We'll still have to struggle against a minority of internal dissidents and counterrevolutionaries supported by the United States. . . . But it will be a more comfortable, a simpler struggle." [7]

Che also underlined the source of the calm. What held up the invasion while Eisenhower was president was the fact that "the USSR and all the socialist countries are ready to go to war to defend our sovereignty." And now, he added, Kennedy has spoken of a "certain form of coexistence. This is positive because it shows the way is open for conversations." [8] On the same theme in his speech on January 20, Fidel had said, "we are not only concerned with . . . Cuba's need for peace but the need for peace of all the governments and peoples who are friends of Cuba. . . . They have tied their fate to ours. . . . We're not worried about counterrevolutionaries. Our only concern is world peace."

It was more than a coincidence that precisely at this time Khrushchev was sizing up the prospects of a fresh start in Soviet-American relations and could ill afford a discordant note from Castro. Evidently, Cuban cooperation with the Russian approach to the Kennedy administration was another item in the deal that Che had concluded in Moscow.

Not for this, however, would Fidel relinquish the spotlight of history. In effect, he was saying on January 20 that the fate of humanity depended as much on Cuba as on the Soviet Union and the United States. Hence Cuba, "not thinking exclusively of our national interests, but of the whole world," would not stand in the way of

7. *El Mundo*, January 24, 1961.   8. *Ibid.*

peaceful coexistence between the two superpowers. Later, Fidel would discover that Khrushchev and Kennedy would settle the fate of Cuba, and of humanity, without consulting Cuba.

Meanwhile, a number of factors seemed to indicate that Cuba could reasonably accept the Soviet approach quite apart from Soviet pressure to do so. Public opinion in most parts of the world—not merely leftist or Communist opinion—was distinctly cool toward Washington in its quarrel with Cuba. The British attitude was explained with considerable candor by the London *Times*. The United States is enraged over the expropriation of American property in Cuba, said the *Times*, according to a UPI London dispatch of August 11, 1960; but why should the British support the United States which prevented England and France from punishing Nasser for having seized properties that were of vital importance to these two countries? The same dispatch reported that most of the British and European press opposed United States armed intervention in Cuba.[9]

From Ottawa a press release on January 3, 1961, revealed that the Canadian government, at the time headed by Conservative John Diefenbaker, had offered to mediate between the United States and Cuba.[10] This followed a clear statement in mid-October 1960 that Canada intended to continue trade relations with Cuba.[11] On December 9, after all American banks had been expropriated, Cuba reached an amicable settlement with the Royal Bank of Canada by purchasing all of its Cuban assets. Over the years, Canadian policy of maintaining normal relations with Cuba paid off. Even though American branch firms and subsidiaries in Canada, under constraint from Washington, did not participate in the Canada-Cuba trade, Canadian exports to Cuba increased manyfold, far outstripping imports from Cuba.[12]

9. *El Mundo*, August 12, 1960.
10. *El Mundo*, January 4, 1961.
11. *El Mundo*, October 20, 1960.
12. Assets of the Royal Bank included twenty-four branches. A friendly settlement was also reached with the Bank of Nova Scotia, which at the time had eight branches in Cuba. Other Canadian holdings, notably the life insurance companies which, at the time, had sold more than 70 percent of the policies held by Cuban nationals, received similar preferential treatment. Harold Boyer, in his doctoral dissertation in progress at Simon Fraser University on Canadian-Cuban relations (from which the above information has been taken) notes that a "Cuban

In Latin America, the governments of important countries, such as Brazil, Argentina, and Mexico, were clearly opposed to American intervention and, from the time Kennedy took office until the very eve of the invasion, were active in various schemes of mediation. In addition, a large number of Afro-Asian countries, as was to be expected, stood behind Cuba.

Thus, for a time there was some ground for Cuban optimism that the invasion plans would not materialize. However, there was less optimism that negotiations with the United States were imminent or that sabotage and infiltration by Cuban counterrevolutionaries based in the United States would not continue. Nevertheless, there was a high degree of confidence that Cuba could handle anything short of a serious invasion attempt in which the United States would become directly involved. Should this happen, then the Cubans could hold out long enough to bring the Soviet Union into the picture. In any event, military training and preparations continued, though on a reduced scale, after the mobilization.

---

peasant carrying a Canadian life insurance policy was not uncommon in prerevolutionary days!" There is no available record of the value of Canadian properties in Cuba at the time of settlement. It was probably less than 10 percent of the value of expropriated American properties. Trade figures, according to Boyer (citing official Ottawa sources), show that for the ten-year period 1949–1958, the Canadian trade surplus was $60.1 million (Canadian). For the period 1959–June 30, 1968, that is, nine and a half years, the surplus was $265.6 million. With respect to American branch firms and subsidiaries, through their parent companies they were subject to the special Cuban Assets Control Regulations of July 8, 1963, supplementary to the general Enemy Trade regulations, which prohibit persons subject to U.S. jurisdiction from dealing with Cuba. As Rainer Hellmann points out, the "American Government hits an especially delicate spot with the extraterritorial application of Enemy Trade regulations," with Canada in the lead among protestors (*The Challenge to the U.S. Dominance of the International Corporation*, [New York: Dunellen, 1970], pp. 228–229). As a result, in the words of Samuel Pisar, "In the case of Cuba, the Treasury has long relied on a program of voluntary compliance whereby American companies are 'invited' to persuade their foreign subsidiaries to refrain from such trade. Experience to date bears out the practical and diplomatic superiority of this noncoercive method of international regulation" (*Coexistence and Commerce: Guidelines for Transactions Between East and West* [New York: McGraw, 1970], p. 138).

The Illusions Vanish

From mid-February on, for any reader of the American press there could be no doubt that an invasion of Cuba was shaping up. By mid-March, practically everything was known except the day and place of the strike. And if any confirmation was necessary, there was a stepping up of CIA arms drops in the hill country to counterrevolutionary bands, hotly pursued by Castro's peasant militia, and a notable increase of sabotage.

On March 13 President Kennedy unveiled his plan for the Alliance for Progress, coupling it with an attack on the Castro government. It was not difficult to surmise that the timing of the announcement was related to the need to build up goodwill in Latin America before Cuba was invaded. On March 22 a Cuba Revolutionary Council was set up in New York. It was headed by Miró Cardona, whom Fidel had appointed as prime minister in January 1959. The meaning of this event was not difficult to interpret: the council would be the provisional government to be set up by the invaders once they had secured a piece of Cuban territory.

On April 4, the State Department issued a white paper on the Cuban situation. It was a shoddy and unconvincing statement, as any attempt to dress up a legally and morally unjustifiable exercise in *Realpolitik* with an ethical veneer was bound to be. It was, moreover, easy to decode. It told Castro that the invasion was now imminent and the wording confirmed previous indications that the invading force would consist mainly of what he called "mercenaries," that is, Cuban exiles. Thus, Fidel was alert and, in keeping with his character, confident, relaxed, and in a jocular mood. It would probably never occur to any other head of state at such a time to discuss golf, as Fidel did in a television appearance on April 10, just a week before the invasion began. He was explaining that the magnificent golf course at the once exclusive country club just outside of Havana was now open to the general public. "I've neglected this sport," he confessed. Fidel, among other distinctive features in his career, had been a baseball player of at least semiprofessional competence, and now and then he still works out with one of the teams and occasionally pitches an inning or two in a game. It has been said, though not confirmed, that when he was a student he was scouted by one of the big league teams in the United States and offered a contract. However that may be, he chose politics and revolution and became the first baseball player in history to head a government and a ruling Communist party.

"The other day I was out there with Che," he continued. "Che was once a caddy and knows how to play golf. So I said to him, 'Let's play a game.' Well, he beat me, naturally. Now if Kennedy and Eisenhower would like to discuss some problems with us over a game of golf," he added with a twinkle in his eye, "I'm sure we'll win. We just have to practice a few days, that's all."

Prelude to Invasion

On April 12 President Kennedy held a press conference during which he said, "There will not be, under any conditions, an intervention in Cuba by the United States armed forces or American civilians. The basic issue in Cuba is not one between the United States and Cuba. It is between the Cubans themselves." [13] Castro had no trouble deciphering this message. Kennedy was reacting to mounting public pressures, particularly by Latin American and Afro-Asian governments, to forestall an invasion of Cuba. At the same time, his statement significantly did not exclude military intervention carried out by Cuban exiles.

That same night (April 12), Fidel, speaking at a meeting said, "The United States has rejected all offers at mediation. They have invested a great deal of money in their plans for aggression and training Cuban counterrevolutionaries. They still have illusions so they don't want to discuss." Earlier, in speculating about whether Kennedy could extricate himself from the trap bequeathed by Eisenhower, he had predicted that Kennedy was "going to have a headache, what to do with these bands of criminals," referring to the Cuban exiles in training in Guatemala.[14]

In retrospect, it is remarkable how well Fidel was able to size up Kennedy's problems for, as was later revealed, "what to do about these bands of criminals" was, indeed, a consideration that entered into his decision to go ahead with the invasion. Actually, Kennedy and Castro were not far apart in their thinking about the political drawbacks of an American, or American-sponsored, invasion of Cuba,

13. *El Mundo,* April 13, 1961.
14. *El Mundo,* January 14, 1961.

which led to Castro's early conjecture that Kennedy would not carry out the Eisenhower project and to Kennedy's reluctance to go ahead with it.

On April 13, El Encanto, Havana's largest and most fashionable department store, was completely destroyed by fire. Inflammable material had been placed in the air conditioning system, so that fire spread throughout the building in a matter of moments. It was a spectacular piece of sabotage, the high point of a campaign clearly coordinated with the invasion plans.

Some 200 suspects were picked up for questioning, the largest such roundup since the early days of the revolutionary government. Castro had built up an effective organization of surveillance called the Committees for the Defense of the Revolution. It was (and still is) a mass network of unpaid neighborhood volunteers that combines snooping with more prosaic social services. After the air attack preceding the invasion, there were thousands of arrests, probably more than 50,000 throughout the island, mainly innocent people who were eventually released; but at the same time enough genuine anti-Fidelista activists were caught to smash the urban counterrevolutionary organizations. Partly because of this massive roundup and partly because of the collapse of counterrevolutionary morale after the Bay of Pigs, these urban organizations never recovered.

The Air Strike

Early Saturday morning, April 15, radio programs throughout the island were interrupted by an official communiqué. "Today, April 15, at 6 A.M., American B-26 aircraft simultaneously bombarded points situated in Havana, San Antonio de los Baños [37 miles southwest of Havana], and Santiago. . . . Our country has been the victim of a criminal imperialist aggression which violates all the norms of international law. . . . The Cuban delegation at the United Nations has been instructed to accuse the government of the United States directly as guilty of this aggression. . . . The order has been given for the mobilization of all combat units of the Rebel Army and the National Revolutionary Militia. . . . *patria o muerte, venceremos*. Fidel Castro."

Later it was learned that eight B-26 planes had participated in the raid. They had flown in from Puerto Cabezas in Nicaragua, and their mission was to destroy the Cuban air force in a kind of minia-

ture Pearl Harbor operation. An elaborate cover scheme was arranged by which the air strikes could be imputed to planes seized
at Cuban air bases by defecting air force personnel.

Some sixty casualties were inflicted, an ammunition dump was
blown up, and a number of planes were destroyed; but the operation
was a failure. Castro's aviation, tiny enough to begin with, was not
eliminated; and the cover story, thin enough as it was, was quickly
blown when one of the attacking planes, damaged by antiaircraft
fire, had to limp back to Key West instead of returning to Nicaragua.

A prominent victim of the air strike was Adlai Stevenson, at the
time the United States ambassador to the United Nations. Ironically
enough, along with Senator Fulbright and Chester Bowles he was
one of the few with some prior knowledge of the invasion project
who was completely opposed to it. However, he was kept in the dark
about the actual plans and so on the very afternoon of the attack, in
a verbal duel with Raúl Roa at an emergency meeting of the United
Nations Political Committee, he accepted as truth the misinforma-
tion he received from Washington.

"These two planes," he informed the committee, referring to
the damaged B-26 and another that had also turned up in Florida,
"to the best of our knowledge, were Castro's own air force planes,
and, according to the pilots, they took off from Castro's own air force
fields." [15] Then, bolstering his case with faked photographs that had
been rushed to him, he hit back at Roa with the full force of the
cover story.

What then happened is told by Herbert J. Muller: "shortly after
his speech friends found Stevenson in a shocked daze: he had at last
been told the truth, learned that unwittingly he had told the U.N.
a clumsy lie. . . . He felt worse when gossip had it that Kennedy
had referred to him 'as my official liar.' " [16] This was one of the
hazards of the business for a professional diplomat, as Stevenson
must have realized after recovering from his shock; he managed to
carry on long enough to take his revenge on Soviet Ambassador Zorin
in a similar situation at the United Nations during the missile crisis
of 1962.

15. *El Mundo*, April 18, 1961.
16. Muller, *Adlai Stevenson: A Study in Values* (New York: Harper
and Row, 1967), p. 283.

For Fatherland and Socialism

On Sunday morning, April 16, the day after the attack on the air-fields, Fidel spoke at the funeral of seven soldiers who had been killed at the Havana air base. To expose himself at this moment was an obvious risk, although somewhat lessened by the concentration of antiaircraft batteries on the perimeter of the cemetery. However, the feeling of anger, combined with that of indignation and grief, added to Fidel's moral stature and enhanced the political impact of his speech. No doubt it provided a final psychological boost before the impending ordeal.

Fidel had an easy time of it since the situation was made to order for a devastating and convincing indictment of the United States. The implausable cover story was readily demolished. The shedding of innocent Cuban blood, the Pearl Harbor type of treachery except that "the Japanese did not hide their responsibility nor did they attack a small, defenseless country"—these and similar themes Fidel developed to maximum advantage. With emotions running high, he told his listeners that this was just the beginning, "the prelude to aggression by the mercenaries."

There was also fulsome praise of the Soviet Union and the great feat of Gagarin who a few days earlier had been the first human being to orbit the earth. However, Fidel scrupulously avoided any reference to the Soviet promise to defend Cuba, to the oft repeated "Cuba is not alone" theme. Twenty-four hours had elapsed since the air strikes and the invasion was sure to come at any moment, but no thunder and lightening emanated from the Kremlin. Now that the chips were down, when and how the Soviet Union might intervene was a large question mark.

Before concluding his funeral oration, Fidel made an unexpected announcement. In his appeal to defend the Revolution and the Fatherland, he addressed himself almost exclusively to the "common people," the people of "humble means," the "workers and peasants" who have been given arms to defend themselves against the "imperialist exploiters" and the native "millionaries." At a moment of national peril, it seemed strange that Fidel would insist that Cuba was engaged in a class struggle, but he had a special purpose in mind: an ideological buildup for an official proclamation that Cuba was a socialist state.

"What bothers the United States most is that we have made a socialist revolution right under their noses," he exclaimed. "Workers and peasants, comrades, this is a socialist and democratic revolution of the poor, by the poor, and for the poor."

Why drag socialism into the picture at this time? Was he trying to get a message across to the Soviet Union and the socialist camp? On April 17, the day after the funeral, *Revolución* came out with a headline splashed across the top third of the front page: "Long Live Our Socialist Revolution."

10
∎

A Fierce Battle and a Rare Celebration

Kennedy's Dilemma

A FEW HOURS BEFORE DAWN on Monday, April 17, Brigade 2506, consisting of 1,400 Cuban exiles fully equipped for battle, with an arsenal of weapons and equipment including artillery, tanks, and aircraft, began to disembark on two beaches in the Bay of Pigs, situated on the south coast of the island, about 140 miles southeast of Havana. A fierce battle began almost immediately and ended on Girón Beach in the late afternoon of Wednesday, April 19, less than seventy-two hours after the landing. The invasion was crushed and eventually close to 1,200 prisoners were rounded up. So rapidly had the action taken place that when word reached Washington that the brigade was in mortal danger, it was too late to provide effective help.

It seemed incredible that the mightiest power on earth, with the greatest experience of any nation in amphibious landings, could not secure a beachhead when, how, and where it wished on the well-mapped territory of a neighboring island in the throes of a profound social and economic reorganization and which had an immeasurably smaller military capability. Looked at in this way, the American defeat would appear to have been the result of monumental stupidity and colossal bungling. Yet it was not that simple.

On taking office, one of the first decisions President Kennedy had to make was whether or not to go ahead with the operation he had inherited from his predecessor. It is surprising to find how some otherwise competent scholars have misjudged the complexity of the problem Kennedy had to grapple with at this moment. For example, Professor Hans J. Morgenthau, writes about "the fiasco of the Bay of Pigs" as follows:

> The United States was resolved to intervene on behalf of its interests, but it was also resolved to intervene in such a way as not openly to violate the principle of non-intervention. . . . Had the United States approached the problem of intervening in Cuba in a rational fashion, it would have asked itself which was more important: to succeed in the intervention or to prevent a temporary loss of prestige among the uncommitted nations. Had it settled upon the latter alternative, it would have refrained from intervening altogether; had it chosen the former alternative, it would have taken all the measures necessary to make the intervention a success, regardless of unfavorable reactions in the rest of the world. Instead, it sought the best of both alternatives and got the worst.[1]

The rationality suggested here presupposes the kind of situation Castro was in rather than the one Kennedy faced. Castro had to decide between the possibility of survival if he resisted and the certainty of nonsurvival if he did not. Kennedy had the more difficult task of matching a number of options and risks, of which the least was whether or not "to prevent a temporary loss of prestige among the uncommitted nations."

Options and Risks

I have already noted that in the months prior to the invasion American policy toward Cuba had, on the one hand, drawn no significant support abroad and, on the other, had created a good deal of international apprehension. In this situation, military intervention in Cuba, whether successful or not, would inevitably entail a moral and political setback of varying dimensions for the United States in a considerable number of countries. However, in two areas, the repercussions could be of a different order of magnitude.

In Latin America, given the prevailing climate of nationalism and radicalism—that is to say, hostility to "Yankee imperialism"

1. Morgenthau, *A New Foreign Policy for the United States* (New York: Praeger, 1969), p. 123.

—and the considerable prestige of the Cuban Revolution at the time, it was entirely conceivable that an invasion of Cuba—especially with direct and open American participation—could set off disturbances that would seriously threaten American property and lives, undermine friendly governments, and generally set back relations between the "good neighbors" for years. As it was, even the more prudent type of invasion that took place set off scores of massive demonstrations with ominous potentialities, but which lost their momentum when Castro's victory was announced.

Then there was the question of the Soviet Union. That it had by then made a significant political and economic investment in Cuba was evident. How far it would go to protect its investment either directly or through countermeasures in other parts of the world, such as in Laos or West Berlin, were matters of conjecture; but they could not be lightly dismissed.

Thus, major risks, not only matters of prestige, were involved. To what extent were they worth taking? How urgent was it that Castro be destroyed? What were the real dimensions of the Communist menace in Cuba? Were there alternative ways of overcoming this menace? In the event of a successful invasion, what if Castro reverted to guerrilla warfare and held out for months or years in the mountains? What headaches would be faced in Cuba after Castro was eliminated?

But Kennedy's situation was even more complicated. There was no time for a thorough study of all the pieces in these interlocking puzzles. The reason was that military action against Cuba had to be taken before May, when Castro's air force was due to be greatly strengthened with up-to-date Russian military aircraft manned by Cuban pilots trained in the Soviet Union. Finally, for Kennedy to conclude that the most "rational" decision under the circumstances would be to cancel the invasion almost certainly would have meant, at the very start of his administration, exposing himself and all he hoped to accomplish to a severe pounding from the Congress, the "military-industrial complex," the media, and a host of powerful political enemies. This was another risk that could not be brushed aside.

Kennedy's decision was to go ahead with the invasion on condition that the international political risks be reduced to a minimum. Given the fact that the preparations for the invasion had been widely publicized in the press, American involvement would be no secret; but this inconvenience could be managed if the direct participation of the armed forces of the United States was scrupulously avoided. Unprovoked direct aggression would be a flagrant violation of the United Nations Charter, as well as that of the OAS and of all international law. It would immediately whip up passions and place heavy pressures on foreign governments to take some action. Indirect aggression does not provoke the same urgent response. It can be denied, even if unconvincingly, or it can become entangled in the issues of a civil war. The debate over facts, allegations, motives, and credibility can be sufficiently complicated and lengthy, so that the sharpness of the question itself fades away. From the moral point of view, the distinction between direct and indirect aggression is slight; but in the marketplace of international politics the distinction is real.

The American Plan of Operations

Except for the Sunday morning quarterbacks analyzing Saturday's game with the benefit of hindsight, the invasion blueprint worked out by the Pentagon and the CIA, from the technical point of view, could be considered reasonably competent. The Bay of Pigs is a long, narrow body of water with several good beaches. The entrance to the Bay is from the south. In all other directions, the Bay is hemmed in by vast stretches of treacherous swampland. Between the eastern shore and the swampland there is a piece of dry land containing a sizable air strip and sufficient space for the brigade to assemble and set up its command headquarters. Access to the area by land at the time was limited to a couple of trails through the eastern swamps and to a single paved road that traversed the northern swamp, a stretch of about twenty miles. The entire zone was thinly populated, principally by charcoal makers and a few fishermen. It was a quiet and isolated spot, well suited for an inconspicuous landing.

According to the plan, once Castro's air force had been eliminated, the landing operations and the supporting vessels lying off shore would be immune to air attack. Paratroopers, supported by bombing and strafing of the brigade's B-26 planes, would be dropped far up the paved road, to be reinforced by artillery and tanks coming up from the beach, thus effectively sealing off the area. With a bridgehead secured, the Cuban Revolutionary Council, previously assembled in Miami, would be flown in and proclaimed as the provisional government of Cuba. What happened next would depend on the strength of supporting counterrevolutionary activity in various parts of the island and the extent to which Castro would be able to cope with the crisis. In any event, with a piece of Cuban territory firmly in the hands of the rump government, recognition could be extended by the United States and such assistance supplied as necessary to topple the Castro regime.

The Best Laid Plans of Mice and Men

In February 1962 the Cuban government completed the publication of a four-volume report on the aborted invasion, entitled *Playa Girón: Derrota del Imperialismo* ("Girón Beach: defeat of imperialism"; the Cubans named the episode after the beach on which the final action occurred). The work contains some indispensable background, neglected by most foreign writers, for an understanding of what went wrong with the Pentagon-CIA plan. Particularly useful are sections of the more than 100 pages of the verbatim text of Fidel's television report, accompanied by a series of maps, delivered on April 21, two days after his victory.

Although the Bay of Pigs was, on the whole, well chosen as the site of the type of invasion contemplated, it was not without its drawbacks. To begin with, it was one of a number of locations that Fidel and his staff had considered likely in some degree to be selected by the invaders as a landing area. There was some element of chance in this coincidence but also of good judgment by those preparing to repel the invasion. Although Cuba has some 2,000 miles of irregular shoreline, there are only a limited number of sites that could be logically considered as suitable for the type of operation Castro had every reason to expect.

A matter the Pentagon-CIA might easily overlook, or to which they might attach small importance, was the fact that the charcoal makers of the area, one of the most impoverished segments of the Cuban population prior to the Revolution, had especially benefited from the Castro regime and were intensely loyal to it. In addition, there were some 200 "alphabetizers" working in the zone; and like all those participating in the literacy campaign, they were totally dedicated to the Revolution.

As a result of these factors, the invaders met with resistance from the moment the first landing craft approached the shore. The area was not fortified, but a day-and-night patrol had been on the lookout for several weeks. As soon as the landing occurred, and before the brigade could cut communications, the news was transmitted to an infantry battalion stationed at a sugar mill at the northern terminal of the paved road dissecting the swamp. At the same time, the local militia, consisting of several platoons of well-armed charcoal makers, went into action. Thus, the invaders lost some of the element of surprise, as well as the time required to subdue the militia.

A more important setback took place early in the morning of the same day when Castro's aviation, supposedly eliminated in Saturday's air strikes, appeared on the scene. What happened was that Fidel, anticipating an attempt to destroy his air force, had previously dispersed his dozen or so serviceable combat planes. At the same time, a number of permanently grounded planes were conspicuously lined up in close formation as decoys. The result was that relatively little damage was inflicted on Castro's real air power. As a matter of fact, as Castro claimed, his problem was that he had more planes than pilots.[2]

Another problem facing him was how to use his aviation; for although it included a couple of fast jet trainers while the enemy had only slower moving bombers, the latter outnumbered the planes Castro could put in the air at any one time. In addition, during the first day of fighting, Castro's infantry lacked antiaircraft equipment and from early morning on began to take severe punishment from enemy bombing and strafing.

Fidel's decision was to leave his infantry unprotected and attack the enemy flotilla. In this operation he lost two planes and two pilots, but succeeded in destroying a number of small craft, thereby disrupting the landing of men and supplies. He was also able to sink a 5,000-ton supply and communications vessel lying off shore. This was a hard blow to the invading force and later made escape by sea

2. Commemorating the tenth anniversary of the battle, Castro said, "The enemy tried to destroy the few old planes we had and, in fact, they succeeded in destroying a few. On the morning of April 17 [1961] we had nine planes—if I remember correctly—which could possibly get into the air, and some seven pilots" (*Granma Weekly Review*, May 2, 1971).

impossible, but it was not necessarily fatal. Castro did not achieve control of the air until the third day, and this was accomplished primarily by antiaircraft artillery which arrived only on the second day of battle. Meanwhile, the brigade's aviation, until it was eliminated, inflicted heavy casualties on Castro's troops and downed a number of his planes. Castro claimed that, at the rate his planes were being shot down, he would have lost all his pilots (who displayed exceptional courage and endurance) if the battle had lasted a short while longer.

Conflicting figures have been given concerning the exact number of casualties on each side. Nevertheless, all indications are that the killed and wounded on the government side out-numbered those of the brigade by a wide margin.[3] Morale is an imponderable factor in war. Sometimes it can be decisive. In Castro's victory at the Bay of Pigs it undoubtedly played a very significant role. But Fidel and his staff must also be given credit, beginning with the day-and-night training of artillery recruits months before the invasion, for effective planning and use of limited resources. In any battle, or ping-pong match for that matter, victory or defeat does not depend on only one of the contestants.

An Evaluation

From the point of view of the Cuban Revolution, except for the heavy casualties, the Bay of Pigs incident could not have turned out any better. Cuba's international prestige zoomed upward. National pride soared and with it popular confidence in Fidel's leadership. Counterrevolution on the island received a setback from which

3. Hugh Thomas fairly well sums up what is known about this matter: "The brigade lost 80 men in fighting and perhaps 30 to 40 in the disembarcation. Nine had died while *en route* to Havana. . . . Castro announced that his losses had been 87, but the implication of his speech on 19 April was that the losses were greater. . . . The chronicles of the invaders from the estimate of an unnamed Cuban doctor reckoned Cuban revolutionary losses as 1,250, with another 400 dying of wounds, and 2,000 wounded. It is in fact hard not to believe that the . . . government did not lose many more men than they announced" (*Cuba: The Pursuit of Freedom* [New York: Harper and Row, 1971], pp. 1370–1371). One additional detail can be added to the puzzle. In a speech on the tenth anniversary of the battle, Fidel nearly doubled his original estimate of losses when he referred to the "149 comrades who died at Girón" (*Granma Weekly Review*, May 2, 1971).

it never recovered. In later and more difficult years, the memory of the victory, assiduously kept alive by the regime, would serve to bolster a sometimes lagging spirit of nationalism and enthusiasm for the Revolution among the Cuban people.

Does this mean that, from the point of view of the United States, it could not have turned out any worse? Nobody can say what might have occurred had Brigade 2506 succeeded in establishing and maintaining a bridgehead. As good a guess as any is that the United States would have become involved in a nasty and protracted civil war, with unpredictable consequences. Equally unpredictable would have been the course of events had there been open and direct American military intervention to guarantee the success of the invasion. The only thing hindsight reveals with unimpeachable logic is that no invasion would have been better than the one that took place.

Looking back dispassionately, the underlying miscalculation of Kennedy, his political experts, and his military planners was an underestimation of the enemy's capacity to resist, a failure to take into account the military capability that the leadership of a technically deficient but aroused and highly motivated society can frequently generate out of its limited material and human resources. It was a historically and culturally conditioned error, and particularly so in the context of inter-American relations—the kind a great power can make when it undertakes to apply punitive measures against a small, backward nation. It was, in part, the same error that turned the American intervention in Vietnam into a savage war of unexpected dimensions and tragic futility.

The Marathon Interrogation

It has been customary since the dawn of history for the winning side in a war to celebrate its victory with various kinds of military and religious ceremonies, but never before with the type of spectacle that took place in Havana after the battle of the Bay of Pigs. To begin with, there was a marathon televised interrogation of prisoners on four successive and long nights beginning on April 21, two days after the end of hostilities. Some forty captives appeared in small groups before a panel of ten local journalists set up in a large theater filled to capacity with spectators. The verbatim text was published in the newspapers. Reprinted in book form, it covered more than 400 pages.

The men were apparently selected among consenting prisoners with the idea of obtaining a wide coverage of recruitment history, training procedures, and battle assignments of brigade combatants, as well as of stressing the participation of former Batista soldiers and upper class Cubans. Nevertheless, it is clear from the text that the selection was hastily made and the prisoners were unrehearsed. As a result, a very human picture of complex backgrounds and motives emerged, and more than once long discussions ensued between a number of remarkably self-possessed and opinionated prisoners and the journalists.

There was the case of a prisoner who had been an officer in Batista's army. He had fought in several engagements against Fidel's guerrillas and had left Cuba the very day that Batista had left. At the Bay of Pigs he was a battalion commander. He refused to concede that revolutionary morale or patriotism were significant factors at the Bay of Pigs or for that matter in Fidel's success against Batista's troops.

Long discussions developed about several of the skirmishes where he commanded troops against the guerrillas. "How do you explain that you had to retreat," he was asked in one instance, "when you outnumbered the guerrillas five to one?" "Numbers aren't everything," he replied. "Position is sometimes more important." A technical discussion about some of the fighting then ensued. Having a better grasp of the details than his interlocutors, he made a plausible case for his thesis. And how do you explain your defeat a couple of days ago? In any battle, he answered, plans can go awry. He handled himself with the dignity and stubbornness of an old-time Prussian officer.

Then there was the twenty-nine-year-old parachutist who admitted that he had been misled to believe that the brigade would be welcomed by the Cuban population. "And now what do you think of the Revolution?" he was asked. "Well, maybe I'll be here long enough to form an opinion." On the same theme, another prisoner, when asked why the Cuban people did not rally to support the brigade, replied, "We had no chance to meet the people. You pushed us back before we could establish contact."

Still another prisoner, a former member of the exclusive Havana Yacht Club, refused to accept the assertion of his interrogator that there were no workers in the brigade, that the "Cuban people" were not represented. "Well, that's your opinion," he replied. "Mine is that all social classes and political views were represented. . . . I saw many workers in our group." The following week, in his May Day speech, Fidel said that among the prisoners there were 75 whom he classified as "lumpen proletariat," and also that 135 were officers and soldiers from Batista's army and some 200 were members of the island's wealthiest families.

One of the stranger cases was that of a prisoner who turned out to be a winner of the Congressional Medal of Honor in World War II. He was a Communist and joined the American army to fight against fascism. Having acquired American citizenship in the army, he stayed in the United States after the war but came back to Cuba with the body of his son who had been drafted and killed in the Korean War. At the burial in Havana, he made a speech blaming the death of his son on American imperialism. Then he returned to the United States. He had known the leaders of the PSP and three of his brothers were still members of it. Two of his grandsons were in the militia unit that captured him. He refused to say what induced him to join the brigade, though he did mention that he was out of work at the time of his recruitment. Without prompting, he declared he was a traitor and asked to be executed for his crime.

Some of the prisoners appearing before the panel were clearly shady characters, and the majority were unimpressive and compliant. Some appeared to cooperate out of disillusionment, while a larger number probably hoped to have their punishment mitigated. If we can draw any conclusion from this sampling and from the sequel to the interrogation described below, it would be that the members of the brigade were not the heroes they were proclaimed to be in the United States or the scum they were made out to be by their captors. As often happens, there can be a considerable discrepancy between the black-and-white judgments that are politically expedient and the gray realities of human conflict.

The Free-for-All with Fidel

On April 26, the day following the end of the marathon interrogation, Fidel literally took on about 1,000 prisoners, assembled in the
sports arena, in a five-hour televised free-for-all discussion. In a matter
of minutes the ice was broken and the atmosphere quickly became
that of a teach-in, with good-natured student-prisoners and Professor
Castro debating a wide range of social, political, and ideological
issues.

A black man argued with Fidel about racial discrimination in
prerevolutionary Cuba. A discussion arose over whether in the old
days a tobacco tenant farmer gave the landlord a third of his profit
or a third of his crop. A prisoner who said he was a fisherman
claimed he was satisfied with the way things were before the Revolution. Another prisoner said he had heard that "you have salted away
a lot of money in Swiss banks." One prisoner asked Fidel if it was
true that he was a Communist. "Socialist," answered Fidel, to which
the prisoner responded, "What's the difference?" Fidel dodged the
question with a dissertation on the virtues of socialism. The prisoner
interrupted, "Pardon me, Dr. Castro, but I believe that democracy
is better than socialism."

Fidel never lost his calm or his patience. Although he lost a few
points, he was more than a match for his prisoners. The television
and radio audience for whom he was primarily performing could
only be convinced that Cuba had a wise and benevolent leader.
Even the prisoners must have been convinced that he was an unconventional leader. "Now be honest," he said during a discussion
with one prisoner, "surely you must realize that you are the first
prisoner in history who has the privilege of arguing in front of the
whole population of Cuba, and the entire world, with the head of a
government which you came to overthrow."

There was an epilogue to this undeniably unique event. To find
a precedent, one would have to go back to the good old times when
knighthood was in flower and chivalry played a role in warfare. Fidel
proposed to free his captives on payment of what he called an in-
demnity for damages inflicted, but which in the days of yore was
known as ransom. After months of negotiations with private donors
in the United States, an agreement was reached to exchange the

prisoners for $53 million worth of food and medicine. They returned to Miami in time for Christmas, 1962. Before they left Cuba, Fidel promised that in case of another invasion, no prisoner would be taken alive.[4]

4. "[The ransom] brought back 1,113 prisoners for $53 million, or $48,000 a head. The money was raised semipublicly under the auspices of the United States Government. The sum was about 2½% of the Cuban national income or about 8% of exports" (P. J. D. Wiles, *Communist International Economics* [New York: Praeger, 1969], p. 363). Castro later claimed that the Americans swindled him by delivering goods valued at only $43 million.

11
■

From the Military to the Political Arena

What Next?

In Cuba, in the United States, and in the Soviet Union, the same question was being asked: What next? The answer, we know, was the missile crisis of October 1962; but when the last shot was fired at the Bay of Pigs, there was no human mind or electronic computer capable of predicting it.

In Cuba, for a time at least, the prevailing mood was one of optimism, despite a worsening of economic conditions. Both the American trade embargo and the reorganization and disorganization of production and distribution were beginning to take effect. On July 4, 1961, the first rationing of foodstuffs was announced (permanent and systematic rationing of most consumer goods was introduced on March 19, 1962). This was an unfortunate postscript to Fidel's proclamation that Cuba was a socialist state. However, victory on the battlefield had come at the right time to boost the prestige of the government and the patriotic fervor of the people. Socialism or no socialism, Cuba had repelled a Yankee invasion and had inflicted a decisive defeat on the Colossus of the North.

Then again, it was confidently believed that the economic difficulties were bound to be temporary. Massive aid would be coming from the Soviet Union and other socialist countries, and very soon Cuba's planned economy would move into gear. *Revolución* on May 25, 1961, quoted Che as saying, "In 1965 we shall double our standard of living" (a prediction to be fulfilled in reverse). With equal naiveté, Fidel said at the celebration of the "First Socialist 26th of July": "How can we fail when all the means of production are in the hands of the people?"

With respect to American intentions, the signals reaching Cuba were mixed. President Kennedy made a strong statement on April 20. Cuba must not be abandoned to the Communists, he said in effect, and we do not intend to abandon it: "let the record show that our restraint is not inexhaustible. . . . If the nations of this Hemisphere should fail to meet their commitments against outside Communist penetration, then I want it clearly understood that this Government will not hesitate in meeting its primary obligations, which are the security of our nation." [1]

The threat could be discounted, at least in part, as necessary political muscle flexing under the circumstances. However, strong pressures on the president were being exerted, publicly and privately, to take direct action against Cuba. Richard Nixon, for example, who spoke with Kennedy on April 21, later revealed that he urged him to "find a proper legal cover . . . and go in." [2]

On the other hand, *Time* magazine reported on July 7, apropos of an OAS meeting scheduled for the following month, that "a shift in U.S. policy toward Latin America" was taking place. "The old hard line . . . that the American Republics must agree to bring down Castro as the first order of business, was disappearing." *Time* went on to say, "the struggle against Communism and Fidel Castro must be waged the long way around, building up Latino good will through development cash and the Alliance for Progress." [3]

Prudence prevailed in Washington for the time being at least, and understandably so since Cuba's international assets were not negligible. Public opinion in most of the world had condemned the aborted invasion. Cuba's participation at the first conference of Non-Aligned Countries, held in Belgrade from September 1 to 6, placed on record the continuing growth of Cuba's influence and prestige in the Third World. It was the only Latin American country among the twenty-five voting members, which included India, Egypt,

1. *El Mundo,* April 21, 1961.
2. Nixon, "Cuba, Castro, and John F. Kennedy," *Reader's Digest,* November 1964, pp. 281–284.
3. *Time* (Atlantic Edition), July 7, 1961.

Morocco, Tunisia, and Yugoslavia, among others. Particularly in the important countries of Latin America, it was difficult to imagine any support for new military intervention against Cuba. In Mexico, Brazil, Argentina, Uruguay, and Chile, even in some less prestigious countries such as Bolivia and Ecuador, both public and official opinion on this subject was unambiguous.

The Russian Posture

In Moscow there was, of course, glee but mixed with feelings of relief and caution. On April 18, while the outcome of the battle hung in the balance, Khrushchev had sent the following message to Kennedy:

> It is no secret that the armed bands which have penetrated [Cuba] have been trained, equipped and armed in the United States. . . . It is still not too late to prevent the irreparable. The United States still has the possibility not to permit the flames of war which the interventionists have ignited in Cuba to be transformed into a fire which it will not be possible to put out. . . . With respect to the USSR, there should be no confusion about our position: we shall lend the Cuban people and their government all the help necessary to repel armed aggression.[4]

While the message preserved the Soviet posture toward Cuba, it was considerably less than the ultimatum Castro would have hoped for. Khrushchev must have felt enormously relieved when the fighting ended the next day and extricated him from a put-up-or-shut-up dilemma.

On April 22, three days after the end of hostilities, Khrushchev sent another message to Kennedy. It contained a sharp criticism of American policy toward Cuba and China, and a pointed reference to American bases on the borders of the Soviet Union. However, he declared, "We have no bases in Cuba or any idea of creating them. . . . We sincerely wish to reach an agreement with you . . . on disarmament and other problems whose solution would contribute to peaceful co-existence, . . . to true respect for the wishes of peoples and nonintervention in their internal affairs." [5]

It would be reasonable to surmise that Castro had mixed feelings about this statement. Khrushchev's larger interest was to achieve

4 *El Mundo*, April 19, 1961.   5. *El Mundo*, April 23, 1961.

a settlement on more important areas of conflict than Cuba. One could discern an implication that he was ready to use Cuba to his advantage in negotiating with Kennedy. His first offer seemed to be a guarantee against setting up a Russian base in Cuba in return for some unspecified concession by the United States elsewhere, perhaps the elimination of one or more "American bases on the borders of the Soviet Union." Would his next offer be the demilitarization of Cuba? Would peaceful coexistence between the two superpowers once more relegate Cuba to the status of "docile pawn"?

These were matters that would come to a head later. Meanwhile, the Bay of Pigs quickly faded into a minor irritant in Soviet-American relations. In early June, Khrushchev and Kennedy met in Vienna. It was the chairman who took the initiative for the meeting. Later accounts revealed that Cuba was scarcely mentioned in the conversations. In Havana, an editorial in *Revolución* dutifully concluded that the Vienna summit conference was a "positive step forward." [6]

Punta del Este I: Peaceful Coexistence?

From August 7 to 17, 1961, an inter-American economic conference was convened at the Uruguayan seaside resort of Punta del Este. For Cuba, still under the spell of Soviet policy, this was no time to rock the boat. At the same time, although American reluctance to modify its attitude toward Cuba could be expected, pressures favorable to Cuba from the leading Latin American governments could be anticipated. Thus it was that Castro's foreign policy made another detour into the quicksands of peaceful coexistence. As if to make the point more convincing, Che Guevara, now minister of industries but better known as Latin America's leading exponent of guerrilla warfare, was chosen to head the Cuban delegation and to make the live-and-let-live offer.

The main business of the conference was to set up guidelines for the implementation of the Alliance for Progress. Earlier, the alliance had been invariably denounced in Cuba as a fraud. Che, however, took a new approach. "We are not interested in the failure of the Alliance for Progress," he declared in his opening statement on August 8, "so long as it represents a real improvement for the

6. June 6, 1961.

200 million inhabitants of Latin America." [7] This was not an un-qualified endorsement, but it set the tone of Cuban participation in the conference. In the day-to-day proceedings, Che and his colleagues were businesslike and avoided unnecessary polemics. As a result, with the exception of the United States delegation, which ostentatiously ignored the presence of the Cubans, some of the other delegations were at times eager to accept Cuban voting support and at other times voted for measures initiated by Cuba.

In the final vote, which gave all but unanimous approval to the Charter of Punta del Este—the document that summarized the agreements reached at the conference—Cuba abstained. Nevertheless, the charter contained some points introduced by Cuba and others supported by Cuba during the voting on individual measures. This prompted Che to say in his closing remarks on August 16, that "we believe that the first precedent of real peaceful coexistence in the Americas has been established." [8] In the same spirit, Che had earlier made what amounted to an offer: "We cannot stop exporting our example, as the United States wants. . . . We cannot ensure . . . that the idea of Cuba will not take root in some other [Latin] American country, and . . . unless urgent social measures are taken, the Cuban example will take root. . . . *What we do guarantee is not to export revolution; we guarantee that not one rifle will leave Cuba, that not one weapon will go to another country.*" [9] The *quid pro quo*, of course, was that Cuban sovereignty, hence its socialist form of government, be respected.

One is tempted to speculate on the course of events had the proposition been taken up. Cuba would have dismantled its guerrilla operations, which were already under way and which eventually cost the United States, directly and indirectly, millions of dollars to suppress.[10] Normal trade and diplomatic relations would have been resumed. Given the simple facts of geography and the far greater capacity of the United States to supply Cuba with essential imports, this would inevitably have meant a weakening of economic and,

7. *Ernesto Che Guevara: Obra Revolucionaria*, prólogo y selección de Roberto Fernández Retamar (Mexico: Ediciones Era, 1968), p. 426.
8. *Ibid.*, p. 445.   9. *Ibid.*, p. 440. (emphasis added.)
10. The *New York Times*, on July 27, 1968, reported Bolivian President Barrientos as saying, "It cost us $3 million to win the guerrilla war against Che and our economy was badly damaged."

consequently, political and military ties with the Soviet Union and the other Communist countries. There would have been no missile crisis, although this might have been regrettable since it turned out to be a profitable experience for all mankind. Cuban socialism, even under these more favorable conditions, would still have had hard sledding (particularly if Fidel continued to manage it), as socialism everywhere has had for more than a half century. The example of Cuban socialism, at peace with Yankee imperialism and deprived of its evangelical mystique, would have been far less attractive to Latin Americans than Che imagined or American policy makers feared.

Fidel, if he could have survived the new tension-free political climate, might have become a tropical Tito. As for the uprooted Che, who could say? Certainly there would have been no posters or banners with his brooding countenance to excite the imagination of restless youth around the globe.[11]

On the other hand, the long-run solution to fundamental problems in Latin America would not have depended on the course of Cuban-American relations. Such phenomena as the deterioration of the Alliance for Progress over the years, the ever-sharpening crisis in Brazil, and the expropriation of vast American properties in Peru in 1968 and in Bolivia in 1969 by the very generals who had destroyed Cuban-supported guerrilla uprisings in their respective countries would have occurred even if Cuba in 1961 had been totally and permanently inundated by a cataclysmic tidal wave.

At Punta del Este, Che, in addition to his larger proposal, also made a more modest offer in an informal conversation with Richard Goodwin, President Kennedy's special assistant on Latin American affairs. The hijacking of American airplanes to Cuba, which in the

11. In a speech on July 26, 1970, Fidel announced that a shrine containing Che's hands and his death mask, secretly shipped to Cuba from Bolivia, would be set up in a special room in the monument to José Martí which dominates the Plaza de la Revolución. "Che's hands are in a perfect state of preservation," Fidel explained. "Our country's traditions are well known. We bury our dead. . . . Each people has its own traditions. But we wondered what to do with Che's hands." The decision was to preserve "in a sober design that has been made—framed by the olive-green sleeves of his uniform and his Major's stars and enclosed in a glass urn—Che's death mask and his hands" (*Granma Weekly Review*, August 2, 1970).

years to come was to develop into a major international travel hazard involving aircraft of countries and destinations far removed from Cuba, had already begun. At the time, hijacking was very much of a one-way problem, with more Cuban planes being diverted to the United States than vice versa. Che proposed that the United States and Cuba negotiate an agreement for the return of hijacked planes and hijackers.

Years later, Juan de Onis, speculating in a *New York Times* Washington dispatch on the possibility that the epidemic of hijacking would open the door for the no longer unthinkable settlement of Cuban-American differences, recalled that in August 1961 "Mr. Goodwin came away with the clear impression that the Cuban leader was proposing negotiations on hijacking as a first step toward broader talks and the Cuban suggestion went officially unanswered." [12]

The final episodes in Che's coexistence gambit took place immediately after the end of the conference. On August 18, Che was secretly flown in an Argentine plane to Buenos Aires for a private meeting with President Frondizi. He returned the same day to Montevideo and on the next flew to Brasília. Here he was officially received by President Quadros, who decorated him with the National Order of the Southern Cross, Brazil's highest award. Both visits added to the impression that Che's performance at the inter-American conference was profitable. He returned to Havana "with not inconsiderable political capital," in the words of the *New York Times:* "His activities at Punta del Este helped assure that, following the Alliance meeting, the American Republics would not embark on a political conference designed to punish Cuba in some form for her links with the Soviet bloc—as Washington had fondly hoped at an earlier stage." [13]

Back to Normal

The prediction of the *New York Times* was based on one kind of logic, but American policy was determined by another kind. Preparations began almost immediately in Washington and the capitals of Latin America for the punitive political conference. President Quadros, assailed for his ostentatious pro-Cuba gesture, resigned from office just six days after his meeting with Che. Frondizi lasted

12. *New York Times*, February 16, 1969.
13. *New York Times*, August 20, 1961.

a few months longer, fighting a losing battle, until he was overthrown by a military coup d'etat.

By mid-September, the Havana press was back to "normal," denouncing new conspiracies by Yankee imperialism. Fidel, weary with speeches on production failures, absenteeism, and black-market speculators, perked up. On September 26, back in top form, he declared to a graduating class of officers, "If they invade, we'll annihilate them. We are much better prepared now and we are not alone." The day before, Foreign Minister Roa, speaking at the United Nations, warned that the United States was planning a new military aggression against Cuba and that "Cuba is not alone." [14] On October 13, *Revolución* carried a banner headline "ATTACK AGAINST CUBA DOOMED TO FAILURE," attributing the statement to Radio Moscow.

On November 12, Venezuela broke relations with Cuba, making it the seventh Latin American country to close its embassy in Havana. Five days later, Fidel, in a stinging attack on American policy, condemned the break as part of Washington's plan for collective intervention against Cuba. "We are armed to the teeth," he shouted.

On December 1, Fidel announced, "I am a Marxist-Leninist and shall remain a Marxist-Leninist until the day I die." Paradoxically, the news was suppressed in Moscow but greeted with great enthusiasm in Washington. Some Latin American governments were dragging their feet in getting on with the project to excommunicate Cuba from the OAS, and Fidel's profession of faith made the job easier. Thus, on December 5 a majority of the governments approved a motion to convene the Eighth Consultation of Foreign Ministers of the OAS.

Punta del Este II: Cuba Expelled

The OAS meeting took place, once more at Punta del Este, during the last week of January 1962. The arm twisting, horse trading, and bribery that went on behind the scenes reached unusual dimensions, reflecting the extreme urgency that the United States attached to the business at hand and the reluctance of a number of the "good neighbors" to concede the urgency. In the end the United States had to drop its proposal that all member states which had not already done so break relations with Cuba (excepting Mexico this aim

14. *Revolución,* September 26, 1961.

was achieved later). On the suspension of Cuba from the organization, which only Cuba directly opposed, the United States had to be content with an unimpressive majority since six states abstained, among which were Argentina, Brazil, Chile, and Mexico.

However, on the main issue of principle, the United States scored heavily. Except for the opposition of Cuba, on January 31, 1962, unanimous approval for the following resolution was secured:

> 1. The adherence of any member of the Organization of American States to Marxism-Leninism is incompatible with the inter-American system and the alignment of such a Government with the Communist bloc breaks the unity and solidarity of the Hemisphere.
> 2. The present Government of Cuba, which has identified itself as a Marxist-Leninist Government, is incompatible with the purposes and principles of the inter-American system.

Whatever was to follow, it would not be peaceful coexistence.

In anticipation of the results of the second Punta del Este meeting, Che did not attend and the Cuban delegation was headed by President Dorticós. Midway through the meeting he declared his conviction that the conference was the prelude to further armed aggression against Cuba, "by mercenary forces or by Latin American armies" or by the "powerful country itself." [15] This conviction was the starting point of the events leading to the extraordinary Soviet-American confrontation of the following October, which in turn, by a curious twist of fate, provided Cuba with immunity from the armed aggression it had predicted at Punta del Este.

Thus, as often happens in history, today's success paves the way for tomorrow's failure, or vice versa from the Cuban perspective. There was little reason for anyone, including Dorticós, to have confidence in his parting words at the meeting: "You may expel us [from the OAS] but you cannot remove us from the Americas. . . . The United States will continue to have a revolutionary and socialist Cuba ninety miles from its shores." [16] Nevertheless, as the years passed, the prophecy was fulfilled. After the missile crisis, a period of angry coexistence set in, to be replaced by one of annoying coexistence. As the 1960s came to a close, lowered tensions in Cuban-

15. *Revolución*, January 26, 1961.
16. *Cuba Socialista* 2, no. 7 (March, 1962): 98.

American relations ushered in a period of bored coexistence, while Chile, Colombia, and the new governments in Venezuela, Peru, and Bolivia cautiously explored the possibilities of peaceful co-existence.[17]

17. Chilean feelers occurred toward the end of the Frei regime—that is, even before the election of Marxist Salvador Allende as president, who renewed diplomatic relations with Cuba on November 12, 1970.

12
■

Prologue to the Missile Crisis:

Cuban-Soviet Dissonance

A Year of Economic Disaster

IN JANUARY 1962, on the fourth anniversary of Fidel Castro's seizure of power, the year was officially designated in the revolutionary calendar as "El Año de la Planificación," that is to say, the year of economic planning. In this respect, it was to be the year of disaster.

The reasons were multiple, and among them were a number of improbable assumptions. The first assumption was that Cuba could be rapidly industrialized, even though it was notably lacking in both the natural and human resources for such an undertaking. The second was that dependence on sugar, thus far the mainstay of the economy, had to be drastically and immediately reduced by converting some of the sugar croplands to diversified farming. The third assumption was that the Soviet model for planning and operating a socialist economy—or the Czech version, since the job of introducing the model was assigned to the Czechs—would work in Cuba, whose geography, physical endowments, and culture had nothing in common with either the Soviet Union or Czechoslovakia.

Looking back on the scene, one is still dumbfounded by some of the incredible bungling that took place. A few simple facts sum up what happened. The complicated, highly centralized economic planning and control machinery was set up. The Czech experts were technically competent, but rigid, as rigid as the system of which they were a part. They were under tight reign from Prague (in the last analysis, Moscow) which, to put it mildly, did not encourage the type of imagination and initiative that would have been required to adapt to Cuban conditions. Paradoxically, they were transplanting a system whose inflexibilities had already become a matter of serious concern to some of the leading economists in Czechoslovakia, Russia, and other eastern European countries.

As for the enthusiastic young Cuban amateurs who mainly staffed the Central Planning Board and the new ministries, they were unsuited by temperament and habit to the kind of methodical, disciplined approach the task required. In addition, statistics, the basis of any kind of accounting let alone planning system, were rudimentary; and the urgency for improvement went unrecognized. Meanwhile, above the ministries hovered Fidel, constantly disrupting plans with his free-wheeling intrusions; and below were the managers of state enterprises, a considerable proportion of whom had less than a sixth-grade education.[1]

When the harvest was over, sugar production, the source of more than 80 percent of export income, had failed to reach five million metric tons. This figure was 16 percent less than in 1960 and close to 30 percent under the 1961 figure, with no compensating increases to speak of in other agricultural endeavors. At the year's end, the trade deficit, which along with sugar output is a prime indicator of the state of the Cuban economy, was a whopping 238.6 million pesos, as compared with a 20 million surplus in 1960 and a 14 million deficit

1. Fidel from time to time has stressed the exodus of Cuban technicians and competent managerial personnel as an important contributing factor to the economic problems of his regime. This no doubt is true. However, it is my impression that many who departed would have remained and accepted Fidel's revolution if they had not been unnecessarily badgered and pushed around, let alone had they been encouraged to stay. In addition, the skills of those who remained were frequently wasted when they were arbitrarily shifted from job to job irrespective of specialization, or sometimes allowed to "lie fallow" for months at a time between jobs, meanwhile drawing full pay.

in 1961. Significantly, only a small proportion of the 1962 deficit was due to imports of capital goods for new production.[2]

One can readily understand the lively optimism with which Fidel and his associates plunged into socialist planning on the Soviet model. It was ready-made, credit was easy, and they were ignorant. As for the Russians, even though they were drawn into the Cuban vortex by political considerations, it is more difficult to understand how they allowed themselves to get involved in some of the more obvious follies incorporated into the plans for Cuban economic development.

A typical example of irrational investment on the most elementary level was the failure to calculate the cost of importing raw materials for new plants created to produce goods formerly purchased abroad. To cite a well-known case, when a pencil factory, the first in Cuban history and celebrated as a landmark in the drive for import substitution, went into production, it was discovered that the foreign exchange outlay for wood and graphite was greater than it would have been to import the pencils ready-made.

The question, then, is, Why did the Czech—or the Soviet, Polish, and Hungarian—technicians[3] fail to prevent such simple but costly blunders? The answer is that, apart from specific problems in individual projects, it was the Cubans who made the decisions. The methods of planning and running the economy, the expertise in the construction and operation of new plants, and the equipment were supplied by the east Europeans; but the *content* of the planning—the type, number, and locations of new projects, within the limits of the overall credit agreements between the governments—was determined by the Cubans.

In other words, the Cubans were cheerfully, and stubbornly, exercising their sovereign right to make their own errors; and it was politically inexpedient for the Russians, who ultimately had to foot the bill, to stand in their way. Here was one of the early manifestations of a strange phenomenon that developed in Cuban-Soviet rela-

2. *Cuba, 1968: Supplement to the Statistical Abstract of Latin America*, Latin American Center, University of California, Los Angeles, 1970, p. 168.

3. The tenth anniversary of the arrival in Cuba of the first team of Soviet technicians (presumably nonmilitary) was celebrated in Moscow at the Cuban embassy on June 7, 1971. *Granma Weekly Review*, June 13, 1971.

tions: that of the tail wagging the dog. How it came about that the tail aspired to wag the dog can be better understood if viewed in the broad context of the special conditions that helped create the patterns of Soviet-Cuban relations.

Geographic Restraints on Soviet Policy

Apart from the personality of Fidel Castro, two circumstances, absent in Soviet relations with all other Communist countries, gave a distinctive character to the development of Soviet-Cuban relations. The first was geography, that is to say, Cuba's proximity to the United States and the great distance separating it from the Soviet Union. Hence, simple prudence called for an element of ambiguity in Soviet pronouncements of its readiness to defend Cuba in case of attack.

This ambiguity, understandably a source of acute anxiety for Castro, could have been removed at any time by a formal Russo-Cuban military alliance or Cuban membership in the Warsaw Pact (although the latter procedure might have required costly pressure on the east European *tovarishchi*). Neither of these steps was ever taken and, from the Russian point of view, for very good reasons. If Cuba were invaded by a superior force, there would be no way to provide direct military assistance except by a nuclear strike against the United States. While the threat of such a deterrent could give pause to the United States, circumstances that might require making good the threat had best be avoided. Hence, a firm and unequivocal defense commitment to Cuba would not be realistic.

In view of the limits imposed by geography, the weapons Russia could deploy in defending Cuba—in addition to supplying the island with the means of self-defense and subsistence as long as the sea lanes remained open—were essentially those of political and psychological warfare. On the one hand, such tactics involved a combination of intensive international propaganda and more or less explicit warnings of counterpressures in other parts of the world readily accessible to Soviet power. On the other, the Russians held out the possibility of a general accommodation with the United States—peaceful coexistence—of mutual advantage to both countries. A settlement of the Cuban problem would, of course, be part of such an accommodation. For Fidel, once he could grasp the subtleties of his situation, the prospect of ending up as a pawn in big power politics was extremely unpalatable.

Geography also played another significant role in Soviet-Cuban relations. It was a major obstacle preventing the Russians from exercising the kind of control over Cuban affairs that at one time they had hoped to have, and without which their ability to maneuver in their confrontation with the United States would be impaired. While their control problems in the "fraternal" countries of Europe and Asia became increasingly widespread and acute in the post-Stalin era, nowhere except in Cuba (and possibly Albania) was military intervention, the ultimate recourse—or even the threat of it—for all practical purposes excluded. The reason was not only a matter of logistics but, even more important, the proximity of Cuba to the United States. Any serious political or military upheaval on the island would in all likelihood tempt American intervention. If overt or covert Soviet participation were detected, American intervention would be certain.

As geography began to impose its twofold pattern of restraints on Soviet policy, tensions developed between Fidel and his benefactors, at first only faintly visible and then rising to the surface. At the same time, interlocking with geography in this process was a second circumstance which, for want of a better name, we shall call the politico-ideological considerations.

Politico-Ideological Considerations

By the beginning of 1961, when the Soviet Union had become deeply involved in Cuba, the Cuban economy by any reasonable definition was already a socialist economy. Before the year was out, Fidel announced, first, that Cuba was a socialist state, and then that he personally was a Marxist-Leninist, which was intended to be a final clarification, if one were needed, of the kind of socialist state over which he presided. However, the Soviet Union was extremely reluctant to acknowledge Fidel's claims. For if it were to do so, it would imply an ideological commitment to defend Cuba, which would further complicate an already difficult situation. It would be one thing to let down a "progressive" or even "socialist-oriented" Cuba but quite another to desert a bona fide socialist Cuba, a member of the socialist family whose safety it would be the sacred obligation of the Soviet Union, the mightiest bulwark of international proletarian solidarity, to guarantee at all costs, etc., etc.

There was still another reason, equally important and more complicated. From the point of view of ideology, to concede that

Fidel Castro had created and was ruling over a socialist state would be tantamount to negating a fundamental principle of Marxism-Leninism, namely, that at some point in a revolutionary process the leading role in setting up the new socialist state is inevitably assumed by the "vanguard party of the workers and peasants," in other words, the Communist party, which in Cuba had been the PSP, the legitimate Marxist-Leninist vanguard for over thirty-five years. The day on which a Communist party takes power signals the real and final transformation of a bourgeois into a socialist state. The socialist state then proceeds with the task of building socialism.

Hence, it was not easy to swallow this embarrassing Cuban proposition. In fact, before the Cuban Revolution, the classical pattern had prevailed without exception. In all socialist countries, state power had been seized by their respective Communist parties, or placed in the hands of the parties by the Russian army. Since 1917, the socialist world has been plagued by countless doctrinal disputes, but not even the most formidable heretics, within or outside the Soviet Union—such as Trotsky, Tito, and Mao—had ever questioned the dogma of the "leading role."

At the same time, the ideological problem raised by Cuban socialism had serious political implications of a practical nature. Any corrosion of the leading-role principle would weaken the authority of the world network of Communist parties in the Soviet sphere of influence. Particularly vulnerable would be the Communist parties in Latin America, where the Cuban Revolution early became a source of doctrinal and tactical disputation both within the parties and between them and other leftist groups.

Finally, in Cuba itself even more was at stake. Once Cuba had moved into the Soviet orbit and with Castro depending more and more on PSP organizational and political expertise, it was natural for the Kremlin to hope that the experienced and trustworthy leadership of the old Communist party would take power in a relatively short period of time. At that moment, Cuba would at least be under control; and all decisions, including whether or not and when it might be expedient formally to proclaim the Marxist-Leninist orientation of the state, could be made "rationally."

There is evidence that there was serious debate in the inner circles of the PSP, and one can assume in the Kremlin, about whether these expectations were realistic and what risks they entailed. In any event, the entire process in the shift of power, if it could take place, was anticipated as part of a gradual, normal transformation obeying well-known Marxist "laws" of historical development. There would even be a role for Fidel to play in the new order, and some preparation for this was visible. Ignoring Fidel's socialist and Marxist pretensions, official Soviet statements consistently described him as Cuba's "national hero." Thus enshrined, he could remain floating above the power structure as a figurehead, as long as he behaved and was needed.

Fidel Presses for Recognition of Cuban Socialism

It is difficult to determine when Fidel became fully aware of the geographic and politico-ideological complexities that affected his relations with the Soviet leadership. Certainly, after his showdown with the PSP in March 1962 and the termination of the missile crisis eight months later, he was perfectly clear about his assets and liabilities in dealing with Moscow. It appears, however, that he began to suspect somewhat earlier that Cuban interests, as he saw them, and those of the USSR were not always identical.

Earlier, I suggested that Fidel's unexpected announcement on the very eve of the Bay of Pigs invasion that Cuba was a socialist state was addressed more to the Soviet Union than to the Cuban people. An explanation for this announcement was attempted by President Dorticós in a speech delivered on June 14, 1961. He noted that in Cuba, unlike the course of events in other countries, first a socialist revolution took place and only later was it publicly proclaimed to be socialist; he went on to say, "a large part of our population—let us mention this with complete frankness—even a large part of our workers were frightened by the very word [socialism]. . . . After socializing the principal sectors of our economy . . . the people and the entire working class applauded this transformation of our economy, and one fine day they discovered or confirmed that what they were applauding . . . was a Socialist Revolution." [4]

The president's candid admission that most Cubans were allergic to the word "socialism" makes the rest of his statement less than convincing. To be sure, eventually socialism would have to be acknowledged, and in time the even less palatable term, "communism." The new economic structure existed, a new vanguard politi-

4. *Cuba Socialista* 1, no. 1 (September 1961): 28.

cal organization was already on the drawing board, and massive ideological indoctrination of the population to create acceptance of the new order and submission to it had to get under way. The word for all this could not be "humanism," not only because it would be absurdly inaccurate but also because it could not serve the interests of foreign policy which required Cuban identification with the Communist world and a popular consciousness of this identification.

What Dorticós failed to explain is Fidel's timing. Why did he use the dread word, by Dorticós' own definition, at a moment of supreme national peril? Did he believe that by his charisma he could suddenly convert it into a glowing symbol for which his soldiers would gladly sacrifice their lives? This was extremely unlikely There was no mention of socialism in his exhortations when the missile crisis occurred, only "patria o muerte." Just as in the Soviet Union, during the entire course of the war against the Nazi invaders, there was no appeal to defend socialism, communism, or Marxism-Leninism. The basic slogan was "For the Fatherland and Stalin."

Thus, it seems almost certain that Fidel's proclamation of the "Socialist Revolution" on April 15, 1961, was addressed to the Soviet Union; in other words it was dictated by foreign policy and not domestic considerations. Apparently already uneasy about the extent to which the Soviets would give assistance if the impending invasion threatened to destroy his regime, his dramatic announcement was a desperate and naive attempt to force the Russians to recognize a "fraternal" obligation to defend Cuba at all costs.[5] With the quick annihilation of the Bay of Pigs invasion, the Soviets were taken off the hook, but only temporarily. Fidel continued to press for a 100 percent Russian commitment for the survival of his regime.

Fidel's next ideological leap came in his speech of December 1, 1961, in which he declared for the first time that he was a Marxist-

5. Although Khrushchev, in his memoir, claims not to have grasped the meaning of Fidel's signal, his comments on the subject lend support to the hypothesis that Fidel was indeed addressing himself to the chairman: "We had trouble understanding the timing of this statement [in regard to the "socialist revolution"]. Castro's declaration had the immediate effect of widening the gap between himself and the people who were against Socialism, and it narrowed the circle of those he could count on for the support against the invasion. . . . From a tactical standpoint, it didn't make much sense." *Khrushchev Remembers* (Boston: Little, Brown, 1970), p. 492.

Leninist. As with his earlier socialist proclamation, eventually acknowledgment of Marxism-Leninism as the official state ideology had to come as a logical step in the process of completing the political and ideological identity of the new order. As a matter of fact, some preparation for this eventuality had already been under way. Two months preceding Fidel's speech, *Revolución* began to print a regular column entitled "Marxist Vocabulary," a glossary as indispensable for veteran guerrilla leaders as for schoolchildren of the perplexing terminology of the Marxist-Leninist classics on prominent display in all bookstores.

Thus, once more the question is not why Fidel openly embraced Marxism-Leninism, but why he did so at that moment, when he could easily have anticipated that his "confession" would shortly facilitate the expulsion of Cuba from the OAS.

With respect to the OAS, he had undoubtedly already given up hope. Cuba's adoption of the Soviet line of peaceful coexistence at the August meeting in Punta del Este had signally failed to achieve its purpose. On the contrary, a new and more powerful invasion was in the cards, as Fidel read them. Meanwhile, his socialist proclamation of April had thus far been completely ignored by Moscow and the rest of the camp, and only reluctantly and somewhat ambiguously accepted by the PSP leadership. Hence, Fidel's Marxist-Leninist pronouncement was primarily another and more spectacular effort to break the continuing ideological blockade that compromised Cuba's security in the face of what he believed to be a growing external danger. I shall scrutinize this pronouncement after examining another development that also had some bearing on it.

The New Vanguard Party

The situation was further complicated by the fact that a new vanguard party was being organized—the Organizaciones Revolucionarias Integradas, or ORI (Integrated Revolutionary Organizations)—to replace the loose confederation of the three recognized revolutionary organizations: the Movement of July 26th, the PSP, and the Revolutionary Student Directorate. In his speech on July 26, 1961, commemorating the eighth anniversary of the attack on Moncada, Fidel proposed that the ORI be considered the forerunner of the Partido Unido de la Revolución Socialista, or PURS (United Party of the Socialist Revolution). "All in favor, raise your right hands," he exclaimed to the great sweltering throng below him. Up went the hands, and the motion was "unanimously" carried.

The main task of setting up the ORI was entrusted to the PSP, and more particularly to Aníbal Escalante. Although he did not hold the formal title of secretary-general, he was possibly the most influential and certainly the most energetic figure in the old Communist leadership, not always admired by his peers in the PSP but highly regarded in Moscow.

As far as can be known, Fidel had no misgivings about turning over this job to the PSP, and even if he did, he had little choice. Of the three amalgamating revolutionary organizations, only the PSP had the experience, the disciplined membership, and the ideological background that were needed in setting up the ORI-PURS. There was also another, and very significant, advantage from Fidel's point of view. The enhanced role of the PSP would inspire more confidence in the Kremlin concerning his own reliability, while the PSP in turn would be more willing and in a better position to persuade the Kremlin to recognize the legitimacy of Fidel's claim to full membership in the socialist club.

But there was also a disadvantage, even a potential danger, in this situation. Fidel could never have intended to transfer any real power to the ORI or PURS, nor did he do so to their successor, the new Communist party of Cuba, which he himself set up and inaugurated in late October 1965. Power has always been a strictly personal matter for Fidel; and even though from time to time he would discourse on the benefits of collective leadership—perhaps sincerely when he was in a mellow mood and could objectively assess some of the costly failures stemming from his one-man rule—he would be temperamentally incapable of submitting to any kind of truly collective decision-making body, however reduced in numbers it might be.

Thus, once it became a question of moving from acceptance of the prescribed theory of the vanguard party to its actual construction, for Fidel—who took power without a party and by the end of 1961 had been governing without a party for three years—the ORI-PURS could not be the kind of traditional ruling party that existed in all Communist states. It would have a limited, though not insignificant, role to play. In international affairs, it would have a decorative and legitimizing function in Cuba's relations with the Communist world, essentially for protocol and for communicating with the fraternal parties of other countries and participating in interparty meetings. In domestic affairs, its task would be to promote and coordinate the civic and ideological mobilization of the population for goals defined by the regime, that is to say, by Fidel Castro. This, in effect, was the way the party was to operate once Fidel decided to bring it under his personal control.

On the eve of his I-am-a-Marxist-Leninist speech, Fidel was already aware that Aníbal Escalante was building a PSP-dominated power machine. On several occasions he had publicly shown his dissatisfaction. For example, on November 10, speaking to the Revolutionary Orientation Committee (COR), the new party's information-propaganda-censorship department presided over by Aníbal himself, Fidel declared, "It is important for us to bear in mind that Marxism is not a catechism," and then went into a long disquisition on this theme. "Dogmatism," he pointed out, was at the root of the trouble. It was responsible for the poor quality of the press. We must, he said, fight against stereotype expressions and ideas. Then, still within the context of "catechism" and "dogmatism," he wound up with a startling indictment of overzealous revolutionary vigilance: "Arbitrary arrests must stop!"

These and similar warnings went unheeded, nor was the time ripe for Fidel to crack down for he needed Escalante and the PSP in his strategy vis-à-vis the Soviet Union. It was a delicate and urgent problem, which he decided to tackle by making a dramatic profession of faith. This, he expected, both would hasten the Kremlin's recognition of Cuba as an authentic Marxist-Leninist socialist state and at the same time would establish his personal ideological credentials in anticipation of the moment when he would have to purge Escalante and his comrades and assert his full authority over the party.

13

■

Political Juggling in Havana, Moscow, and Peking

"I am a Marxist-Leninist"

SPEAKING AS USUAL without a prepared text, it took Fidel five hours on the night of December 1–2, 1961, to define his position, most of which was spent in attempting to develop an elaborate rationalization of the process that had led him and the Cuban Revolution to embrace Marxism-Leninism.[1] There was a good deal of autobiographical explanation, a blending of fact and fiction designed to establish some knowledge of and an intuitive predilection for Marxism-Leninism from the time of his youth. This explanation need not detain us since we have already seen that Marxism-Leninism had practically nothing to do with his political and intellectual development prior to 1959.

A more difficult problem for him was how to incorporate the history of his successful insurrection into the mainstream of Marxist-Leninist revolutionary theory. Without explicitly dealing with PSP charges of "petit bourgeois adventurism," some admission of having

1. Castro's speech is reported in *Revolución*, December 2, 1961, as well as *Hoy* and *El Mundo*. The reader is reminded that, unless otherwise indicated, quotations from Castro's speeches and other remarks of his are taken from the version published in *Revolución* the day after they are made. If a speech continues after midnight, the date of publication is the day following the beginning of the speech.

committed errors was required. At the same time, in order to maintain his political authority, as well as for reasons of pride and probably conviction, he could scarcely afford to tell his Cuban and Latin American following and his admirers throughout the world that he had merely blundered his way into power, that the Cuban Revolution was an accident and not a model for revolution in other Latin American countries.

As a result, this part of his performance was a fascinating hodgepodge of extemporaneous reminiscences, explanations, and unavoidable incongruities. At one point he made an unexpected admission: "When we reached the Sierra Maestra, we had made no previous study of the situation. . . . We did not know a single peasant." At another point: "We did not think that we would take power with a handful of men. We thought that we would keep up the guerrilla struggle until we took power with the help of the masses."

Then how did they manage to take power with no previous study of the situation and with a handful of men? The answer is that they began their struggle on an "assumption" which turned out to be "correct because it corresponded to reality," and then they "simply took advantage of the existing objective conditions." Another twist in the story came an hour or so later in his discourse: "Little by little, [our] struggle was converted into the struggle of the whole people. . . . The people was the sole protagonist [in the revolutionary drama]."

All of this was no doubt interesting, and some of it useful for the historian, but scarcely edifying for the Marxist-Leninists in the PSP and the Kremlin. It added up to the same heresy he and Che in particular had been promoting for well onto three years: the Cuban Revolution was the model for revolution in Latin America.

"It's good to go over these things," Fidel said, "so that it can serve as an example to other exploited peoples. . . . Conditions in our country are similar to those of many other countries in Latin America. . . . When . . . people become convinced as we did . . . [and create] a revolutionary movement . . . and this movement obeys the rules of guerrilla warfare, it will then be the spark that will set the country on fire." The most distressing element in this unacceptable departure from orthodoxy—and on this both Mao and Khrushchev could agree—was the clear implication that the "revolutionary movement" need not be a Marxist-Leninist political party.

There was no way for Fidel to draw on the Russian Revolution for historic analogies with his own revolution. He therefore turned to the Chinese Revolution to link up with previous, and now authoritative, Marxist-Leninist experience. In a burst of candor, he exclaimed, "Was the [Cuban] Revolution, when it took power, an organized, disciplined movement? No!" As an explanation, he made a farfetched comparison between the Cuban and Chinese revolutions: "The Chinese had time to acquire experience, . . . to adminster a large territory, . . . to discuss problems long before taking power. . . . It was a twenty-year struggle."

It was a clever bit of insinuation, chacteristic of his skill in the manipulation of innuendo. The myth was already abroad that the Cuban Revolution was a peasant revolution and hence resembled the Chinese Revolution. Fidel was not adverse to reinforcing the myth. By expounding the "difference" as he did between the two revolutions, the similarities could be taken for granted. Fidel, of course, knew the facts. The real difference was that twenty years before Mao took power, he had "an organized, disciplined movement," in fact, a bona fide Marxist-Leninist party.

The Chinese, as we shall see, were not impressed by Fidel's reference to their revolution, and the Russians were probably annoyed. At the same time, in attempting to legitimize his own past and that of the Cuban Revolution, Fidel could probably foresee that neither China nor the Soviet Union would be convinced. Nevertheless, he hoped that they—and in particular the Soviet Union—would accept, if only tacitly, his effort for what it was meant to be: an invention of historical credentials with which they could rationalize Cuba's admission as a full member of the socialist club.

Something more was required, however, and this was a pledge that henceforth, through its participation in the ORI-PURS, the former PSP would now have full partnership in the new power structure that would govern the country. He had, he said, unfortunately misjudged the PSP in the past: "I remember when we launched the call for a general strike in April, 1958. . . . It was premature because the objective conditions [for its success] did not exist. . . . We made an error." He did not mention that, at the time, the Movement of July 26th blamed the disaster on the PSP which, in fact, had boycotted the strike. However, now, by admitting his "error," the PSP was in fact absolved. Even after his pact with the

PSP and after taking power, he said, he still had had "some preju- dices" against the Communists. It was wrong and harmful.

After giving the PSP a clean bill of health, he declared, possibly sincerely—in which case he was deceiving himself as well as others— that the time had come for a change from personal decisions, "almost always taken because of the trust placed in the prime minister," to a "system of government built on the foundations of a revolutionary party, democratically organized and through collective leadership."

No one could doubt any longer that "collective leadership" in- cluded the former PSP or that the Marxist-Leninist system he had in mind was the Soviet model; "read Khrushchev's reports to the Twenty-Second Congress," he advised, for they "constitute a real textbook of politics." With this he signed off: "I am a Marxist- Leninist and shall remain one until the last day of my life."

Remarkable as the speech was, even more remarkable was the silence that followed, in both Cuba and the socialist camp. After publishing the speech, *Hoy* understandably waited for a signal from Moscow. *Revolución*, which also printed the speech and on such occasions would normally follow up with laudatory comments and a protracted exegesis, apparently received immediate negative feedback. Had Fidel overreached himself? Had the populace, grumbling over food shortages, annoyed by the new ORI bureaucracy, and always distrustful of the Communists, reacted unfavorably? Did the veterans of the Movement of July 26th, already alarmed by the way they were being pushed into the background by Aníbal Escalante's control of the ORI, suspect that Fidel had indeed decided to sacrifice them to appease the Kremlin? In any event, there was no exuberance over the sensational speech by *Revolución*.

A month passed with no visible or audible reaction from Moscow, Peking, or the other capitals of the socialist world. Then, in the first days of January 1962 came the customary congratulatory messages commemorating the anniversary of the Revolution. They differed little from the previous year. Not a word about Fidel's "socialism," to say nothing of his "Marxism-Leninism."

The Second Declaration of Havana

On February 4, 1962, the Second Declaration of Havana appeared. Like the First on September 2, 1960, it was Cuba's answer to an OAS pronouncement, this time the resolutions adopted four days previously, on January 31, at the second Punta del Este conference, condemning Cuba's adherence to Marxism-Leninism and expelling the country from the organization. However, unlike the first, aimed at the United States and Latin America, it included another target: the Soviet Union. And whether it was coincidental or deliberate, it injected Cuba into the now flourishing Sino-Soviet ideological dispute.

In its wrath and indignation over the misery inflicted on Latin America by the United States and the native oligarchies and in its great length—some 9,000 words—it very much overshadowed the first declaration. Hurling anathema at the forces of evil, the document reached a climax at the end of some 6,000 words:

> What this nightmare in [Latin] America adds up to is that in this continent of almost 200 million human beings, two-thirds of whom are Indians, Mestizos [of mixed Indian and white ancestry], and Negroes [earlier mulattos were also mentioned], the discriminated races in this continent of semicolonies, the death rate from hunger, curable diseases, and premature old age amounts to approximately four persons per minute, 5,500 per day, 2 million per year, 10 million every five years. . . . Meanwhile an unending torrent of money flows from Latin America to the United States: some $4,000 per minute, $5 million per day, $2 billion per year, $10 billion every five years. For each thousand dollars they take from us, they leave us a corpse. A thousand dollars per corpse: that is the price of what is known as imperialism! $1,000 per corpse, four times per minute! [2]

The arithmetic was dubious but the invective was superb and very much in Fidel's personal style. Distributed in hundreds of thousands of copies throughout Latin America and broadcast countless times by shortwave radio, it was undoubtedly effective propaganda. As for the Kremlin, thus far at least, it could have little quarrel with the substance of the document, although the savage tone of the indictment would not correspond to Soviet policy, which aimed to leave the way open for an accommodation with the United States.

Some analysts have speculated that the unusual emphasis given to Indians and Negroes was a deliberate appeal for Chinese support, but this seems hardly likely. In the context of the document—which

2. *Cuba Socialista* 2, no. 7 (March 1962): 21.

earlier referred to the Ku Klux Klan—the stress on the colored peoples and racial discrimination reinforced the attack on the United States.

The final quarter of the declaration was an exhortation for immediate armed struggle against the oppressors and represented the most significant statement thus far of the Castro-Guevara thesis on revolution. After the familiar disclaimer that Cuba did not want to export its revolution—although for some time it had been helping to organize and arm rebel bands on the continent (see below, chapters 28–29)—and after repeating the equally familiar assertion that Cuba only provided an example to Latin America, the document asks, "And what does the Cuban Revolution show? That revolution is possible, that the people can do it. . . . The socioeconomic conditions [which ensured our triumph] exist to an even greater degree in a considerable number of Latin American countries." [3]

The problem, then, is to know how to go about it. To begin with, "the national bourgeoisie cannot head the antifeudal and anti-imperialist struggle, . . . although its interests are opposed to those of Yankee imperialism. . . . It is paralyzed by fear of social revolution." As for the working class, "it is in general relatively small, . . . but there is a social class that has a decisive importance in the national liberation struggle: the peasants. . . . But the peasant needs revolutionary and political direction by the working class and the revolutionary intellectuals. . . . Alone he cannot begin the struggle and achieve victory." [4]

Where does the struggle take place? Primarily in the countryside. "When the army, trained and equipped for conventional warfare, . . . has to engage in an unconventional type of struggle with the peasants in their natural habitat, then it becomes absolutely impotent: it loses ten men for each revolutionary fighter and it becomes quickly demoralized."

And how is the war finally won? "The struggle begins with small groups of fighters which keep growing in size. A mass movement then begins to take shape, the old order little by little begins to crumble in a thousand pieces and that is the moment when the working class and the urban masses enter the fray and decide the outcome of the battle."

The thesis was not only a call to arms, and as such a threat of answering United States aggression against Cuba with a military

3. *Ibid.*, p. 22.   4. *Ibid.*, pp. 22, 23.

counteroffensive in the southern continent, but also a direct challenge
to the Kremlin's leadership of the revolutionary movement in Latin
America. To make this crystal clear, a sharp warning was added:

> where repression of workers and peasants is fierce [and] the
> Yankee monopolies most powerful, the first and most important
> thing to understand is that it is neither just nor correct to lull the
> people with the vain and comforting illusion that by legal means,
> which do not exist and will not exist, they can seize power . . .
> from the monopolies and oligarchies who will defend themselves
> with their police and armies, no matter what the amount of blood-
> shed and destruction. We know that [eventually] the revolution
> will triumph in [Latin] America and the world but this does not
> mean that revolutionaries should sit on their doorsteps and wait
> to see the corpse of imperialism pass by.[5]

In the years that followed, the Second Declaration of Havana
was enshrined in Cuba as if it were a second Communist manifesto,
a sequel to the classical pronouncement of 1848; and its flamboyant
prose became the source of many a revolutionary epigram. The "revolutionaries sitting on their doorsteps" became a favorite taunt in the
extensive polemics with Latin American Communist parties. Another
passage was frequently cited in connection with the Havana Tri-
Continental Conference in 1966: "What is the history of Cuba if
not the history of Latin America? And what is the history of Latin
America if not the history of Asia, Africa and Oceania? And what is
the history of all these peoples if not the history of the most pitiless
and cruel exploitation by imperialism in the entire world?"

And all school children from one end of the island to the other
could repeat the closing words of the document: "Porque esta gran
humanidad ha dicho 'Basta!' y ha echado a andar" ("because this
great mass of humanity has said, Enough! and is already on the
march").

The Chinese Stake in Cuba

The first significant foreign response to the Second Declaration of
Havana came from Peking. To place it in its proper perspective, a
brief recapitulation of the triangular relationship between Cuba,
China, and the Soviet Union is in order.

5. *Ibid.*, p. 25.

The year that Castro came to power marked the beginning of the Sino-Soviet dispute. It led to the withdrawal of Soviet technicians from China in April 1960; and by November of that year, at the meeting of eighty-one Communist parties in Moscow, the Chinese attack on the Soviet thesis concerning peaceful coexistence and peaceful transition to socialism brought the conflict into the open. In later years Fidel Castro was among those who most vociferously deplored the break between the two Communist powers. Nevertheless, it was in fact a situation that offered him opportunities, though not without problems.

While for the Soviet Union, Cuba was primarily a front in the cold war with the United States, for China it was mainly a front in its cold war with the Soviet Union. The Chinese, to be sure, were eager to support the challenge Cuba presented to the United States. However, Cuba was not Korea and it was obvious that only the Soviet Union could effectively cope with the United States in this part of the world.

Thus, with the Soviets having to bear the brunt of the confrontation, and since all-out confrontation with imperialism had become the keystone of Chinese foreign policy and a principal source of the Sino-Soviet quarrel, the Chinese tactic in the Cuban situation was designed to encourage Cuba's anti-American belligerency. This was a way of exerting pressure on the Soviets and thereby, they hoped, of sharpening Soviet-American antagonism. Concurrently, the Chinese aim was to establish in Cuba a base from which to subvert the Moscow-oriented Communist parties in Latin America.

Beginning with the first postrevolutionary exchange of visiting delegations between Cuba and China in mid-1959, the Havana revolutionary press, including *Hoy*, gave exceptionally large and favorable coverage to news from China, frequently overshadowing news from Russia. Cubans, moreover, were familiar with the Chinese. Since approximately 1850 some 150,000 Chinese had settled on the island. In Cuba, where xenophobia is practically nonexistent, Chinese immigrants intermarried freely with their dark- and light-skinned neighbors, and their offspring were readily assimilated into the Cuban culture. Fulgencio Batista, for example, is partly of Chinese ancestry, as is Wilfredo Lam, avant-garde painter and the most prestigious of contemporary Cuban artists.

Nevertheless, China itself was unknown to the great mass of

Cuban readers, hence the stigma attached to Russian communism, and related phenomena such as Stalinism and the Hungarian uprising, was absent. Chinese communism could be portrayed as more tolerant, more benign. China could be presented as an underdeveloped country, a nation of peasants struggling heroically and successfully to build a new, prosperous, egalitarian society. In addition, China, like Cuba, was the object of unrelenting hostility by the United States.

In other words, China appeared to be a more relevant and appealing model for Cubans than the Soviet Union. From both public and private comments made by Cuban officials returning from both China and the Soviet Union, it was clear that the simplicity of the Chinese and the unaffected warmth of their hospitality made a better impression on them than the efficiency and ostentation of the Russians. As one Cuban diplomat said to me confidentially, "The Russians remind me too much of the Americans."

Although Chinese economic aid to Cuba was very much overshadowed by that of the Soviet Union, judged in terms of their respective capabilities the Chinese effort was considerably greater. In fact, it was something of a paradox that China, whose people lived in grinding poverty, should provide any aid at all to Cuba whose entire population, by comparison, was living in the lap of luxury. At the same time, although the Chinese could not compete with the Russians on a material basis, they could make a convincing display of their higher morality.

In Che Guevara's long television report on January 6, 1961, following his grand tour of the socialist countries, including China and North Korea, his earlier enthusiasm for Yugoslavia had disappeared and was replaced by a new enthusiasm for Far Eastern communism. China, he explained, had granted Cuba credits amounting to $60 million on exceptionally generous terms: repayment in fifteen years with no interest charge. Moreover, said Che, "I was told that if we couldn't meet the payments when they fell due, it wouldn't matter." This was something other than the strictly businesslike transactions with the Russians, who also asked for a 2.5 percent interest charge.

Che also made another observation on the difference between the Chinese and the Russians, without, of course, mentioning the Russians. He told how, when the final joint communiqué was drawn up, the Cubans had inserted in the draft a reference to Chinese "disinterested aid" to Cuba, a formula always used by the Russians on such occasions. The Chinese, however, objected. "We most certainly have an interest," Che quoted them as saying. "Cuba is in the vanguard of the struggle against imperialism and imperialism is our common enemy. We have an interest in the defeat of imperialism." [6]

In the months that followed, only occasionally—and very circumspectly—did the Sino-Soviet jockeying for position in Cuba appear on the surface. For one thing, Peking was just as reluctant as Moscow to acknowledge Fidel's "socialism." The reasons, however, were not entirely the same. To grant its ideological imprimatur to Fidel's pronouncement, as long as Fidel appeared to be firmly in the grip of Moscow, would risk legitimizing another voice in the chorus of Russian "modern revisionism." At the same time, the Chinese, like the Russians, were deeply interested in the possibility that the PSP, in the process of taking control of ORI, would in fact take power from Fidel. As we shall presently see, the Chinese were not merely spectators in this process. Hence, until the outcome was known, it would be premature to make a formal commitment on the socialist character of the Cuban state.

An Unreported Episode

On September 6, 1961, *Revolución* printed a brief TASS dispatch originating in Moscow the same day saying that "The First Secretary of the Central Committee of the Communist Party of the USSR, Nikita Khrushchev, and Presidium members Alexei Kosygin and Mikhail Suslov, met with one of the leaders of the ORI of Cuba, Blas Roca. They held a friendly and cordial conversation."

Blas Roca had been, until the merger of the PSP in the ORI, the secretary-general of the old party, a position he had held for more than twenty-five years. At the moment he was a member of President's Dorticós' delegation, which had been at a meeting of nonaligned countries in Belgrade. In October he was to be the chief spokesman of the ORI at the Twenty-Second Congress of the Soviet Communist party. It was probably because of the latter function that his official reception by Khrushchev could be justified by proto-

6. *El Mundo*, January 7, 1961.

col, for important figure as he was, he was no longer secretary-general of a Communist party, nor was he a key figure in the Cuban government.

The substance of Roca's conversation with Khrushchev and his colleagues was not revealed in the TASS dispatch. Nevertheless, I was reliably informed at the time—quite by accident—that China loomed large in the conversation. Specifically, Roca told the Russian leaders that members of the Chinese embassy in Havana had been attempting to persuade certain elements of the former PSP, among others, to seize power by a military coup. The argument of these zealous Chinese was that Castro was an incorrigible petit bourgeois romantic whose rapid elimination was necessary to ensure Cuba's transformation into a genuine socialist state. With mass discontent rising and Fidel's charisma at a low ebb, according to their view, and with the ORI now in an advanced state of organization and removed from Fidel's control, the time was ripe for the change.

Whether the attempt at subversion originated in the Chinese embassy or was undertaken on a directive from Peking was not revealed. It may be noted that Chinese activity in Havana would not be inconsistent with the generally aggressive mood of Chinese foreign policy at the time, notably in Africa and Asia, and which would reach a climax in September 1965 with the disastrous attempt by the Chinese-oriented wing of the Indonesian Communist party to seize power in Jakarta. In any event, Roca considered the situation to be sufficiently dangerous to request that Khrushchev personally take the matter up with Mao Tse-tung.

No further details concerning this affair are available (early in 1966, when the Chinese embassy was again caught in flagrante delicto, Fidel turned it into a major scandal without mentioning the earlier trouble). Since Khrushchev and Mao were still on speaking terms in late 1961, it is possible that some exchange on the matter took place between them. The incident, in any case, failed to develop and was quietly swept under the rug. On the surface Chinese-Cuban relations remained unruffled. President Dorticós was received in Peking at the beginning of October with the customary honors. The official communiqué issued at his departure, published on the front page of *Revolución* on October 3, stated in part that "China notes with satisfaction that the heroic Cuban people . . . led by Fidel

Castro has chosen the path of socialist development." This was the same formula used by the Russians, and it left the Cubans where they were before: sitting on the doorstep of the socialist camp but not admitted.

At the Twenty-Second Congress of the Soviet Communist party later in the month, Blas Roca, speaking officially in the name of the ORI, went all out for the Khrushchev line, including an endorsement of the latter's attack on the Albanian party. Sino-Soviet tensions were rising. Chou En-lai, it will be remembered, left the congress in a huff before it was over, placing a wreath on Stalin's new grave prior to his departure for Peking. As the year 1961 came to an end, the Cuban stock in Peking could not have been especially high.

The Chinese Reaction to the Second Declaration of Havana

Such was the state of Sino-Cuban affairs when the Second Declaration of Havana was broadcast to the world. A week later, in record time for such an important reaction, a mass meeting was organized in Peking in honor of this "solemn proclamation." A lengthy resolution was adopted and Deputy Prime Minister Ch'en Yi, one of the notables on the platform, also made a speech. The next day, on February 13, *Revolución* carried the story on the front page, with the full texts of the resolution and the speech on an inside page.

The heart of both statements was contained in the following passage of the resolution: "[The Second Declaration of Havana] has correctly pointed out the road the peoples of Latin America must take in their struggle for liberation. The declaration has emphasized that there must be no illusions concerning Yankee imperialism and its lackeys. . . . The people must take up arms and wage armed struggle against the enemy. The Chinese people support the just struggles of the peoples of Cuba and Latin America."

It was, of course, the "armed struggle" thesis, a major issue in the Sino-Soviet dispute, that attracted the attention of the Chinese and accounted for the unusual pomp and circumstance with which the second declaration was endorsed. There were other points the Chinese might have dealt with, such as the document's emphasis on the exploitation of the nonwhite peoples and the role of the peasantry in the armed struggle, both important questions in their polemic with the Russians. For the Chinese, however, Latin America, with its

numerically and politically significant white population, did not fall
into the same racial category as Asia and Africa. With respect to the
peasantry, the Chinese view stressed their incorporation into a
"People's War" under the leadership of a Communist party, a
strategy modeled on their own experiences or that of Vietnam.
Hence, they could not support the Castro-Guevara theory that small,
scattered guerrilla nuclei, operating without benefit of a central Communist political authority, would "ignite" a general revolution, which
in turn would create the conditions for the emergence of a Communist party.

The implications of the Chinese statement were not lost in either Havana or Moscow. In Havana, the statement was prominently
displayed, as we have seen, but prudently it was not followed by
any meaningful commentary. After all, the solution to Fidel's problems, economic and military, lay in Moscow and not Peking. As for
the Kremlin, the statement further complicated the task of meeting
the pressure exerted by Fidel through the second declaration.

The Soviet Reaction to the Second Declaration of Havana

The Soviet Union was faced with other complications as well. Moscow had not yet replied to Cuba's expulsion from the OAS and the
related anti-Soviet resolutions at the second Punta del Este conference. Tensions between Cuba and the United States were building up. On February 3, President Kennedy cut off the remaining
trickle of Cuban-American trade with a total embargo. On February
8, Argentina broke relations with Cuba. At the United Nations,
Cuba was denouncing United States "plans for a direct and uni-
lateral military intervention," while the Soviet representatative once
more felt obliged to repeat, "Everybody knows that Cuba is not
alone." On February 15, a Czech-Rumanian resolution calling for
the United States and Cuba to resolve their differences peacefully,
despite strong support by Afro-Asian countries, was voted down,
46 to 39, with a dozen abstentions. Apparently, stormy weather lay
ahead which, combined with Fidel's nagging and Mao's needling,
would lead Khrushchev within a few short months to decide on his
desperate missile gamble.

On February 18, the long-awaited Soviet pronouncement was
issued. It bore the solemn title of "Declaration of the Government
of the USSR." The next day it was splashed across the front page
of *Revolución* under a banner headline, although it was hardly the

kind of statement the Cubans had hoped for. Despite its loud bark-
ing and occasional growling, it carried no bite. It was, in effect, a
prudent statement befitting a great power 6,000 miles from Cuba,
addressing another great power 90 miles from Cuba. On the main
issue it said no more than that the United States was wrong, Cuba
was right, the Soviet Union was virtuous and textually repeated the
well-worn enigmatic formula, "Cuba is not alone."

With an eye on the Chinese, there was a sprinkling of references
to the national liberation movements in Asia, Africa, and Latin
America. However, there was one paragraph, tucked away in the
middle, that must have raised blood pressure in Havana and sar-
donic guffaws in Peking: "The peaceful and profoundly human aims
that inspire the Cuban people have been set forth with burning conviction in the Second Declaration of Havana, which has proclaimed
before the entire world the desire of the Republic of Cuba [the
declaration spoke of "socialist Cuba"] to base its relations with all
states on the principles of peaceful coexistence and nonintervention
in the internal affairs of other countries." This was the only reference to the second declaration. It was a complete distortion of its
meaning and intent.

The Cubans could do no less than spread the Soviet statement
over the front pages of the Havana press, giving it greater prominence
than the more palatable Chinese statement. Anything else would be
an open affront to Moscow, which could hardly be afforded at that
moment. Besides, the innocent Cuban reader, that is to say, the
vast majority of Cubans, would not be able to catch the subtle points
at issue and would take the document at its face value, namely, as a
smashing rebuke administered to Yankee imperialism.

However, Fidel, an expert in verbal fencing, had a way of
handling this situation. On February 26 *Revolución* published a full
page reply to the Soviet declaration of the previous week. Signed
by Fidel himself, it was nothing less than a masterpiece of carefully
worded insinuation inserted into an irreproachable expression, in
Fidel's words, "of profound gratitude for Soviet solidarity with
Cuba." With a slight twist here and there of the Soviet document,
Fidel put the teeth into it which it lacked and then expressed his
entire agreement:

There is no doubt that the United States intends to attack
Cuba. . . . The interests of peace demand that a serious warning

be given, . . . as the Soviet government has done, . . . to the imperialists that the crime against Cuba will not go unpunished, . . . that the people of Cuba can count not only on their own strength to defend their independence, but also on the strength of the peoples who defend peace and peaceful coexistence. . . . The people and revolutionary government of Cuba, with the deepest emotion, thank the repeated offers of Soviet aid, . . . the explicit condemnation of any kind of attack against our country, . . . and the good wishes of the Soviet government for our final triumph.

Then followed a concluding sentence spelled out in capital letters: "Cuba Will Not Fail." The words and typography carried an unmistakable message: We trust that Nikita will not fail, either.

14

■

A Turning Point in the Revolution

Preparing for the Purge

IN THE YEAR 1962 EVERYTHING was destined to be overshadowed by the events in the month of October. Nevertheless, Cubans will long remember the month of March. Scarcely a day passed without reminders in the press and other media that the United States was preparing a new invasion, coupled with the reassuring news that the USSR stood shoulder to shoulder with Cuba. Khrushchev himself was quoted in a front-page banner headline of *Revolución* (March 17) as saying that the "Soviet Union Has Given and Will Give Maximum Support to the Just Struggle of the Republic of Cuba." At the same time, two new "fronts" in the war against imperialism were given top billing: "Guerrillas Battling Against Venezuelan Government" (March 12) and "Guerrillas Take Guatemalan Towns" (March 15). The Cuban example, it appeared, was beginning to bear fruit in the rest of Latin America.

If the *Sturm und Drang* of new and bigger conflicts helped raise the spirits of many Cubans—as it probably did given the country's aroused and still potent nationalism—the announcement of comprehensive food rationing was undoubtedly depressing news, unalleviated by the now recurrent promises that abundance was just around the corner. However, there was still bigger news to distract their attention. Fidel had decided the time had come to settle scores with the by now almost universally detested "old Communists" entrenched in the ORI—and to remove whatever illusions remained in the Kremlin that it would in the foreseeable future call the tune in Havana.

It began, as if by accident, during his speech at the University of Havana on the night of March 13, in commemoration of the fifth anniversary of the ill-fated student attack on the Presidential Palace. Somewhere in the middle of his discourse, Fidel paused and said,

> I am going to criticize something that took place here tonight . . . and will provide an example for a revolutionary analysis. . . . The master of ceremonies was reading the political testament of José Antonio Echevarría [slain organizer of the attack]; . . . while he was reading we were following the text . . . and noticed he skipped three lines which said . . . "may God grant we succeed in establishing the kingdom of justice in our fatherland." When he finished reading, I asked him about it, and he said: "*They* gave me instructions."

At this point in his narration, Fidel exploded: "Is this possible? Can this cowardly act be called the dialectical conception of history? Can such a manner of thinking be called Marxism? Can such a fraud be called socialism? . . . What a myopic, sectarian, stupid, and crooked conception. . . . No, we can't let this go by. . . . What are they trying to do this revolution? Transform it into a yoke for oxen or a school for puppets?"

Parenthetically, contrary to the practice in the Soviet Union and other socialist countries, in Cuba all speeches by Fidel and other leaders, and all historical documents, have invariably been reproduced without omission or alteration. In other respects, Cuban journalism over the years degenerated so that its products became as pompous, platitudinous, and "disciplined" as any in the Communist world.

Fidel did not mention who "they" were, though it was hardly necessary. Still, anybody who wanted to could still pretend that "they" were simply low-ranking, hard-shell dogmatists who had somehow crept into the bureaucracy. Then two days later, an editorial entitled "War Against Sectarianism" appeared on the front page of *Revolución*. It was a signal that something serious was up and that "sectarianism" somehow involved the former PSP.

On March 16, speaking at the graduation exercises of 300 girls who had completed a one-year accelerated teachers' training course,

Fidel again digressed with a tirade against "them," but this time openly involving the ORI: "There are people who have the idea that to belong to the ORI gives them the right to be giving orders, to fire and appoint [government administrators], to create chaos in the management of the state." According to Fidel, these were the same people who "think that to make a revolution means to make everybody unhappy, . . . who can't distinguish between friend and enemy . . . or between the enemy and the person who is neither friend nor enemy, but whom the revolution must not convert into an enemy."

When Fidel spoke of "chaos," he was complaining of an authority competing with his own. Chaos, as a matter of fact, was already endemic in the revolutionary administration, largely reflecting his own style of leadership. As for the question of "making everybody unhappy," a matter about which he was undoubtedly genuinely disturbed, Fidel at the time could never have imagined that five years later he would merit the same reproach, and that from governing on the principle that "those who are not against me are for me," he would turn to the more drastic rule that "those who are not with me are against me."

Be that as it may, probably nine out of ten Cubans listening over the radio or watching television, to one degree or another already repelled by the arbitrary and heavy-handed intrusion of the ORI into their daily lives, must have literally or figuratively given a great cheer for Fidel. Long after the ORI affair was over, Fidel would from time to time assume the role of the champion of the people against bureaucracy or even the government, as if he were outside of them. In troublesome situations, this would help bolster his charisma.

A Shuffling of Personnel

Earlier in the month, the public was informed that the National Directorate, or governing council, of the ORI had been formed. Of the twenty-five members, ten could be identified as former PSP stalwarts, and they included Aníbal Escalante. However, on March 23 the press reported that six of the twenty-five were selected to form the ORI Secretariat, corresponding to an executive committee. Significantly, it contained only one "old Communist." It was Blas Roca, not Aníbal Escalante, and he ranked next to the last in the list that began with Fidel Castro as first secretary, his brother Raúl as second secretary, followed by Che Guevara and President Dorticós, in that order. Che, incidentally, remained in number three position until his departure from Cuba, after which Dorticós moved up into Che's niche. Roca eventually slipped out of the top circles altogether.

The next day, *Hoy*, now edited by Blas Roca and assumed to be the organ of the ORI, that is, the voice of the party (while *Revolución* presumably spoke for the government), properly heaped praise on the Secretariat and categorically declared that today "Fidel is the soundest Marxist-Leninist in Cuba, the leading representative of the working class and the most dependable of Communists." The last lingering doubt—in Cuba, at any rate—concerning Fidel's ideological purity and primacy was removed.

Meanwhile, on the same day, the news broke that Faure Chomón, earlier summoned from Moscow where he was Cuba's ambassador, had been appointed minister of communications, making it the first time that the former Revolutionary Student Directorate was represented in Fidel's cabinet. His main job, however, was to give political support to Fidel in the unfolding drama. For many months following his cabinet appointment, Chomón, an effective speaker and prerevolutionary foe of the PSP, spent a great deal of his time holding forth on the perils of "sectarianism" at meetings large and small throughout the island.

Sectarianism Denounced

With the stage now completely set, on March 26 Fidel addressed the nation over radio and television on the subject of sectarianism. Without mincing words this time, he accused Aníbal Escalante, as organizational secretary of the ORI, of staffing the new party with former PSP members and of "deliberately and consciously" using the party as an instrument with which to gain personal control over a wide spectrum of civilian and military organizations and institutions.

While Escalante bore the brunt of the attack (Fidel fired him then and there and shipped him off to Prague on the next plane), it was clear from the speech that others shared responsibility with him and that Escalante did not invent the model, the type of "straitjacket" in Fidel's words, which he had tried to impose on the Cuban Revolution.

As for sectarianism, Castro defined it as the "belief that the only true revolutionaries, the only ones sufficiently capable and trustworthy to run a farm, or cooperative, or hold any important job in the state apparatus are the members of the old Communist party." As a result, the ORI became a "nest of corruption" where favors and privileges were traded by those on the inside.

"What is the function of the party?" he asked. "To orient . . . and not to govern. . . . It got so that it became impossible for a minister to change a functionary or administrator without clearing with ORI headquarters. . . . No minister could make any decision without prior discussion with the local ministerial party nucleus, or going all the way up to ORI headquarters." However, he added, Escalante and company guessed wrong. "Obviously, this type of disease can't get very far in our country because we don't go for this kind of meek submission; we are not easily domesticated." Here and elsewhere in his speech, as when he mentioned the "personality cult" in the USSR, it was quite plain that, without saying so directly, Fidel was associating sectarianism with the ugly features of Soviet-style socialism.

What particularly incensed Fidel was the scorn heaped on some of his best-known guerrilla leaders by PSP upstarts running the ORI with the "mentality of a Nazi gauleiter," as he phrased it. He gave as an example a certain Pompa, whom Escalante named party secretary in Oriente Province and who, according to Fidel, was overheard to say that "one fine day we'll get rid of all these nobodies" cluttering up the ORI. "How was Pompa to know these people who were fighting," Fidel exclaimed, "while he was hiding under the bed? If it weren't for them, he'd still be hiding. With all the atrocities going on in Oriente, he could have reached and joined the the Rebel Army in one day's walk." And there are others like Pompa, he concluded.

Fidel gave many other examples of sectarianism. One day he ran into a group of Rebel Army officers, "veterans of many battles." "What are you doing here?" he asked them. "Aren't you in command of troops? No, their political level was too low for them to command troops—and these fighters actually made the Revolution!"

However, Fidel's speech contained one major contradiction. While 90 percent of it was a merciless attack on the former PSP, 10 percent was simultaneously a rehabilitation of the old party, almost a plea for an appreciation of its virtues. Escalante and "others" had wrecked the ORI and were about to destroy the country, but the bulk of old Communists were honest, sincere revolutionaries. Fidel went into the history of the party and dwelled on the selfless dedication and courage of its great martyrs, such as the student Julio Antonio Mella, a founder of the party, assassinated in Mexico in 1929, and black Jesús Menéndez, leader of the Sugar Workers Union, gunned down in 1948. "What should be our attitude toward the old Communists?" Fidel asked. "It should be an attitude of respect and recognition of their merits. . . . And what should their attitude be? They should be modest."

Thus the speech ended on a note of unity. The purge that followed was quiet and controlled, although in a final broadside against sectarianism, delivered in Matanzas on April 10, Fidel confessed that since his March 26 speech he had discovered that the situation was worse than he imagined, that there was not one, but five hundred Escalantes, that ORI terrorism and corruption were turning the people against the Revolution and affecting production.

Nevertheless, except for a complete overhaul of the ORI, a good many old Communists in the higher echelons of the various ministries retained their jobs (a drastic elimination would begin only in 1966). Carlos Rafael Rodríguez, for example, was appointed head of the Instituto Nacional de la Reforma Agraria, or INRA (National Agrarian Reform Institute), a cabinet post; while Aníbal Escalante's brother, César, succeeded Aníbal as director of the Comité de Orientación Revolucionaria, or COR (Committee of Revolutionary Orientation), the key propaganda and censorship office.

At the same time, but also slowly and quietly, the leading Fidelista anti-Communists who had been sacrificed in the early days of the Soviet-Cuban partnership—men like Faustino Pérez, Marcelo Fernández, and Enrique Oltuski—began to move out of obscurity and once more into positions of prominence.

The Strategy of the Purge

The purge of the old Communists, as we have noted, was carefully controlled. It was also just as carefully attributed not to a conspiracy to seize power, but to personal and ideological aberrations. There was, to be sure, no need for harsher measures since Escalante's ORI crumbled like a house of cards. Nor has it been customary for Fidel to indulge in vengeful and arbitrary brutalities,[1] although the next time Escalante ran afoul of Fidel, in 1968, he was sentenced to fifteen years in prison. Nevertheless, what primarily dictated Fidel's strategy was the need to sugarcoat the bitter pill that he wanted the Kremlin to swallow.

This Fidel managed brilliantly. Without exception, the old Communist leadership immediately lined up behind him, accepting his supremacy both ideologically and politically, and in terms that spelled out unconditional surrender. There was little choice for the Kremlin, all circumstances considered, but to accept defeat and adjust more or less gracefully to the situation.

On April 12 *Revolución* gave top billing to a *Pravda* editorial of the previous day. *Pravda* praised Fidel's "perfectly correct criticism of sectarian errors," declared his March 26 speech to be authentically Marxist-Leninist, referred to him again as the "national hero of the Cuban people" and for the first time called him "tovarishch." The full blame for the episode was put on Aníbal Escalante. *Pravda* denied that any "scission" had taken place in the Cuban revolutionary ranks and, in turn, offered a bit of advice: "The use of proven revolutionaries [PSP] in responsible positions is very important during the period of the tempestuous development of the Revolution, of sharp ideological struggle. At the same time, the young cadres formed in the revolutionary struggle must be used more boldly for leading political work." On the surface, the statement was a nicely balanced formula, but in effect a reminder to Fidel that the Kremlin expected him to refrain from any wholesale purge of the "proven revolutionaries."

On April 15, when *Pravda* published the slogans for the forthcoming May Day celebration, Cuba was discovered to have moved up to twelfth place, that is, one notch above Yugoslavia, in the hierarchy of countries receiving fraternal greetings. However, whereas all the other socialist countries were said to be "building socialism," Cuba was still listed as "having embarked on the path of building socialism," a subtle but meaningful distinction. Fidel was a "tovar-

1. The same probably cannot be said of his regime. While Castro has denied that prisoners in his jails are tortured and otherwise given inhuman treatment, released and escaped political prisoners have testified to the contrary. See Jean Cau, "Cuba a ses camps de mort," *Paris-Match*, June 12, 1971.

ishch" but the title was apparently honorary. He was still not a member of the club.

The Chinese also came out strongly in support of Fidel, but for some reason the Cuban press failed to mention a word of it. However, two weeks later, when a Chinese delegation arrived in Havana for the May 1 festivities, *Revolución* (April 26) gave front-page prominence to a statement by the head of the delegation who said, "The struggle against sectarianism by the Cuban people under the leadership of Fidel Castro is a just and healthy struggle for the socialist revolution." Like the Russian formulation, the "struggle for the socialist revolution" was something less than the acknowledgment desired by the Cubans, although from a practical point of view the Chinese phraseology was much less important than the Russian.

It was a rare occasion when Cubans, Russians, and Chinese could agree on what sectarianism was and denounce it in unison. The explanation, obviously, is that sectarianism had little or nothing to do with the situation. The real issue was power. Fidel proved he had it and would keep it, and his foreign backers registered their acceptance of the fact.

From the Old to the New Orthodoxy

The Escalante affair was a turning point in more ways than one. It revealed the gulf that separated Fidel's homespun Marxism-Leninism from that of its long-time practitioners inside and outside the socialist camp. Escalante (whose side of the story was never made public) was no upstart conspirator but a veteran, a top-ranking professional functionary of a fully accredited Communist party. Once he and his collaborators were entrusted by Fidel himself with the task of organizing and managing the new Marxist-Leninist party, it was normal for them to assume that the historic moment had arrived to set up an authentic Communist party, run by bona fide Communists, such as existed in all Communist countries. They could not imagine any other kind of Marxist-Leninist party.

Fidel's indignation, which was clearly genuine, among other things revealed that he knew next to nothing about the function and role of the party in a socialist state, that he was unaware of the extent to which official Marxism-Leninism had become the self-serving ideology of entrenched bureaucracies, and that he himself still harbored some of his old "humanist" ideas. Thus, following the Escalante episode, Fidel set about to create his own brand of Marxism-Leninism, cautiously (at first) groping toward his goal by the pragmatic method of trial and error.

When the gloom of Escalante's short-lived "dictatorship of the proleariat" began to lift, it seemed as if in Cuba a return to some measure of joy and freedom under Marxist-Leninist socialism were possible, and that in time the spirit of the carnival would once more prevail. In the arts, the danger that "socialist realism" would strangle creativity vanished as abstractionism and surrealism again could function without inhibitions. And for several years there was an astonishing amount of public debate on a wide range of topics.

Then, as the economy continued to falter and Fidel, to safeguard his regime, had to depend less on his charisma and more on discipline and authority, one by one the avenues of discussion and critical inquiry were eliminated. A shrill idealism, grounded in austerity and stressing patriotism, heroism, and the salvation of all mankind, gripped the island and imposed total conformity. By 1966 a new dogmatism, Fidel's and the mysteriously absent Che Guevara's version of Marxism-Leninism, had taken the place of the old orthodoxy discarded in the spring of 1962.

In turn, the new orthodoxy receded and something akin to the old orthodoxy returned. What remained fixed in these transmutations was the source of wisdom and authority from which they flowed. "Can anybody analyze or study the theoretical questions raised, for instance, by philosophy; the roads to communism; or any field of culture, mainly those of social sciences and philosophy, without taking into account the ideas and concepts of Fidel and Che?" It was Armando Hart, national organizing secretary of the party, speaking at the University of Havana in late September 1969. Che had been dead for two years, now only a ghost to be invoked as needed. "Whoever thinks he can do so . . . will fail for several reasons. First of all, because of the information at the disposal of the Revolution's leadership. Secondly, because of Fidel's capabilities and his ideological insight. . . . Discipline based on trust in the leadership of the Revolution is the only guarantee of serious scientific work [in philosophy, the social sciences, and the humanities]." [2]

2. *Granma Weekly Review*, September 28, 1969.

One of the most notable of Fidel's revisions of standard Marx-ist-Leninist practice was the system he devised for restructuring the party after the banishment of Escalante. Like all Communist parties, the leadership was self-appointed. In addition, a small elite group was directly opted into the party by the leadership. Here the similarity ended. Candidates for membership in the new Cuban scheme were nominated from among the workers, including the managerial staffs, by majority vote at open mass meetings in each work center or institution. To be eligible for nomination, a person had to be an "exemplary" worker, an active member of a number of mass organizations including the militia, and familiar with Fidel's important pronouncements and those of Che after his canoni-zation, and had not to have voted in the election Batista mounted in 1958 (this presumably eliminated "collaborators with the tyr-anny"). Conspicuously missing among the required qualifications was a knowledge of any of the classics of Communist literature, includ-ing the works of Marx, Engels, and Lenin. At the same time, candi-dates and all others were given to understand that membership in the party would require selfless devotion to the collective welfare but would provide no privileges. Finally, nominees were screened by party authorities before receiving their membership cards.

From a practical point of view, there seemed to be considerable logic in this novel system. In all other socialist countries, the ruling Communist parties originated as small, more or less clandestine rev-olutionary groups, organized for the purpose of taking and holding state power. However, the job given to Fidel's party was neither to seize nor to wield power, but to activate and consolidate mass support for an existing power structure. Hence, by having the masses themselves participate in choosing the most worthy among them for party membership, the new Communists would presuma-bly inspire confidence among the people whom they would effectively mobilize in the constant stream of campaigns set in motion by Fidel. Furthermore, it was Fidel's often expressed hope that his Com-munist party would not generate a new class of privileged card-holders with a hankering for good living and power.

Nevertheless, from the beginning there were enough symptoms of emerging bureaucratic vices to suggest that the classical patterns of privilege would eventually take hold and prove difficult to sup-press. Meanwhile, it is interesting to observe that as late as 1969, that is, seven years after the process got under way, the construction of the party had not been completed. For example, the party "nucleus" in the cinema industry (ICAIC) was set up on August 4, 1969, although as Director Alfredo Guevara explained in the speech of the day, with the required homage to the party and its leader, "we have always worked closely with the party, first and foremost . . . with our Commander-in-Chief [Fidel] from whom we have received our basic orientations." [3] Nor as of mid-1971 had the continually postponed first party congress yet taken place or a date for covening it been announced, although the new Communist party of Cuba was created and its Central Committee, of mainly army officers, appointed (not elected) in late 1965.

Clearly, Fidel was considerably less in a hurry than Escalante in getting the job done, and this is understandable. For Escalante, the party was to hold power while the government implemented party directives. For Fidel, for most purposes himself the government, it is vice versa; and having once been bitten, he is twice shy about letting the Marxist-Leninist "vanguard" get out of hand.

3. *El Caimán Barbudo* (Havana), no. 34, September, 1969.

15

■

The October Crisis—I:

Missiles and Motives

Cuba Seen from the Kremlin

TAKING STOCK OF THEIR CUBAN OPERATION in late March 1962, the Russians could scarcely have failed to conclude that thus far they had mainly accumulated liabilities, with few if any tangible assets, to show for their investment. Supplying Castro with military aid and keeping the Cuban economy from collapsing, let alone developing it, turned out to be a far more costly undertaking than had been anticipated. In addition, the aftermath of the ORI purge, coupled with growing consumer-goods shortages, for the first time brought popular disaffection to the surface. There was some reason for the Russians to become apprehensive about the stability of the regime.[1]

Meanwhile, Cuba's expulsion from the OAS in early January was followed by a hardening of American policy and attitudes toward Cuba. Strong pressures were being exerted in the NATO countries, as well as in the western hemisphere, to embargo trade with Cuba. Hit-and-run attacks by small craft based in Florida and manned by Cuban exiles were increasing, as was the infiltration of men and military equipment to counterrevolutionary peasant bands operating

1. Food riots occurred in June in a number of towns in the western provinces, including Cárdenas, a sizable urban center and seaport about 100 miles east of Havana. Here, at a mass meeting on June 17, President Dorticós had to be protected by tanks during a speech he made to calm the inhabitants.

in the Escambray hills of central Cuba. Responsible business and political leaders in the United States were publicly urging President Kennedy to "get tough" with Cuba or openly calling for an invasion of the island. Large-scale military and naval maneuvers in the Caribbean were scheduled to take place in early April.

With the benefit of hindsight, it is evident, as I shall shortly explain, that the likelihood of military intervention on the scale necessary to overthrow the regime was remote. At the time, however, these and other symptoms of an increasingly aggressive mood in the United States, as well as clear indications that the Republicans would make Kennedy's failure to eliminate Castro a prime issue in the November congressional elections, were understandably matters of deep concern in Moscow and of uninhibited expressions of alarm in Havana. Finally, to complicate matters still further for the Russians, Fidel was becoming more and more difficult to deal with. The hope of "domesticating" the Cuban Revolution waned with the elimination of Aníbal Escalante and some of his old Communist following from the political scene. Fidel's response to the American threats was to shake his fist under Kennedy's nose while insisting on an irrevocable guarantee that the Soviet Union come to his rescue if Cuba was attacked.

For the Kremlin, its Cuban investment also had to be considered in the context of the larger world picture. For four years now, Khrushchev had been alternately threatening and cajoling the western powers in attempts to eject them from Berlin, but to no avail. He had no real bargaining power beyond the promise to force the issue, which the western powers correctly discounted. Hence, despite his solemn pledge to sign a separate peace treaty with East Germany, which would be the legal grounds for the elimination of the West Berlin enclave and its access routes across East German territory, the peace treaty remained unsigned.

Soviet credibility, and hence prestige, had been weakened. To add to the embarrassment, Ulbricht was beginning to show his dissatisfaction in public. According to Michael Tatu, at the time Moscow correspondent of the Paris *Le Monde* and one of the keenest observers of the east European political scene: "At the end of 1961 and the beginning of 1962, Moscow's relations with East Germany were deteriorating. . . . On January 17 a spokesman on East German television acknowledged for the first time that differences existed with the USSR, by saying in effect that the Soviet Union was trying to preserve peace on the international level, whereas the German Democratic Republic also had national problems to settle." [2]

Meanwhile, relations with China also had to be taken into account. Tatu points out that "during a Warsaw Pact meeting in Moscow in the summer of 1961 the Albanians [speaking for the Chinese] had demanded that the USSR sign the German peace treaty." [3] Now the mounting tension in the Caribbean could provide the Chinese with another opportunity to discredit the Russians for their reluctance to stand up to the American "paper tiger."

Finally, in the larger picture loomed the problem of improving the Soviet position in the strategic "balance of terror" on which depended the credibility of its military and political posture in the cold war with the United States. In an astute and convincing article entitled "The Cuban Missile Crisis: An Analysis of Soviet Calculations and Behavior," Arnold Horelick explains,

> The Soviet Union acquired a very potent nuclear capability against Western Europe. . . . But the Soviet heavy bomber and ICBM forces—that is, the long range weapons required to reach the United States—did not attain the strength levels that Western observers anticipated. . . . Deceptive Soviet claims . . . tended, until the fall of 1961, to deprive continued and an ever growing U.S. strategic superiority of much of its *political* value. But . . . the 'missile gap' was found, in Secretary McNamara's words, to be a 'myth.' Confidence was restored in the West; moreover, it became apparent, both from Soviet behavior and from the modification of Soviet strategic claims, that the Soviet leaders knew that the West had been undeceived about the strategic balance.[4]

Weighing the Alternatives

It was in this setting that Khrushchev had to consider the alternatives available to deal with the Cuban item on his agenda. One was to strengthen the credibility of the Soviet threat to defend Cuba with Russian-based intercontinental ballistic missiles. There were three ways to do so:

2. Tatu, *Power in the Kremlin: Khrushchev to Kosygin* (New York: Viking, 1969), p. 232.
3. *Ibid.*
4. *World Politics*, April 1964, pp. 374–375; emphasis in original.

(1) To acknowledge Cuba as a bona fide member of the socialist family; this would represent a costly politico-ideological concession to the Fidelista heresy, as I have previously explained.

(2) To bring Cuba into the Warsaw Pact, something that many if not all of the Soviet Union's co-members would have been most reluctant to accept, particularly when the risks at this time would have seemed to be very high.

(3) To conclude a separate, formal military alliance with Cuba, probably the most provocative move of all and hence entailing the greatest danger of a belligerent reaction by the United States.

However, what was perhaps most important about any one, or all, of these measures taken simultaneously was the fact that they would still leave the initiative in the hands of Washington and little room for Moscow to maneuver. If Cuba were attacked—this time it would not be a Bay of Pigs romp—there would be no escape from the dilemma of putting up or shutting up, that is, either launching the unthinkable nuclear war (in which the obliteration of Cuba would be only a minor episode) or losing Cuba and in the process suffering a disastrous political defeat.

Another alternative that would have logically occurred to Khrushchev, if it had not already been proposed by Fidel, would be to provide Cuba with sufficient missile power to deter an American attack. How much would be required? A very small number, probably no more than a score of properly deployed and concealed mobile tactical units—that is, with a range of some two hundred miles and the capability of destroying Miami—would do the trick. As soon as they were operational, an appropriate public announcement could be made that they existed and, although manned by Russian personnel, were the property of the Cuban government.

The next move would be up to Washington, which would be hard put to find a punishment to fit the crime. In fact, it would be difficult to convince international public opinion that any crime had been committed or intended. The small number and limited range of the weapons would clearly give them a defensive character in the context of Cuban-American relations. There could be no question of a threat to the security of the western hemisphere, of an attempt to shift the balance of power. In the game of nuclear bluff, a threat by Washington that, should Miami be attacked if Cuba were invaded, it would hold Moscow responsible and take "appropriate measures" against the Soviet Union would not be credible. However, the point of basic importance in this scheme would be the altogether reasonable assumption that the threat of the destruction of Miami would be an unacceptable risk to take should the United States contemplate an invasion of Cuba.

This was almost certainly the kind of missile arrangement the Cubans would have had in mind when, in January following the crisis, Fidel informed Claude Julien, a friendly French journalist, that "We had discussed among ourselves the possibility of asking the USSR to provide us with rockets." [5] As for the Russians, for whom the crux of their Cuban problem was how to restrain the Americans and how to satisfy Castro and at the same time avoid being pushed into a blind alley, this kind of arrangement, although not without its hazards, would have merit, particularly if compared with the alternatives described above.

Converting a Liability into an Asset

Khrushchev, however, came up with another solution. Apparently against the better judgment of some of his military and political advisers, he pushed through approval in the party Presidium of a plan to establish a major strategic missile base in Cuba. This probably occurred before the end of April 1962.[6] The next step was to

5. In an interview, datelined "Havana, March," and published in *Le Monde* in two installments on March 22 and 23, 1963, under the heading: "Sept Heures avec M. Fidel Castro." From other evidence (discussed in a later chapter), it seemed very unlikely that the interview could have taken place in the month indicated. In reply to a request for the precise or approximate date of the interview, M. Julien was kind enough to explain in a letter to me (Paris, September 16, 1970) that "the interview with Fidel Castro took place in the month of January 1963 but I do not remember the exact day."

6. Michel Tatu (*Power in the Kremlin*, p. 236) points out that General K. S. Moskalenko, commander of strategic rocket troops, was relieved of his command in April and soon after lost his post as deputy minister of defense, but he was reinstated in the latter job in November, following the dismantling of the Soviet missile base in Cuba. "It is not at all unreasonable," declares Tatu, "to link Moskalenko's case with the Cuban affair. The decision affected him directly as commander-in-chief of strategic rockets. It is a safe bet that a man anxious to preserve his equipment intact could not have been happy at the prospect of having his most secret weapons shipped with their nuclear warheads to a

get Fidel's approval. Fidel, as I shall presently argue, was at first reluctant but then yielded. This must have taken place not later than the end of May or very early in June, since preparations for clearing the ground for the missile sites could not have started any later given the amount of work done when the sites were discovered by a U-2 reconnaissance plane in mid-October.[7]

Considering Khrushchev's Cuban headache, both in the narrow context of the alternatives available to him for dealing with this single ailment and in the broader context of the multiple problems he faced in other areas, his motives and objectives in setting up a strategic base in Cuba are not hard to discern. To begin with, the emplacement in Cuba of several score of Soviet-manned and -controlled missiles in the medium and intermediate categories—that is, with ranges up to 2,200 nautical miles, hence capable of reaching any part of continental United States and thus equivalent to the much larger intercontinental missiles deployed in the Soviet Union (potentially even more effective because of their proximity to targets in the United States)—such emplacement would considerably upgrade the strategic posture of the USSR and greatly enhance its po-

---

highly exposed site such as Cuba. . . . Moreover, these rockets had to be withdrawn from current supplies, or, if they were only on order, diverted from their original destination." Another demotion occurring at the same time was that of General F. I. Golikov, director of the Main Political Administration of the Armed Forces. His task, according to Tatu, "would have been to explain to the officers and men involved the reasons for this 'agonizing reappraisal' of traditional Soviet policy with respect to foreign bases. In any event, like Moskalenko, he suffered notable ups and downs in the course of 1962, and these corresponded with the development of the Cuban crisis."

7. According to Theodore C. Sorenson, special counsel to President Kennedy and a prime source of information and analysis concerning the missile crisis, "forty-two Soviet medium- and intermediate-range ballistic missiles—each one capable of striking the United States with a nuclear warhead twenty or thirty times more powerful than the Hiroshima bomb —were enroute to Cuba [in the first week of September]. Judging from the rapidity with which they were assembled, the planning and preparations for this move had been under way within the Soviet Union since spring and within Cuba all summer. The sites had been selected and surveyed, the protective anti-aircraft missiles moved in, the roads improved and the local inhabitants evicted." *Kennedy* (New York: Bantam, 1965), p. 753.

litical prestige. Second, it would be accomplished with far greater
speed and at a much lower cost than it would take to keep abreast
of the United States in the arms race by increasing Russia's stock of
intercontinental ballistic missiles.

Third, several benefits would immediately flow from the establishment of the new outpost of Soviet power. One would be a large
boost in bargaining strength on the Berlin question and other areas
of friction with the United States.[8] Another benefit would be the
checkmating of Chinese propaganda about Russia's. fear of the
American "paper tiger." Finally, of course, there would be convincing proof of Soviet intentions concerning the defense of Cuba.

It was, in short, a scheme by which Cuba would be converted
from a liability into an asset. For Khrushchev, with a large degree
of personal responsibility for the Soviet presence in Cuba, the conversion would be a triumphal vindication for what at the moment
clearly appeared to have been a profitless and hazardous venture
into the Caribbean area.

Cuba's "International Proletarian Duty"

From Fidel Castro's point of view, Khrushchev's proposition went
considerably beyond Cuba's needs. Moreover, it raised some embarrassing questions. To being with, introducing a veritable arsenal
of long-range missiles instead of a modest shipment of tactical weapons vastly increased the danger of premature discovery, which it was
essential to avoid. In the second place, to set up, maintain, and protect the strategic emplacements would require stationing a large
contingent of fully equipped Soviet troops, probably 20,000 or
more.[9] A Russian garrison of this size could conceivably inhibit
Cuban policy making or play a role in case of internal dissension.

8. Tatu is convinced that the main objective of Khrushchev's Cuban
missile gambit was to obtain leverage with which to oust the western
allies from Berlin; he presents as evidence the coincidence of a definite
stiffening of tone in Soviet pronouncements on the Berlin issue with
the decision to set up the strategic missile base. *Power in the Kremlin,*
p. 232.

9. "At one time, the Soviet forces [in Cuba] probably numbered
from 30,000 to 40,000 men, although the U.S. government never admitted . . . the presence of more than 17,000 to 22,000. . . . [In-
cluded were] four highly mechanized and armored units . . . equipped
with tanks and field artillery and FROGS (Free Rockets Over Ground)."

Finally, after all the verbal fireworks denouncing the American base at Guantánamo as an infringement of Cuban sovereignty, to permit another foreign military base to be set up several hundred miles to the west would bring into question in Latin America and other parts of the Third World the sincerity of the Cuban claim that there were no strings attached to the aid it was receiving from the Soviet Union. However, no doubt under pressure by Khrushchev, on the one hand, and on the other convinced that the United States was planning an invasion of Cuba, Castro concluded that the advantages of the Russian offer outweighed its disadvantages.[10]

Fidel's explanations of how the decision to set up the Russian missile base on Cuban soil came about were often enigmatic and seemingly inconsistent. For example, on a dozen or so different occasions, ranging from his speech on the fourth anniversary of the Revolution on January 2, 1963, to a conversation at the end of October 1967 with Herbert Matthews,[11] Fidel declared that the missile deal was (1) a Cuban idea, or (2) a Russian idea, or (3) a joint idea. Actually, all three answers are in all likelihood technically correct, depending on the stage in the decision-making process, beginning with the Cuban discussion "among ourselves," mentioned to Claude Julien, proceeding to the Russian offer on quite a different scale and then the final agreement of the two parties to the Russian scheme. Which way he put it would depend on what he judged to be expedient at the moment—a practice not restricted to Castro among political leaders.

At the same time, a significant thread of consistency can be detected in his more extended comments on the subject. Here he emphasized, and at no other time denied, that Cuba, in addition to being motivated by self-defense, was fulfilling "an international proletarian duty." This duty was spelled out in his remarks to Her-

---

Hanson W. Baldwin, "A Military Perspective," in *Cuba and the United States,* ed. John Plank (Washington: Brookings Institution, 1967), p. 205.

10. In this connection, the fact that the Soviet-Cuban commercial agreement for the year 1962, under discussion since the fall of 1961, was not signed until May 14 may well have reflected politico-military discrepancies as well as economic bargaining.

11. Matthews, *Fidel Castro* (New York: Simon and Schuster, 1969), p. 225.

bert Matthews in October 1967 as being "in the interests of the Soviet bloc" [12] and elsewhere, in effect, as being payment for favors received. "It was explained [by the Russians]," he told Claude Julien, "that by accepting them [the missiles] we would strengthen the socialist camp on the world scale. *And since we are getting a large amount of help from the socialist camp, we felt that we could not refuse.* That is why we accepted them. It was not in order to ensure our own defense, but primarily to strengthen socialism on the international scale. That is the truth, even if different explanations are given elsewhere." [13]

If Fidel here preferred to discount "our own defense" as a motive for granting the Soviet request, it was probably due to the freshness of the wound his pride had suffered when Khrushchev failed to consult with him about pulling Russian missiles out of Cuba. Still, Fidel was not too far off the mark, for in complying with the Soviet request for a strategic base on Cuban soil, he went considerably beyond, and obviously after some prodding, the needs of "our own defense."

Soon after the event, however, Khrushchev gave a different and much simpler version of the transaction, but one that can be safely discarded. In a lengthy report to the Supreme Soviet on December 12, 1962, he stated that the weapons were sent to Cuba solely at the request of the Cubans, exclusively for their protection, and were removed when President Kennedy's pledge not to invade the island made their presence unnecessary. Interestingly enough, a few months after Khrushchev's fall, the Kremlin, in the devious manner that is often its custom, rectified the ex-chairman's statement.

The occasion was a speech Fidel delivered in Havana on March 13, 1965. Fidel not only repeated what he told Claude Julien two years previously about "strengthening the socialist camp," but spoke about "strategic" missiles, a terminology consistently avoided by the Russians, and spilled a few more beans. "We did not vacillate in risking the dangers of thermonuclear war," he declared, "when we agreed to the installation of strategic thermonuclear missiles on our territory. And moreover . . . we were opposed to their removal! I believe this is absolutely no secret to anybody." *Pravda,* never known

12. *Ibid.*
13. *Le Monde,* March 22, 1963; emphasis added. As already noted, Castro made these remarks to Julien in January 1963.

to be careless about such things, unexpectedly reprinted this part of the speech.[14] The only reason for this indiscretion that makes sense is that it offered an opportunity to discredit Khrushchev, a matter sufficiently important at the time to risk puzzling the Soviet reading public hitherto unexposed to any other than the official explanation.[15]

14. Tatu, p. 230.

15. However, this was a temporary lapse. The Khrushchev version reappears intact in a Soviet history published in Moscow in 1967 (*A History of International Affairs*, edited by I. A. Kirilin, 3:410–411; cited by Robert G. Wesson, *Soviet Foreign Policy in Perspective*, [Homewood, Ill.: Dorsey, 1969], p. 247). There is, to be sure, no mention of Khrushchev as if he never existed. That this kind of historiography was still flourishing in the year marking the fiftieth anniversary of the Bolshevik Revolution makes the foreign scholar despair of ever being able to take Soviet historians seriously.

16
■

The October Crisis—II:

Profits and Losses

The Six Days of Brinkmanship

THE MISSILE CRISIS PROPER covered a period of slightly less than two weeks, as the White House reckoned it, but only six days as seen from Havana and Moscow. On October 16, as a result of a U-2 flight over Cuba two days before, President Kennedy first received incontrovertible evidence of a number of completed missile sites and others under construction. On October 22, he addressed the nation, informing the American people and the whole world of the existence of the missile buildup and the measures to be taken to meet the threat, including in his words "a strict quarantine [nonbelligerent euphemism for *blockade*] on all offensive military equipment under shipment to Cuba." The next day an official proclamation to this effect was issued.

On October 28, after six momentous days of hair-raising brinkmanship by the two superpowers (though in retrospect remarkably well controlled), Khrushchev capitulated: "the Soviet government," he stated in a letter of that day to Kennedy, "in addition to earlier instructions on the discontinuation of further work on weapons construction sites, has given a new order to dismantle the arms which you describe as offensive, and to crate and return them to the Soviet Union." [1]

1. According to United States military reconnaissance photos, the forty-two missiles were distributed among four sites: at San Cristóbal and

Thus, for all practical purposes, the crisis ended. Khrushchev stalled at removing two score IL-28 bombers, which Kennedy had included in the demands. The problem was Castro, who made a distinction between the missiles, which he acknowledged to be Russian property, and all other weapons obtained from the Soviet Union, which he claimed to be Cuban property. With Kennedy publicly pressing Khrushchev and the latter privately pressing Castro, an agreement on the removal of the bombers was finally reached. The rest was a matter of verifying the removal of the missiles and bombers, made difficult by Fidel's refusal to allow inspection on Cuban soil, and generally unwinding after the accumulated anxiety.

On November 20, the naval quarantine was lifted. On January 7, 1963, in a letter to United Nations Acting Secretary-General U Thant that was signed jointly by Ambassador Adlai Stevenson for the United States and First Deputy Foreign Minister Kuznetsov for the Soviet Union, the two countries officially declared the incident closed.[2] A discordant note came from Cuba. In a separate letter to U Thant on the same day, Cuban Ambassador Lechuga declared that "the conduct of the government of the United States . . . makes it impossible for us to agree that a real solution to the crisis has been reached."[3] However, nobody paid much attention to the Cuban statement.

Khrushchev Disparaged

Once the two great powers were in confrontation, it was a matter of sheer good luck that the ultimate responsibility for avoiding or unleashing the fearsome destruction of an atomic war lay in the hands of two highly capable and essentially sober leaders. Khrushchev, to be sure, although widely and understandably praised for drawing back from the edge of disaster,[4] could not escape worldwide censure for

Guanajay, respectively 65 and 30 miles west of Havana; and Sagua la Grande and Remedios, 200 milest east of Havana. (Robert F. Kennedy, *Thirteen Days: A Memoir of the Cuban Missile Crisis* [New York: Norton, 1969], pp. 143–150.)

2. Moscow also promised to withdraw "several thousand troops" from Cuba before March 15, as disclosed later by Washington. (See Tatu, *Power in the Kremlin* [New York: Viking, 1969], p. 323).

3. *Política Internacional* 1, no. 1 (January–March, 1963): 244–245.

4. As he put it in his speech to the Supreme Soviet on December 12, 1962, "if one side or the other had not shown restraint, had not

setting in motion the scheme that threatened to bring on a universal holocaust. It was predictably a hazardous undertaking at best, and the hazard, as it happened, was compounded by hasty and imperfect execution. Nor could he escape the blame for the loss of prestige inflicted on the Soviet Union by the exposure of the extraordinarily reckless duplicity with which he tried to conceal his gamble [5] and by the humiliation, only partially mitigated by President Kennedy's qualified promise not to invade Cuba, of accepting the American ultimatum to withdraw his lethal weapons from the island.

---

done everything necessary to avert the outbreak of war, an explosion would have followed with irreparable consequences." (Supplement to *Soviet Union Today* [magazine], Ottawa: USSR Embassy in Canada, p. 16. No date given; presumably December 1962 or January 1963). Examining the confrontation from the point of view of international jurisprudence, Professor Edward McWhinney places less emphasis on personalities by noting that "the actual peaceful resolution of the Cuban conflict conformed exactly to the pre-existing cold war 'rules of the game,' amounting almost to an agreed code of minimum inter-block rules of public order." Thus the "most positive gain" from the crisis was "acceptance and reaffirmation by the United States and the Soviet Union equally . . . of a common interest in minimum rules of world order governing East-West differences." " 'Coexistence,' the Cuba Crisis, and Cold War International Law," *International Journal* [Canadian Institute of International Affairs, Toronto] 18, no. 1 (winter 1962–63): 67–74.

5. In his historic address to the nation on October 22, President Kennedy referred to "the repeated assurances of Soviet spokesmen, both publicly and privately delivered, that the arms buildup in Cuba would retain its original defensive character and that the Soviet Union had no need or desire to station strategic missiles on the territory of any other nation." He went on, citing chapter and verse to document a series of barefaced and irrefutable deceptions which considerably exceeded even the cold war norms of political and diplomatic cynicism. No less damaging, in this connection, was a Stevenson-Zorin verbal exchange at a meeting of the U.N. Security Council on October 25. After Zorin labeled Stevenson's reference to Soviet missiles in Cuba as "falsified information of the U.S. Intelligence Agency," Stevenson replied, "All right, sir, let me ask you one simple question: Do you, Ambassador Zorin, deny that the U.S.S.R. has placed and is placing medium- and intermediate-range missiles and sites in Cuba? Yes or no—don't wait for the translation—yes or no?" When Zorin refused to answer, Stevenson pulled out a set of large photographs. The evidence was solid, and for Zorin's reputation, devastating.

There was no little embarrassment for Khrushchev when Fidel, enraged by what he privately denounced as cowardice and betrayal, flatly rejected inspection by the United Nations on Cuban soil. Posters displaying a photo of Lumumba undergoing martyrdom and he legend "Cuba is not the Congo!" sprang up all over the island, a pointed reminder of the disaster that befell Lumumba and his regime during the United Nations intervention in the Congo. Nor did it enhance Soviet prestige when Anastas Ivanovich Mikoyan, Khrushchev's deputy premier, rushed to Havana on November 2, where he spent more than three unrewarding weeks (not even interrupting his visit to attend his wife's funeral) trying to soothe Fidel who for most of the period ostentatiously ignored his presence.

Particularly mortifying were the charges hurled at Moscow by Peking, which had noisily pledged its support of the Soviet Union when the missile crisis began.[6] John Gittings, in his *Survey of the Sino-Soviet Dispute: A Commentary and Extracts from the Recent Polemics*, 1963–1967, aptly summarized what happened when the Russians agreed to withdraw their missiles from Cuba: "China lost no time in denouncing the arrangement as an example of the 'cowardice' of modern revisionism. . . . Massive rallies were held in China, at which Chinese support was pledged for Cuban sovereignty. China's argument, that the Soviet Union was guilty of 'adventurism' in sending the missiles to Cuba, and of 'capitulationism' in withdrawing them, touched the Soviet leadership on a sensitive spot." [7] These and other unfavorable repercussions fell most heavily on Khrushchev personally, and almost certainly paved the way for his removal from office two years later.[8]

6. "Stop New U.S. Imperialistic Adventure," *People's Daily*, October 24, 1962. The next day the paper carried an official government statement pledging support for the USSR in the Cuban crisis. (Cited by William E. Griffith, *The Sino-Soviet Rift*, [Cambridge, Mass.: M.I.T. Press, 1964], p. 60). It was probably more than a coincidence that *Pravda* (Oct. 25) temporarily modified its pro-Indian "neutrality" by endorsing a Chinese three-point proposal for ending the Sino-Indian border conflict then under way.

7. London: Oxford University Press, 1968, p. 176.

8. In *Khrushchev Remembers* (Boston: Little, Brown, 1970), the chairman modified some of the statements he made when in office, such as, for example, those concerning who originated the idea of setting up

Kennedy Criticized

President Kennedy also did not escape criticism, by some for over-reacting to the Russian move and by others for excessive caution—that is, for not taking advantage of the provocation by invading Cuba and eliminating the missile emplacements and Castro in one operation. However, opinion overwhelmingly expressed in the United States and elsewhere in the non-Communist world was that Kennedy had displayed a rare combination of cool judgment, superb tactical skill, and just the right amount of aggressive response to achieve the maximum result in a situation of extreme danger and essentially without precedent.

The "maximum result" left the Castro regime intact. In his letter to Khrushchev of October 27, Kennedy stated that, in line with the chairman's proposal of the previous day, upon the removal of "these weapons systems from Cuba under appropriate United Nations observation and supervision, . . . we, on our part, would

---

atomic missiles in Cuba. "It was during my visit to Bulgaria that I had the idea of installing missiles with nuclear warheads in Cuba without letting the United States find out they were there until it was too late to do anything about them. I knew that first we'd have to talk to Castro and explain our strategy to him in order to get the agreement of the Cuban government" (p. 493). With respect to the Bulgarian visit, Michel Tatu notes that on "the 21st [of May 1962] Khrushchev signed a Soviet-Bulgarian communiqué in Sofia that was particularly aggressive on the Berlin issue" (p. 234). Incidentally, Khrushchev here makes it difficult to assume that failure of the Russians to camouflage the construction sites and otherwise to take sufficient measures to prevent premature exposure was due to a plan by which the "missile sites were meant to be discovered by American espionage planes," as argued, among others, by Anatol Rapoport in *The Big Two: Soviet-American Perceptions of Foreign Policy* (New York: Pegasis, 1971, p. 183). The reason was haste and calculated risk—poorly calculated this time. Khrushchev also admits, although almost parenthetically, that the defense of Cuba was not his only consideration in deciding to emplace missiles on the island: "In addition to protecting Cuba, our missiles would have equalized what the West likes to call 'the balance of power.'" Altogether he wants to leave the impression with posterity that he covered himself with glory in the great confrontation with the United States: "The Caribbean crisis was a triumph of Soviet foreign policy and a personal triumph in my own career as a statesman and as a member of the collective leadership" (p. 504).

agree . . . to give assurances against an invasion of Cuba. I am confident that the other nations of the Western Hemisphere would be prepared to do likewise."

Thus, Khrushchev requested and Kennedy granted the "assurances" that would permit the chairman to retreat without a total loss of dignity. From Kennedy's point of view, this concession was consistent with his strategy throughout the crisis of trying to avoid pushing Khrushchev into a corner where he would be faced with the alternatives of unconditional surrender or shooting his way out. Moreover, it was a concession easily granted for two reasons: first, by its wording, the president's no-invasion agreement was sufficiently qualified by inspection provisos and sufficiently informal with respect to the definition of American obligations, so that there could be no question of who was forcing whom to back down; second, Kennedy, in fact, had long ago discarded the idea of invading Cuba (as I shall presently explain) and, oddly enough, it was only in the context of a great and deadly crisis, successfully overcome, that he could obtain sufficient acceptance of this view by the American public and thus to a considerable extent neutralize the efforts of his Republican opponents to exploit the issue.

Meanwhile, in the months that followed the missile crisis, and stimulated by the studied ambiguity of statements emanating from Washington on the subject, the no-invasion agreement stirred up a hornet's nest of polemics in Communist and leftist circles throughout the world. Khrushchev stoutly maintained he had obtained a real commitment from Kennedy, while the Chinese heaped further abuse on the chairman for pretending to lend credence to what they claimed was obviously no commitment at all. Nowhere was Kennedy's promise received with greater skepticism than in Cuba. By the strangest of ironies, when the elusive security from invasion that Fidel had so arduously and fruitlessly pursued since before the Bay of Pigs fell into his lap, he refused to recognize it. However, this was not purely a matter of disbelief on his part.

A Basic Misconception

Looking back, the October crisis seems to have come about as the result of a number of misconceptions and miscalculations, of which two were of decisive importance: one, of course, was Khrushchev's decision to establish a strategic missile base in Cuba; the other concerned the likelihood of American armed aggression against Cuba. In retrospect, it is clear that prior to the period of the crisis itself, during which a military assault on the island was narrowly averted,[10] no real prospect of an invasion existed. It is true that tensions had risen to what appeared to be dangerous heights in the summer and fall preceding the October crisis. As the November congressional elections grew closer, the Cuban problem, as anticipated, became a central issue in Republican attacks against the administration. In addition, the issue was considerably sharpened by the Soviet-Cuban flaunting of high-level military consultations in Moscow[11] and by

10. Robert F. Kennedy, in his posthumously published *Thirteen Days* which is a revealing and moving inside account seen from the White House, wrote: "The Soviet Union had been adamant in its refusal to recognize the quarantine. At the same time, it was obviously preparing its missiles in Cuba for possible use. The President in response ordered a gradual increase in pressure, still attempting to avoid the alternative of direct military action. . . . But privately the President was not sanguine about the results of even these efforts. . . . The feeling grew . . . that a direct military confrontation between the two great nuclear powers was *inevitable* [emphasis added]. Both 'hawks' and 'doves' sensed that our combination of limited force and diplomatic efforts had been unsuccessful. . . . Recognizing this, Friday morning [October 26] President Kennedy ordered the State Department to proceed with preparation for a crash program on civil government in Cuba to be established after the invasion and occupation of that country." The president was still extremely reluctant to mount an invasion, even assuming it would not trigger a nuclear exchange with the Russians. His brother quoted CIA Director John McCone as having warned that "an invasion was going to be a much more serious undertaking than most people had previously realized. 'They have a hell of a lot of equipment,' he said, 'and it will be damn tough to shoot them out of those hills, as we learned so clearly in Korea' " (pp. 83–86).

11. For example, Fidel's brother, Minister of Defense Raúl Castro, heading a Cuban military delegation, spent the first two weeks of July in the Soviet Union. His visit was given major coverage by the Russian and Cuban press. He was ostentatiously wined and dined by Khrushchev, Minister of Defense Marshal Malinovski, and the Central Committee of the Communist party. Then, from August 27 to September 2, Che Guevara was in Moscow, where he was also received by Khrushchev and other top dignitaries. At the end of his visit a joint communiqué was issued stating, among other things, that in view of the "threat of imperialism," Cuba had asked for and the USSR had agreed to supply weapons and technical specialists to train the Cubans in the use of the

other evidence that the flow of military equipment and technicians from Russia to Cuba was rapidly increasing. Although it was assumed to be a conventional-type military buildup (except for a few passionate anti-Castroites who began to "see" nuclear missiles a year before the first one arrived, apparently on September 8), it was enough to heat up the atmosphere in the United States.

Finally, there was a new bellicosity in Soviet admonitions against an invasion of Cuba, combined with a heightened shrillness and bristling defiance in Fidel's reiterated charges that an American invasion was imminent. It was almost as if Moscow and Havana preferred to raise rather than try to lower the level of polemics in order to justify the secret missile base in Cuba, once it was unveiled.

Much of the world at the time was led to believe that the United States was indeed planning another invasion of Cuba. Kennedy's statements to the contrary notwithstanding, it was feared that even if he were sincere, pressures for military action exerted on him might be too strong to resist. At the same time, his sincerity could also be brought into question. His role in the Bay of Pigs episode and the continuing political and economic offensive by his government against the Castro regime could raise doubts about his intentions to refrain from military action. Meanwhile, Fidel, having correctly predicted the invasion of the previous year, enjoyed a certain amount of credibility not only among the various shades of sympathizers with the Cuban Revolution but also among governments not unfriendly to the United States.

Under these circumstances and lulled by Soviet denials that strategic missiles were being deployed in Cuba, denials reinforced by a disbelief that Khrushchev would engage in so mad an adventure, a good deal of public opinion in many parts of the world considered Kennedy's address of October 22 as the opening move of the long-planned assault predicted by Fidel. Some of this public opinion, recalling the admittedly faked pictures Stevenson displayed at the United Nations at the time of the Bay of Pigs invasion, was skeptical concerning the same Mr. Stevenson's photographic evidence of the missile sites in Cuba. A notable case was that of Conservative Prime

---

weapons. Probably the main reason for the communiqué was to admit what could not be concealed, that is, the increased flow of military equipment and personnel. This "candor" would then lessen suspicions that anything but conventional weapons were involved.

Minister John Diefenbaker of Canada, who was clearly suspicious of the photographs and only reluctantly gave his government's support to President Kennedy's quarantine proclamation of October 23.[12] He was, however, the only NATO leader to respond in this manner.

A Proper Perspective

Theodore Sorensen, who worked more closely with Kennedy than anyone, excepting his brother Robert, later placed Kennedy's policy toward Cuba in a proper perspective. In his invaluable account of the Kennedy years to which we have already referred, he is altogether convincing when he writes, "The presence in Cuba of Soviet weapons *incapable* of attacking the United States was obnoxious but not sufficiently different from the situation which had long existed in Cuba . . . to justify a military response on our part." [13] The president, he further noted, "refused to give in to the war hawks in the Congress and press (and a few in the Pentagon) who wanted to drag this country into a needless, irresponsible war without allies against a tiny nation which had not yet proven to be a serious threat to this country." [14]

In addition, Sorensen relates, the president was concerned "about the possibility that Khrushchev hoped to provoke him into another entanglement in Cuba which would make a martyr out of Castro and wreck our Latin American relations while the Soviets moved in on West Berlin." [15] Finally, Sorensen points out that "America's allies also warned over American hysteria over Cuba. Neither Latin America nor western Europe showed any signs of supporting—or even respecting a blockade or other sanctions." [16] Such support came only when the Russians were caught in flagrante delicto building a strategic missile base in Cuba, and it enormously strengthened Kennedy's hand in dealing with Khrushchev.[17]

12. It was only after a delay of forty-two hours that Diefenbaker, under severe pressure from Washington and within his own cabinet, granted the United States request to station nuclear-armed aircraft on Canadian soil. (Robert W. Reford, *Canada and Three Crises* [Lindsay, Ontario: John Deyell, Ltd., 1968], p. 169ff.)

13. Sorensen, *Kennedy* (New York: Bantam, 1965), p. 756. Emphasis added.

14. *Ibid.*   15. *Ibid.*   16. *Ibid.*, pp. 756–757.

17. Particularly important was the *unanimous* support by the OAS, a surprising change from the attitude at the Second Punta del Este meet-

Thus, Kennedy's "assurances against an invasion of Cuba," despite the fact that they were contingent on United Nations inspection of the removal of the weapons, which Castro refused to permit, were honored in his lifetime and in the years that followed. They had, in fact, been built into the structure of American policy toward Cuba ever since the failure of the Bay of Pigs invasion. And to a large extent, the same political factors that in 1961 inhibited the rescue of the Cuban exile brigade remained operative during the following decade. The repercussions of direct American military intervention in Cuba would create unacceptable political risks for the United States in many parts of the world, and more than political risks in its relations with the USSR. The near catastrophe experienced in the October nuclear crisis, immediately followed by a notable relaxation in Soviet-American tensions, reinforced an existing policy, rather than created a new one.

It should be made clear, of course, that in no sense was it a policy of peaceful coexistence with Cuba. President Kennedy, after the missile crisis, by and large remained committed to "harass, disrupt and weaken Cuba politically and economically," as Sorensen relates, "while he dismissed in his own mind more firmly than before the possibility of bringing Castro down through *external* military action." [18] However, shortly before his assassination he began to reexamine the possibility of an understanding with Castro, but the reappraisal was cut short by his death, as I shall presently relate.[19]

---

ing nine months earlier when the vote in favor of excluding Cuba from the organization was 14 to 6 (not counting the Cuban vote). Among NATO leaders, there was immediate support from Charles de Gaulle, not known to give rubber-stamp approval to U.S. foreign policy. As Sorensen explains the strong political backing of American policy, it "was due in part to the shock of Soviet perfidy, and their futile attempts to deny the photographic evidence of attempted nuclear blackmail. It was due in part to world-wide recognition that this was an East-West nuclear confrontation, not a U.S. quarrel with Cuba" (p. 796).

18. *Ibid.*, p. 814; emphasis added.

19. Kennedy badly misjudged Castro's staying power. Sorensen states that "the effort to isolate his regime continued with increased success," quoting the president as saying: "I don't accept the view that Mr. Castro is going to be in power in five years. I can't indicate the roads by which there will be a change, but I have seen enough change . . . to make me feel that time will see Cuba free again." One alternative

Further reinforcement of the no-invasion policy came with the passage of time. Cuba, with the help of the Soviet Union, continued to increase its defensive capabilities, leading to rising estimates of casualties and other costs that an invasion of Cuba would entail. Then, again, beginning in 1965, the escalation of the Vietnam war created a sufficient drain on American material resources and strain on its moral resources to further discourage military activity against Cuba.

Finally, the failure of Castro-supported guerrilla warfare in a half dozen Latin American countries—climaxed by the defeat of Che Guevara's Cuban expedition in Bolivia in late 1967—coupled with the sharp decline in the prestige of Castro's system as a model for economic development, gave Washington additional ecouragement to look on the Cuban Revolution as a tolerable nuisance, rather than the threat it once appeared to be.[20]

Who with the foresight in 1962 to imagine that Richard Nixon would one day be president of the United States could have had the additional clairvoyance to predict that President Nixon's first major foreign policy report to the Congress, on February 18, 1970, in which a whole section was devoted to the western hemisphere—and with Fidel still in control of his island—would have no mention of Cuba or even an oblique reference to it?

Sorensen says was rejected was "the possibility of enticing Fidel into becoming a Latin-American Tito with economic aid" (p. 814). Actually, Kennedy was in the process of rethinking this alternative on the eve of his death.

20. Once Castro was confined to "building socialism in one country," several western hemisphere governments, such as those of Chile (prior to the election of Marxist President Allende), Venezuela, Colombia, Peru, and Trinidad-Tobago, began to take an interest in normalizing relations with Cuba. The principal motive appears to have been economic (Chile, for example, agreed to sell Cuba in 1970 nearly $11 million worth of agricultural products). It was also politically useful in these countries as an inexpensive sop to leftist and nationalist public opinion. Castro, needing time to back away gracefully from his Latin American revolutionary commitments, played hard to get without discouraging these moves.

Castro with Khrushchev at the Lenin Stadium,
Moscow, May 23, 1963

[All photographs are from ¡*Viva Cuba!*]

Muscovites cheer Castro's arrival in Red Square, April 28, 1963

Uzbeks welcome Castro to Tashkent, May 8, 1963

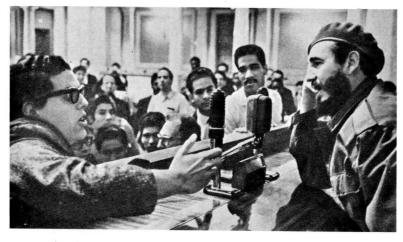

Castro talks with Cuban students in Kiev, May 20, 1963

Castro visits a collective farm near Kiev, May 20, 1963

Castro and the top Communist leaders at the "Soviet-Cuban Friendship Meeting," Lenin Stadium May 23, 1963

Castro in dress uniform, sporting his new decorations—Hero of the Soviet Union and the Order of Lenin, with Gold Medal—immediately after receiving them. With him are Khrushchev and Brezhnev. The Kremlin, May 23, 1963.

17

■

The October Crisis—III:

Cuba's Psychological Preparation

"We Can Hurl Back the Enemy"

On Monday evening, October 22, 1962, immediately after President Kennedy's "quarantine" broadcast, Fidel decreed full mobilization of the armed forces and citizens' militia. It was the climax of months of psychological preparation during which tensions over domestic issues were submerged as the consciousness of external danger gripped the population. Thus, on July 26 at a huge rally in Santiago de Cuba celebrating the ninth anniversary of the attack on the Moncada barracks, close to the scene of the rally, Fidel spoke about the imminence of an American attack with the kind of fervor and conviction that Cubans had not heard since the eve of the Bay of Pigs invasion.

Sweating profusely under the broiling midday sun and fingering the battery of microphones that carried his voice over a nationwide radio and television network, Fidel hammered away at his theme: "The mercenaries [Cuban exiles] are no longer any danger because with our present combat strength we'll wipe out any mercenary invasion." Hence, "the danger of direct imperialist aggression against us increases," especially since Kennedy and the United States government have absolutely refused to give assurances of any kind that "at any given moment our country will not be victim of an aggression." Obviously, then, "we must organize our defenses to defeat a direct invasion by the imperialists."

Then followed a passage whose real meaning was difficult to

decipher at the time and which the American intelligence community apparently failed to notice. Until then, Fidel had spoken in terms of resisting and defeating an invasion, that is, a defensive operation; but now for the first time in more than two years of confrontation with the United States, he gave a broader meaning to this operation. Speaking about Cuba's accelerated military preparations, he declared, "When our Revolution will be able to say that we are capable of *hurling back* [he gave great emphasis to this expression] a direct invasion, the last danger for the Revolution will have disappeared." The Spanish word was *rechazar* and in the context of the speech suggested a capacity to go beyond successful resistance and mount a significant counterattack.

This potential indiscretion was followed by another: "Of course, we run the same risks as all progressive humanity. Any war unleashed by the imperialists, . . . in any world war, . . . the war unleashed will be against us too. Therefore we have to get ready, not only because imperialism threatens us, not only because Mr. Kennedy . . . is obsessed with the idea of attacking our country, . . . but because . . . the progressive nations live in danger of war which the imperialists threaten to unleash."

None of his more than a million listeners across the length and breadth of the island, except a handful privy to the secret, realized that by getting ready to "hurl back" the enemy and run the risks of the "progressive nations" Fidel was referring to the preparations, at that moment under way a fairly short distance from Havana, for the installation of Soviet ballistic missiles equipped with nuclear warheads.

A Small Episode Blown Up

At about 11:30 P.M. on the night of August 24, the inhabitants of Havana were startled by the sound of heavy gunfire coming from the direction of adjoining Miramar. Members of the militia, men and women, rushed into the streets lugging their rifles. The neighborhood bars emptied as the customers dashed home, grabbed pistols and knives, and began moving toward the shore. The long expected invasion, it seemed, had finally come.

However, it turned out to be something less than an invasion. One or more hit-and-run launches, manned by Cuban exiles, had slipped in under cover of darkness to within a half mile of the shore and shelled a seaside luxury hotel housing resident Russian and other east European technicians and their families. The hotel and other buildings close by were hit, but the damage was slight and there were no casualties. Indignation, nevertheless, ran high, and the next morning it was fanned by very large headlines and a story covering the entire front page of *Revolución* and spilling over onto the inside pages. The highlight was a solemn "Declaration," signed by Fidel, denouncing the "treacherous and cowardly attack" and "holding the government of the United States responsible." The Cuban Revolution, he added, unyielding in the face of American-sponsored attacks by Cuban counterrevolutionaries, will resist "and also hurl back" any direct attack. Once more the term *rechazar* added a new sense of optimism and confidence to Fidel's exhortation.

In September real and fancied provocations by the United States, combined with ever more fulsome praise of the Soviet Union, dominated the media. Few Cubans failed to respond with more pride than apprehension to the words in heavy, black, jumbo-sized type which took up the entire first page of *Revolución* on September 12, and which read: ROCKETS WILL BLAST THE UNITED STATES IF THEY INVADE CUBA. It was Khrushchev's deceptive message to Kennedy promising to protect Cuba with Soviet-based missiles. It came only five days after another headline and lead story, with eagerly believed but spurious information about fourteen bases in Central America, Haiti, and the Dominican Republic where Cuban counterrevolutionaries were in training, presumably to participate in the forthcoming aggression by United States forces.

On September 29, Cuba issued a lengthy "Declaration" in reply to the joint resolution of Congress on Cuba, approved by the United States Senate on September 30 by a vote of 86 to 1, and by the House on September 26 by a vote of 384 to 7. Coming shortly after President Kennedy's request to Congress for standby authority to call up reserves, essentially made for purposes of domestic political expediency, the joint resolution—"to prevent by whatever means may be necessary, including the use of arms," Cuban efforts to subvert any part of the western hemisphere and to prevent the "creation or use of an externally supported military capability endangering the security of the United States"—seemed in Havana a more candid variation of the white paper that preceded the Bay of Pigs invasion. Thus the Cuban declaration spoke of "this indisputable danger of direct armed aggression by the government of the United States authorized by the congressional joint resolution" and warned the United States that "it will not find a people unprepared, but one that is vigilant, ready for combat, and prepared to defend house by house and inch by inch our territory, the independence of the nation and the sovereignty of the fatherland." In addition, Cuba will not be alone: "Thus we reply to this threatening and insolent resolution that the Cuban people . . . will not be alone . . . and in resisting is prepared to use whatever means may be necessary." [1] Not mentioned were the ballistic missiles already on Cuban soil.

Dorticós Returns from the United Nations

Something close to a national holiday was declared when President Dorticós appeared before the General Assembly of the United Nations on October 8. For the first time since the break in relations with the United States, radio and television connections between New York and Havana were set up, permitting all Cubans to watch and listen to the president as he stated Cuba's position to the dignitaries of a hundred nations. It was the same message Cubans had heard many times during the past few months, which was already convincing; but to hear it coming from New York and to see the eyes of the delegates focused on Dorticós as he extolled Cuba and excoriated the United States reinforced its meaning. Cuba was in the center of the world stage, and the spotlight of history was on David as he issued his challenge to Goliath.

The next day Dorticós returned and was greeted as a conquering hero. That evening thousands gathered in front of the Presidential Palace in downtown Havana to hear Fidel, with Dorticós at his side, for nearly three hours "review" the highlights of the "battle," as Fidel put it, that the president had waged on behalf of Cuba. One of the themes to which Fidel gave major emphasis was the Soviet Union, "defender of peace, . . . of the sovereignty of peoples, of the rights of humanity." When our president declared our readiness to negotiate our differences with the United States, what did Stevenson say? "That if we wanted to negotiate we must first break our ties with the Soviet Union." Spontaneous shouts of "no" from the listeners interrupted the speaker. "What do you think?" he added. A roar of "no" arose from the multitude. "Never," Fidel shouted back. This

1. *Cuba Socialista* 2, no. 15 (November 1962): 132–139.

was greeted by wild cheering, followed by the now familiar chant: "Fidel, Khru'cho'/e'tamo' con lo' do' [We stand with both Fidel and Khrushchev]." [2]

The response to Fidel was genuine. After the intense buildup of the Soviet image during the summer and fall, the sense of being linked to this great, generous, noble, and powerful country as the big crisis approached had taken hold of the Cuban people. "Why has this tremendous multitude of our people, . . . stronger and more resolute than ever, . . . gathered here tonight?" Fidel asked rhetorically at one of the climatic points of his speech. "To back the Revolution," he cried. "To back the measures of the revolutionary government for the defense of the fatherland! To back the support given by the Soviet Union! To say most emphatically 'yes,' it does accept the arms the Soviet Union sent us." The mention of Soviet arms set off a frenzy of wild applause and shouting.

Ben Bella's Visit

The month of October in Cuba is normally the last month of the hurricane season. The sun no longer scorches, the torrential rains have let up, the nights are less humid and the approach of the New Year revelry and the balmy winter all combine to raise the spirits of the population. It was this way in October 1962, only much more so as the consciousness that Cuba was the focal point of a world crisis added patriotic excitement to the seasonal mood.

Thus, when Ahmed Ben Bella arrived in Havana on October 16, his reception could only be described as spectacular. Never before or after did the Cuban Revolution provide so tumultuous a welcome to a high-ranking foreign official. In contrast, the reception given to Soviet Deputy Prime Minister Anastas Mikoyan six weeks later was merely correct and to Premier Kosygin in 1967 downright rude.

Ben Bella's visit, to be sure, was a spectacular undertaking. He had been released from a French prison in March 1962. In early July France gave formal recognition to the independence of Algeria. Ben Bella, as prime minister of the Algerian Peoples' Democratic Republic, in early October headed his country's first delegation to the

2. In Spanish the name of the chairman is written "Jrushchov" (*j* is the exact equivalent of the Russian gutteral *x*, rendered in English by *kh*) and pronounced with the stress on the final syllable, which approximates the Russian much more closely than the English version.

General Assembly of the United Nations. From New York he went on a state visit to Washington, where his meeting with President Kennedy was described as cordial. Then, without pausing for breath and in a kind of reckless gesture of political unconventionality worthy of Fidel himself, he flew straight from the White House to Havana.

The day before his arrival all the media gave top billing to the hero of Algerian independence. *Revolución* devoted a half page to a map of the route that the procession would follow from the airport to the statue of José Martí in the great plaza. The next morning a more than life-size drawing of the head of Ben Bella covered the entire front page of an early edition of *Revolución*.

At the airport Ben Bella and his retinue were met by Fidel, Dorticós, all the ministers, and the entire ORI leadership. There was the traditional twenty-one-gun salute for a chief of state, after which Fidel spoke, the words and scene transmitted over a national radio and television hookup. "To visit Cuba," he said turning toward his guest, "at the moment when the rich and powerful Yankee empire redoubles its hostility and hatred toward our country . . . and more-over threatens to attack our country at any moment . . . is a courageous act, and one of unswerving political commitment on your part, Señor Prime Minister, . . . and a gesture of friendship that we shall never forget." (In late 1962 Fidel had still not completely lost the habit of using "señor" as a friendly salutation.) It was a dramatic demonstration to the Cuban people that their cause indeed had acquired universal appeal. Fidel did not forget it.

With no one available to translate from Arabic to Spanish, Ben Bella replied in French. "Comrade Fidel Castro," he began, "our National Liberation Front has awarded only one Medal of Honor, and it was to you. Not a single Algerian, myself included, has received this medal." Fidel, no doubt, remembered, but many had forgotten: It was on March 2, 1959 that *Revolución* reported that representatives of the then hard-pressed and bedraggled Algerian NLF, on a tour of Latin America to drum up support for their cause, had stopped off in Havana and presented Fidel with a medal, in the words of the newspaper, "the first given by this heroic people, and the first accepted by the leader of the Cuban Revolution." It is possible that Fidel made a financial contribution, in addition to giving strong political support to the Algerian Revolution at the United Nations. In any event, three and a half years later, here was Ben

Bella, head of a sovereign state, courted by the White House, paying back a debt with interest. "And thus," Ben Bella concluded his brief remarks at the airport, "just as Cuba gave unstinting support to Algeria, so Algeria supports and will support Cuba."

Standing side by side at the microphones, in some respects they made an unlikely pair. The broad shouldered, heavily bearded Fidel, dressed in his usual olive green army fatigues, was a head taller than the slender, smooth-shaven, and well-tailored Ben Bella. At the time nearly forty-three years old, the Algerian was ten years older than the Cuban, but less experienced. Castroism antedated Ben Bellism and influenced it. In a sense, Ben Bella was the disciple paying his respects to the master. But they had other things in common as well, including charisma and dreams of continental leadership, Castro in Latin America and Ben Bella in Africa. Seen from Moscow or Peking, they were both "socialist" mavericks.[3] They were drawn to each other, so much so that, as Fidel disclosed three years later when Ben Bella was overthrown, he had revealed to Ben Bella the secret of the strategic missiles, which Fidel and the Russians believed had not yet been detected and which Ben Bella faithfully kept to himself.

The visit was short. Twenty-seven hours after his arrival, Ben Bella departed. The next day the press carried the joint communiqúe signed by both leaders and dated October 17. It gave Fidel everything he needed and pulled no punches, going so far as to speak of the "undeferrable need for the evacuation of troops and the dismantlement of foreign military bases in other countries, including the naval base at Guantánamo."[4] Each country recognized that the other was in one or another stage of "socialist construction" and that both were joined by "indestructible bonds of brotherhood."

3. Like Castro, Ben Bella clipped the wings of the local Communist party, was in the Kremlin's doghouse for a while, and then emerged to receive Moscow's highest honors. Ben Bella's ideology was even more eclectic and original than Castro's. At first under strong Trotskyite influence, he then tinkered successively with what he called "Castro-style socialism," "specific socialism," "scientific socialism," and "Arabo-Islamic socialism." In his last pronouncement on the subject, shortly before Boumediène locked him up, he said, "I accept the Marxist economic analysis, but I reject the analysis of scientific materialism." David and Marina Ottaway, *Algeria: The Politics of a Socialist Revolution* (Berkeley and Los Angeles: University of California Press, 1970), pp. 54–55, 81 n. 33.

4. *Revolución*, October 18, 1962.

That same evening, in a speech to a group of medical students, Fidel called for fifty doctors to volunteer for service in Algeria. "Most of the doctors there were French," he explained, "and many left. Thus with four million inhabitants more than we have, they have less than a third the number of doctors." This was the beginning of Cuban technical aid to Algeria, although Cuba could scarcely afford it. Many of the doctors on the island had already emigrated.

18
■

The October Crisis—IV:

Aftermath in Cuba

Bad News

AT ABOUT NOON ON SUNDAY, OCTOBER 28—a cloudy, sticky day, as I remember—I was visited in my seaside Miramar apartment by a couple of neighbors in uniform, members of the civilian militia on leave from an unspecified "front," probably one of the shore batteries a few hundred yards away. They were collecting money to buy cigarettes for the boys "in the trenches," as they put it, and asked for a contribution. "Con mucho gusto," I replied; "although the war is over. The boys should be leaving the trenches any minute now."

They stared at me in disbelief while I cheerfully explained that Khrushchev and Kennedy had reached an agreement by which the Soviet Union would ship home its missiles and the United States would not attack Cuba. This I had learned in a newscast originating in New York and transmitted by the CBS outlet in Key West.

"But this is Yankee propaganda," said one of them. What struck me was not only their incredulity, but the feeling that if it were true, it was bad news. The next morning, when the news was confirmed by the Cuban media, I discovered this was the general reaction. Walking into the office of a vice-minister and warmly congratulating him that we were both still alive and that Cuba had escaped destruction, I was met with a glum stare and a less than cordial handshake. "You think so? You trust Kennedy?" the young man asked. He was a friend and admirer of Che.

"It's not a question of trusting or not trusting Kennedy. You have to consider the whole situation created by the crisis. He can't afford to do otherwise than go along with the agreement. I wouldn't want to guess for how long, but I would say you have immunity from attack for at least the rest of Kennedy's term in office, which would be to the end of 1964. That gives everybody a lot of time to cool off and think things over and maybe come up with a reasonable solution." Carried away by my optimism, I added, "Now that you have security, you can put all your energy into building up the economy and creating the socialist showcase for Latin America which Che promised last year at Punta del Este. The Soviet Union will certainly approve and increase their financial and technical assistance."

The vice-minister was visibly irritated. "Look, my friend," he said in a way that indicated he was deadly serious, "you don't understand the Cubans. Security and material goods are not all that important to us. Honor, dignity, trustworthiness, and independence—without these neither economic growth nor socialism mean a damn."

A Remarkable Record

All week I had tried to understand the Cubans. Listening to the fear and panic building up over the Florida radio broadcasts, to the news of civil defense preparations, of hoarding of food, and of mass flight from American cities, I wondered what was wrong with the people on my street, on crowded buses, and jam-packed at the ubiquitous coffee and refreshment stands in downtown Havana. They went about their daily chores as if there had been no mobilization, as if they did not see the antiaircraft batteries that had been wheeled into strategic locations throughout the city or the sandbagged machine gun nests and barbed wire set up along the shore.

It was not a question of indifference. People talked about the situation. Monday night on television Fidel had once more, and very pointedly, spoken about "hurling back" the enemy. They did not know exactly what it was but Fidel had a surprise in store for the Yankees and, of course, the Russians would back up the Cubans. Nobody, however, seemed to notice or care that in the event of a bombardment, there would be nowhere to hide, no shelters stocked with medical supplies, and no trained personnel to take care of the wounded, put out fires, and bury the dead. Perhaps the very lack of preparation for disaster kept them from visualizing the disaster and hence fear was not provoked. Or maybe it was patriotism and confidence in Fidel and the Russians, feelings very much in evidence, which kept them so calm. Or perhaps it was ignorance. This occurred to me when I noticed men and young boys with butcher knives, meat cleavers, or more often machetes stuck in their belts. They were geared up for hand-to-hand combat without the slightest suspicion that they could be blown to bits by an invisible enemy.

Once again, as at the time of the Bay of Pigs invasion, Washington failed to grasp the mood of the overwhelming majority of Cubans. Near the close of his quarantine speech, President Kennedy addressed "a few words to the captive people of Cuba, to whom this speech is being directly carried [in Spanish translation] by special radio facilities." He spoke of his "deep sorrow" that "your nationalist revolution was betrayed . . . and fell under foreign domination. . . . These new weapons are not in your interest. . . . Most Cubans today look forward to the time when they will be truly free," etc., etc.

The next day, October 23, replying to the quarantine speech, Fidel easily made these remarks of Kennedy's boomerang: "Perhaps the most insolent part of Mr. Kennedy's statement are the two paragraphs he addresses to the Cuban people, which I am going to read to you so you can see how cynical and shameless this gentleman really is." Reading and commenting as he went along (for example, "*the captive people of Cuba*; he is talking about a people that has hundreds of thousands of men under arms; he should have said *the armed captive people of Cuba*"), Fidel took full advantage of whatever speech writer it was who once more sold President Kennedy this defective bill of goods. Later, on November 1, reporting to the Cuban people immediately after the two-day visit of U Thant, Fidel spoke of the remarkable spirit of the Cubans during the crisis:

I must say that the attitude of our people surpassed anything that the most optimistic could ever have imagined by their firmness, bravery and discipline. . . . Thousands of men who . . . in these four years of revolution had not joined the militia, did so during this crisis. . . . I must say that the enemy could not find allies of any kind within our country, . . . that in those days of the greatest crisis it was not necessary to arrest a single person [in contrast to the Bay of Pigs crisis].

Why, even men and women who were criticising the Revolu-

tion revealed their basic patriotism at the decisive moment . . .
and signed up to take part in a struggle which, according to all
appearances, was to be . . . a tremendous struggle. . . . The
president of the United States tried to intimidate our people . . .
whom he called a "captive people"; . . . the result was that more
people joined the militia than ever before, that there were more
militant revolutionaries than ever before.

It must also be said that women and . . . old men went to
work to substitute for the men in the trenches. . . . In spite of
it having been the greatest mobilization ever, it was the one that
least affected production.

As remarkable as these claims by Fidel were, equally remarkable was
the fact that, according to the abundant evidence available, the claims
were the simple, unvarnished truth.

Saving Face

Khrushchev's deal with Kennedy, bypassing Castro, confronted the
Cuban leader with a number of serious problems. Fidel had been
careful to protect his credibility by neither denying nor affirming
the emplacement of Soviet strategic missiles, always stressing tiny
Cuba's defensive posture vis-à-vis the aggressive Yankee giant and
Cuba's sovereign right to have whatever weapons it pleased. However,
once it was public knowledge that the missiles on Cuban soil were
admittedly owned and operated by the Russians, that they clearly far
exceeded Cuban defense needs, and that the arrangement for their
removal had been made without consulting Fidel, the immediate
reaction abroad was that revolutionary Cuba, instead of achieving
independence, had merely traded masters. In Cuba itself, the letdown
was noticeable but it took a different form. The immediate, almost
instinctive, reaction was not that Fidel had blundered or sold out but
that the Russians had betrayed Fidel and the Revolution. This, too,
was a difficult problem to handle.

It required all of Fidel's political acumen and agility to save face
both at home and abroad and, at the same time, not to upset the
applecart—that is, not really to obstruct the Kennedy-Khrushchev
agreement on the removal of the missiles or to jeopardize the still
indispensable assistance of the Soviet Union. Over the course of five
days, he pretty nearly accomplished this trick.

His first move on learning of the Russo-American agreement was immediately to send a letter to U Thant requesting that it be circulated as an official document of the General Assembly. Dated October 28, it declared that "President Kennedy's guarantees that there will be no aggression against Cuba are meaningless" unless he agrees, in addition to ending the "quarantine," to implement the following five stipulations: "1. Lift the economic blockade. . . . 2. Stop all subversive activities . . . carried on from the territory of the United States and from a few other countries cooperating with it. 3. Stop the attacks by pirate vessels based in the United States and Puerto Rico. 4. Stop all violations of our air space and territorial waters by United States aircraft and warships. 5. Withdraw from the Guantánamo Naval Base and return the Cuban territory occupied by the United States.[1]

The five-point program, given maximum publicity by all the media, including powerful shortwave transmissions which covered the globe, was a brilliant *tour de force*, a nose-thumbing gesture toward both superpowers, explicit in the case of the United States and implicit in the case of the USSR—a piece of audacity that would appeal to the Cuban people and refurbish the image of Cuban sovereignty abroad, but would not and was not expected to be treated as more than a petty annoyance by both the United States and Soviet governments.

In any event, with the broadcasting of the five points, Cuba ceased to be merely a piece of real estate, the status to which it was relegated during the height of the crisis, and emerged as "the third party" in the great confrontation.

The new status was reinforced by the arrival of U Thant in Havana on October 30. Just four days earlier, during the darkest hours of the crisis, he had sent an urgent message to Fidel. "Your Excellency," he wrote, "can make a significant contribution to the peace of the world at this present critical juncture by directing that the construction and development . . . in Cuba [of] installations designed to launch medium-range and intermediate-range ballistic missiles, be suspended during the period of negotiations which are now under way."[2]

Having thus far been shunted aside by both Kennedy and

1. *Política Internacional* 1, no. 1 (January–March 1963): 235.
2. David L. Larsen, ed., *The Cuban Crisis of 1962: Selected Documents and Chronology* (Boston: Houghton Mifflin, 1963), p. 153.

Khrushchev, Castro must have received a psychological boost from the letter. Dated October 27, his answer, unlike the hard-hitting five-point statement of the following day, was a model of courtesy and sober statesmanship. "The Revolutionary Government of Cuba would be prepared to accept the commitment you request . . . ," he declared, "provided that at the same time, while negotiations are in progress, the United States government desists from threats and aggressive actions against Cuba, including the naval blockade of our country." [3] He further indicated a willingness to consider any new suggestions, provided "respect for the sovereignty of Cuba" was maintained, and he invited U Thant to come to Havana "should you consider it useful to the cause of peace."

Apparently, U Thant was unaware that the missile installations were completely under Russian jurisdiction, and possibly Fidel also was still unaware of how little influence he could have in any kind of decision affecting them. In any event this exchange of corre-spondence must have greatly exacerbated Fidel's wrath and frustration twenty-four hours later when a radio broadcast from Miami gave him his first news of the Soviet-American agreement. It was also a source of embarrassment for the historical record. When the first number of the new *Política Internacional* (January–March 1963), official quar-terly of the Ministry of Foreign Affairs, published all the documents "fit to print" concerning the crisis and its immediate aftermath, Fidel's answer to U Thant was printed, but U Thant's message was omitted. Cubans never discovered what the "commitment" was which Fidel was willing to accept and lacked the power to imple-ment.[4]

The presence of the acting secretary-general of the United Nations and his retinue in Havana understandably was exploited by Fidel to boost the diminished prestige of his government and to re-store the buoyance of Cuba's injured national pride. No less im-portant at this moment than Ben Bella's journey from the White House to Havana a fortnight earlier, it nevertheless required a dif-ferent kind of handling. Two meetings between the parties were

3. *Política Internacional* 1, no. 1 (January–March 1963): 234.
4. Actually, Fidel let the cat out of the bag during his November 1 radio and television appearance when he read the transcript of his Oc-tober 30 meeting with U Thant; but at the time few, if any, listeners would have been sufficiently alert to have noticed it.

scheduled. Fidel obtained permission in advance from U Thant to make public the stenographic report of the discussion at the first meeting. What occurred at the second meeting was to remain confidential. U Thant and company departed on October 31 and the next day Fidel appeared on a national television and radio hookup. Even judged by the high standards of effective communication and persuasion set by Fidel himself, this was an extraordinary performance. First, he led off with a low-keyed verbatim reading of the stenographic report of the first meeting—altogether an impressive display of candor and "open diplomacy" even if one remembered that it was a controlled candor to be supplemented by confidential discussions. He then launched into a passionate elaboration and defense of the Cuban position, continued with a high-pitched plea for a restoration of public confidence in the Soviet Union, and ended with a panegyric on the virtues of the Cuban people during the crisis (which I have already cited).

Some Revelations by U Thant

The purpose of U Thant's visit, as far as it was revealed, was to solicit Fidel's cooperation in permitting United Nations inspection of the missile installations in order to verify their dismantlement, a request that, as has already been noted, Fidel refused. As they discussed this matter, U Thant made several interesting revelations. Thus, when Khrushchev announced that he would request the United Nations to send an inspection team to Cuba, it was U Thant who first raised an objection. "I answered the Soviet representatives," he told Fidel as he unfolded the background of his mission, "that before sending a team . . . the most important point was to get the prior consent of the Cuban government . . . and that no action could be taken which would violate its sovereignty." [5] Apparently, Khrushchev, in his haste to satisfy Kennedy, had overlooked this small point, which did not help improve his image with the one million or more Cubans listening to Fidel that night.

Strangely enough, the image of the United States as it emerged in U Thant's report to Fidel, in contrast, was altogether respectable. The United States, he explained, hoped that U Thant could organize a temporary arrangement, "naturally with the authorization and consent of the Cuban government," during the week or two it would

5. *Política Internacional* 1, no. 1 (January–March 1963): 13.

take for the dismantling and loading of the missiles for the return voyage to the Soviet Union. Concretely, the United States made two inspection proposals:

> The first United States proposal, subject to the consent of the Cuban Government, is that [an on-the-spot] team of U.N. representatives be set up, composed of persons whose nationalities would be acceptable to the Cuban government. The second proposal would be to employ a U.N. reconnaissance plane manned by persons acceptable to the Cuban, American, and Russian governments. It was even suggested that the crew of the plane would consist of a Cuban, a Russian, and an American. I replied to the United States that I would also present this proposal to Prime Minister Castro.[6]

At this point, the transcript that Fidel was reading revealed a matter of more than anecdotal interest. "The United States told me," continued U Thant, "that as soon as this system was set up they would make a public declaration, and if necessary in the Security Council, that they would relinquish any aggressive intentions against the Cuban government and would guarantee the territorial integrity of the nation. They asked me to tell you this." [7] A few moments later, U Thant repeated the American proposition, adding that "they would also lift the blockade [quarantine]." [8] In addition he told Fidel that, at his request, the United States had lifted the quarantine during the forty-eight hours he would spend in Cuba.

There was no clarification of what the United States meant by the phrase "relinquish aggressive intentions" (in the Spanish text, "no mantendrián intenciones agresivas," which in turn was a translation from the language spoken by U Thant, almost certainly English). Fidel asked for no clarification and appeared to assume that it meant "no invasion." In any event, the offer by the United States of a formal and solemn pledge of no invasion and a "guarantee of territorial integrity" might have appeared, to anyone except Fidel, as a real turning point in revolutionary Cuba's uncertain and extremely costly struggle for survival. It provided the binding juridical commitment lacking in Kennedy's statement to Khrushchev. It certainly would have seemed worth exploring. It might have paved the way for negotiations for a reasonable modus vivendi with the United States,

6. *Ibid.*, p. 14.   7. *Ibid.*   8. *Ibid.*

and it would have cost little or nothing in the way of prestige or status. The procedures suggested by the Americans clearly provided for full respect for Cuban sovereignty. U Thant, both in his official capacity and as an individual always a great stickler for the sovereignty of small countries, obviously considered the American suggestions as above reproach. Nor was Fidel's comparison of the inspection proposition with the United Nations military intervention in the strife-torn Congo in 1961, however effective as a propaganda device, a sound analogy. There was not the remotest possibility that a handful of unarmed multinational inspectors could have the slightest effect on the stability of the Castro regime, let alone threaten Fidel with the unhappy fate that befell Patrice Lumumba.

Castro Blows Cold and Hot

Fidel's reply, stripped of the familiar expressions of indignation against the United States and determination to defend Cuba's sovereign rights—not completely relevant to the negotiation of the moment but good copy for the transcript he planned to read—boiled down to the following: the Cuban government does not prevent the withdrawal of the missiles; the United States knows that the Soviets fully intend to keep a commitment made in the full glare of world publicity; hence, "as I see it, inspection is just another attempt to humiliate our country. Therefore we do not accept it. . . . We do not accept dictates that can only be imposed on a defeated country." [9]

Whether or not Fidel believed the reasons he gave U Thant, he had at least one additional powerful motive for refusing to cooperate, the same one that earlier prompted the proclamation of the five points, and that was the Soviet Union. Short of obstructing the removal of the missiles—a suicidal undertaking—it was the most dramatic means at his disposal to demonstrate that Cuba was not a Russian puppet. And from all accounts, it gave him a great deal of personal satisfaction to force Khrushchev to perform an undignified maritime striptease by which his missiles were unwrapped and displayed on the high seas for the benefit of American aerial inspection.

Nevertheless, there was a limit on how far Fidel could afford to annoy the Soviet Union. Thus, after blowing cold, he also blew hot in the direction of Moscow. When he concluded reading the transcript of the meeting with U Thant, he took up the question of

9. *Ibid.*, p. 16.

Cuba's relations with the Soviet Union: "During the course of this crisis, some differences arose between the Soviet government and Cuban government. But I want to say one thing to all Cubans: this is not the place for us to discuss these problems. . . . This we must do on a government and party level . . . because . . . we are Marxist-Leninists! And we are friends of the Soviet Union!" [10]

This had to be said, but it was not too easy to put across at this moment. Hence, he made an extraordinary appeal, the kind he had never had to make before: "In this confused situation . . . what advice can I give you? . . . Above all, have confidence, full confidence in the revolutionary government, in the leadership of the revolutionary government, . . . that everything will be discussed at the proper time and place, all problems, all questions." [11]

At this point something more positive was needed, but without losing sight of the negative: "In all sincerity, I want to say that at this moment when a certain *disgusto* may have arisen because of these misunderstandings or differences," he declared, lingering on the word *disgusto*, "it is good to remember what the Soviet Union has done for us." [12]

He then recalled the economic, technical, and military assistance received from the Soviet Union, for which "we are grateful," giving prominence to the weapons received: "the basic weapons of our armed forces are all weapons that the Soviet Union has sent us and which it has provided us free of charge. I must tell you that a few months ago the Soviet Union decided to cancel the entire debt incurred by the purchase of weapons." [13]

The Moral Projectiles

Finally, he moved into his peroration, praising the people for their patriotic response during the crisis and culminating in his long-remembered double-edged metaphor with its unflattering connotations for Soviet "morality": "Such a people [the Cuban people] is

10. *Ibid.*, p. 31.   11. *Ibid.*   12. *Ibid.*, p. 32.
13. *Ibid.*, p. 33. In a speech on April 22, 1970, Fidel said that Cuba had received "$1,500 million in armaments" from the Soviet Union. Presumably, this does not include the cost of training Cubans in the use of the armaments and of other instruction in military science. This sum is "double the amount of direct U.S. military aid to all the rest of Latin America" over the same period, according to Juan de Onis (*New York Times*, May 10, 1970).

invincible . . . [and] has a right to maintain its dignity and prestige unsullied! Because we possess long-range moral projectiles that cannot be dismantled and will never be dismantled! And these are our strategic weapons, our defensive strategic weapons, and our most powerful offensive strategic weapons!" [14]

A week later, there was evidence that Moscow had not discounted Fidel's "moral projectiles." While Mikoyan, now in Havana, was trying to soothe ruffled feathers, somebody in the Kremlin—more than likely Khrushchev himself—hit upon a special piece of flattery. Here is how novelist Juan Arcocha, at the time Moscow correspondent of *Revolución*, described it in a dispatch dated November 8, the day after the forty-fifth anniversary of the Bolshevik Revolution:

> Yesterday morning in Red Square the Soviet Union paid the greatest possible homage to the Cuban Revolution. It was totally unexpected. Nothing like it had ever happened before. . . . Never in 45 years had a foreign anthem been played during this parade. Suddenly, after the band had played three marches, Red Square reverberated with the notes of the *Hymn of the 26th of July*. In front of Lenin's Mausoleum, on which Khrushchev and the principal leaders of the Soviet state were standing, the flower of the Red Army marched by to the strains of our glorious hymn.[15]

It was the lead story in big type on the front page of *Revolución*. However, another dispatch, much smaller, was tucked away at the bottom of the same page. It quoted Khrushchev as saying at the reception given in the Kremlin on November 7: "We believe in Kennedy's word. The Cubans reply they don't believe. We consider that a president of the United States cannot go back on his word in such a serious moment. We must believe him because otherwise it means world war." Whoever made up the front page must have done so with malice aforethought. Let us enjoy the flattery, he seemed to be saying, but not be fooled. It will take more than music to end our *disgusto*.

The Soviet Cultural-Scientific Offensive

During the rest of the year, the front pages bristled with alarm and warnings. New plans for an invasion of Cuba were reported and

14. *Ibid.*, p. 35.   15. *Revolución*, November 8, 1962.

Kennedy and U Thant were reminded that "CUBA WILL DEFEND ITS SOVEREIGNTY." [16] Meanwhile, Revolución gave full coverage to Peking dispatches offering enthusiastic support to Fidel's five points and scorching indictments of Soviet "adventurism and capitulationism."

Mikoyan left for New York on November 26, having gone on record with a pro forma endorsement of Fidel's five points, a gesture that became the subject of crude jokes in the upper levels of the government bureaucracy. In some offices, photos of Mao sprouted where once Khrushchev appeared alongside some living Cuban hero or martyr. A new popular ditty was widely repeated: "Nikita, Nikita/ Lo que se da/ No se quita" ("Nikita, Nikita, when you give somebody a gift, you're not supposed to take it back").

On December 1, Yevtushenko gave a poetry reading (with the help of a translator) to an overflow audience at the University of Havana. His provocative verse and his ebullient histrionics (on and off stage) gave a much needed boost to Soviet prestige in the student population, even though he had some difficulty during the question period with queries on freedom of speech and Trotskyism. Yevtushenko was the start of the post-missile-crisis Soviet cultural-scientific offensive in Cuba which in short order brought David Oistrakh, Russia's top-ranking violinist, and cosmonaut Pavel Popovich to Havana.

Fidel reciprocated with an "offensive" of his own. In mid-December he sent Enrique Oltuski and Faustino Pérez to Moscow as part of a four-man commercial delegation. Both had played a leading role in Fidel's insurrection (Oltuski in the underground while Pérez was one of the "twelve" survivors of the Granma expedition); both had been outspoken anti-Communists, held top positions during the first year of the revolutionary government, had been sacrificed by Fidel at the start of the honeymoon with the Soviet Union, and had been quietly "rehabilitated" after the purge of Aníbal Escalante. On the surface the choice of the two men was innocent and unobjectionable. However, nobody with a modicum of political sophistication, least of all the men in the Kremlin, failed to get Fidel's message.

Among the top figures who rolled out the red carpet for the Cuban delegation was Mikoyan, whose recent presence in Cuba as well as his earlier visit in February 1960 made him more deeply aware than his peers of what the Kremlin was up against. According to Che

16. Headline in Revolución, November 17.

Guevara, Mikoyan had confessed to him at the time of his first visit to Havana that the Cuban Revolution "is a phenomenon that Marx had not foreseen." [17]

17. *El Mundo*, July 29, 1960.

19

■

Prelude to Reconciliation

The Need for Accommodation

FIDEL CASTRO ARRIVED in the Soviet Union on April 27, 1963. Thus ended the visible and audible friction between Cuba and the USSR generated by the October missile crisis, although an incompatibility of interests and temperaments remained to plague their relationship for a number of years to come.

Neither party had any real choice but to patch up the quarrel. From the Cuban point of view, there were no substitutes for the life-sustaining Soviet economic and military subsidies. Fidel, in his anniversary speech on January 2, had declared 1963 to be the "Year of Organization." Coming after the "Year of Planning" (in both cases with the principal focus on the economy), it was a way of admitting that little had been achieved thus far in bringing order into the main branches of economic activity. As it turned out, the cumulative failures of a year of planning and another of organization were impressive. In 1963 sugar production, the prime indicator of the Cuban economy, was to fall to 3.8 million metric tons. This was not only a decline of 20 percent from the already depressed amount (4.8 million) registered in 1962, but the lowest figure in absolute terms since 1945, and in per capita terms, since 1933.[1] Only an unprece-

1. With an estimated population of 7.2 million in 1963, per capita production amounted to 0.53 metric tons. Production in 1945, when the population was a shade under 5 million, was 3.5 million metric tons

dented rise in the price of sugar on the world market and a substantial increase of Soviet assistance (I shall comment on these phenomena later) were able to reverse the consequences of the disaster in production.

As for Moscow, after the missile crisis it had become essential to appease Fidel. It was not merely a question of maintaining the Soviet presence in Cuba—this was in no danger for all of Fidel's gestures of "independence"—but of rehabilitating Soviet prestige in Cuba and concerning Cuba. The immediate objective was to demonstrate by Castro's physical presence in Moscow and a solemn joint Soviet-Cuban declaration that, on the one hand, the USSR remained committed to support and defend the Cuban Revolution and, on the other, that Cuba had given a vote of confidence to Moscow at a time when, in China and Rumania [2] and among Communists and

---

(3.4 million Spanish large tons). Hence, per capita production in 1945 was 0.7 tons, or some 30 percent higher than in 1963. Production in 1933 was the equivalent of 2 million metric tons, at a time when the population was 4 million. Per capita production was thus 0.5 tons, or slightly less than in 1963. Leví Marrero, *Geografía de Cuba* (Havana: Editorial Selecta, 1957), pp. 152–155, 675.

2. According to Stephen Fischer-Galati, a "decision to exploit Moscow's embarrassment and weakness resulting from the Cuban crisis was made at a special plenum of the Central Committee held [in late November 1962]. . . . By March 1963, the Rumanian leaders had adopted the actual Chinese interpretation of the Moscow Declaration of 1960 . . . on the vital issues of national self-determination and sovereign rights" (*Twentieth Century Rumania* [New York: Columbia University Press, 1970], pp. 173–174). Unlike the other Warsaw Pact countries, Rumania from the beginning resisted Soviet pressure to export goods to Cuba, unless exchanged for goods of equivalent value that were needed in Rumania. As a result, trade between the two "Latin" socialist countries was minimal and diplomatic relations merely correct. In late 1967 and early 1968, at the height of Castro's great controversy with Moscow, there was a sudden flurry of mutual enthusiasm between the two countries, involving Rumanian technical and financial assistance in prospecting for Cuban oil (see W. Raymond Duncan, ed., *Soviet Policy in Developing Countries* [Waltham, Mass.: Ginn-Blaisdell, 1970], p. 130). As of the middle of 1971, no significant oil deposits had been discovered, by either the Rumanians or the Russians, who began explorations much earlier. After August 1968, when Cuba and Rumania took opposite positions on the Soviet intervention in Czechoslovakia, relations between Havana and Bucharest went back to normal.

leftist activists elsewhere, the legitimacy of Soviet leadership in the "world revolution" was being questioned. The longer range objective was to move Fidel toward creating a viable economy and accepting "peaceful coexistence," under the Soviet protective umbrella, as a rational foreign policy goal.

Fidel Presses His Advantage

All the post-missile-crisis indicators, including the effusive greetings sent by Khrushchev and Brezhnev to Castro and Dorticós for the anniversary of the Revolution on January 1, 1963—there was even a mention of the "notable achievements . . . in the *construction of socialism*" (emphasis added)—told Fidel that he was in a strong bargaining position. He therefore pressed his advantage. Mao Tse-tung's New Year's message to Castro—"you have defended the sovereignty of Cuba and the honor of a *socialist country*" (emphasis added) and obtained "a victory for the revolutionary [Chinese] line of Marxism-Leninism"—was conspicuously featured in the press and given considerably more coverage than the Russian greetings.[3]

In mid-January, speaking at a Latin American women's congress in the Chaplin Theatre, Fidel challenged Soviet policy in the sharpest terms. Once more he insisted that Latin America was ripe for armed struggle. As for Cuba, it would never bow to atomic blackmail, nor was it hoodwinked by the Soviet-American settlement of the missile crisis. "For us," he repeated, "the Caribbean crisis has not been re-solved. . . . We don't believe in the word of Kennedy; moreover Kennedy hasn't given any word; and if he did give his word, he has taken it back." Finally, striking hard at "intriguers and divisionists," that is to say, the Kremlin-oriented old Cuban Communists, he de-clared to be "an act of treason against the Revolution" any deviation from the "line of our party, of its leadership." Here, it would appear,

3. The Chinese lost no opportunity to outdo the Russians in courting Cuban favor. At the Third Afro-Asian Solidarity conference, held at Moshi, Tanganyika. February 4–11, 1963, at which both China and the USSR were represented, while the Russians dragged their feet it was the Chinese delegation that pushed through acceptance of Cas-tro's invitation to hold an Afro–Asian–Latin American conference in Havana. (See William E. Griffith, *The Sino-Soviet Rift* [Cambridge, Mass.: M.I.T. Press, 1964], p. 125.) When the turbulent Tricontinental Conference was finally held three years later, Fidel rode roughshod over both the Russians and Chinese.

Fidel was flexing his muscles needlessly. The leaders of the now defunct PSP were basically powerless to stir up any trouble; and in any event, like Fidel, they could easily recognize the appeasement signals coming from Moscow. However, this was Fidel's manner of displaying his power and, like the rest of his speech, part of the larger effort to refurbish, at home and abroad, the Cuban image of unwavering sovereign self-determination and uncompromising revolutionary militancy—before the inevitable compromise would be negotiated.[4]

The Turning Point

On February 28, Cubans were startled by a banner headline in *Revolución*: THE USSR WILL FIGHT ANY AGGRESSION AGAINST CUBA. There followed a report of a speech by Khrushchev in Moscow in which he was quoted as saying that the Soviet Union "will not allow the big sharks of North American imperialism to swallow heroic Cuba." The context in which the new pledge to defend Cuba was made was almost as startling. "If they attack Cuba," the chairman continued, and then significantly added "or the People's Republic of China, . . . the Democratic Republic of Korea, the Democratic Republic of Vietnam, the German Democratic Republic or any other Socialist country," then the Soviet Union "will come to the aid of its friends and deliver a devastating blow to the aggressors."

Thus was the turn in Cuban-Soviet relations first announced.[5] To what extent Fidel at this moment gave credence to Khrushchev's bellicose "nonsectarian" and "internationalist" definition of Russia's

4. The speech at the Chaplin Theatre was delivered on January 15 and, as usual with Castro's pronouncements, published verbatim in the press on the following day. The special importance attached to this address was underscored by the fact that the usual one- or two-day editorial commentary and exegesis in *Revolución* was prolonged for nine days straight, beginning with the issue of January 18.

5. Three weeks earlier (February 7), the signing of a Cuban-Soviet trade protocol and a new agreement on Soviet credits no doubt paved the way toward reconciliation. Likewise, an important trade agreement between Cuba and the German Democratic Republic, concluded on February 15, must have played a role in softening up Fidel. The deal with the Germans apparently depended on the conclusion of negotiations with the Russians, since the GDR commercial delegation arrived in Havana on January 2.

obligations would be difficult to say. What mattered more to Fidel was that it allowed his reconciliation with the Kremlin to appear to be consistent with principle, and not a pragmatic or opportunistic move. If this was indeed the case, then Khrushchev had gone to extraordinary lengths to accommodate his wayward Cuban protégé. But it would be only the beginning of an extraordinary series of accommodations, as we shall presently see.

Hostility in the United States

Meanwhile, the need for the new turn in Cuban foreign policy had been made more plausible by the stepping up of the Cuban polemic in the United States during the months of January and February. Anti-Kennedy hawks in both parties called for military intervention, once and for all, to eliminate Castro and the Russian garrison in Cuba. The administration, while conscientiously pursuing its short-of-war policy to bring down the Castro regime, felt it expedient to simulate hawkish noises from time to time. To complicate matters further, Venezuela and Guatemala, among other Latin American republics, had lodged complaints with the OAS that Cuba was furnishing arms and money to subversive movements in their countries. These and similar charges were scornfully rejected in lengthy declarations sent by Raúl Roa to U Thant. In confrontations of this kind, either side was capable of straying from the truth. Some years later, the Castro regime in effect admitted that the evidence against Cuba was not "tainted," but at the time, Roa's posture of injured innocence was effective in misleading sections of public opinion in many parts of the world. As a result, when an OAS committee meeting in Washington on February 12 recommended new measures to tighten up antisubversive vigilance and Cuban isolation from the continent, Cuban propaganda that this was preparation for new and unprovoked aggression carried with it a certain amount of credibility. In the meantime, a United States counterinsurgency base took shape in the Panama Canal Zone, which the Cuban media could exploit as part of the evidence of a grand design to crush the Cuban Revolution and any support for it that might arise in Latin America.

Finally, a continuing series of shooting and near-shooting incidents in Cuban coastal waters and the adjacent shoreline added significantly to the irritation on both sides of the Straits of Florida. In February, several such incidents—on the 9th, 13th, 20th, and

23rd—were given prominence in the Cuban press and were the subject of sharp diplomatic exchanges between the United States and Cuban governments, channeled through the Swiss embassy in Havana and the Czechoslovak mission in Washington.

The incidents themselves were petty and due mainly to free-wheeling actvities by Florida-based Cuban counterrevolutionaries and overzealous Castrophobic American officers operating in the zone, and in both cases they were stimulated by the storm that the hawks in Washington were raising over the administration's "soft" line against the Communist challenge in Cuba. Nevertheless, added to the verbal threats coming from influential sources in the United States and from the OAS, they provided the kind of setting that would permit Khrushchev once more to raise his voice (this time with little risk since Cuba was clearly in no danger of being invaded) and would facilitate Fidel's reconciliation with the chairman without losing face.

The *Baku* Episode

A more serious incident followed that finally provided President Kennedy with the opportunity of bringing under greater control the irresponsible activities, which not only better served Soviet and Cuban than American purposes but which now threatened to disrupt Soviet-American relations at a time and under conditions that were scarcely in the American interest. At dawn on March 26, an attack by an unidentified launch against the Soviet freighter *Baku* occurred, in which the bridge was raked with heavy caliber machine gun fire and the vessel itself was damaged by a mine that exploded alongside. The ship was still in Cuban waters and had just sailed from Caibarién, on the north coast, with a load of sugar bound for Leningrad. In an official declaration issued the following day over his signature, Castro blamed an "agency of the United States" for financing and equipping the armed launch.[6] "If these attacks continue," he added, "Cuba will have to consider acquiring long-range bombers, as well as naval equipment . . . to protect our supply routes and repel the aggressors. . . . The cowardly and criminal aggression demonstrates the irresponsibility of those who govern the United States and the dangers to world peace created by their policy of banditry and aggression."

The answer to Castro and to Khrushchev as well was not long in coming. Early in April the United States Navy began to inter-

6. *Revolución*, February 28, 1963.

cept counterrevolutionaries heading for Cuba and on the 10th, amid a tremendous uproar in Washington, the news broke that Kennedy had ordered all American support withdrawn from the Cuban Revolutionary Council, a quasi government-in-exile headed by Fidel's one-time prime minister, Miró Cardona. That very night, speaking at a graduation exercise in the Chaplin Theatre, Fidel, waving a batch of news dispatches freshly printed out by UPI telex receiver, began to read snatches with obvious relish: "Kennedy and Castro coexist. . . . U.S. government refused request by Miró Cardona for $50 million. . . . Support for invasion withdrawn. . . . Kennedy opposed to having Cuban exiles determine U.S. policy."

Fidel was in a mellow mood that evening. On the eve of his trip to Moscow (still unannounced), was he already beginning to respond to the siren call of peaceful coexistence? This he could not afford to admit. "Can we say that the imperialists have abandoned their plans of aggression against Cuba?" he exclaimed. "No!" was his answer. But as he went on, an air of conciliation could be detected in his remarks. He explained how, two weeks before, Cuban planes had mistakenly harassed a United States freighter, believing it to be manned by Cuban counterrevolutionaries, and how the Cuban government had apologized for the error. Finally, he delivered a reasoned assessment of the dispatches he had read at the beginning of his speech: "Objectively, however, we can say that the measures taken by the U.S. government . . . are a positive step . . . a small step to lessen the risks and crisis of war." [7]

The Eve of Fidel's Departure

On April 16, the front-page headline of *Revolución* announced that Fidel had accepted an invitation by Khrushchev to visit the USSR "this year." Three days later, on the second anniversary of the Bay of Pigs victory, in his last speech before leaving for Moscow, Fidel gingerly turned his listeners toward the new horizon. In the midst of resounding denunciations of the enemy and impassioned praise for the revolutionary patriotism and heroism of the Cuban people—to be expected on this occasion—he again dwelt on the meaning of the break between Washington and Miró Cardona's Cuban Revolutionary Council.

    7. Speech published as usual on day following delivery (*Revolución*, April 11, 1963).

"The counterrevolutionaries accuse Kennedy of wanting to co-exist with Cuba," he declared, thus proving that "the aggressive policy of the United States against Cuba is bankrupt." Nevertheless, he added, "We are not campaigning here for coexistence; we don't want war, we want peace, we are no obstacle for peace." Time and again in the past, Fidel and his spokesmen had declared that Cuba favored peace over war with the United States. However, in this new context, Fidel's denial that he was "campaigning" for coexistence could be interpreted as a signal to Washington that he was, indeed, proposing coexistence, that is, a normalization of relations based on mutual concessions.

In any event, given the announcement of his projected visit to the Soviet Union, it was no longer a secret that he was also preparing the ground for the anticipated new look in Cuban-Soviet relations. This was confirmed by another point made in the same speech: for the first time Fidel explained the emplacement of strategic missiles in Cuba in terms that Khrushchev could approve. Leaning on Miró Cardona's charges that Kennedy had betrayed a promise, made after the Bay of Pigs failure, to invade Cuba (charges denied by the president), Fidel declared, "And now the whole world will have to recognize that Cuba acted in legitimate self-defense, that the measures jointly adopted by the governments of Cuba and the Soviet Union were just and necessary measures."

20

■

Fidel in the Soviet Union

An Unprecedented Reception [1]

ONE WOULD HAVE TO COMB the annals of all recorded history, eastern as well as western, to find a precedent for the magnificence of the reception that the Soviet government provided for the Cuban prime minister. Certainly, in the 800 years since the founding of the Duchy of Moscow, no Russian czar, emperor, or ruler of the Soviet Union had received a visiting head of state or any other foreign guest with anything remotely resembling the pomp and ceremony, and out-pouring of attention and honors, that Nikita Khrushchev bestowed on Fidel Castro.

As part of the elaborate security precautions taken to ensure his safety, Fidel and his retinue left unannounced on the regular Friday weekly return flight of the TU-114 which, since early January of that year, provided a direct link between Cuba and the Soviet Union. It was Saturday, April 27, 1963, in Murmansk, where the huge turbo-prop landed after an uneventful twelve-hour nonstop flight. From that moment until Fidel's return to Havana by the same route thirty-seven days later, every day would be jam-packed with

1. Most of the material in this chapter is drawn from ¡Viva Cuba!: Visita de Fidel Castro a la Unión Soviética (Moscow: Ediciones "Pravda," 1963). The circumstances of its publication are explained later in the chapter.

extraordinary events and no less extraordinary accounts of these events in the Russian and Cuban press.

No sooner off the plane and embraced by the waiting Anastas Mikoyan, Fidel was called to the telephone. It was Nikita, bidding him welcome to the Soviet Union, adding, "Moscow awaits you." It was their first conversation since their meeting in New York in the United Nations General Assembly in the fall of 1960. At the time, Khrushchev had invited Castro to visit him in Moscow. Little did he imagine the circumstances that would impel him to receive Fidel, not as the quixotic ruler of an indigent and beleaguered tropical island, but as if he were the sovereign of a great power whose favor be humbly sought, hat in hand.

An overnight stay in Murmansk was arranged so that Fidel could reach Moscow rested and ready for a strenuous Sunday afternoon reception. Nevertheless, there were speeches in Murmansk, a visit aboard the atomic icebreaker *Lenin,* and a large reception at the naval base attended by the top brass of the northern fleet.

The next day, when Fidel in an IL-18, escorted by a squadron of fighter jets, circled over Red Square and then landed at Vnukovo airport, an unimaginable event in Soviet journalism had already occurred: the entire first page of *Pravda* (circulation, eight million) was dedicated to a biography and eulogy of Fidel Castro. At Vnukovo, there were greetings according to protocol, much more effusive than customary, by Khrushchev, Leonid Brezhnev (at the time president of the Supreme Soviet, with who knows what dark thoughts about Nikita concealed behind his bushy eyebrows), and a score of top party and government dignitaries, with three astronauts thrown in for good measure.

Then came an additional ceremonial welcome that again shattered all precedent. From the airport, Fidel and Nikita and their respective entourages were driven to Red Square where 100,000 Muscovites were waiting to cheer the two great leaders and applaud their speeches, in which each showered the country and person of the other with superlative praise. Nothing like this Red Square arrival celebration had ever happened before—nor has it happened since—but this was only the beginning.

On May 1, Fidel stood atop Lenin's tomb to review the May Day parade. Red Square was bedecked with Cuban flags. Standing side by side with hands clasped, Castro and Khrushchev waved their free hands as the cheering throngs marched by. From time to time, a military band would play the Cuban national anthem. At other times several hundred Cuban students, their normal exuberance and unruliness accentuated in the Muscovite setting, would chant from the grandstand opposite the mausoleum: "Fidel, Khrushcho', e' tamo' con lo' do'," at which the marchers, infected by the tropical turbulence, would shout back their Russian approximation of the strange Spanish name: "Fee-dell, Fee-dell," stressing the first syllable and pronouncing the final "l" like the "ll" in the English word "million."

That night there was a great banquet in the Kremlin, at which Khrushchev and Castro exchanged soaring compliments in resounding toasts. The next day the inseparable two leaders went to a soccer match in the Lenin Stadium, where they were acclaimed by the masses, and the same evening attended a variety show in the new Palace of Congresses, the enormous glass and concrete building erected on the exquisitely beautiful Kremlin grounds. By the time Fidel left for Volgograd on May 6, there had been a dozen formal and informal receptions, dinners, and luncheons, in addition to a visit with Khrushchev, his wife, children, and grandchildren at the chairman's country dacha and a hunting party in the Zaviodovo woods. During the entire eight days that had elapsed since Fidel's arrival in Moscow, it is doubtful whether Khrushchev had any time left to attend to government and party business.

The Grand Tour and Honorary Doctorate

Leaving the chairman behind to catch up on his homework, Fidel, accompanied by his Cuban staff, representatives of the host government, and the usual contingent of newspaper reporters and photographers, departed on an eleven-day tour of the Soviet Union. It began with a two-day stop at Volgograd. On May 8 the party reached Uzbekistan, spending a couple of days in Tashkent and one in Samarkand. On Saturday the 11th, Fidel arrived in Irkutsk, in south central Siberia. There was an excursion to nearby Lake Baikal and then he made the short trip west to Bratsk by train. After briefly visiting the giant hydroelectric installation on the Angara River, he flew west to Krasnoyarsk and then to Sverdlovsk, in the Urals, arriving in the evening of the 13th.

Everywhere it was much the same story: official receptions,

flowery oratory, inspections of factories, schools, historic monuments, and such natural phenomena as were worthy of notice. And everywhere there was an outpouring of genuine enthusiasm by the masses who were not merely stirred by the tremendous barrage of propaganda, but were truly fascinated by this strange Marxist-Leninist potentate from the distant west—young, tall, erect, bearded, and handsome, smoking long cigars (the symbol of affluent imperialism), informal in dress, manner, and speech (even in Russian translation so much more lively and colorful than a *Pravda* editorial), his black eyes now sharp and piercing, now relaxed and twinkling with amusement.

On the 17th, Fidel returned to Moscow after spending two days in the Urals, followed by two extraordinary days in Leningrad, where from all accounts it could be said that he took the city, still looking westward as in the time of Peter the Great, by storm. It was a killing pace, 10,000 miles of speeches, banquets, embraces, hydroelectric plants, collective farms, and tractor plants in eleven days; but Fidel was up to it. It even seemed as if he thrived on the adulation; and as at each stop the chorus of "Fee-dell, Fee-dell" appeared to grow louder, he responded with ever more extravagant praise for the Soviet Union and Nikita Khrushchev.

After a brief pause, Fidel was on the hustings again. On May 20, Kiev, bedecked with flags and flowers, paid its tribute to the great hero and to the "Isle of Liberty," as Cuba had been dubbed by the Soviet media. Back in the capital the next day, Fidel went directly from the airport to the skyscraper that houses the University of Moscow. Here, in the main auditorium filled with students, the rector bestowed on him the honarary degree of doctor of laws, "in consideration of the distinguished contribution made by Fidel Castro to the application of Marxist-Leninist doctrine in matters involving the state and law," in the words of the rector. For the historian, if not for those present, the irony of the citation was as impressive as its solemnity; for from Fidel down to the lowliest bodyguard in the Cuban delegation, there was not a single bona fide Marxist-Leninist, according to the Russian definition. Fidel, presumably to underscore the extent of the concessions, ideological and otherwise, that he was forcing on the Kremlin, had carefully omitted from his entourage anyone identified with the old Communist PSP.

The Rally at Luzhniki

The concessions, however, were reciprocal. The fallout from the acclaim showered on Fidel enhanced the revolutionary leadership claims of Soviet foreign policy and, on the domestic scene, helped refurbish the somewhat tarnished image of the chairman. In fact, Khrushchev had converted Castro's visit into a juicy political plum, as the next and climactic event made entirely explicit. It was on Thursday, May 23, that an enormous rally dedicated to the "eternal, unbreakable friendship of the Cuban and Soviet peoples," etc., etc., was held in the Lenin Stadium at Luzhniki, on the banks of the Moscow River. *Pravda* reported that 125,000 Muscovites were present, while in Havana the figure was raised to 150,000. An aerial photo of the ovular amphitheatre showed grandstands, bleachers, and playing field jam-packed with humanity. Close-ups revealed that it was a humanity bedecked with flags, pennants, and banners and sweltering under a hot sun. On the speakers' platform, bald-headed, roly-poly Nikita was in his shirt-sleeves, the long end of his unevenly knotted tie tucked under the belt of his trousers. Next to and towering above him was Fidel, wearing his usual beret and army fatigues, shirt collar open, understandably not impressed by the heat. Although the two men were separated by the great gulf of age, physical stature, language, and culture, they had one thing in common as they faced the multitude: the visible evidence of sartorial neglect.

Khrushchev's speech [2] was a major pronouncement addressed to the world at large. Although it was mainly a restatement of familiar Soviet policy and of the nation's "unparalleled achievements" and the "radiant future" it would shortly enjoy, the fact that Fidel was there beside him gave special meaning to much of what he said. "Prometheus," he declared, "gave humanity a gift of eternal fire. You, valiant fighters for the liberty of Cuba, have ignited the sacred fire of the Great October Revolution in the western hemisphere." It was now officially one big blaze, and as the speech wore on it was clear that the keepers and protectors of the holy flame were the progeny of its Russian creators in "October." The evidence was there at Khrushchev's side: Fidel, inspired, nurtured, delivered from peril, and now anointed by the heirs of Lenin. (When his turn came to speak,

2. Summary and quotation from ¡*Viva Cuba!*, pp. 92–102.

Fidel, who had undoubtedly seen an advance copy in Spanish of the chairman's address, found it necessary to explain that, "Of course, it never occurred even to the imperialists to say that the USSR exported revolution to Cuba.") [3]

The events of the day were being transmitted live by shortwave radio to Europe, the Orient, and Cuba. From Havana they were simultaneously rebroadcast to all Latin America. In addition to the Cuban delegation and all the top-ranking members of the Soviet hierarchy, there was a contingent of Communist party leaders from abroad, such as the venerable Tim Buck of Canada, the blind and black Henry Winston of the United States, and, significantly, several stalwarts from Latin America, including the Uruguayan Rodney Arismendi and the Argentine Victorio Codovilla. Four years later, when Fidel exploded with titanic wrath against the Soviet Union (who could have predicted it on this day of glory?), each had a separate role to play on behalf of the Kremlin: Arismendi as conciliator and pacifier on the political front and Codovilla as hatchet man on the ideological front.

Khrushchev on Peace and China

Once more Khrushchev repeated his version of the missile crisis, which ended "in a victory for the policy of peace and peaceful coexistence, thanks to which the revolutionary conquests of the Cuban people were safeguarded." From here he moved on to a broader defense of peaceful coexistence and a critique of those who saw in this policy a betrayal of the national liberation struggle of the oppressed peoples of the Third World. On the contrary, "Our party has always maintained that peaceful coexistence creates favorable conditions . . . for the constant development of the national liberation movement. . . . It was precisely under conditions of peaceful coexistence between states with different social systems that the glorious Cuban Revolution triumphed." The record does not state whether, at this point, Khrushchev turned toward Fidel or whether Fidel squirmed with embarrassment. Khrushchev, in a desperate rebuttal of the Chinese heresy, had pulled a non sequitur of large dimensions out of his hat, exploiting Fidel's presence on the platform to give it credibility. Perhaps Fidel, under the illusion prevalent in some Communist circles that the relative lull then prevailing in the Sino-

3. *Ibid.*, p. 103.

Soviet controversy foreshadowed the end of the quarrel, was less disturbed than he might otherwise have been. His complicity in Khrushchev's distortion of history would soon be forgotten.

Finally, the chairman dealt explicitly with the question of Sino-Soviet relations:

> In the bourgeois press not a few absurd rumors are being published concerning the relations between the Communist parties of the Soviet Union and China. As you know, in the near future the delegations [of the two parties] will meet. . . . We express our hope that this meeting will strengthen even more the cohesion of our parties and of the whole international Communist and workers' movement. The great cause of communism will overcome all obstacles as it marches ever forward and will triumph in the entire world.[4]

The rumors, as we know, were far from absurd. A few moments before, Khrushchev himself had cited Lenin on the need for an "intransigent struggle against all manifestations of nationalism" and had warned against dividing the working classes "on the basis of continents or skin color." This he had said for the benefit of the Chinese and their backers, and it could only have increased their anger and resentment.

At Luzhniki, however, when Khrushchev expressed his optimism about Soviet-Chinese relations and the triumph of communism, a great applause burst forth. Even mightier was the applause when Khrushchev, skilfully enveloping the Cuban in the web of his argument, added, "We rejoice because the visit of comrade Fidel Castro to the Soviet Union has contributed to the unity not only of the Cuban and Soviet peoples, between our two parties, but also be-

4. By the time the meeting mentioned by Khrushchev took place, on July 5 in Moscow, relations had again openly deteriorated, practically to the point of no return. The discussions were "suspended" on July 20 and not resumed. William E. Griffith comments on the meeting as follows: "probably always intended by both sides as a manoeuvre from which each hoped to profit by fixing the blame for its prospective failure on the other, and which had in any case been agreed to largely as a result of pressure from other Communist parties, [it] was almost certainly doomed to failure in advance." *The Sino-Soviet Rift* (Cambridge, Mass.: M.I.T. Press, 1964), p. 155.

cause it has contributed to strengthening the cohesion of the entire socialist community and the whole international movement."

Fidel Reads His Speech

Among the notable and unprecedented feats performed in connection with Fidel's visit was the publication by the *Pravda* press, on the eve of Fidel's departure from the USSR, of a 200-page book in hard covers and richly illustrated, containing the full TASS coverage of the Cuban leader's visit. A copy was presented to Fidel before leaving for Cuba. A short time later, a Spanish version of the book, somewhat expanded with coverage of Fidel's homecoming television report in Havana, and a *Pravda* article reporting the speech, was circulated in the Cuban capital.

In *¡Viva Cuba!*, as the Spanish edition of this remarkable volume was entitled, Fidel's speech covered about one-third the space taken up by the chairman's discourse.[5] For its brevity it was thus a record-breaking performance, no doubt in part explained by another unusual occurrence—he read the speech from a prepared text. "It seemed to me it would be easier this way for you, for the translator, and for me," he explained to his listeners, "since I can't speak your language." This was most likely not the reason. Speaking in Moscow on the same platform with Khrushchev was serious business. The chairman, and the Presidium committee that cleared Khrushchev's speech, would certainly want advance notice of what Fidel intended to say.

Under the circumstances, Fidel fulfilled his obligations with no ambiguities, with his usual eloquence, and with unusual dispatch. Speaking of the United States, he declared that the imperialists have not "resigned themselves to the idea of leaving our country in peace. There are still a number of problems to be solved if the risks of a [nuclear] conflict are not to arise again." Nevertheless, he continued, after listing the continuing hostile activities against Cuba, "Faced as we are with this policy of blockade, isolation, and aggression, Cuba has proclaimed its desire to live in peace and maintain normal relations with all nations [of the western hemisphere], including the United States. An example of those relations are those of Cuba with Canada, Mexico, Brazil, and other Latin American countries."

5. Pp. 102–106.

Fidel did not refer directly to the issue of peaceful coexistence and national liberation on which Khrushchev spoke at length; but considering the relative moderation of Fidel's remarks and the general context of the situation in which they were made, it was clear he was not supporting Chinese intransigence nor was he ruling out an accommodation with the United States. His reference to Canada could not be overlooked in this connection. Cuba had amicably settled all Canadian claims arising from the nationalization of Canadian enterprises and properties. It set a precedent for a future settlement of American claims.[6]

Fidel also refrained from any specific reference to the Sino-Soviet controversy and from any elaboration on the issues involved. In a very short paragraph he called for "the unity of the international Communist movement." It will strengthen the "power of the socialist camp," he declared, "thereby safeguarding peace and creating more propitious conditions for the struggle of the peoples against the colonial and imperialist yoke." Here again, one could discern an echo of Khrushchev's speech. In any event, Fidel's very presence at this great demonstration of "unity" clearly implied the judgment that the obstacle to unity did not lie in Moscow.

In Praise of Russia and the Chairman

With respect to the Soviet Union, Fidel spoke only in superlatives, and of the magnanimous "solidarity of the Communist party of the USSR, of the government and Soviet people with the Cuban Revolution." Reaffirming the Khrushchev version of the missile crisis, he pulled out all stops to convey "in all its grandeur" the nobility of the "gesture of a country which, in defense of a small nation many thousands of miles away, at the risk of a thermonuclear war, placed in jeopardy the well-being achieved in forty-five years of creative work and of immense sacrifices. . . . The Soviet Union . . . did not vacillate in accepting the risk of a cruel war in defense of our little country. History knows of no such example of solidarity. This is internationalism. This is communism." Nor, we may add, does his-

6. As for Brazil, it broke relations with Cuba after the overthrow of the Goulart regime on April 1, 1964. Mexico continued to maintain relations with Cuba over the years, although imposing strict surveillance of air traffic between Mexico City and Havana and an informal near-total trade embargo.

tory know a more complete reversal of judgment in so brief a period of time.

As *¡Viva Cuba!* described the scene, if there had been a roof over the Lenin Stadium, the applause and shouting that followed this panegyric would have raised it. But Fidel had not yet finished. When the tumult died down, he continued his speech. Thus, there was to be another climax when he reached the end. I must express "our deepest gratitude," he declared, "to the one who has been the indefatigable builder of friendship between our two peoples, Nikita Sergeevich Khrushchev. It is to him that we Cubans owe countless deeds of solidarity and friendship. With all our heart we congratulate him, and through him, the Central Committee of the Communist party of the USSR for the success achieved by the Soviet Union, under his leadership, along the road to communism." Then, in Russian, "Thank you very much, my Soviet brethren." And finally again in Spanish, "¡Viva el comunismo! ¡Patria o muerte, venceremos!" A thunderous ovation greeted these words. Most people were on their feet shouting "¡Viva Kuba! ¡Fee-dell!" and it was several minutes before the crowd began to disperse.

A New "Hero of the Soviet Union"

It would seem that after the jamboree at Luzhniki, there would be nothing left to do but release the joint Cuban-Soviet declaration which was signed on that day. But more was to come. That evening a gala reception was held in the Kremlin in honor of Fidel and the Cuban delegation. Present were marshals of the armed forces, admirals of the fleet, academicians, poets, scientists, and artists—the cream of the Soviet intelligentsia—as well as the top leadership of the Soviet state and party. At the appropriate moment, Brezhnev came forward and, according to *¡Viva Cuba!*, "As the entire hall broke out with applause, the chairman of the Presidium of the Supreme Soviet pinned the Gold Medal of Hero of the Soviet Union and the Order of Lenin on Fidel's Castro's jacket." [7] A full-page photo shows a smiling Fidel, unexpectedly well-groomed and sporting his medals on the chest of his dress uniform, while at his side,

7. The value of the decorations was somewhat depreciated a year later when both Nasser and Ben Bella became "Heroes of the Soviet Union." On May 1, 1961, along with Sékou Touré and others, he had been awarded the much lower-ranking Lenin Peace Prize.

grinning widely, stood Nikita, his dark coat properly buttoned and wearing his own medals. Slightly behind Nikita, and partly obscured by him, was Leonid Brezhnev.

Thus ended this day of glory, destined to be soon forgotten, not even worthy of a footnote in the works of either Cuban or Russian historians. Less than a year and a half later, Khrushchev would become a nonperson in his native land; and not long after, Cuba would achieve a new place in the sun when Fidel would simultaneously hurl defiance at the United States, China, and the Soviet Union. Even after the next Russo-Cuban reconciliation, publicly formalized by Fidel's approval of the Soviet invasion of Czechoslovakia in August 1968, the great outpouring of mutual love and admiration in this month of May 1963 would remain a nonevent, and nothing remotely resembling its warmth would be revived.

The Joint Declaration: Cuban Socialism Approved

The joint Cuban-Soviet declaration was almost as long as Khrushchev's extended discourse at Luzhniki, hence far more lengthy than Fidel's speech. It was largely a formalized version of what Khrushchev had said concerning the views of the USSR on international relations and relations between Communist parties. In this respect, the document as a whole need not detain us except to note that it was also officially declared to be the Cuban position, a matter that at the time was considered by the Kremlin to be a significant contribution to its efforts to maintain primacy in a less than monolithic international Communist movement. In the concluding words of the declaration, "The visit of comrade Fidel Castro serves the interests of the final consolidation of the monolithic unity and cohesion of the great socialist community."

In return, the document provided unequivocal Soviet acceptance of Cuba as a member in full standing of the "great socialist community," and of its party, the PURS, as a genuine Marxist-Leninist "vanguard." According to the text, "The relations between the PURS and the CPUSSR are based on the unbreakable principles of proletarian internationalism and fraternal solidarity, of equality between the parties," followed by more in the same style. Thus, the ghost of the Kremlin-chartered PSP, the one-time "vanguard" whose taking of power should have been the sine qua non of a genuine socialist revolution, was quietly laid to rest. The legitimization of Cuban socialism, was, to be sure, a reluctant concession by the Kremlin. However, much of the rest of the declaration was a form of payment. Still, for Fidel it was a good bargain at the time. Membership in Moscow's "socialist club" appeared to add something to Cuban security and a good deal more in the way of political and ideological status, a useful asset in the internecine warfare among the Marxist-Leninist parties and movements.

There was also a sharp statement concerning the defense of Cuba "if in violation of the obligations undertaken by the president of the United States not to intervene in Cuba, aggression against her takes place." In this case, the document continues, "the Soviet Union will fulfill its international obligation . . . and will provide the necessary aid, with all the means at its disposal, to defend the liberty and independence of the Republic of Cuba. The organizers of aggression must bear in mind that intervention in Cuba will confront humanity with the danger of thermonuclear war." After the October missile crisis, it was a moot question whether this statement added to Cuban security, but it did not in any event weaken it. And besides, what else could be said on this subject on this occasion that could better satisfy Cuban apprehensions and rehabilitate Soviet prestige?

Retroactive Increase in the Price of Sugar

In a section in which, in glowing terms, "both parties express their satisfaction" with Soviet economic and technical assistance to Cuba, a significant announcement was made. In view of the rising price of sugar on the world market and "to strengthen the socialist economy of Cuba," as the text explained, the Soviet government proposed "on its own initiative to increase the price of the sugar purchased in 1963 to the level of the price on the world market." On his return to Havana, Fidel offered more details on this deal, as I shall shortly explain.

As soon became evident, the new price agreement was part of a larger joint decision by which the ambitious plans for Cuban industrialization would be drastically modified and the island would give priority to agricultural development in which the restoration and expansion of sugar production was to play the principle role.[8] It was

8. It appears that the initiative for the new economic orientation came from the Cubans, not the Russians. A Canadian economist who

an eminently sound decision in principle, although its implementation was characteristically and sufficiently erratic so that the economy became more and more dependent on Soviet subsidies and less and less able to meet the daily necessities of the Cuban people. Be that as it may, meanwhile plans would be discussed and Fidel would unexpectedly return to Moscow the following January to draw up the new long-term sugar agreement.

Political Concessions to Fidel

The Cuban press made much of the fact that the joint declaration spelled out and endorsed Fidel's famous "five points" for "normalizing the situation in the Caribbean" and that it gave its blessing to the two declarations of Havana. These pronouncements, the document stated, "have historic importance for the national liberation struggle of the peoples of Latin America and correctly indicate the course of events." [9] In the context of the joint Cuban-Soviet declaration as a whole, they appeared to be mainly face-saving concessions

---

was in Cuba at the time recalls that by mid-1962, Fidel, Che, and others were beginning to reemphasize the importance of sugar as "fundamental to the economy, its cornerstone, the principal export." (F. W. Park, "Development Policies of the Cuban Revolution." Centre for Developing-Area Studies, McGill University, p. 29; paper presented at the meeting of the Canadian Political Science Association, University of Manitoba, June 1970.) However, a new sugar policy could take shape only after the Soviet Union, the world's leading producer of sugar (derived from sugar beets) and by this time normally a net exporter, agreed to provide a market for the bulk of Cuban sugar. An American economist, working in the Ministry of Foreign Trade in Havana and involved in a study of possible markets for Cuban sugar in 1962 and early 1963, explained Cuban thinking on the subject as follows: "Why, then, shouldn't Cuba try to promote a large market for her sugar in the socialist countries? . . . The Soviet Union was financing Cuba's trade deficit. Unless sugar exports were expanded, the deficit would continue indefinitely. Before the Cuban Revolution, large sugar imports might not have been desirable from a Soviet economic point of view. But now the choices were not the same. Better to take sugar even though there might be some disadvantages than just to continue financing the deficit." (Edward Boorstein, *The Economic Transformation of Cuba: A First-Hand Account* [New York: Monthly Review, 1968], p. 199.) Ironically, the Russians did both, for many years. There was not enough sugar to cover the deficit, or even come close to covering it.

9. *¡Viva Cuba!*, p. 120.

to Fidel, two or three small paragraphs submerged in the long-winded elaboration of the Soviet doctrine of peaceful coexistence and its numerous corollaries. Thus, it was not illogical to conclude that by signing the declaration, Fidel in fact was renouncing his five points and muting the declarations of Havana and concurrently submitting to the other requirements of economic and political rationality. In the long run, it would turn out that to survive, socialist Cuba, like capitalist Cuba, would have to move in the orbit of a great power and to produce sugar. Celebrated and flattered by the Russians beyond measure, Fidel, nevertheless, could only be an appendage and not a prime mover where imperial decisions were made. Eventually, in his relations with the Soviet Union Fidel did yield, grudgingly, to the "rationality" envisaged by the joint declaration of May 23, 1963, but not before an amazing attempt to free himself from it.

It was announced that Fidel Castro's official visit ended on May 23. The next day Nikita and his honored guest flew to the chairman's summer residence near Sochi on the Black Sea. A week later they visited a strategic missile base (location not revealed) and then spent two days in Tbilisi, capital of Georgia, where according to TASS, as reported in ¡Viva Cuba!, they received a "tumultuous welcome," leading to the suspicion that Fidel had resumed his official visit. For Khrushchev it must have been both a very pleasurable and profitable experience, since he was not popular among Stalin's fellow countrymen who still worshipped the dead Georgian as a national hero, notwithstanding the fact that Khrushchev had ordered his mummy to be moved out of the Lenin Mausoleum. Needless to say, Khrushchev and Fidel steered clear of Stalin's birthplace maintained as a shrine in Gori, easily accessible from Tbilisi.

Finally, the two prime ministers flew to Murmansk where Khrushchev and a large group of Soviet notables escorted the Cuban party to the TU-114 that was waiting to take Fidel and his retinue back to Havana.

21

■

A Report to the People—I:

Concerning Russian Virtues

The Main Objectives

On June 4, the day after his return to Havana, Fidel spoke over a national television and radio hookup about his trip to the Soviet Union. It was one of those classical performances, then becoming rare and soon to disappear, set up in the form of a meet-the-press interview, part of the American cultural heritage that lingered on in Cuba and that, along with Fidel's habit of speaking extemporaneously on all occasions, amazed the brethren from the socialist countries of both Europe and Asia. Of course, it was a modified form of the American institution. In the first place, the moderator and the three journalists on the panel could scarcely afford to be hostile to or even critical of the person being interviewed. Nor, in the second place, could they lead Fidel with their questions, which they had little opportunity to interject in the stream of his exposition and which, in any case, Fidel good-naturedly brushed off most of the time. Finally, in the United States there would be no sponsor willing or able to foot the bill for a four-hour interview over a national hookup on prime time; and if such a sponsor could be imagined, where would he find a latter-day version of William Jennings Bryan able to talk four hours at a stretch and hold the attention of 90 percent of the adult population?

In giving his report that evening, Fidel seemed to have had

three main objectives in mind: first, to remove what remained of popular Cuban resentment and suspicion of the Soviet Union, which he himself had helped to generate following the missile crisis; second, to convince the Cuban people that the reconciliation with the Soviet Union would provide the Cuban Revolution with far greater security and economic opportunity than it had thus far known; and third, to let it be known that the time had now come for Cubans to get to work seriously and give first priority to the economy. Developing his major points, as well as a number of significant digressions, at great length, Fidel produced a report of unusual interest.

Admiration for the Soviet Union

As Fidel began to talk, it was apparent that in the course of his visit he had fallen under the spell of the visible economic and military power of the USSR and its vast geography. This was not difficult for any visitor to do who arrived in 1963 with a reasonably open mind and whose guided tour systematically accentuated the positive. Recalling the backwardness of czarist Russia, the destruction and chaos following the Bolshevik Revolution, the civil war and foreign intervention, and finally the horror and decimation inflicted during World War II, the visitor could easily conclude that what he had seen represented a series of monumental achievements, without being aware that they obscured equally monumental failures in many areas of material production and human relations. Thus, apart from the extraordinary circumstances of his visit, Fidel was no doubt sincere when he told the Cuban people that, although "we had a very high opinion" of Soviet achievements before the visit, "the fact is that when we actually came into direct contact with it, what we saw gave us an even higher opinion of the Soviet Union."

An annoying and persistent problem that Fidel had had to face since the day he took power arose from the fact that most Cubans, to a greater or lesser extent, had had direct experience with American consumer goods. In addition, most Cuban either by living in or visiting Havana, or through the movies and other media, or through reports from the thousands of their relatives who had migrated to the United States long before the Revolution knew something about the standards of living in the adjoining "Colossus of the North." By comparison, Mao Tse-tung, for example, has had no problem at all in this respect, for undoubtedly 99 percent or more of the Chinese cannot begin to imagine the relative opulence in which even the depressed populations of the industrialized societies live.

By mid-1963, the Cuban people had had ample opportunity to discover that consumer goods imported from the Soviet Union were by and large shoddy and expensive, compared with those they used to receive from the United States. In the case of foodstuffs, taste and habit would sometimes enter into the comparison. With respect to Russian canned meat, for example (by any standard it would have to be rated as of poor flavor), Cubans would invariably "remove the curse," as they expressed it—that is, mask the flavor with various combinations of available condiments—before eating it. When fresh herring packed in brine appeared in the foodshops, even though it was unrationed, low priced, and an excellent source of scarce protein, it found no takers. Fidel was so disturbed that he located an elderly Polish Jew who, he was told, knew how to prepare the strange fish; and one day he knocked on his door, unannounced, with a bundle of herring. After sampling the old man's concoction, he sent word to the minister of foreign trade to cancel all shipments of herring still undelivered.

Thus, in addition to telling his listeners about enormous hydroelectric plants and giant construction equipment at work in temperatures of 55 degrees below zero, Fidel had to spend a great deal of time explaining that, although there was no "infinite" abundance of goods, the masses had "everything that was indispensable and necessary," including "an average daily per capita consumption of nearly two pounds of bread." By comparison, Cubans consumed very little bread and Fidel appeared to be trying to impress his fellow countrymen with Russian affluence in this department. Here Fidel undoubtedly used poor selling judgment, since Cubans are traditionally rice eaters and have always used bread sparingly, if at all.

Fidel went on to explain that the Soviets were not "investing in luxury goods, but in the means of production"; that feudal and bourgeois exploitation having been eliminated, "the masses own what they make"; and that the "standard of living has been going up." When he ventured to make an explicit comparison between the Soviet Union and the United States, he picked a sure winner: "take the subway in Kiev, the Metro, as they call it, which is the one I visited. I know the New York subway and it is nowhere near in the same class as the Kiev subway. . . . What do you have in New York? Darkness, filth, and deafening noise. . . . In Kiev you go down and come up on an escalator, you know, a moving staircase, like the one in [Havana's] Sears, Roebuck [at the time permanently out of order] and everything clean, bright, spotless; you don't see a single scrap of paper. That's how they've solved the transportation problem, and what's more you really enjoy riding in the Metro. I took a little ride myself." [1]

Production, Party, and Classless Society

At this point, he returned to the more serious theme of the "basic means of production," and with mounting enthusiasm. "Here lies the real basis for calculating that they will surpass the production of the United States," he declared, and going beyond even the rash Soviet prophesies, Fidel predicted that at the "end of the present twenty-year program they will have a larger production than the present production of *all the capitalist countries put together*" (emphasis added). And what made all of this possible? To begin with, the party. "The party made a great impression on me," he declared; "magnificent party workers everywhere, competent, enthusiastic, completely dedicated to their work. . . . The decisive role of the party is a basic principle of Marxism-Leninism. . . . The development of the Revolution, the construction of the economy, the leadership of the country, . . . only the party can perform these tasks."

But also the new society "without classes" made a deep impression on him. There was a "type of men," he explained, "men and women, full of enthusiasm and optimism, . . . strong, . . . hardworking, frugal, willing to sacrifice, . . . with great organization and great efficiency. . . . You can really appreciate the human quality of the people, which is the result of a revolution." Fidel, with his customary self-assurance and excessive volubility, clearly could not have remotely suspected how in a short time his views concerning the Soviet party, the classless society, and all the human

1. Listening to Fidel, I was reminded what a Russian friend told me when I expressed my admiration for the Moscow Metro: "Yes, we have succeeded in building socialism under the ground. With our aircraft, sputniks, and submarines we have successfully built socialism in the air, in space, and under the water; all that remains is to build socialism on the surface of the earth."

virtues he was extolling would radically change. For very likely he was sincere, on the whole, when reporting his impressions of the visit. His selective enthusiasms and conspicuous exaggerations were conditioned and motivated by special circumstances, not by a deliberate intention to falsify (which is not to say that he was incapable of lying when it suited his purposes). Understandably, he had looked at the Soviet Union through rose-colored glasses, but he had also made an important decision. He had quite clearly returned from the Soviet Union determined to turn over a new leaf. Thus, his praise of the Soviet Union was also a springboard from which to launch a sharp critique of the state of affairs in Cuba and to exhort his fellow countryment to emulate the Russian virtues.

A Salute to *Pravda*

It must have come as a shock to most Cuban journalists and intellectuals when Fidel, paying his respects to *Pravda*, in effect proposed that it should be a model for the Cuban press. It was "a newspaper with only two sheets [four pages]," he explained to his listeners familiar with the sixteen or more pages of the papers then circulating in Havana, "where they condense all the important news. They have marvelous editors, I can tell you." He also made a big point of the way the Russians saved newsprint. "With their enormous forests, their newspapers are much smaller than ours, and we don't even have a single, tiny forest." There was also the question of quality. "Magnificent editors," he repeated; "they collect and synthesize the most important things, . . . very well organized, . . . efficient, . . . no advertisements; *I don't read Russian* but that's my impression. . . . Let's see if we can't set up some kind of comradely competition [*emulación*] between the two papers" (emphasis added).

This tribute could have been dismissed as another effusive gesture of friendship for his erstwhile hosts (he had actually toured the *Pravda* plant), if it were not for a disquieting coincidence. On May 14, from Sverdlovsk in the Urals, Fidel had sent a message to *Hoy*, the old PSP daily, on the occasion of the newspaper's twenty-fifth anniversary. Addressed to "Dear Comrade Blas"—that is, Blas Roca, the editor and, it will be recalled, the venerable leader of the PSP until its merger in the PURS—it was the first time since taking power that Fidel expressed such high esteem for an organization that on some occasions he had only faintly praised and on others severely criticized.

"From the land of the Soviets," the message read, "where we have had the opportunity of . . . admiring the creative work of this society of giants, we send our greetings. . . . *Hoy* for twenty-five years preached the ideas of Marx, Engels, and Lenin. . . . It armed the Cuban revolutionary movement with ideas. . . . With the reunification of all our revolutionary forces in the United Party of the Socialist Revolution, . . . *Hoy* plays an extremely important role in the struggle. . . . It places special emphasis on economic problems and . . . production which are the fundamental questions confronting socialism." [2] Meanwhile, at *Hoy*'s elaborate twenty-fifth anniversary celebration on May 16 in Havana, among the notables who spoke was President Dorticós and Acting Prime Minister Raúl Castro. The latter seemed to take it for granted that *Hoy* would become the official organ of the PURS and clearly implied that this was Fidel's idea.[3]

Although it is entirely possible that this was Fidel's intention at the time, *Hoy* never received the official designation. When the first flush of his new-found admiration for the Soviet Union and its orthodox Cuban disciples wore off, Fidel discovered that such a move would estrange the writers and intellectuals of the more libertarian left. This would be a high price to pay since, unlike the old-line Communists, their basic loyalty was to him, personally. Fidel wrestled with the problem of creating a press that would be "responsible" in the *Pravda* sense, but also responsible only to him and therefore controlled by his own people. He finally solved the problem in October 1965, when the PURS was transformed into the new Communist party of Cuba. Both *Hoy* and *Revolución* (and their editors) were scrapped and replaced by a single daily, *Granma*, officially designated as the organ of the new party and edited by a faithful, but also domesticated, Fidelista.

Granma, it will be recalled, was the name of the formerly Florida-based yacht on which Fidel and his band sailed from Mexico to Cuba in late November 1956. A column under the heading "Granma" appeared for several months in *Revolución* during 1959. The new party organ, in addition to the vernacular American derivation of its

2. *Cuba Socialista* 3, no. 22 (June 1963): 142.
3. *Hoy*, May 17, 1963.

name, has no precedent in the Communist world. Although like *Pravda* it is a no nonsense paper, and in this sense more like a house organ than a newspaper, it still resembles *Revolución* by its flamboyant tabloid-style makeup, lavish pictorial embellishments, florid prose style, and generous consumption of newsprint. It also publishes a widely distributed twelve-page *Granma Weekly Review* in English, French, and Spanish, an extravagance that the Kremlin has been unable to control. By 1965, Fidel was again vigorously projecting the image of a nationally conscious and independent Cuba, and apparently decided to tropicalize rather than emulate *Pravda* standards in all their austerity.

22
■

A Report to the People—II:

Concerning Economics,
the United States,
and Khrushchev

The New Priority

TOWARD THE VERY END of his television appearance, Fidel returned to his preoccupation with Cuban press standards, as we shall presently observe. Meanwhile, he focused his attention on the topic that was clearly uppermost in his mind. "I must tell you," he said, "that everybody over there is dedicated to the development of the economy . . . in a very serious way, so that a Cuban visitor can't help feeling a little ashamed because we haven't yet . . . paid enough attention to the economy. We are somewhat idealistic revolutionaries: very revolutionary, to be sure! We make a lot of noise and keep stirring things up; we hold big meetings; we're very patriotic. . . . But it seems as if we're doing all this with our heads in the clouds, without realizing that we must have a base for all this, that an economic base is absolutely essential."

It would seem that somebody had reminded Fidel of what Lenin used to say on the subject, although it was, of course, an old principle, as old as Aristotle who advised that "We must first secure a livelihood and then practice virtue." [1] If Fidel more often honored this dictum in the breach than in the observance, it was not on philosophical grounds but because he found that his efforts to "secure a livelihood" were so unrewarding and frustrating. Che Guevara, on the other hand, by late 1964 fed up with his own and Fidel's constant planning and management blunders, concluded that a new systematic approach to the problem was required, the reverse of Aristotle's. I discovered that he bluntly told his friends, including Fidel, that he considered economics of secondary, or less, importance for the Cuban Revolution. What is the point of developing the economy, he would say, if we do not create the new socialist man whom it is supposed to benefit? Apparently Che was already contemplating disengagement from Cuba's domestic affairs.

"And it's really a shame," Fidel continued, "that we have many good revolutionaries here who don't have the slightest idea that there is such a thing as economics. They are a special breed of revolutionary: they eat, sleep, wear shoes and clothing, and don't know that all of this has something to do with the economy." Addressing himself to administrators, party members, and other leaders, he added, "It often happens that a man who is doing some job or other makes a big mistake, and stays right on the job just the same . . . or he's shifted to another job with the same salary . . . or a higher salary. . . . We must insist on responsibility, which we haven't been doing."

This was not the first time nor would it be the last that Fidel publicly exposed the real shortcomings of some of his own vanguard, although without admitting or perhaps being unaware that they were to some extent the reflection of his own unchecked irresponsibility and his disorganized work style. This time, however, there was a special urgency in his words. Not only had Fidel discovered economics in the USSR, but in connection with his discovery he had made some important arrangements with Khrushchev. This had to be explained so that the Cuban people would truly understand that a new start in economic development was about to begin; that Russian commitments—solid and magnanimous—guaranteed the success of the development, but only if Cubans gave priority to working efficiently, using wage incentives to improve productivity (later,

1. Cited by John A. Hobson, *Imperialism* (1902; Ann Arbor: University of Michigan Press, paperback edition, 1965), p. 91.

when there would be less and less available for wages to buy, Fidel would discover that only moral incentives were worthy of a society aspiring to become Communist[2]), and only if Cuba would invest the surplus in expanding the means of production rather than spending it on more consumption. In a word, from now on "we must use our resources . . . in a rational manner," as Fidel put it.

The Sugar Deal

The key to the new economics was sugar, and Fidel went into great detail about how Cuba had always had difficulties with the United States over sugar prices and quotas, how the Yankees thought they would ruin Cuba by cutting off all imports of Cuban sugar, how the Soviet Union came to the rescue "paying us four cents a pound . . . when the price on the world market was under three cents . . . and when they didn't need the sugar. The Soviet Union is making enormous strides in beet sugar production in Ukrania." In fact, although Fidel did not mention it, the USSR outproduced Cuba for the first time in 1959, thereby becoming the world's largest sugar producer. It has maintained this position ever since.[3] When the price of sugar on the world market started going up, Fidel continued, "we felt it would be incorrect for us to raise the question of a price increase with them" in view of what they had done for us and also "because we had not shipped the amount of sugar we had promised them . . . and were running a large trade deficit with the Soviet Union, between $150 million and $200 million."

Where, then, did the initiative for increasing the price of our sugar come from? he asked. "The enemy claims we made a deal, . . . charging the Soviet government and party a high price in return for giving them political support [meaning in the Sino-Soviet quarrel]."

2. And still later, after the near collapse of the economy, he would change his mind again, under Russian "guidance."

3. In 1959 the Soviet Union produced 6.5 million metric tons as against 5.9 million for Cuba. By 1965 Soviet production was 9.7 million tons, close to the 10 million goal which Cuba failed to meet in 1970. Not counting its political imports of sugar from Cuba, the USSR is normally a net exporter of sugar, with countries such as Finland, Afghanistan, Iraq, Iran, Egypt, and Algeria among its regular substantial customers. Sources: *The World Sugar Economy in Figures, 1880–1959*, FAO, 1960, p. 29; *Sugar Year Book* (London: International Sugar Council, 1967), pp. 261–264.

At this point he became very indignant. "Everybody knows our position," he declared, "that we are struggling for the unity of the socialist camp; and especially those who know us well also know perfectly well that we never take an unprincipled position in order to secure economic benefit, and they know very well that we have our own opinions and will defend our opinions and we are capable of defending our opinions at any price." After this outburst, Fidel then explained that it was Khrushchev himself who suggested raising the price of sugar from four to six cents a pound to include deliveries for 1963 already contracted at four cents.[4] The chairman proposed this figure, Fidel went on to say, because at the time of their conversation the price of sugar on the open world market was fluctuating around six cents a pound.

A Fictitious Explanation

Here Fidel revealed more than he intended, although his slip went largely unnoticed. The record shows that the upward movement of prices could be described as fluctuating around six cents from late February to mid-March at the latest, and that by the end of March it was fluctuating around seven cents. It also shows that the average (mean) price for April, the month before Fidel's arrival, was approximately seven and a half cents; and for May, the month of

4. Approximately 975,000 metric tons were delivered to the Soviet Union in 1963 (*Sugar Year Book*, p. 56). The readjusted price thus gave Cuba an additional $32.8 million. According to the earlier agreement (February 13, 1960), covering sugar sales from 1961–1964, the USSR would pay 20 percent in convertible currency and the rest in Soviet merchandise at "world prices." Hence, $6.5 million of the increase was in hard cash to be spent in capitalist markets. For practical purposes, as it turned out, the rest of the benefit was visible only in the clearing accounts where it appeared as a credit against a steadily mounting trade debt. Cuban imports from the USSR were determined by what Cuba needed and what the USSR could provide and not by the value of sugar deliveries. The convertible currency stipulations, in part, represented reimbursement for sugar production inputs available only in capitalist markets, although mainly they were a form of economic aid. This arrangement was continued in the new agreement of January 1964, covering the period of 1965–1970. During this period, due to the sharp decline of sugar prices on the world free-market, it provided Cuba with a significant proportion of its hard currency earnings.

his sojourn in the Soviet Union, the average rose to a shade under ten cents a pound.[5]

Hence, if Fidel is to be believed concerning the basis on which the six-cent price was chosen, the agreement must have taken place before mid-March. On the other hand, if Fidel is to be believed concerning the time when the Khrushchev "offer" was made, then the basis could not have been the April-May price of sugar on the open market. The chances are that the price of sugar was largely determined in the preliminary discussions that must have taken place between Havana and the Kremlin before Fidel's departure for Moscow. It must also have been more than a coincidence that the six-cent figure resembled one in an earlier Cuban trade agreement. Prior to Washington's embargo in 1960, the price of Cuba's sugar allotment on the American preferential market was 5.45 cents a pound,[6] which in most years represented a substantial premium over free-market prices. Now that Cuba had switched to the Soviet preferential market, with a long-term agreement in the offing, the starting point in a new price discussion would logically be the former price paid by the United States. Six cents would thus be the upper limit of a "reasonable historic" price, as the Russian economists could argue, while politically it looked good since it was somewhat better than the former American price. However, in 1963 six cents turned out to be over 25 percent less than the record annual average of 8.29 cents a pound. It was only in 1965, when the free-market price averaged 2.03 cents, and in the following years of normal and lower than normal prices [7] that the six-cent level looked good. By that time, Cuban deliveries of sugar were so far below the plan and the Cuban trade deficit with the USSR so far above it that the prac-

5. *Annual Report and Accounts for the Year 1963* (London: International Sugar Council, Annex G. 1964), p. 19. The price reached 5.92 cents per pound on February 7, dropped to 5.86 on February 20, rose to 6.09 on February 25, and stayed well above 6 cents until mid-August, resuming its upward movement in early September. After March 15, when the steadily rising price reached 6.26 cents and a continuing climb could easily be predicted, by no stretch of the imagination could it be said that the price was fluctuating around 6 cents a pound.

6. Leví Marrero, *Geografía de Cuba* (Havana: Editorial Selecta, 1957), p. 240.

7. *Sugar Year Book*, p. 362.

tical importance of the six-cent price, as earlier noted, was restricted to the 20 percent paid in hard currency.

Thus, in his television account Fidel tried to elevate an expedient politico-economic transaction to the level of high socialist virtue. That he felt impelled to twist the facts is almost a certain confirmation that some hard bargaining did take place. Further confirmation was his inordinate display of outrage that the "enemy" had accused him of such conduct. On this point the record is clear. Fidel did pay a political price for what he received from Khrushchev, though not a big price in terms of what he received, and not as big a price as it first appeared to be. He had managed a deal that was binding on the Russians but from which he could, in a large measure, withdraw, as he later proved. But at the time, he clearly did not in any way anticipate that he would again fall out with the Russians. He was therefore extremely anxious to preserve the image he had built up of himself as an independent, principled, revolutionary leader. It was an important part of his stock in trade, both among his own people and radicals throughout the world.

When the next dramatic reconciliation with the Russians occurred, in an unusually labored and entangled argumentation (speech of August 23, 1968), Fidel again insisted that he had made no compromise with principle. This time, however, his attempt to save face was obviously and completely cynical. Coming after two years of sharp denunciation of Soviet foreign policy, after Che Guevara's Bolivian debacle in October 1967, and after the precarious situation of the Cuban economy in mid-1968, his turnabout was less a deal, as in 1963, than a surrender. In addition, in 1968 the issue on which he sacrificed principle—the right of small countries, including socialist countries, to self-determination and national sovereignty—far transcended the political and ideological accommodations he made in 1963.

A Problem of Extreme Urgency

Having disposed of the question of the new price for Cuban sugar on the Soviet market (shortly to be adopted by all of Cuba's socialist customers), Fidel went on to explain that much more was involved in his discussions with the chairman, both about sugar and a broad range of economic questions. With respect to sugar, he informed Khrushchev that "we had a problem of extreme urgency and difficulty to solve, . . . the question of cutting sugarcane with machinery." Fidel was right. After the Revolution, the professional cane-cutting labor force became seriously depleted as easier and better paid job opportunities opened up in public works, construction, new industries, and custodial and other menial services for the mammoth bureaucracies that had sprung up almost overnight. Already volunteer cane cutters had been mobilized to assist in harvests. Some were more or less willing volunteers and others, in effect, were drafted; but they all had one thing in common: they cut cane slowly and poorly. In addition, they continued to receive their normal wages while on sugar harvest leave from their jobs, wages that on the average were several times higher than what the professional fulltime cane cutters were earning. At the same time, the government had to foot the bill for transporting, feeding, and housing the volunteers, in many cases equipping them with boots and gloves, and providing medical care. Accidents and illness were much more frequent than in the case of the hardy old-timers. Finally, time taken off by the volunteers from their normal occupations could not be fully compensated by placing extra loads on the staffs remaining on the job. Thus, the real cost of producing sugar was extremely difficult to calculate. It was possible that even at six cents a pound, it was produced at a loss.

Socially and ideologically, the government probably derived some benefit from using amateurs in the cane fields (until later years when almost the entire able-bodied male population was compelled to endure long and hard stints in the cane fields, under military discipline). The mobilization was portrayed as an exercise in selfless patriotism and as a step in the creation of "the new socialist man." Another by-product, less glamorous, was the fact that the system helped break down the rigid separation between rural and urban cultures and between manual and nonmanual labor, characteristic of prerevolutionary Cuba and most underindustrialized societies. However, all of this was a way of converting necessity into a virtue. What mainly concerned Fidel when he contemplated returning to sugar as the chief source, for years to come, of the funds with which to develop a prosperous socialist Cuba was how to produce sugar efficiently and more abundantly. For this, the mechanization of all field work, and particularly cane cutting, was the crucial factor.

"And in solving this problem," Fidel continued, "the Soviet

government and especially comrade Khrushchev took an extraordinary interest. Khrushchev has great experience in agricultural matters, . . . in machinery. . . . So I shouldn't have been surprised, as I was, when he himself, as we discussed the characteristics of sugarcane and different types of agricultural machinery, came up with an idea for designing a single machine that would both cut the cane and lift it at the same time."

Fidel went on to explain how Khrushchev spent a whole day working on this problem, and then organized a team of top specialists to go into all the details and produce a blueprint for the mass production of these machines. "All the technological and industrial resources of the Soviet Union have been mobilized to solve this problem," he added. Fidel, who has always had a predeliction for dramatic breakthroughs and miracle-producing shortcuts in solving the most difficult problems, was clearly carried away by the magnitude and grandeur of this crash program. Moreover, this time he was moved by more than a personal brainstorm. According to Fidel, the chairman himself had promised that, "without the slightest doubt, no later than two years from now the problem of mechanizing the sugar harvest will be completely solved." And, indeed, who could doubt it? As comrade Khrushchev explained, continued Fidel quoting him verbatim, "We have solved the problems of cosmic travel; how can we fail to construct machines for harvesting sugarcane, which is an incomparably simpler problem?"

For Fidel and his now spellbound listeners it was a beautiful and inspiring vision. Soon there would be no need for volunteers to work to exhaustion under the blazing sun. Instead of hundreds of thousands of men wielding machetes, a couple of thousand combines would go zipping through the green stalks, cutting, trimming, and lifting the cane as they went, dumping it at intervals in trucks that would haul it to the mills. One could even imagine the combine operators comfortably seated in air-conditioned cabs. In subsequent discussions, Fidel would predict that only 20,000 men would be needed to harvest enough cane to produce ten million tons of sugar. "Just imagine what it will mean," he finally exclaimed, "when the news will reach Latin America [where they will still be cutting cane by hand] that we have completely mechanized our sugarcane agriculture!"

The Power of the Imagination

Only the rare chance that brought together two minds whose great imaginative powers were equaled by their naiveté in matters of agricultural technology, and whose leadership role in their respective countries gave them immunity from discouragement by experts, could account for the wild optimism concerning the mechanization of Cuban sugar harvests. It was as if Khrushchev, who had never seen sugarcane growing, was thinking about wheat and Castro, ignorant about wheat which is not grown in Cuba, failed sufficiently to impress on his host and benefactor the special characteristics of Cuban sugarcane. Unlike the even alignment of sugarcane as, for example, in Louisiana and Australia, where practically the entire crop is cut by machine (a recent achievement in Australia), in Cuba the great bulk of the cane grows in dense, massive clusters and frequently not on level ground.[8] Hence, a more realistic approach would have called for adapting Cuban sugarcane culture to meet the requirements of existing mechanical cane harvesters, without the need of

8. The experience of Hawaii provides perspective on the Cuban problem. In Hawaii, where much of the sugarcane grows in tangled clumps, similar to those in Cuba, the typical method of harvesting, after burning the cane fields to eliminate the foliage, is by a "bulldozer that merely pushes the cane with a rake that shears off the cane at ground level," as described by Frederic Middleton, chief engineer of the Hawaiian Sugar Planters' Association. However, this system results in considerable sugar and soil losses. Consequently, over the past twenty years the association has been developing "a harvester to cut and pick up cane in the field similar to other harvesters in the world [e.g., the Australian machine and the one Khrushchev dreamed of building]." Although in use by some companies in Hawaii, it has not been widely adopted "due to the complexity of the machine relative to the bulldozer and also due to the much higher cost of operating than the bulldozer push rake. Our efforts will continue on harvester improvements as well as reduction of losses with the standard push rake system. . . . Still, it will take a lot of development to surpass our present system in spite of the high losses involved." (The information from Mr. Middleton was received in a letter to me dated December 22, 1970, at Honolulu.) Thus, Khrushchev promised to produce in two years a type of machine that in Hawaii has been under development for twenty years and apparently is still less than satisfactory. And Khrushchev's harvester took on the additional handicap of attempting to cut unburned cane.

inventing new equipment.[9] However, this would have been a complex, tedious process, probably stretching into a number of years. It would have conflicted with the goal of rapid advancement with moderate investment, and it would have been unworthy of socialist ingenuity in the age of the sputnik.

Watching Fidel on the television in the privacy of my apartment in Havana, I smiled broadly when Fidel quoted Nikita on the relative difficulty of solving space problems and building a proper sugarcane harvester. It was the classical trap into which amateurs fell when extolling the wonders of the Soviet technology and economy. I recalled during a stay in Moscow coming across an article in a San Francisco Communist publication by the one-time well-known American novelist, Michael Gold. The author was chiding Mayor George Christopher of San Francisco, who, on returning from a visit to the Soviet Union in 1960 or thereabouts, reported that the new dwellings going up like mushrooms in Moscow were shoddily built. This was true and easily verified. A Russian wag had said, "Our new apartment buildings have never known the bloom of youth; they are born old and decrepit." "Now Mr. Mayor," Gold wrote, "do you mean to tells us that the people who put sputniks in orbit around the earth don't know how to hang a door correctly?" The fact, of course, was that the development of space technology—a very advanced but also narrow field of specialization—once it was given top priority by the Soviet state and thereby supported by the most qualified human and most abundant material resources at its command, was incomparably easier than creating a modern, mass construction industry involving, in addition to other complexities, the training and management of hundreds of thousands of unskilled workers.[10]

9. After the disastrous experience of the hand-cut giant harvest of 1970, something of this approach was adopted and resulted in the Cuban purchase, on an experimental basis, of twenty sugarcane harvesters from Australia. (Vancouver *Sun*, May 12, 1971.)

10. Foy Kohler, one-time American ambassador to the USSR, apropos this paradox very aptly remarks: "One cannot help being struck by the remarkable contrast of a society which produced better cosmonauts than mechanics, more sophisticated electronics than plumbing, better 'Sputniks' than automobiles." *Understanding the Russians: A Citizen's Primer*, New York: Harper & Row, 1970, p. xiv.

Theoretically, given top priority and unlimited resources, a harvester adapted to Cuban sugarcane fields might have been possible, which is another way of saying that, realistically, it was impossible. Thus, the Khrushchev machine never materialized. Fidel, nevertheless, went ahead with a great, irrational plan for the expansion of sugar production. The cane in the extended do-or-die militarized harvest, which ended in 1970, was cut by hand. Fidel had staked "the honor of the Revolution" on a goal of ten million tons of sugar, "not one ton less," but fell short by 1.5 million. It was the biggest harvest in Cuban history (in absolute but not in per capita terms), but it was also one of the least profitable. As Fidel himself explained, among its costs was a colossal 500,000 man-years of labor, that is, the equivalent of half a million individuals working for an entire year.[11] Compared with the decade preceding the Revolution, it represented more than double the expenditure of work per unit of sugar produced.[12] The losses that this labor drain inflicted on the rest of the Cuban economy could not be calculated, although there was no doubt that they were exceedingly heavy. Fidel only skimmed the surface when he revealed that milk production declined by 25 percent, delivery of steel by 38 percent, and cement output by 23 percent; and he gave similar data for a number of other activities.

The traumatic experience of the 1970 harvest, followed by a serious lag in the seven-million-ton production schedule for the 1971 harvest, led Fidel to announce on January 25, 1971, that henceforth all cane fields would be burned over to eliminate the foliage before cutting the stalks. The immediate purpose was to reduce the cane-cutting labor force from "300,000 to 100,000," since burned-over cane could be cut more easily and rapidly than green cane. At

11. *Granma*, August 24, 1970.
12. With a sugar production of 8.5 million tons and, according to the Cuban census of 1970 (the first since 1953), a population of 8.5 million in 1970, per capita output was one ton. In 1952, when the previous record of 7.2 million tons was produced and the population numbered 5.8 million, per capita output was 1.24 tons. In the 1950s, on the average, a labor force of 500,000 working for three months produced 5 million tons (see Leví Marrero, *Geografía*, p. 225). This comes to 40 tons per man-year. In the 1970 harvest, 500,000 persons working for twelve months produced 8.5 million tons. This amounts to 17 tons per man-year.

the same time he stated that "there is no machine that can cut cane unless it is first burned. . . . We cannot . . . mechanize cane harvesting . . . unless we burn over the cane fields." [13]

For all practical purposes, Fidel was right (Louisiana cane fields are perhaps the only important exception) and his announcement was hailed by *Granma* as a great discovery, although the facts about burning were easily available in 1963. However, Fidel was still not out of the woods, as he himself realized when he pointed out the problems created by the burning method. The most serious one was the need for a very high degree of coordination in cutting the cane immediately after burning, transporting it to the mills, and grinding it in the shortest possible time. The reason is that burned cane, before and especially after cutting, loses its sugar content much more rapidly than unburned cane. Coordination, precisely, had been one of the weakest points in the harvests of recent years. Other problems included the need for much larger quantities of fertilizer and for the frequent replanting of cane. New cane, however, could bring dividends through the use of higher yielding varieties maturing at different periods of the growing season and properly aligned for machine cutting, which Fidel implied was still his goal but in some unspecified future.

Thus, the great vision of Castro and Khrushchev in 1963, unmentionable since 1965, was finally buried in 1971. There would be no mechanical harvester for some time to come. It was still premature, for reasons that Fidel should have grasped years before and for others that only an accumulation of bitter experience might reveal. For as an unusually keen observer pointed out, following a visit to Cuba and a bit of reading on the subject, given the general state of the Cuban economy and what he called "the fascination with technological innovation combined with supreme disdain for cost-accounting and all other kinds of economic calculation" and given the low motivation and low productivity of labor which in early 1971 Fidel highlighted as Cuba's most serious problem, in these conditions the mechanical harvester could not be expected to pay its way:

Experimentation with mechanical cane cutters seems to have been promoted by the belief that the low efficiency of labor could be

13. *Gramma Weekly Review*, January 31, 1971.

compensated for by large-scale use of sophisticated automatic equipment. . . . Such hope is hardly justified. Careless handling and poor maintenance of machinery, buildings, and all other kinds of fixed capital goods is one of the surest signs of an insufficiently motivated labor force. So long as moral incentives continue to work as badly as they apparently have up to now, large-scale introduction of costly new equipment might aggravate the economic difficulties of Cuba instead of alleviating them.[14]

Relations with the United States

Toward the end of his report, Fidel linked up the glowing prospects for Cuba's economic growth with his new estimate of Cuba's situation vis-à-vis the United States. Cuba, he explained, was now practically immune from any kind of major attack. The Soviet nuclear protection was "a solid shield," and then he repeated, "solid, solid, and we had an opportunity to see it and size it up." In addition, there was a further Soviet guarantee: "Our armed forces will be maintained in optimum combat condition . . . in case of imperialist aggression." As a result, "at the present time our country can count on a very high level of security, and this gives us the possibility of dedicating a great part of our energy to the building of our economy."

As Fidel described it, a new era had dawned, which called for another look at relations with the United States: "As we declared on many occasions and at the meeting in the Lenin Stadium, we are ready to normalize relations, if they want to. . . . If they don't want to, we can wait indefinitely, we are not in a hurry." Actually, Fidel was calling for a fresh start. Along with the expected ritualistic flag waving in which he claimed that American policy toward Cuba was "bankrupt" and that Cuba had "triumphed," there was a message to Washington that was not difficult to decipher: the time for negotiation had come and we could make it worth your while.[15]

14. Wassily Leontief, "The Trouble with Cuban Socialism," *New York Review of Books*, January 7, 1971, p. 21.
15. *I. F. Stone's Weekly* of June 10, 1963 reported: "On the eve of his trip to the Soviet Union, so we are informed by a trustworthy source, Fidel Castro went to the Swiss Embassy in Havana, which represents U.S. interests there, and proposed that he visit Switzerland on his return from Moscow for a discussion of how Cuban-American relations might be improved. . . . The Swiss were ready to act as hosts but the State

There was another intriguing part of the message. At the very end of his remarks on Cuban-American relations, and with clear reference to them, Fidel pointedly explained that

> We discussed all problems, all questions and details with comrade Khrushchev. . . . We had the opportunity of reading many reports, of getting data, documents, and a tremendous amount of information, all of which contributed to providing us with a general understanding of the situation. . . . We can say with the greatest satisfaction in reply to the imperialists [who want us to break our ties with the Soviet Union] that all the conclusions we have reached are the result of conversations, discussions, . . . what we have seen and were given in the USSR.

There was thus a strong implication that Fidel's offer to negotiate was based on Soviet advice and had their approval. Was there also a hint that a settlement was no longer a matter of bilateral but of tripartite agreement and would be facilitated by direct Soviet participation in the negotiations?

The Chairman Extolled

If any further evidence were needed that Castro's visit to the Soviet Union marked what gave every appearance of being a great and definitive turning point in Cuban-Soviet relations, it was supplied by Fidel's inordinate praise of Khrushchev: "One of his characteristics is that he is an extraordinarily human individual." Fidel then went on in a great stream of superlatives: "Khrushchev at 69 years of age has an extraordinary mental energy, . . . not only great mental clarity, but great mental agility, . . . without doubt one of the

---

Department turned thumbs down" (p. 3). Later asked if he could identify his source, Mr. Stone replied by telephone (September 28, 1970) that it was "an individual with close contacts in White House circles." However this may be, it is entirely possible that Fidel did take this initiative. The story went on to say, "Castro's original itinerary was to have included Peking, Algeria and Sweden as well as Moscow. . . . We are told he wanted to visit Sweden for purposes of trade and to demonstrate his desire for close ties with the non-aligned world. . . . But the Swedish trip was dropped after the Swiss visit fell through. The Russians talked him out of a trip to Peking, and the visit to Ben Bella . . . was then also dropped in order to have a face-saving excuse for not visiting China."

most brilliant minds I have ever known. . . . As a militant revolutionary for many years, he represents a perfect combination of profound theoretical knowledge and great practical experience."

There followed a biographical sketch of the chairman, born in a peasant family, "a proletarian who emerged from the coal mines," a party leader in the Ukraine and then in Moscow, and a veteran of the battle of Volgograd. One could almost sense a feeling of envy by the Cuban revolutionary who, born with a silver spoon in his mouth, would never be able to acquire the credentials of a peasant or worker. "The Soviet people have a great affection for Khrushchev," he continued. "We could see it. We know something about these things because we've had a lot of contact with people, with the masses." However, something that impressed Fidel even more was the attitude of the party leaders toward the chairman. "There really exists a spirit of collective discussion there," he explained; "nevertheless, Khrushchev's authority and prestige are easily detected within this collective leadership. He speaks with great authority at high-level meetings. Everywhere he is received with great respect by party cadres and members, and by the people." Here, then, was an example, a model of leadership, for which Fidel had a natural affinity and which the Cuban people could recognize with pride as one already invented and functioning in their own country.

Another one of his host's outstanding virtues, according to Fidel, was that he was "a man of great honesty, of extraordinary honesty." Obviously addressing himself to Peking, although without saying so, Fidel stressed the importance of this virtue in estimating the position and intentions of Khrushchev "in all of the problems that are related to the unity of the socialist camp." Underscoring several times his opinion that Khrushchev was "a serious opponent of imperialism" and with equal emphasis the chairman's genuine and wholly laudable "preoccupation with the problems of preserving peace . . . and avoiding thermonuclear war," Fidel launched a great plea for the honest exchange of opinion, reasons, and arguments in the socialist camp, and with it he made an appeal—again principally meant for the Chinese—to trust Khrushchev.

"I am certain," he declared, "that comrade Khrushchev is a person with whom you can discuss things, on account of his general attitude and his willingness to listen. I speak from personal experience. I had a great many discussions with him, I observed how he took into consideration our points of view, the things we said . . . and how he would agree that we were right every time we gave him a solid argument."

As immoderate as was the praise that Fidel had heaped on the Soviet Union, in his panegyric to Khrushchev he had gone far above and beyond the call of duty. To be sure, with the memory of the October missile crisis and of the earlier purge of Escalante and his PSP cronies still vivid in Cuba, some warmth was required in attempting to rehabilitate the reputation of the Russians in general and of Khrushchev in particular, and in convincing the Cuban people that the new era of cooperation with the USSR would guarantee the security and welfare of the country and elevate the prestige of the Revolution. In addition, some special effort was needed to persuade the Chinese that Khrushchev was on the level, a most difficult task.[16]

Nevertheless, Fidel could have easily met his needs and obligations with a much more modest and prudent display of enthusiasm, one that would have been less damaging to his reputation later when his relations with the Soviet Union would take a sharp turn for the worse. How then does one explain Fidel's behavior? It is very simply that Fidel was expressing his real and genuine feelings, that it did not even cross his mind that relations with the Soviet Union could ever again deteriorate, that he was immensely pleased and flattered by the historical role he imagined he was playing to bring about the unification of the socialist camp, and that in keeping with his character he was carried away by his high spirits.

16. "The Chinese printed the joint Cuban-Soviet Declaration but not Castro's subsequent speech [of June 4]." Andrés Suárez, *Cuba: Castroism and Communism,* 1959–1966 (Cambridge, Mass.: M.I.T. Press, 1969), p. 183.

23

■

A Report to the People—III:

Concerning Journalism
and the Soviet Model
of Socialism

The Censure of *Revolución*

IT WAS GETTING LATE and Fidel had to postpone further details of the
Khrushchev portrait for "some other day," as he put it, but would
not leave the topic without mentioning what he claimed to be his
own reluctance to praise people excessively and stressing in particular the modesty in such matters practiced by the Soviet media.
"Very likely," he said, "in the Soviet Union they won't publish
what I've been saying [about the chairman] because generally
their policy is not to heap praise on their leaders." Alas, according
to the long-standing Soviet tradition, historically anchored in the
veneration accorded to the reigning czar, the glory heaped on Khrushchev was reproduced in full in the Soviet press and, ironically, in
¡Viva Cuba! only a short space removed from Fidel's unfortunate
prediction.[1]

However, Fidel's sudden and unaccustomed preoccupation with

1. In a commentary on Fidel's television report in *Pravda*, June 8,
reproduced by ¡Viva Cuba! pp. 186–188. According to Suárez, p. 183
(see chapter 22, n. 16), both *Pravda* and *Izvestiya* published the complete report on June 6 and 7, respectively.

the virtues of modesty was aimed at another target, for he at once launched into a sharp and for all but a handful of listeners a totally unexpected and astounding censure of *Revolución*, his own guerrilla newspaper, born in the mountains during the insurrection and edited by its creator and one of Fidel's closest collaborators, Carlos Franqui. "Sometimes we [our press] fall into the habit of excessive adulation. . . . And I myself was the victim of an exaggerated build-up during the time I was in the USSR," he went on to say with an injured air. "I almost blushed when I read the newspapers. . . . The way they praised me was immoderate—and I'll be more specific so that there'll be no doubt what I'm talking about—the newspaper was *Revolución*. I think it is important that I express this opinion, important for our people and for everybody." [2]

Puzzled by this unusual and, taken at face value, unfathomable public reprimand, I decided to examine the coverage of Fidel's trip in *Revolución* in search of a clue. I soon noted what prompted Fidel's displeasure. At this point a digression from the main chronology of our narrative is indicated.

The Arcocha Dispatches

At the time of Castro's visit to the USSR, the young translator and novelist Juan Arcocha,[3] at the time an ardent Fidelista, was the resident correspondent of *Revolución* in Moscow. Well educated, cosmopolitan in outlook but nationalist in feeling, with an alert and critical mind and a fine sense of humor, he typified the Cuban radical intellectual of Fidel's generation who, although without roots in Marxism and intensely hostile to Stalinism, accepted socialism and supported the Cuban-Soviet alliance on the premise that under Fidel there would be no Russification of Cuba. A top-notch journalist, Arcocha's eyewitness dispatches in *Revolución* on Fidel's adventures in the Soviet Union were frequently gems of perceptive reporting.

Knowing Fidel's informal and mischief-prone personal life style, on the one hand, and the extreme sensitivity of his hosts in matters

2. Fidel alluded to this matter at the beginning of his television performance, but without details, saying, "well, we won't discuss it now because it's not the place to discuss the problem." Apparently, he was uncertain of how to handle this delicate question, making up his mind as he went along.

3. Author of *A Candle in the Wind* (New York: Lyle Stuart, 1967).

of protocol and security, on the other, Arcocha was alert to the likelihood that Fidel's first night in the Kremlin would not pass without
some incident taking place that would deserve at least a footnote in
the history of Russo-Cuban relations. And so it was. Sunday night,
April 28, Fidel and a few of his Cuban companions finished their
dinner around ten o'clock. As Arcocha tells the story, Fidel decided it was too early to go to bed and suggested they go out for a
walk. A short time later they had left the Kremlin grounds and were
strolling toward the middle of Red Square.

"There was general consternation in the old palace," Arcocha
wrote.[4] "The servants went crazy and rushed up and down the cor-
ridors. Telephones rang in darkened offices in various parts of the
compound. The sentinels were suddenly jerked out of their boredom,
their eyes popping. What was going on? It was not in the program.
The worst of it was that nothing like this had ever happened before.
As a result they had no clear idea of what they ought to do."

As the Cubans were crossing Red Square, a breathless interpreter
caught up with them and with great excitement offered to show them
some rare Byzantine murals in one of the cathedrals on the Kremlin
grounds. By this time the word somehow had spread like wildfire
and a tremendous throng of Muscovites, who could scarcely believe
their eyes, had gathered around Fidel in the usually deserted Red
Square at that hour. A squad of police also suddenly appeared on the
scene, but before any serious shoving and pushing between the law
and the citizenry could take place, Fidel and his companions ducked
into the Hotel Moskva, "to the amazement of the few people in the
lobby at that hour which in Moscow is considered to be very late,"
Arcocha added so that the Cuban reader could better appreciate the
incongruity of the scene. The story ended with Fidel sneaking out
the back door, taking a cab, and joining an impromptu fiesta of
Cuban students and the main body of his delegation in their quarters at a nearby hotel, where he stayed until the early hours of the
morning.

In the same dispatch Arcocha describes another incident that
took place the next day. Coming out of Lenin's tomb escorted by a
group of high-ranking dignitaries, Fidel noticed in the distance that
Red Square was filled with people, held back by police barricades.
"Why don't we talk to these people?" Fidel asked and started off

4. *Revolución*, April 30, 1963.

without waiting for an answer. Seeing Fidel approach, people pressed forward and despite police reinforcements crashed through the barricades. Arcocha describes a bedlam of shouting and shoving by the police, interpreters, chauffeurs, protocol officials, and the masses chanting, "Fee-dell, Fee-dell." Castro tried to speak, but the noise and commotion were too great. Finally, he turned to the police and shouted, "Quit your shoving! If you'd stop pushing, the crowd wouldn't push either." When the interpreter got the message to the police, according to Arcocha, "the police looked at Fidel as if they were seeing visions." Eventually, Fidel made it back to his car and as he got in Arcocha noticed that he wore the grin of a roguish boy.

On May 10, *Revolución* published a dispatch sent by Arcocha from Tashkent:

> Fidel's greatest victory in the USSR, was achieved in his battle against protocol. . . . It is difficult for anyone who has not lived in this country to understand the tremendous impact that Fidel's "style" has had on the Soviet people, the simple and amiable manner of his behavior, his interest in human problems, and in the people who surround him. And above all, this habit of his, completely unheard of here, of improvising his speeches. . . . And he is moving across the Soviet Union like a real whirlwind. Until now foreign chiefs of state who had visited the USSR were people of a different type, solemn and governed by protocol, who were driven from place to place at high speed in black automobiles with curtains drawn.

It can be assumed that Arcocha was not completely "objective" with respect to the image of Fidel's impact on the Soviet Union that he wished to project. He valued the "humanist" elements, somewhat faded it was true, but still lurking just below the surface of Fidel's newly acquired Marxism-Leninism and setting him off from all other leaders in the socialist camp. Arcocha was also reacting against the deeply entrenched czarist and Stalinist patterns of behavior in the Soviet bureaucracy. Nevertheless, anyone who knew Fidel and his Cuba, and also the Soviet Union, immediately recognized that Arcocha had undoubtedly caught the real spirit behind the enthusiasm of the Soviet masses for the Cuban visitor. Unfortunately, in so doing Arcocha exposed some of the bleak reality of political life in the Soviet Union. Herein lay the sting in these dispatches that must have brought sharp cries of protest from the Kremlin.

A week or so later, *Revolución* printed a couple of dispatches from Leningrad that surely added considerably to the irritation of the Soviet propaganda watchdogs. "In Leningrad, yesterday was the day of apotheosis," wrote Arcocha in the issue of May 16. "Some old Bolsheviks who had watched the demonstrations in other cities on the television told me that they could only be compared to the way the masses responded to the presence of Lenin. . . . Nowadays the only receptions that come anywhere near are the ones the cosmonauts get." The next day's story from Leningrad was even more explicit: "When Fidel moved away, a little old man, his chest covered with medals, took out his handkerchief and rubbed his eyes which were bathed in tears. 'Why are you crying?' the reporter asked him. 'Because it has been a big day for me,' the old Bolshevik replied. 'Fidel is a great revolutionary.'" It was not necessary for Arcocha to add that the old Bolshevik was also mourning the unfulfilled promise of the Russian Revolution.

The Motives Behind the Censure

Thus, it was not a sudden onset of modesty that moved Fidel to make his extraordinary statement concerning *Revolución*. He was greatly annoyed with the newspaper for disturbing the deep harmony achieved in Cuban-Soviet relations; for the Kremlin, extremely sensitive about such matters, must have made sure that Fidel was aware of its indignation. Hence, to begin with, he felt obliged to appease the Kremlin and this, he decided, required a public reprimand of the newspaper. However, it had to be handled in a manner that would not draw attention to the real reason for the reprimand, which would have further spread Arcocha's "poison" among the Cubans and would have revealed that Fidel was yielding to Russian pressure.[5]

5. This incident can serve as an example of the problems involved in deciphering Castro's speeches, a principal source of information about the Cuban Revolution. In this case his attack on the newspaper was sufficiently awkward—which is no reflection on his skill since the situation itself was very awkward—to raise doubt concerning Fidel's credibility in even a moderately sophisticated listener or reader. However, only someone with a professional interest would invest the time and effort

At the same time, if we recall the extraordinary warmth of his anniversary message to *Hoy* and his ostentatious praise of *Pravda*, an additional and perhaps deeper motivation for his criticism of *Revolución* is suggested. This was not the first troublesome incident in which Franqui's newspaper had been involved. Two years earlier, intellectual Havana was rocked by the crisis of *Lunes* [Monday] *de Revolución*, a weekly literary supplement that *Revolución* had been publishing since mid-1959. Enthusiastically eclectic and antidogmatic within a wide leftist spectrum, it published writings by Jean-Paul Sartre, Albert Camus, André Breton, and Trotsky, as well as Marx, Lenin, early Soviet classics, and Cuban vanguard poets, novelists, and critics.

The Russians, at the time already deeply committed in Cuba, were understandably disturbed. So was the Consejo Nacional de Cultura, a quasi ministry for cultural affairs controlled by the old Communists, which set out to destroy *Lunes*. On June 30, 1961, with the struggle between the two opposing cultural-ideological factions getting out of hand, Fidel decided to intervene. Declaring that he was against imposing a "cultural" line on intellectuals supporting the Revolution, he settled the quarrel with the dictim: "For those within the Revolution, full freedom; for those opposed to the Revolution, no freedom." At the time, it was hailed by the antidogmatists "within the Revolution" and radical intellectual circles outside Cuba as a blow against neo-Stalinist obscurantism. However, Fidel also suppressed *Lunes*, giving other than ideological reasons for doing so. Because of their confidence in Fidel, whom they considered to be "one of their own," the backers of *Lunes* accepted Fidel's decision as one based on pragmatic considerations that would not affect principle.[6]

Now, in June 1963, Fidel was still bothered with the same problem but in a more serious form. The foreign policy of the Revolu-

---

needed to discover what lay behind the incident. On the other hand, an unsophisticated or inexperienced person, or one predisposed by political conviction to accept anything Fidel says at face value, would simply swallow Fidel's mystification without further thought. Castro over the years has built up a great reputation for candor in his speeches, which has been only partly justified, for it frequently has been a calculated, tactical candor.

6. For the best account of this incident, see K. S. Karol, *Les guérilleros au pouvoir* (Paris: Robert Laffont, 1970), pp. 238–242.

tion had been compromised at a particularly inopportune juncture. Thus, by attacking "his own" newspaper, Fidel had also issued a stern warning to those writers "within the Revolution," or those who wished to remain there, that the Revolution was entering a new era of political, ideological, and cultural responsibility and discipline, to match the responsibility and discipline that would henceforth prevail in the advancement of the economy. It was a drastic decision. Carlos Franqui was sacrificed and Juan Arcocha left Cuba.[7] Although it was to take time before Fidel could effectively tame his intellectuals, it seemed to be an inevitable process. Fidel, for all his earlier humanist intellectual traditions, was now running a large corporation or conglomerate known as socialist Cuba. He was, so to speak, in business, with a payroll to meet, property to protect, production to supervise, sales to promote, public relations to manage, and so forth—an enterprise in which all his personal "capital" had been irrevocably invested. The interests of the business, as he saw them, determined what was good or bad, permissible or proscribed. Thus, as time went on, he became increasingly impatient with his intellectuals; although they served him well in the past and were still supporters of his business, they did so as intellectuals, that is, as practitioners to one extent or another of their traditional critical functions.

Che Guevara also became impatient with Cuban intellectuals.

7. The announcement that Franqui had been replaced as editor of *Revolución* was printed in the issue of September 23, 1963. Apparently he had not been functioning as an editor for some time before that, possibly since Castro's television reprimand. No reason for his separation was given, nor was it accompanied by any expression of commendation or gratitude for his outstanding contribution to Fidel's insurrection and his new regime. Franqui remained "within the Revolution" and performed odd jobs for Fidel, such as purchasing books in France, negotiating with an Italian firm for the publication of Fidel's projected but unrealized autobiography, and serving as liaison with the new left French intellectuals at times when Castro and the Kremlin were estranged. Arcocha, relieved of his Moscow assignment, continued to work for *Revolución* in Cuba for several months, then left for Europe. On the staff of UNESCO at its Paris headquarters (as of mid-1970), Arcocha technically also remained "within the Revolution," although he has lived and worked abroad continuously since early 1964. In 1971, as will be explained in a later chapter, both Franqui and Arcocha publicly broke their ties with Fidel.

Typically (and unlike Fidel), he "theorized" about the problem. In an essay entitled Socialism and Man in Cuba, published in Havana in April 1965, Che wrote of the "hidden meaning behind the word 'freedom' " as "a reflexion in consciousness of bourgeois idealism . . . frequently maintained" among intellectuals supporting the Revolution. While deploring the attempt made in other countries "to combat these tendencies with an exaggerated dogmatism," his final verdict against the freedom-obsessed intellectuals in Cuba was harsh and could have met the approval of Andrei Aleksandrovitch Zhdanov, Stalin's cultural hatchetman in the late 1940s. "To summarize," Che declared, "the culpability of many of our intellectuals and artists lies in their original sin; they are not authentic revolutionaries. . . . The new generations will arrive free of original sin." [8]

Evaluation

Looking back, it can be safely assumed that the major points in the agreement between the two countries had been decided before Fidel set out on his trip; and in any case, negotiations could have been concluded through normal trade and diplomatic channels. Thus, as we have seen, there was a special purpose in the trip. Fidel accepted Khrushchev's invitation for two reasons: (1) because more than a routine declaration of reconciliation was needed after the hard feelings generated by the earlier Escalante affair and Fidel's bitter resentment, broadcast to the world, over Soviet conduct during the missile crisis; and (2) because the honors he anticipated receiving in the USSR would, on the surface at least, prove that Cuban independence was not sacrificed by the reconciliation.

A significant demonstration of independence was, as previously noted, the conspicuous absence in Fidel's entourage of a single person identified with the former PSP. Considering the occasion and the skills of many old Communists—for example, men like Blas Roca or Carlos Rafael Rodríguez—this omission could not have been accidental. However, at a certain point during the visit he must have regretted the decision, the meaning of which was not lost on the Russians; for he had changed his mind about the Soviet Union in

8. Ronaldo E. Bonachea and Nelson P. Valdes, eds. Che: Selected Works of Ernesto Guevara (Cambridge, Mass.: M.I.T. Press, 1969), pp. 164, 166.

situ, so to speak. It was not only an ally that ensured Cuban survival, but he had unexpectedly discovered the true power and the real virtues of socialism as practiced in the Soviet Union. Whereas before his trip he had been skeptical about the Soviet model of socialism, he had now become truly convinced it was a good and efficient model, a worthy economic, political, and intellectual model, and he would strive to emulate it in Cuba.

This was how Fidel frequently made important decisions and later unmade them. It could be almost on the spur of the moment and with little or no consultation. What seemed to move Fidel during his stay in the Soviet Union was the need he felt and expressed from time to time for his own and the Cuban life styles to become more orderly and more efficient. Here, the example of what he was shown was extremely impressive. There seemed to be another factor as well—his reaction to the extraordinary tribute that the Russians paid to the Cuban Revolution and his personal leadership. "When the name, the cause, and the flag of a very small country are received [with respect, admiration, and affection] by hundreds of millions of people," he remarked early in his television report on June 4, "I can tell you that you get a tremendous feeling of national pride." And he confessed the same kind of satisfaction over the personal attention he received from the head of one of the world's two great superpowers. "Comrade Khrushchev," he said, "devoted a great deal of time to us; you can say he devoted almost the entire forty days . . . that we were there. . . . He treated our whole delegation with unusual cordiality." Probably he could relish this experience even more, thinking back to his visit to Washington in April 1959, when shortly before his arrival President Eisenhower ostentatiously left town for an extended period of golf.

Finally and perhaps most important, there was the forty-day exposure to the Khrushchevian magic. Surrounded mainly by associates slower witted than himself, and whom in any case he dominated by virtue of his supreme authority, Fidel since coming to power had not experienced the challenge of a demonstrably superior intellect, supported by a strong and ebullient personality and buttressed by decades of important experience. In Khrushchev, Fidel met his match, or rather more than his match. The new-found and enormous admiration he expressed for the chairman was entirely sincere.

Later, when disillusionment with the Soviet Union again struck

Fidel, his admiration for Khrushchev turned to resentment. The chairman had taken advantage of his inexperience and had used him to promote Soviet foreign policy and to bolster his personal position in the party Presidium. In addition, the chairman had "sold him a bill of goods" that turned out to be defective: Fidel's offer to negotiate with the United States was ignored; peaceful coexistence did not prevent American intervention in Santo Domingo or American bombing of North Vietnam; the lull in the Sino-Soviet conflict in the spring of 1963 was the prelude not to the settlement of the quarrel but to its aggravation; and, of course, the miraculous sugarcane harvester was sheer fancy.

Thus, in the years that followed Khrushchev's ouster, Fidel was less than chivalrous in his treatment of his fallen idol. In a conversation with Herbert Matthews in October 1967, he called him *torpe* several times, a term Matthews translated as "clumsy" but which carries connotations of stupidity.[9] A few months earlier, in an interview with the French journalist K. S. Karol, Fidel raked the ex-chairman over the coals. "He was a man who really had no principles," Karol quoted him as saying and went on to mention that Fidel told him that he considered Kosygin "more interesting and more serious" than Khrushchev, a comparison that perhaps carried even more malice than his reference to Khrushchev's lack of principle.[10]

9. Matthews, *Fidel Castro* (New York: Simon and Schuster, 1969), p. 225.
10. Karol, *Les guérilleros au pouvoir*, p. 342.

24
■

The Tenth Anniversary of Moncada

Assets and Liabilities for the New Year

On January 2, 1964, the day after the fifth anniversary of the fall of Batista, the editorial on the second page of *Revolución* exuded joy and optimism. The headline above the text read "JANUARY, MONTH OF EUPHORIA"; and in the body of the text Cubans were told, "There are well-founded hopes that international tension will diminish."

The editorial quite faithfully reflected the mood in high quarters and low, yet it seemed strange because many events in the months since Castro's return from Russia gave little promise that the New Year would dawn in an aura of high spirits and expectations. Relations between Cuba and the United States appeared on the surface to be getting worse, not better, and in Havana the assassination of President Kennedy raised fears of further deterioration. There were signs of friction between Havana and Moscow as the glow of Fidel's triumphal reception in the USSR began to fade. The most destructive hurricane in Cuban history devastated Oriente Province. Finally, despite Fidel's stern admonishment in his early June television appearance, a cultural-ideological dogfight of major proportions broke out in Havana.

On the other hand, there were also grounds for satisfaction. There was no real threat to Cuban security. Cuban-inspired or directly promoted guerrilla activity was spreading in Latin America. The Cuban-Algerian partnership was blooming, promising a profitable political relationship. Trade with capitalist countries was picking up despite increasing American efforts to prevent it. The Chinese continued to be friendly, which meant that Fidel still had this source of leverage in his dealings with Moscow. And last but not least, the phenomenal rise in the price of sugar replenished the coffers of the National Bank with great quantities of convertible currency, which in turn provided the wherewithal for a grand splurge of holiday feasting throughout the length and breadth of the island.

July 26, 1963: The Tenth Anniversary

What could be taken as Washington's reply to Castro's thinly veiled normalization signals came shortly after his return from Moscow. On July 3 the council of the OAS approved a series of recommendations aimed at curbing "Castro-Communist" subversion in the western hemisphere. Then, on July 8, citing OAS recommendations, the United States Treasury Department ordered all Cuban assets in United States banks (about $33 million) to be frozen and forbade the transfer of American dollars to and from Cuba, either directly or through third countries. Meanwhile, the Cuban press reported new incidents of counterrevolutionary agents killed or captured in the attempt to infiltrate the island. The responsibility for these incidents was invariably attributed to the United States government.

Such was the climate of Cuban-American relations when Fidel once more addressed the multitudes on July 26 in Havana's ample Plaza de la Revolución. It was the tenth anniversary of the attack on the Moncada barracks in Santiago. Hence, it was a special occcasion, the celebration of the first decade of Cuba's on-going Revolution, as Fidel liked to think of it. There were scores of foreign delegations from far and near—from the Soviet-bloc countries, from China and Algeria, from friendly nations of Africa and Asia, from fraternal parties of Western Europe and Latin America; and there was even a contingent of American students (including two or three on the FBI payroll, as was later revealed) who had defied the State Department ban on travel to Cuba. Alternately sweltering and then mercifully drenched by sudden rainfall as they sat in the grandstand behind Fidel, at the base of the gigantic prerevolutionary monument to Martí, their presence told Fidel that Cuba's fame transcended even Moscow's mighty month-long tribute, and that Cuba's place in the sun (and his own) was secure.

The setting and the circumstances must have stirred all the hopes, fantasies, and audacity that had carried him along in his quest for the salvation of Cuba and Latin America, and the glory of achieving it. He had even brought to the celebration his recently ailing mother, a pious old lady from Oriente Province, to witness his triumph. Ten years earlier to the day, she had wept when the news of Moncada first reached her, presuming that he had been killed.[1] It was thus a curious speech he gave that day, one might say almost schizophrenic, as he oscillated between his commitment to the guidelines of the Soviet-Cuban joint declaration two months earlier and his impatience with the constraints they imposed.

In Praise of the Soviet Union

His praise for the Soviet Union and its decisive role in ensuring the survival of the Cuban Revolution was unconditional. "The devastating power of the Soviet Union," he declared, is what placed "Yankee imperialism . . . [in] a very difficult situation because it can neither go to war nor can it prevent the revolution of the peoples." By sheer coincidence, the Anglo-American-Soviet nuclear test-ban agreement

1. Señora Lina Ruz viuda de Castro died suddenly eleven days after appearing with Fidel at the Plaza. She was staying at his younger sister Juanita's home in the Miramar suburb of Havana prior to returning to Oriente. The news was reported on the front page, bordered in black, of *Revolución* (August 7). The next day the paper carried a report of the burial in Marcané, Oriente Province, not far from Fidel's birthplace, and where his father had been buried seven years earlier. The report named Fidel, Raúl, and other members of the family and close relatives who attended the funeral. Missing or unidentified was Fidel's fourteen-year-old son, Fidelito, who had accompanied his father in his triumphal entry to Havana after the fall of Batista. Some time lafer he was secretly placed in a school under an assumed name and disappeared from public sight. Fidel and the boy's mother, who under pressure from her conservative family had turned against her husband, were divorced in late 1954 or early 1955, while Fidel was in prison on the Isle of Pines. The funeral of Fidel's mother was the last time any mention of Fidel's private life was made in the Cuban media. Juanita Castro's spectacular defection in Mexico in 1964 was unreported, although the news circulated in Cuba when it was featured in Spanish language radio broadcasts from Florida, which regularly bombard the island and penetrate the jamming screen. Data concerning Fidel's personal life up to the time of taking power are found in Luis Conte Agüero, *Fidel Castro: Vida y Obra*, Havana: Editorial Lex, 1959.

had been announced on July 25, the day before Fidel's speech. No doubt Khrushchev had discussed with him the eventuality of this agreement, since the tripartite negotiations were already well along at the time of Fidel's visit to the Soviet Union. One can imagine Fidel explaining to Nikita his reluctance to become a signatory while the United States was conducting economic, political, and paramilitary warfare against Cuba. In any event, Fidel in his address incorporated the news with considerable tact. Without promising to sign, he broadcast to the world his opinion that the agreement was "a victory for the peace-loving conscience of the world and a victory for the peace policy of the Soviet Union." Khrushchev could have no objection to this statement. Five days later its value for the Russians was greatly enhanced when the Chinese came out with a blistering denunciation of Moscow for having perpetrated "a big fraud to fool the people of the world." [2]

Flattering though a bit worrisome to the Russian dignitaries [3] sitting behind Fidel was his assurance that "We know, by experience and conviction, that any people which does what the Cuban people have done will have the complete support of the Soviet Union." And what has that support meant for Cuba? he asked. "It has been such an extraordinary aid that possibly what they gave us in a year is larger than the aid that imperialism has given to all the oligarchies put together." Without pursuing the somewhat vague comparison, he went on to mention fishing boats and commercial aircraft supplied by the Soviets, the new thermoelectric plants they were building, and the fact that "they are going to solve our country's problem of mechanizing the cutting of sugarcane . . . which in the future will permit us to have enormous harvests. . . . And the Soviet Union is solving this problem, at the cost of great effort and sacrifice."

2. Chinese government statement on test-ban treaty, July 31, 1963. Cited by William E. Griffith, The Sino-Soviet Rift (Cambridge, Mass.: M.I.T. Press, 1964), p. 326. Later, Cuba's refusal to sign the treaty was explained in sharper terms, more in line with the Chinese position.

3. The Soviet twelve-man delegation was headed by Alexei Fyodorov, minister of social security of the Ukranian Soviet Republic, probably chosen because he was a famous forest guerrilla leader during World War II. Nevertheless, the delegation also had political weight because it included Pavel Satyukov, editor-in-chief of Pravda, and Alexei Adzhubei, editor-in-chief of Izvestiya and Khrushchev's son-in-law.

The Example of Canada

Once more, Fidel echoed his previous invitation for normalizing relations with the United States, again invoking the example of Cuban-Canadian coexistence: "We said that we are ready to discuss. Well, we are ready to discuss formulas for indemnification [of expropriated properties] as we did with the Canadians. Our relations with them can be considered as a model of relations between a socialist and a capitalist country . . . and any difference between us we've always been able to settle in a friendly way."

Good relations with Canada was to become a recurring theme, even after Fidel abandoned his coexistence overtures to the United States. Canada became an important source of supplies for Cuba, including all its wheat and flour (purchased and shipped directly to Cuba by the Soviet Union in Soviet boats) and practically all the blooded breeding stock for an overly ambitious—and low yielding, as it turned out—meat and dairy development project. Canada was also the source of unrecorded quantities and varieties of industrial equipment produced in the United States or American branch plants and exported to Cuba via clandestine routes by commercially motivated and well-rewarded Canadian entrepreneurs.

Mention of Quebec separatist, to say nothing of "revolutionary liberation," movements was taboo in the Cuban press. When in late 1970, Cuba granted asylum to the Quebec terrorists responsible for the kidnapping of the Montreal-based British trade commissioner, in a celebrated case in which the captive was released in exchange for a one-way direct flight from Montreal to Havana for his captors, the Cuban government, in an official statement, took pains to make crystal clear that Cuba consented to provide asylum solely at the request of the Canadian government.[4]

As Fidel warmed up to the theme of good relations with capitalist countries, he spoke hopefully of Britain and Switzerland. "And we also explained to the British ambassador," he added, "that we are ready to discuss . . . some kind of economic agreement that would

4. According to a Havana dispatch by Patrick Nagle (*Vancouver Sun*, December 15, 1970), "The Cuban government does not want them [French-Canadian refugees] in the country. They are an embarrassment to current foreign policy."

include indemnification for properties that were nationalized. And the same goes for the Swiss." This was true. Sugar was in short supply on the world market; the price of sugar had gone sky high; and Washington was clearly having no success, outside of Latin America, with its pressures to recruit other countries to join the embargo on trade with Cuba. It was the right moment to settle accounts. Shell was paid off and an arrangement was worked out to liquidate Cuba's prerevolutionary debt to Switzerland. It was a sensible policy. It circumvented the Americans but could also serve as a convincing example of the right path to follow. It was consistent with the Soviet-Cuban orientation agreed on by Khrushchev and Castro, of working for détente in international affairs and concentrating all Cuban energy on internal economic development.

Dr. Jekyll and Mr. Hyde

Thus, the burly Soviet dignitaries seated behind Fidel, had they known the work of Robert Louis Stevenson, could have said in retrospect that this was the Cuban prime minister speaking in his Dr. Jekyll incarnation, while for half of the speech, if not more, it was Mr. Hyde who took possession of the sweating and gesticulating prime minister on that humid day. Fidel speaking as Mr. Hyde gave the impression that he had never been to Moscow or that he had repudiated most of the Soviet-Cuban joint declaration. Certainly Vice-Minister of Defense General Lio Ya Lau and the rest of the Chinese delegation on the platform behind Fidel must have been encouraged to think so. The Chinese had adopted an attitude of patience and forbearance following the great Russo-Cuban reconciliation. They must have noted with satisfaction that the full text of the 15,000-word Chinese critique of the Soviet position in the sharpening Sino-Soviet controversy had been published, without delay, in the June 17, 1963, issue of *Revolución*.[5]

After the Soviet reply in the form of an "open letter" of similar

5. The document was entitled "A Proposal Concerning the General Line of the International Communist Movement: Letter from the Central Committee of the Communist Party of China in Reply to the Letter from the Central Committee of the Communist Party of the Soviet Union of March 30, 1963." It was dated June 14, 1963. For the complete text in English see Griffith, *The Sino-Soviet Rift*, pp. 259 ff.

dimensions was published in *Revolución* on July 17,[6] the Russians were no doubt aware of what was then common gossip in Havana, namely, that Fidel had been extremely and volubly annoyed with one of the letter's paragraphs. In a lengthy argument against the Chinese accusation of Russian "adventurism" and "capitulation" in the Cuban missile crisis, the letter introduced Fidel's endorsement of the Soviet thesis as a prime bit of evidence: "Why then do the Chinese comrades stubbornly ignore the assessment which the leaders of the Cuban Revolution themselves give to the policy of the government of the Soviet Union, which they call a policy of fraternal solidarity and genuine internationalism?" Fidel's vexation was understandable. It was one thing, in the interests of reconciliation with Khrushchev and in the belief that the Sino-Soviet quarrel was about to end, for him to subscribe to a harmless deception when he put his signature to the Soviet-Cuban joint declaration two months earlier, and quite another thing for the Russians to pull out his inconspicuous fabrication, throw a spotlight on it, and then use it as ammunition against the Chinese.

Fidel's resentment against Khrushchev was undoubtedly comforting to the Chinese. Mainly, however, they pinned their hopes on continuing Cuban-American hostility both to revive Cuban-Soviet friction and to promote Sino-Cuban cooperation. On this 26th of July they could find grounds for their hopes. However, they could not anticipate that, when Fidel once again would be seriously at odds with the Russians, he would be even more critical of the Chinese, to the extent of accusing them of acting like the Yankee imperialists when, for political reasons, they drastically reduced their shipments of rice to Cuba.[7] It was to be the supreme insult.

Imperialist Insolence

"What have the imperialists been doing in the Caribbean?" Fidel asked, raising his voice. "Have they taken any steps to lower tensions? No!" His anger grew as he spoke of "new aggressions against

6. The full title: "Open Letter from the Central Committee of the Communist Party of the Soviet Union to Party Organizations and All Communists of the Soviet Union, July 14, 1963." *Ibid.*, pp. 289 ff.

7. In a lengthy statement published in *Revolución* on February 6, 1966.

our country, new economic measures. . . . Once more [the United States] is setting up mercenaries in Nicaragua, creating bases of operations against Cuba, openly and impudently, cynically and insolently, in the way they always behave." He was referring to a well-publicized project headed by a leading Bay of Pigs veteran, released from Castro's prison under the ransom agreement; it was backed openly by Nicaraguan President Luis Somoza but never materialized. The project was more than likely a fund raising scheme rather than a serious plan to mount an invasion.

There was frustration as well as anger in his voice as he spoke of Cuba's offer to come to terms with the United States: "Yes, we said we were ready to discuss matters with the Yankee imperialists. . . . What do the imperialists say? That they won't renew relations with a 'Soviet satellite in the Caribbean.' " He was referring to a standard theme used by the Kennedy administration to explain its Cuban policy. It was a neat formula, which appeased a vociferous sector of American public opinion running strongly against any kind of deal with Castro, put pressure on the Russians, ran down the Cuban image in Latin America, and yet could imply the possibility of coming to terms with Castro in a quid pro quo that the Americans could define as "de-satellization."

Three months later such a possibility appeared on the horizon, as I shall shortly explain; but in the context of his frustration with the results of his coexistence appeals and of the celebration of a glorious revolutionary anniversary, the formula provoked his scorn and deep resentment. "The only country in [Latin] America, the only one," he exclaimed, "where there is not a single bit of foreign property . . . which is the owner of all its wealth, mines, petroleum, lands, factories; which doesn't have to pay a penny's worth of tribute to the Yankee monopolies. . . . And they call this a satellite."

The Great Swindle

What provoked his indignation even more was his claim that the Yankees cheated Cuba out of $10 million in the deal for the release of the Bay of Pigs prisoners. He had made the claim before and would make it again. The issue involved complicated problems of prices assigned to goods delivered and accounting technicalities. For Fidel it was a very simple matter. The mention of it was sure to raise the temperature of his compatriots, and his own as well. "They were supposed to pay $53 million and only paid $43 million. They are dyed-in-the-wool swindlers. . . . And we hold the American Red Cross and the government of the United States responsible." He belabored the theme for several minutes, adding that some of the prisoners released were once more plotting against Cuba. This led him to a sizzling climax: "Let this serve as an example to the world of how the Cuban government behaves and how the government of the United States behaves, how that hoodlum [*rufián*] of a Kennedy behaves. . . . We freed the mercenaries; they haven't finished paying the indemnity, and now they are getting them ready for new aggression."

His reference to President Kennedy must have shocked the Russians and delighted the Chinese. Speaking extemporaneously as he always did, it was the kind of intemperate remark he was apt to make on the spur of the moment and later regret. In the case of John Kennedy, the regret came soon and it was deep.

The American Embassy Expropriated

He had not finished lambasting the Americans. With great flourish he told his listeners how Cuba had just nationalized the American embassy building, the last remaining Yankee property on the island. It was in reprisal for the blocking of Cuban funds. "And they say it is illegal," he added with heavy sarcasm. "What insolence! This government of the United States has no respect for any international law; it is constantly violating our air space, infiltrating saboteurs, agents, spies; . . . and now they claim the government of Cuba, in just and legitimate defense, can't nationalize their embassy. Well, we have nationalized it, and we shall see to it that the decree is enforced."

The decree had been proclaimed three days earlier with maximum fanfare, and in clear violation of international precedent. It was issued without consulting the Swiss, who had occupied the building in the normal course of taking over the representation of American interests in Cuba. It was one of those typical gestures of bravado with which Fidel soothed his feelings and stirred up those of his compatriots. It had no practical value to speak of as compensation for the freezing of Cuban funds in the United States. Still, as a purely symbolic act of revenge, it might have served its purpose if Fidel had been able to leave well enough alone.

However, the urge to defy the United States and international convention on this anniversary of the Revolution was too great, and as a result he stumbled into an awkward situation. In effect, he was threatening the Swiss instead of the United States, as he suddenly seemed to realize; for he then changed his tone and addressed himself to the occupants of the embassy. There was no hurry to vacate the building, he said, "our country is ready to provide the Swiss diplomatic mission with every facility for moving their archives to another location at their convenience, after which they can hand over the building to the Cuban government. Let us hope the Swiss diplomatic mission will recognize this legitimate and sovereign act of the Cuban people." He then repeated, "let us hope, because it is not aimed against Switzerland."

It was predictably a vain hope. The Swiss had taken over custody of the building at the request of the United States and could only agree to relinquish it in consultation with the United States. Thus, the Swiss refused to vacate the premises, Fidel dropped the issue, and nothing further was mentioned in the Cuban press. Most people soon forgot the episode or discounted it as they did his many other eccentric outbursts; and would-be Cuban emigrants seeking American visas continued to form long lines in front of the conspicuous bay-side stone and glass structure, which in Havana everyone simply called "la Embajada," that is to say, "the embassy." [8]

Seven Years Later

Several years after the tenth anniversary of Moncada, a most unlikely series of events gave Fidel an opportunity to profit handsomely from his previous embarrassment. In mid-May 1970, a carefully

8. In a policy that can properly be described as both humanitarian and providing a political safety valve for the regime, some 600,000 Cubans (in the neighborhood of 8 percent of the population) were permitted to emigrate (95 percent went to the United States) from 1959 until the end of 1970. This policy ended May 31, 1970 when the government stopped accepting applications for emigration. Those whose applications were already on file, providing they could meet the usual requirements, would be allowed to leave. Applications on file at the time may have run as high as 100,000. At the customary rate of departure, the last of this number would not leave from Cuba before mid-1972. (See article of March 18, 1971, the second in a series of four by Charles Vanhecke, under the general title of "Cuba: de l'utopie aux réalites," *Le*

staged "spontaneous" demonstration of what the Cuban media reported to be 200,000 persons, performing in well-organized shifts, surrounded the United States embassy building in a ninety-six-hour continuous round of frenzied protest against the old and still convenient enemy, the American government. The latter was accused of complicity in the capture of eleven Cuban fishermen on the high seas by a counterrevolutionary band. They were being held prisoner in a secret location among the hundreds of deserted cays in the chain of the British-owned Bahama Islands, presumably as hostages to be exchanged for infiltrators recently captured by Castro's soldiers. It was clear that both the United States and British governments were thoroughly annoyed by the escapade; [9] and in the normal course of events the British would have forced the release of the fishermen, as they did in any case.

But the timing of the incident and the fact that the Swiss still occupied the American embassy building was a double coincidence which Fidel was quick to exploit. As he himself explained in his harvest report to the nation on May 20, 1970, after the protest at the embassy had ended, it was on May 7 that he finally had decided that his ten-million-ton sugar goal could not be met. News of the kidnapping of the fishermen reached him on the 10th. It was a godsend. There had been no break—not even for Christmas or the New Year —none of the customary revolutionary celebrations, no long speeches since the harvest had gotten under way nearly a year before. Something was needed to divert attention from the long months of strenuous work and bleak austerity, some "legitimate" reason for a pause in the unfinished task, some emotion-releasing political carnival that

---

Monde, March 17–20, 1971.) This would be the first time that emigration policy in Cuba would conform to that of Soviet-bloc states.

9. The wire services distributed a Washington dispatch, dated May 12, 1970 (as cited by Castro in an official statement of the same day), stating that "The United States expressed its regret . . . that an anti-Castro group sank two Cuban fishing boats and seized their crews as hostages. The United States government reminds all those who live within its territory that its laws prohibit them from using the country as a military base against a foreign country. . . . All necessary measures [will] be taken to guarantee respect for those laws." Castro cited this statement as proof that the fishermen were kidnapped, but claimed the United States was not sincere as far as guaranteeing "respect for those laws" was concerned.

would mobilize the country behind its leader and prepare it for the bad harvest news he would soon have to give to his people.

Thus, on May 12 Castro issued a solemn warning to the American and British governments, over his official signature, which all but declared a state of emergency to exist. Immediately, all the media began to whip up patriotic fervor, truckloads of harvest hands started converging on Havana, and by the 15th the embassy building, now dubbed the "lair" (*guarida*) of the imperialist beast, was surrounded. Inside the "lair," a Swiss diplomat and a Cuban employee had been trapped. Their water was cut off; they had no food and none was permitted to be brought in; and they were threatened with dire consequences if they attempted to leave. They were obviously hostages, though this was hotly denied. It was "difficult for the Cuban authorities to curb the people's anger," *Granma* on May 16 lamely explained and then blithely added, "we aren't in Kent [State University] where fascist goons murder students . . . who protest against the war of aggression. . . . No blood will be shed to defend imperialist symbols or Yankee interests on behalf of a so-called international law [concerning protection of foreign embassies]."

Meanwhile, the confinement of the two men added another— and for Fidel's purposes an opportune—international complication. The Cuban media stepped up the tone and scope of patriotic indignation, and the Cuban ambassador to Switzerland was recalled as sharp notes passed back and forth between Berne and Havana. Judged by legal and moral standards, the Swiss easily won on the exchange; but from the point of view of rhetoric they were no match for Raúl Roa's colorful and overreacting diatribes, which added more than a hint of comic opera to the affair. Fittingly, it had a happy ending. On the 18th the fishermen were rescued unharmed, following which the embassy prisoners were quietly permitted to leave, apparently none the worse for their three-day fast.

The next day, Fidel and the fishermen appeared before the masses, still keeping their boisterous vigil around the "Yankee lair" and obviously enjoying the lark. Fidel made a fighting speech, but noticeably and uncharacteristically muddled when he tried to justify Cuban conduct in the unpleasantness with the Swiss and oozing a type of saccharine demagogy he rarely used: "We have won this beautiful battle . . . [to] save the lives of these fishermen and bring peace of mind to their mothers—those mothers who had so much confidence in the people, who set an example of dignity, who displayed that impressive courage, the courage that comes from knowing that one is part of an entire people which is ready for action in defense of one's beloved children."

That same morning (May 19), *Granma* had printed a front-page banner headline, "VICTORY," and beneath it a gigantic photo of the eleven men. The newspaper reported unrestrained rejoicing throughout the island. For those who could remember, it recalled the jubilation after the Bay of Pigs victory, nine years earlier. It was as if a war had been fought and won against a coalition of the United States, Great Britain, and Switzerland. Never before, thanks to his failure to dislodge the Swiss from the American embassy in July 1963, had Fidel been able to make so much of so little. And never before the economic disaster of 1970 had the need been so great.

Familiar Heresies

To return to the tenth anniversary of Moncada, a good deal of Fidel's speech dealt with Latin America. Repeating his familiar ideological heresies, as the Russians saw them, and his shrill exhortation for armed revolutionary struggle at this time was prime evidence that a new Soviet-Cuban dispute was in the making. It was one thing to insult the president of the United States—vulgar outburst of temper that it was, the provocation was nevertheless understandable —and quite another to meddle in the affairs of the Soviet-guided Communist parties of Latin America. And celebrating the tenth anniversary of the start of his own revolutionary struggle provided him with the perfect setting for spreading his gospel.

"What took place in Cuba was no miracle," he declared after explaining that victory over Batista was considered impossible by many theoreticians. "Everything we did in Cuba can be done bigger and better in many other countries of [Latin] America. . . . And in many, . . . prerevolutionary conditions are incomparably better than they were in our country." Fidel elaborated at length on this theme, going into the "unbreakable faith" that sustained his group after the defeat at Moncada and the trials and tribulations following the landing of the *Granma* three years later, and then repeated the challenge to Marxist orthodoxy: "the duty of the revolutionary is not only to study theory, . . . not to wait for a change in the correlation of forces, . . . but to make the revolution!"

Further along, after repeating that Latin America was a "continent where revolution is inevitable," he added an unexpected qualification for the record, which he sometimes appended to his sweeping generalizations: "When we speak of Latin America in general terms, and when we speak of revolution, we don't believe that conditions are exactly the same in all countries. There are some countries that have . . . greater political stability than others [and] a different economic situation than others. We referred to those countries where the oligarchies have clamped an iron dictatorship over the exploited masses and where all [nonrevolutionary] roads for the people are blocked." He then went on to separate the sheep from the goats. Among the latter he listed Argentina, Peru, Ecuador, Colombia, Venezuela, Guatemala, Nicaragua, Honduras, El Salvador, "and other countries that I may have forgotten" and then added what was undoubtedly though not admittedly his key diagnostic criterion, "precisely those that unconditionally supported imperialism in its aggressions against Cuba." As for the more "stable" countries exempt from his armed struggle thesis, with governments that "respect the sovereignty of Cuba, which have not been instruments of Yankee imperialism in its aggressions against Cuba," these he listed as Mexico, Brazil, Chile, Urugay, and Bolivia (the latter among the most volatile of all Latin American republics), the only five that had thus far resisted American and OAS pressures to break diplomatic relations with Cuba.

Some Inconsistencies

Parenthetically, it is worth noting that precisely a year later, following an OAS majority vote requiring member states to sever relations with Cuba, all the holdouts complied except Mexico. Thus, until 1969 and 1970, when leftist regimes emerged in Peru, Bolivia, and Chile, only the Mexican government continued to enjoy immunity from Fidel's barbs, as well as a complete blackout of unfavorable news in the Cuban media, such as the severe and sometimes bloody crackdowns on radical elements, including Fidelista sympathizers. A cooling off of enthusiasm for Mexico occurred during the course of 1969, but it was only in connection with an airplane hijacking controversy and the case of a Mexican diplomat recruited by the CIA who was spotted by Cuban counterintelligence in the Mexican embassy in Havana.[10]

Fidel's treatment of Chile after the 1964 break in relations involved a quarrel with President Frei made notorious by the torrent of abuse Fidel unleashed against him. At the same time, he revoked Chile's exceptional status in a "continent where revolution is inevitable." On March 19, 1966, without referring to his earlier judgment, he stated that Chile did not "point a new way for the revolutionary masses" and "its experience will serve to justify Cuba's course still further to the revolutionaries of the hemisphere." However, this was not to be Fidel's last word on the subject. In mid-1970, anticipating the election of Marxist Salvador Allende, an old friend and unswerving supporter, as president of Chile, Fidel rediscovered Chilean "exceptionalism." Speaking over the Chilean radio in a recording taped in Havana, he said, "elections in Chile may result in a triumph for the left. . . . I believe that conditions in Chile are different from those in Cuba, and I believe things can't be done there as they were here." [11]

That Fidel's views on international affairs have frequently been inconsistent does not fundamentally distinguish him from most political leaders. His inconsistencies have been more colorful and conspicuous because he is more temperamental, more garrulous, and under less restraint than others and because he is plagued (or blessed) by a mission. In the last analysis, as in the case of foreign policy makers in general, he is compelled to take changing circumstances and tactical considerations into account and to be guided more by expediency than principle; and again, as in the case of most heads of government, his overriding objectives are the national interest, as he sees it. All of this, of course, helps explain why, despite his self-proclaimed and constantly reiterated inflexible dedication to the purest international revolutionary idealism, he is still "in business."

10. *Granma Weekly Review* (September 15, 1969) presented the evidence in a special forty-eight-page supplement entitled "The Amazing Case of the CIA Spy in the Guise of Diplomatic Official of the Mexican Embassy in Cuba." The authenticity of the evidence was not seriously challenged either in Mexico City or Washington.

11. Dispatch from Santiago, Chile; *New York Times*, August 23, 1970.

To return to Fidel's speech on the Moncada anniversary, his explicit distinction between the two groups of countries was a purely practical one. He was, in effect, proposing to revolutionaries and would-be revolutionaries that any Latin American government that maintained normal relations with Cuba was ipso facto progressive and deserved to be tolerated, if not enthusiastically supported. At the same time, it was a way of informing the "good" governments that they would not be targets of hostile propaganda or subversion by Cuba so long as they continued to maintain normal relations. For the fact of the matter is that Cuba at that time was already deeply involved in both overt propaganda and clandestine activities against some of the governments on Fidel's publicly announced blacklist.

Exporting Revolution

As he warmed up to his subject, Castro himself pinpointed his major targets of the moment. "From this tribune, face to face with the Cuban people, we send greetings of solidarity and fraternity to the heroic Venezuelan revolutionaries," he exclaimed; and as he went on to expound their virtues with great passion, it was clear that here was the area of his most important commitments and highest hopes. Then with less fanfare, he sent "our fraternal and warm greetings to the heroic guerrillas who are fighting against tyranny in Guatemala." These were the only two Latin American groups singled out for mention by Fidel. It was too early to greet the Peruvian and Colombian movements, still relatively undeveloped, although Cuban influence was making inroads; while Che Guevara's partly Cuban staffed and wholly Cuban trained and subsidized Argentine guerrilla band (destined to be wiped out in its first and only skirmish nine months later) had not yet surfaced.

It was also too early to admit that Cuba was attempting to export revolution to Latin America. This came some years and many defeats later and mainly after Che Guevara's death in Bolivia, when posthumous honors were paid to Cuban "internationalists," as they were called, who fell on foreign soil. Accordingly, on this occasion Fidel echoed the classic Marxist disclaimer. "We smile when the imperialists say we export revolution," he said with cheerful guile. "No, no, all we do from time to time is to expound our ideas and share our ideas with revolutionaries in any part of the world."

There was, however, some truth in what Fidel said. He was not restricting himself to Latin America. American intervention in South Vietnam offered a particularly appropriate target for broadening his political offensive. Two and a half years had passed since United States ground forces had entered the civil war. Compared to what lay ahead, the ten to fifteen thousand troops in 1963 would seem insignificant, but they already represented more than a token commitment. Moreover, the question of larger involvement was on the agenda, since the Saigon regime was in deep trouble (President Ngo Dinh Diem was assassinated three months after Fidel's speech).

Concerning South Vietnam

"Our fraternal greetings . . . to the heroic fighters who struggle against Yankee imperialism in Vietnam," he exclaimed, "and who have sent a delegation that is here with us today." Undoubtedly, it was with a sense of pride and satisfaction that, a mere ninety miles from the Florida coast, he was able to exhibit as honored guests the delegates of a guerrilla army, some of whom had only recently personally inflicted casualties on American soldiers and who would soon return to continue armed struggle against the United States. The importance of Vietnam was to grow in Fidel's strategy. Some six weeks later, on September 5, the Cuban Committee of Solidarity with South Vietnam was established in Havana, the first of its kind in the world. A semiofficial Vietcong mission was also opened in Havana. Occasionally, groups of young, able-bodied South Vietnamese could be seen in Havana. One could infer that they were in Cuba for specialized military training, or perhaps to help with the training of Latin American guerrillas. South Vietnamese heroes and martyrs were given prime billing by the Cuban media.

In fact a special attitude developed toward the South Vietnamese. It was based not only on the circumstance that they were a model of guerrilla resistance against American military might, but also because in their close relationship with the South Vietnamese the Cubans had learned that the two peoples of Vietnam had distinctive ethnic characteristics and that for the southerners, "national liberation" meant precisely that, and not a slogan invented by Hanoi. Even after the American bombings of North Vietnam tightened the bonds between Havana and Hanoi and produced a virtual Cuba–North Vietnam–North Korea axis designed to prod both China and the Soviet Union into more active military participation in the struggle against the Americans, Cuba maintained a consistent policy of distinguishing between the two Vietnamese populations. Early in 1969 Cuba extended formal diplomatic recognition to the National Liberation Front of South Vietnam, several months before it became the Provisional Revolutionary Government. The Havana press published photos of the event: the Cuban ambassador presenting his credentials to Dr. Nguyen Huu Tho "deep in the jungle . . . in a protocol reception tent fashioned out of nylon from captured parachutes"; and nearby, a lean-to under the trees displaying a large Cuban flag and a wooden plaque carrying the double legend EMBAJADA DE CUBA and BAI SU QUAN CU.BA.[12]

Colonel Boumediène, the Guest of Honor

A brief but, as it later became apparent, significant reference to Algeria added another continent beyond the western hemisphere where Fidel could celebrate the virtues of his armed struggle thesis. "Sooner or later as in Algeria, whose delegation headed by Colonel Boumediène is with us today," he said, turning for a moment toward Ben Bella's lean, taciturn deputy prime minister and minister of war seated behind him, "victory awaits those who fight, [those] . . . who have faith in an idea and in . . . [armed] struggle." Of the six hundred foreign guests present (by Fidel's count), only Boumediène had the honor of being mentioned by name. The explanation lay in the recent history of Cuban-Algerian relations. In the years that followed, the history of these relations would take a number of curious turns.

Ever since Ben Bella's spectacular appearance in Havana on the eve of the October missile crisis, news of Algeria had been featured in the Cuban press and traffic between Havana and Algiers had been heavy. Both the news and the traffic were political. There would be a trade agreement; but due first to Algerian commitments to France and later to the USSR, the exchange, on the order of Algerian wine for Havana cigars and minor quantities of sugar,[13] would

12. *Bohemia*, March 21, 1969, pp. 68–69. The ceremony reportedly took place on March 4. The NLF became the Provisional Revolutionary Government of South Vietnam on June 12, 1969, and was granted diplomatic recognition in the next few days by sixteen Communist and far leftists governments, including Cuba.

13. For the five-year period 1963–1967, total Algerian sugar imports were approximately 1,260,000 metric tons. Of this amount, France supplied over 800,000 tons and Cuba a little over 100,000, somewhat less

necessarily not be of great importance to either country, unless Fidel was already dreaming of Algerian petroleum as an alternative to his dependency on Soviet supplies—a dream, in any event, never fulfilled.

Statements of mutual admiration and support between the two countries were a common occurrence. An Algerian military mission had been present at the Havana May Day (1963) festivities and received a more than ordinary red-carpet treatment by President Dorticós and Raúl Castro, the acting prime minister during his brother's absence in the Soviet Union. On July 3, the first anniversary of Algerian independence, Che Guevara showed up in Algiers heading a Cuban delegation including military specialists. A clue about the situation appeared in *Revolución* on May 29, 1963. In a featured story about Ben Bella, he was quoted as saying, "We are helping revolutionary movements in Africa." [14] There was already some reason to suspect that Fidel was doing likewise. There was, for example, a story on the front page of *Revolución* on February 15, 1963, that told of a Congolese student who was then in Havana and who had come "with the noble purpose of being more useful in the struggle for the definitive liberation of his people: the people of Patrice Lumumba." Presumably, he was not studying Cuban poetry, nor were other young, healthy black African revolutionaries in Havana who would turn up from time to time in a hotel lobby or special shopping center reserved for foreigners.

A front-page photo of Colonel Lahovare Boumediène and President Dorticós and an interview with the distinguished visitor were published in *Revolución* on August 3. Two days later the newspaper covered Boumediène's departure. He was seen off at the airport by Fidel, Raúl, and Che. This was, indeed, an extraordinary honor, not

---

than the Soviet Union which began exporting sugar to Algeria in 1963, the same year as Cuba (*Sugar Year Book*, 1967, [London: International Sugar Council, 1967], p. 5). In 1967–1969, when sugar imports from France declined appreciably, imports from Cuba increased somewhat over the peak previous year, but far less than Soviet imports. In 1969 the USSR was by a considerable margin Algeria's largest single supplier of sugar (*Sugar Year Book*, 1969, p. 5).

14. "By September 1963, Algeria was training 1,000 guerrillas from Angola, Mozambique, and South Africa and giving funds and advice to many liberation movements." David and Marina Ottaway, *Algeria: The Politics of a Socialist Revolution* (Berkeley and Los Angeles: University of California Press, 1970), p. 163.

duplicated at the departure of any other delegation. It went far beyond the requirements of protocol, which could easily have been satisfied by the presence of Raúl or Che, singly.

On August 24 *Revolución* carried a front-page interview with Ben Bella in Algiers under the caption, "Ben Bella Ratifies Total Support for Cuba." And so it went week after week, with Algeria very much in the news. On September 19 another Cuban military mission was reported to be in Algiers. The next day came the notice of a Russian $100-million long-term loan to Algeria, still further enhancing Ben Bella's image in Havana. On September 30 Ben Bella was formally sworn in as the first president of Algeria, and a few days later he received Cuba's minister of foreign trade, Major Alberto Mora, who had arrived to conclude a trade agreement with Algeria. On October 14 another Cuban military mission reached Algiers.

On October 15 *Revolución* carried a big front-page story under the heading "Algeria Invaded by the Moroccan Army." An unprovoked attack by the Moroccans was said to have taken place during the night of the 13th to the 14th. Ben Bella was directing the defense of the fatherland; the Algerians were fighting bravely; Cuba was ready to lend its Algerian brothers whatever assistance they needed, and so on. On the 17th the newspaper reported that members of Cuba's medical team working in Algeria had enlisted to fight against the Moroccan aggressors. For the next ten days, the "war" was prominent in the news, overshadowed only by reports of destruction and relief work in Cuba's Oriente Province, which had been hard hit by hurricane "Flora" shortly before the announcement of the clash.

Who fired the first shot was in dispute (not in the Cuban press, to be sure), but it was followed by a Moroccan incursion into Algerian territory. Probably three factors contributed to the outbreak: "Morocco's long-standing claims to a part of the Algerian Sahara along the ill-defined border"; "the Moroccan government was obviously taking advantage of Algeria's internal difficulties [a rebellion in Kabylia] to press its demands"; and Ben Bella's interest in exploiting "the border conflict to rally his supporters, and even some of his opponents, in defense of the nation." [15]

The chances are that Fidel had been informed of the impending

15. *Ibid.*, pp. 97–98.

confrontation in advance. In any event, he boasted later that Cuban military support was the first foreign aid to reach Algeria. At the time, the shipment of men and arms was unpublicized, although the news spread in the upper levels of Havana's bureaucracy where it caused considerable excitement. There must have been excitement in the Kremlin also. Fidel was again taking large risks. If a real war would develop, no one could tell what the consequences for Cuba would be. At the very least Cuba could lose an important market, since Morocco, next to Japan, was Cuba's most important capitalist customer.[16] Fortunately for Fidel—and for all concerned—after a few minor skirmishes, in which probably neither Cuban men nor arms were involved, the miniscule conflict, following a cease-fire agreement on October 30, was settled by arbitration and all but forgotten, except by Fidel who nearly two years later found a special reason to recall the event.

Colonel Boumediène Denounced

On June 26, 1965, exactly one week after the overthrow of Ben Bella, Fidel addressed several hundred "exemplary" young men and women chosen to represent Cuba at the Ninth World Youth Festival. It was due to be held in Algiers in late July, but Fidel told his listeners it would be indecent for them to attend after Boumediène's treacherous seizure of power.[17] Fidel was exceedingly bitter about the fall of his closest ally in Africa (Nasser ranked much lower on Fidel's merit list)—in fact, more than an ally, a spiritual brother, whose daring visit to Havana on the eve of the missile crisis he extolled to his "exemplary" youth. Of immediate concern, which he could not mention, was that Che Guevara was on the verge of taking off for Algiers, which was to be the base from which a Cuban guerrilla

16. In 1961–1963, inclusively, sugar exports to Morocco averaged 236,000 metric tons per annum as compared with 339,000 to Japan and 110,000 to the United Kingdom, in third place (all figures rounded). *Sugar Yearbook*, 1967, pp. 55–56. Morocco broke relations with Cuba (it could do no less) but not for long. Moroccan imports of Cuban sugar in 1964 exceeded 300,000 tons.

17. With the exception of China, Albania, Indonesia, and Syria, the coup d'etat was condemned by all Communist and other extreme leftist governments. As a result, the site of the festival was transferred to Bulgaria, and after a stint of tree planting while the new arrangements were being made, Cuba's "exemplary" youth had its fling after all.

force was to proceed to the Congo. For when Che decided to leave Cuba, Africa and not Bolivia was his first choice as a battlefield against imperialism. Thus, a hasty revision of logistic arrangements was required; and when Che left Cuba the following month, Cairo instead of Algiers was his first stop. As it later turned out, the Algerian crisis made no real difference in the outcome of Che's African adventure since it was doomed from the start.

Then again, speaking at a moment of deepening estrangement from the USSR and China for what he considered to be their failure to meet their sacred obligation to defend socialist North Vietnam at all costs against American aggression, at a time of final and total disillusionment with the Johnson administration following the American intervention in Dominican Republic, and now the last straw after the shocking precedent of a successful military coup d'etat against a great revolutionary hero, founder and leader of a socialist state, Fidel took the ready-made occasion to reveal an edifying example of more than verbal revolutionary virtue—the Cuban model of quiet, unheralded, self-sacrificing international solidarity. "At a moment of crisis for Algeria, for the Algerian Revolution, when they needed our help," he exclaimed, "men and arms from our country, crossing the Atlantic in record time, arrived in Algeria ready to fight side by side with the Algerian revolutionaries! . . . Nor did distance prevent us from being the first to arrive." Here he was taunting the Egyptians for being second to arrive. Then unmistakably addressing Moscow and Peking, though without mentioning their names, he issued the challenge with which he would shortly dispute the political and ideological leadership of the two Communist giants in the Third World: "Proletarian internationalism in fact, with deeds and not the mouthing of cheap words! Small country that we are, constantly threatened by the imperialists, we gave up part of our most important weapons and sent them to the Algerian people!" [18]

Fidel left the door slightly ajar for a reconciliation with Boumediène in case "the improbable and almost impossible" continuation of a revolutionary and anti-imperialist policy would occur.

18. According to the Ottaways (*Algeria*, p. 166), "Cuba sent three ships carrying 40 Soviet T-34 tanks, 4 MIG jet fighters, some trucks, and more than 800 tons of light arms, ammunition and artillery." The number of men remains undisclosed. Nasser sent about 1,000 troops some of whom saw action against the Moroccans.

The brunt of his vituperation fell on Boumediène's foreign minister (who held the same post under Ben Bella), Abdelaziz Bouteflika, whom he called, with juvenile relish, this "Butterfly [which he pronounced *Booter-fly*] or Butterflyka." Relations between the two countries were practically suspended. Cuban-Algerian trade, which totaled over $3 million in 1965, dropped to $200,000 in 1966. Relations improved considerably after Boumediène proved his anti-imperialist mettle by sending troops to Egypt in June 1967, during the Six-Day War, and particularly by refusing to accept the cease-fire. This political gesture especially pleased Fidel, who shortly after told his fellow countrymen that in case of an invasion of Cuba, any Cuban who would negotiate a cease-fire while the enemy occupied a square inch of Cuban soil would deserve to be shot. In November 1968 Foreign Minister Bouteflika showed up in Havana, where everybody conveniently forgot Fidel's insult, and while Fidel's faithful friend Ben Bella was still under lock and key.

25

■

A Spate of
Stormy Weather

Another Quarrel Resolved

A DECADE, AS HISTORY GOES, is a very short period of time; yet even with the benefit of hindsight, no one looking back on Fidel's thoroughly bungled attempt to capture the Moncada barracks can find the smallest clue in that episode, so lavishly extolled in later years, that could have remotely foreshadowed the Cuba over which Fidel presided on July 26, 1963. Two months, as history goes, is less than a moment; but here again as we look back, what sage on the day after Fidel's June 4 television performance could have predicted so rapid a cooling off of Cuban-Soviet relations as was revealed on the occasion of the tenth anniversary of Moncada? To be sure nobody familiar with the character of the Cuban Revolution and its supreme leader, on the one hand, and the fundamentals of Soviet foreign policy, on the other, imagined that the great reconciliation had removed all possibility of friction between the two countries. However, it was unexpected that only in a matter of weeks there would be friction sufficiently serious to come to the surface. To this day, what it was that provoked Fidel's displeasure is not known, though the chances are it was a specific complaint more than a revival of general ideological incompatibility. The reason is that it was not only reflected in his speech of July 26, but made explicit by a special mode of communication that permitted the two parties to conduct and resolve the quarrel in public without acknowledging the existence of the quarrel. How this was done was sufficiently diverting to merit a brief explanation.

There is a well-known custom among the socialist countries—a custom that the Cubans had already adopted—that on the occasion of a national holiday, the press of the celebrating country is expected to release the numerous congratulatory messages sent by the fraternal foreign governments and organizations, and sometimes by capitalist governments as well. The texts, which at times can make subtle political disclosures, are carefully tabulated, scrutinized, and compared far and wide by political specialists versed in deciphering the idiom in which they are written. Thus, when *Revolución* on July 27 printed a page full of greetings, including those of Wladyslaw Gomulka, Janos Kadar, and Gheorghiu Dej but nothing from the Communist party or government of the Soviet Union, and with the Russian official message not showing up a day or two before or after July 27, it was clear that something was amiss. To add to the mystery, another conspicuous omission was the lack of a message from the Chinese party or government.

Then on August 30 *Revolución* carried on its front page a curious dispatch, attributed to Radio Moscow, which reported that Fidel Castro and Osvaldo Dorticós had sent a telegram to Nikita Khrushchev and Leonid Brezhnev in answer to congratulations transmitted on the occasion of the tenth anniversary of the 26th of July. Moreover, it was noted that the Cuban telegram had also appeared on the front page of *Pravda* on August 30, and that among other things it stated that "the heads of the Cuban government expressed their gratitude for the effective collaboration and aid provided by the people and government of the Soviet Union in order to strengthen and rapidly develop the Cuban Socialist Revolution." It was also probably more than a coincidence that the lead story on the same page of *Revolución*, headlined "USSR CONDEMNS PIRATE ATTACKS AGAINST CUBA. THE SOVIET UNION HAS SUPPORTED AND CONTINUES TO SUPPORT CUBA," reported a *Pravda* statement that underscored close Soviet-Cuban relations in the face of continuing American hostility.

Thus, Castro and Dorticós belatedly acknowledged receipt of congratulations from the Kremlin which, contrary to all protocol, had not been published or even mentioned by the Cuban press. Furthermore, the long overdue Cuban message was publicized on the front pages of both *Pravda* and *Revolución*, although replies to congratulatory messages are normally not publicized at all. Finally, it is a safe assumption that an appropriate message from the Chinese party or government had been received in Havana on or about July 26, and that when Fidel decided to suppress the Soviet message, he did not dare print the Chinese message and thereby compound the insult to the Russians. Undoubtedly, the entire charade was effective. When what had been an undisclosed, though apparently serious, dispute was settled, the reconciliation was also undisclosed, except to the experts, among them the Chinese who were no doubt the principal target of the telegram that Khrushchev extracted from Fidel Castro for an undisclosed price.

The Second Memorable October

During the months of August and September 1963 there was no hint that secret conversations were shortly to begin between Cuba and the United States, at the highest levels, to explore the possibility of a modus vivendi. Almost daily the Cuban press featured news of small craft hit-and-run attacks against industrial sites by sea or air. Indignation ran high, although damage was usually light and only an occasional casualty was reported. At the same time, hostile statements against Cuba in the American press were also given prominence. From time to time, an appropriate *Pravda* commentary on the aggressive acts perpetrated on Cuban soil, accompanied by the warning that the Soviet promise to defend Cuba still held, appeared. Meanwhile, Cubans were given to understand that guerrilla warfare in several Latin American countries, especially Venezuela, was making great headway against the despotic governments and their imperialist masters. There was no sign of peaceful coexistence anywhere to be seen. At a mass meeting on September 28, Fidel summed up the situation for his compatriots "We are not at peace with imperialism."

It was purely a matter of coincidence, but October 1963, like October 1962, was a month to be remembered. On the 4th, the Second Agrarian Reform was announced. It will be recalled that under the provisions of the earlier reform of May 1959, only the large estates defined as *latifundia*—that is, properties of more than 402 hectares (1,000 acres)—were expropriated. The new measure reduced the upper limit to 67 hectares (approximately 165 acres). This resulted in the elimination of about 10,000 middle farmers, leaving 150,000 small farmers in the private agricultural sector. It also reduced the proportion of farmland and pasturage in private hands from 50 to 30 percent of the total.[1]

Publicly, the measure at the time was justified as necessary to eliminate various forms of economic sabotage by the "rural bourgeoisie." Privately, it was explained to the bewildered Russian and other east European economists in the various ministries that the "kulaks" were cooperating with an unpublicized and very troublesome guerrilla insurrection in the central provinces by disaffected peasants supported by clandestine CIA infiltrations. No doubt the government had not acted entirely without provocation. As was generally suspected, a sizable military effect had been under way to put down the uprising, which was not finally liquidated until well into 1964.[2] Nevertheless, there was good reason to believe that the expropriations fell into the by then familiar pattern of hasty and drastic decisions lightly taken. A shotgun type of cure was applied where a rifle was needed, and a high price was paid for the damage

1. See Michel Gutelman, *L'agriculture socialisée à Cuba* (Paris, 1967), p. 63; and René Dumont, *Cuba: Socialisme et développement* (Paris: Seuil, 1964), p. 84. The small farmers, understandably alarmed, were given a solemn pledge that there would be no further expropriations, that as long as they or their heirs farmed the land, their property rights would be respected. Having been the chief beneficiaries of the Revolution, and thus far an important source of its political support, as well as a major source of domestically produced staple food, the government could not afford to lose their loyalty. Although it kept its promise and the small farmers retained title to their properties, in later years they lost much of their independence, incentive to work, and relative prosperity as they were progressively incorporated into government planning and control of crops.

2. The impression obtained in usually well-informed Cuban government circles was that over a period of several years some 50,000 troops had been engaged in liquidating peasant disaffection. Speaking on June 6, 1971, on the tenth anniversary of the formal establishment of the Ministry of the Interior, Castro reminisced about "the uprisings that occurred mainly, though not exclusively, in the Escambray Mountains. . . . Organized groups of counterrevolutionaries . . . existed all over the island. . . . There were more than 1,000 armed bandits in the Escambray Mountains alone. . . . That struggle cost hundreds of millions of pesos and hundreds of lives, . . . and the exact time and date when the last bandit was captured is written in the records on file." (*Granma Weekly Review*, June 13, 1971.) Fidel did not reveal the "time and date."

it caused. Apart from social considerations (to the thousands of law-abiding families evicted without warning, it appeared to be an act of arbitrary brutality), the economic consequences of transforming reasonably productive cattle and dairy farms and other agricultural enterprises into notoriously inefficient and mismanaged "people's farms" were predictably catastrophic.

At the same time, the Second Agrarian Reform was symptomatic of the problems that lay ahead: a seemingly unending series of economic blunders rationalized as gigantic moral achievements destined to create a truly communistic society in record time. As *Granma* put it years later, reviewing a decade of agrarian and other expropriations and commenting on the "epoch-making" 1968 nationalization of "more than 58,000 private stores, shops, and vending stands" in one fell swoop: "Capitalism and its final attempt to curb the impetuous [advance] of the Revolution were completely crushed, destined to total extinction from the conscience of the people in this long process of building socialism and communism." [3]

Pondering on the general phenomenon as it unfolded, I recalled a conversation with Ilya Ehrenburg in his Gorky Street apartment some years earlier. I had asked him how he would explain the stupidity of a recently published ex cathedra pronouncement by a leading ideologue of the Soviet Communist party. "Ah, *mon vieux*," the writer replied in slightly accented French, blinking his pale blue eyes and displaying the blackened remains of his sadly neglected teeth, "you must understand something about the history of our revolution. It was very easy to eliminate *les capitalistes* but we've still not been able to get rid of *les imbéciles*."

A second and this time a totally unavoidable disaster struck the island on October 6. It was hurricane "Flora," which zigzagged erratically for nearly a week over southeastern Cuba. It was the most destructive storm in Cuban history. By the time it moved north into the Atlantic, it had left over 1,000 dead and some 2,500 square miles of the country's most productive soil under water. Although the rescue and relief operations were exemplary (it is in this kind of emergency that Fidel's military and mass organizations could perform as no previous regime in Cuba would have been able to), the national economy had been seriously damaged. A spell of austerity

3. *Granma Weekly Review*, January 12, 1969.

was thus unavoidable. Explaining the need for it in an extended tele-vision appearance on October 30, Fidel included Yankee harassment in the account of the obstacles that had to be overcome with pa-triotic abnegation.

The Story of the *Rex*

Specifically, Fidel related the incident of the *Rex*, a 150-foot vessel that was spotted by Cuban radar on the night of October 21 some five miles off the southwest coast of Pinar del Río, at the western ex-tremity of the island. Investigation proved that it was a mother ship that had launched two smaller craft making their way to shore, each towing a balsa raft. On approaching the shore, counterrevolutionary Cuban infiltrators and their equipment were transferred to the rafts. On reaching land and in the process of disembarking, they were fired on by Fidel's militia which eventually rounded up and captured a number of men and all their equipment. Interrogation of the pris-oners left no doubt that it was a CIA operation and, as a matter of fact, the eighth such mission that the *Rex* had undertaken since July. Three days after Fidel spoke, several of the prisoners appeared on television and gave more details.

Considering the island's approximately 2,000 miles of coves, in-lets, and otherwise irregular shoreline and more than 1,000 adjacent cays and islets, the naval and land units of the Cuban coast guard, however well trained and equipped, could not hope to intercept more than a small percentage of what was quite clearly a steady stream of infiltrators, as the history of the *Rex* would show. At the same time, the infiltrating teams were not made up of amateurs. They were men with a high level of professional competence for the tasks they were to perform, provided with sophisticated technology and generally well motivated. The wonder is that they were not more effective, either in physical sabotage or promoting political subversion. Un-doubtedly, the main reason was that they were tilling barren soil. The one region that was giving the Cuban government serious trou-ble, the hill country of Las Villas Province, was sealed off by a cordon of troops while it was in the process of being pacified. Else-where, the disaffection was troublesome but not acute. As a result, the infiltrators had to contend with a largely loyal population. An-other reason was the convincing evidence the media could present in

A Spate of Stormy Weather

identifying the counterrevolutionaries with the CIA. In this connection, it is more than likely that the incursions were not only of little positive value to their sponsors but largely counterproductive.

After telling about the *Rex*, Fidel went on to say,

> They thought it would be easy after the hurricane; they wanted to take advantage of it. . . . It is truly disgraceful for the government of the United States to do this sort of thing while the entire population is mobilized to contend with a situation created by a natural catastrophe. . . . That's why we absolutely rejected the hypocritical help they offered. . . . The Red Cross is an appendage of the American State Department. The Red Cross swindled us out of $10 million at the time of the indemnity payment for [the release of] the mercenaries [captured at the Bay of Pigs].

For good measure, he was repeating the accusation he had made several times before that the value of the goods delivered was $43 million instead of the agreed on $53 million.

However, Fidel went on to explain that Cuba distinguished between the American people and the American government and had accepted a donation from a religious organization: "the Quakers, who we felt were truly sincere, offered to send a plane. . . . That is why the Cuban government authorized the plane and representatives of the organization to come, since our attitude is not one of hatred or contempt toward the American people; it is an attitude against the policy of the government of the United States."

Considering the opportunity offered by the combination of the hurricane disaster and CIA provocation, one could imagine Fidel rising to the occasion with one of his classic fulminations against *el imperialismo yanqui*. Viewed in this light and with the benefit of hindsight, one could conclude that Fidel's remarks were quite moderate, though at the time few would have looked closely enough at the speech to detect the subtle change in tone. It was still very much of a secret that the first steps toward establishing a discreet dialogue between Castro and Kennedy had already been taken.

26

■

The Kennedy-Castro "Dialogue"

The Initial Gambit

PERHAPS NOT MANY WOULD venture to assert that American foreign policy might have been substantially different had John F. Kennedy completed his first and, what would have more than likely followed, his second term as president of the United States. One cannot be sure. A slow starter, Kennedy was, however, rapidly developing the quality of judgment and the flexibility of response characteristic of the mature statesman. He was also in the process of obtaining a firmer grip on the machinery of government and on public opinion, thus gaining the self-assurance he needed to explore new ways of solving old problems.

A case in point is Cuba. In the fall of 1963 President Kennedy began to investigate the possibility of negotiating a settlement with Fidel Castro. On the surface, of course, no hint of this was visible. As in any war, hostilities continue unabated until the moment when the armistice is signed. Even after the president's death, the high-ranking members of his staff who wrote voluminously of the Kennedy era were either silent about this development or offered little in the way of first-hand knowledge and nothing in the way of explanation. Yet for the historian, the fact that Kennedy was quietly encouraging the exploration of the basis for a reconciliation with Castro, while Castro was doing the same with respect to Kennedy, is a matter of considerable interest, even though nothing came of it.

Fortunately, an American diplomat and a French journalist who became involved in the matter have given us a record of what took place. William Attwood, at the time a member of the United States delegation to the United Nations, relates in his book, *The Reds and the Blacks: A Personal Adventure*,[1] that after receiving information from various sources indicating that "Castro wanted an accommodation with the United States," he brought the matter to the attention of Averell Harriman and Adlai Stevenson, suggesting that the overture be probed by establishing "discreet contact" with the Cuban delegation at the United Nations.

"On September 19 [1963]," Attwood wrote, "Harriman told me he was 'adventuresome' enough to favor the idea, but suggested that I discuss it with Bob Kennedy. . . . Stevenson, meanwhile, had mentioned it to the President, who approved my talking to Dr. Carlos Lechuga, the chief Cuban delegate, so long as I made it clear we were not soliciting discussions." A few days later Attwood met Lechuga at a party and set things in motion. Messages concerning how and where to set up an exchange of views went back and forth from Havana and Washington. Lisa Howard, who had interviewed Castro for a television program, was brought into the picture as an intermediary, and she in turn set up telephone communications with Major René Vallejo, Castro's English-speaking personal physician, aide-de-camp, and intimate friend from the days of the Sierra Maestra until his death in 1970.

Bob Kennedy was brought into the picture. He thought a meeting of the two sides could be worthwhile if held "outside Cuba, perhaps in Mexico." McGeorge Bundy was also involved. "On November 5 I went to see him at the White House," Attwood explained. "He said the President, more than the State Department, was interested in exploring this overture, but thought we should now find out just what Castro wanted to discuss before going into a meeting. He thought we should have a preliminary meeting with Vallejo and Lechuga at the United Nations to agree on an agenda."

This led to a telephone conversation between Attwood and Vallejo in which the Cuban said he would be unable to come to New York, but that "Castro would instruct Lechuga to propose and discuss an agenda with me. I said I'd wait for Lechuga to contact me."

1. New York: Harper and Row, 1967, pp. 142 ff.

The next morning, November 19, Kennedy left word with Bundy that he would want to talk with Attwood after his meeting with Lechuga. The president, Bundy said, "would not be leaving Washington, except for a brief trip to Dallas." On November 23, the day after Kennedy's assassination, Lechuga received instructions from Castro to enter into formal discussions with Attwood. Castro's instructions had gone out shortly before the president's death, and Lechuga wondered how this event would affect the situation. "I said I didn't know," Attwood wrote. "But I informed Bundy and later was told that the Cuban exercise would probably be put on ice for a while—which it was and where it has been ever since."

The Mission of Jean Daniel

While the delicate maneuvers for setting up a meeting between representatives of Castro and Kennedy were under way, something akin to a dialogue between the two principals took place. This remarkable exchange of views was transcribed by Jean Daniel, at the time correspondent of the Paris *Express*, who first spoke with the president in Washington and then with the prime minister in Havana.[2] It was only partly a coincidence that two channels of communications were functioning at the same time. Daniel was in the United States and was about to leave for Cuba when he was given an appointment with Kennedy. This was on October 24, a month after Stevenson had apprised the president of Attwood's proposal to talk with Lechuga, to which he had given his consent with the proviso that Attwood make it clear "we were not soliciting discussions."

However, early in Daniel's interview, Kennedy made it clear that his only interest in talking with Daniel was the latter's forthcoming trip to Cuba. After the president had opened the discussion with questions and remarks concerning France and General de Gaulle, as he normally would with a Frenchman, Daniel picked up a reference Kennedy had made to French policy on Vietnam and Cuba, with the idea of exploring this topic further. At this point, Kennedy decided to move on to what was mainly on his mind. "We haven't enough time to talk about Vietnam, but I'd like to talk to you about Cuba," Daniel quotes him as saying. "Incidentally, our

2. Daniel's report was published by the *New Republic* in two installments: "When Castro Heard the News" (December 7) and "Unofficial Envoy: An Historic Report from Two Capitals" (December 14, 1963).

conversation will be much more interesting when you return, because Ben Bradlee (of *Newsweek*) tells me you are on your way to Cuba now." From then on, Kennedy confined his remarks to Cuba. When Daniel left, it was obvious that he had been given a message to deliver to Castro and that Kennedy had invited Daniel to return to the White House with a message from Castro.

Kennedy's message, of course, had to be decoded. It could not be otherwise. To begin with, the president could not even admit that it was a message. Then again, he had to say no more than he could afford to say publicly. He had to convey the impression, both to Castro and all others who would be listening, that he was speaking from a position of strength, moral and otherwise. But he also had to say something new, or what could be perceived as such; otherwise there was no point in saying anything at all. Castro's job—and that of all other interested parties listening in, including future historians —would be to fish out what was new or appeared to be so. A significant novelty could even consist of the omission of a customary formulation or of placing it in a different context. Then, if Daniel could complete the circuit, he would bring back Castro's message, which in turn would also have to be deciphered for similar reasons and in a similar way. Despite these obstacles to clear and meaningful communication—not uncommon in international relations—in this case the important signals could be identified and translated with surprisingly little difficulty.

President Kennedy's Message

What Kennedy told Daniel was in some respects startling. The Frenchman quoted him as saying,

> I believe that there is no country in the world, including all the African regions, including any and all the countries under colonial domination, where economic colonization, humiliation and exploitation were worse than in Cuba, in part owing to my country's policies during the Batista regime. I believe that we created, built and manufactured the Castro movement out of whole cloth and without realizing it. . . . I approved the proclamation which Fidel Castro made in the Sierra Maestra. . . . I will go even further: to some extent it is as though Batista was the incarnation of a number of sins on the part of the United States. Now we shall have to pay for those sins.

Superficially, some of his remarks resembled those of the white paper issued by the State Department on the eve of the Bay of Pigs invasion, as did his reiteration to Daniel, a few moments later, of Castro's betrayal of the original aims of the Revolution and his role as a Soviet agent. But essentially, he was stressing a different point, that of American guilt—and it was even an emotionally charged expression, rather than a cool assessment, of both crime and guilt— and American responsibility to make amends.

Daniel relates how, when he finally sat down to talk with Castro during the night of November 19–20, "Fidel listened with devouring and passionate interest: he pulled his beard, yanked his parachutist's beret down over his eyes, adjusted his maqui tunic, all the while making me the target of a thousand malicious sparks cast by his deep-sunk, lively eyes. . . . Three times he made me repeat certain remarks, particularly those in which Kennedy expressed his criticism of the Batista regime." It must have crossed Fidel's mind that whatever else Kennedy meant, he was saying that he had no intention of promoting the restoration of the ancien régime, with or without Batista.

Although Kennedy understandably made no specific reference to the possibility of a revision of American policy, in effect he threw out two broad suggestions about what it would take to move toward such a revision: "The problem has ceased to be a Cuban one, and has become international—that is, a Soviet problem. I am the President of the United States and not a sociologist." It was a way of saying that the nature and extent of the Soviet presence in the Caribbean affected American security and hence would have to be modified to acceptable limits before matters of "sociology" could be dealt with. Significantly, it was a different formulation than the blunt demand, favored at the time by official and quasi-official spokesmen of the United States government, that Castro sever all ties with the Soviet Union as one of the conditions for restoring normal relations with the United States.

The second suggestion was also related to a familiar theme but was stated in a new way. Daniel raised the question of the purpose and value of the blockade against Cuba. The president at first fell into the familiar pattern of the need to thwart "Communist subversion . . . in the other Latin American countries [and] to contain Soviet expansion," but then paused, according to Daniel, and added,

"The continuation of the blockade depends on the continuation of subversive activities." It was an offer and one that Fidel was ready to accept, as we shall presently see.

The general tenor of Kennedy's message could not be mistaken. It pointed in one direction: the United States could maintain normal relations with a Communist regime in Cuba, and specifically with Fidel Castro's government, provided certain conditions, more implied than defined, were met. Daniel, however, wanted to make sure. He was taking leave of the president when he raised the question directly: "Could the United States tolerate economic collectivism?" Kennedy's answer was less direct but its implications were unmistakable: "What about Sékou Touré? And Tito? I received Marshal Tito three days ago, and our discussions were most positive."

Jean Daniel talked that same evening with two highly knowledgeable American friends, who were as impressed as he was with most of what Kennedy said. "They hesitated to draw any political conclusions," Daniel wrote. "However, they were not surprised at Kennedy's invitation to come and see him again when I returned from Cuba. . . . He had a consuming need for information . . . since experience had taught him not to rely closely on official channels." Neither Daniel nor his friends knew anything about the machinery for secret Cuban-American consultations that Attwood and Lechuga were in the process of setting up with the approval of Kennedy and Castro.

Jean Daniel in Havana

Daniel spent three weeks in Havana. It was his last night in Cuba and he had given up hope of seeing Castro when "Fidel came to my hotel. He had heard of my interview with the President. We went up to my room at 10 in the evening and did not leave until 4 in the following morning [November 20]." This conduct was typical of Fidel, and it was typical also that Daniel then spent two full days with him touring points of interest near the capital.

Such are the idiosyncracies of Fidel Castro.[3] For all his informality, there is much of the *grand seigneur* in Fidel's personal

3. For an illuminating account of many of Fidel's eccentricities, see Lee Lockwood, *Castro's Cuba, Cuba's Fidel*, New York: Random House, 1969. To the foreigner with a sense of humor they can be very amusing, but more often extremely annoying.

habits, including both the abuse of prerogative and the generosity of *noblesse oblige*. In the matter of abuse, he shares an old Latin American tradition—not unknown in other parts of the world—according to which the importance of a politician or a bureaucrat can be measured by how long a person is kept waiting in the antechamber before being ushered into his august presence. Sometimes it can be a matter of days.

Even while Fidel was "supreme commander" of only a small ragged guerrilla band in the mountains, leaders of his underground movement in the cities relate how they would reach his camp with great difficulty and at the risk of their lives, with urgent matters to discuss, and might be kept waiting for two or three days while Fidel moved about the camp in full sight of the new arrival. Later, as prime minister, he would not only summon his cabinet ministers at all hours of the day or night, but would keep them waiting for hours while he received visitors who obviously had only trivial matters to discuss with him.

By way of contrast, in his chance meeting with peasants or factory workers during his constant comings and goings, he would always treat them with a great deal of consideration. "It's not easy to stay calm when a leader like Fidel is talking to you," an agricultural worker in Las Villas Province is reported to have said after a visitation by the prime minister. "You get all shaken up at first, but then you recover from the shock because he talks to you as if he had known you all his life. . . . I can die happy now, since one of my two fondest dreams has come true: to talk with Fidel." (The other dream was to ride in an airplane.) [4] This manner of quickly putting "little people" at ease and hearing them out has been mistaken by some as a manifestation of Fidel's egalitarian spirit, but it is only the reverse side of the same coin: the benevolence of the truly noble ruler toward his most humble subjects.

As for Jean Daniel, he had much of interest to say about the personality of the prime minister and his impressions of the Cuban scene, but more important was his report of Fidel's reaction to Kennedy's "message." The French journalist was with Kennedy at most a half hour, and in the period between November 19 and November 22 he must have spent somewhere in the neighborhood of twenty hours with Fidel. There was also the remarkable coinci-

4. *Granma Weekly Review*, February 28, 1971.

dence that he was having lunch with Fidel in a villa on Varadero Beach, some 80 miles east of Havana, when the news came through of Kennedy's assassination. Fidel's reactions to the flow of radio reports from Miami were extremely interesting and were described at length.

Fidel Castro's Message

If Kennedy had lived to talk with Daniel—or for that matter had only read his articles—he would have concluded that Castro was ready, indeed eager, to resume normal relations with the United States. In a sense, this was not news. For some time, as we have noticed, he had been sending intermittent signals to this effect in his speeches. Then there was also the secret Attwood-Lechuga operation. However, the warmth of his reaction toward Kennedy as a person was unexpected and conveyed an attitude much more conducive to meaningful dialogue than the president could have had reason to suspect. "I believe Kennedy is sincere," was his first response to Daniel's account of what Kennedy had said. "I also believe today that the expression of this sincerity could have political significance. . . . I feel that he inherited a difficult situation. I also think he is a realist."

Later, speaking of the need for a leader to appear in the United States who would be capable of understanding the explosive realities of Latin America and meeting them halfway, Daniel quotes him as exclaiming,

> Kennedy could still be this man. He still has the possibility of becoming, in the eyes of history, the greatest President of the United States, the leader who may at last understand that there can be coexistence between capitalists and socialists, even in the Americas. He would then be an even greater President than Lincoln. . . . Personally, I consider him responsible for everything [economic, political, and paramilitary harassment], but I will say this: he has come to understand many things over the past few months; and then, too, in the last analysis, I'm convinced that anyone else would be worse.

At this point he added, with a broad, boyish grin, according to Daniel, "If you see him again, you can tell him that I'm willing to declare Goldwater my friend if that will guarantee Kennedy's re-election."

As for Fidel's oft repeated views on international affairs, in-cluding the customary invective against the United States, they were understandably present, although somewhat muted, in his message to Kennedy and could be discounted. The important thing was that Fidel was perfectly aware that Kennedy included Cuban export of revolution to Latin America and Soviet-Cuban relations as mandatory topics on any agenda that might be drawn up between them and, being aware, did not reject further dialogue with Kennedy but rather signaled a fervent hope that it could be continued and amplified.

Fidel did not deny the existence of Cuban subversion, but he handled the matter obliquely: "how can the American government seriously believe that Cuban subversion is at the root of explosions taking place all over the South American continent? In Venezuela, for example, are you familiar with the situation there? Do you think the Venezuelans need us to understand what's going on in their country? Do you think we don't have enough problems of our own? Right now I ask only one thing: leave us in peace to better our country's economic situation." It was as if he were saying that he would prefer "socialism in one country" as his goal rather than that of "converting the Andes into the Sierra Maestra of South America." Concluding his remarks on this topic, Fidel told Daniel, "This doesn't mean we do not feel solidarity toward nations that are strug-gling and suffering, like the Venezuelan people. But it is up to those nations to decide what they want, and if they choose other regimes than ours, this isn't our business." It was a far cry from the Second Declaration of Havana!

On the question of Cuban-Soviet relations, Fidel said what had to be said (coincidentally, it was also largely the truth), but in a manner that clearly implied that these relations were not frozen: "We have none but feelings of fraternity and profound, total grati-tude toward the USSR. The Russians are making extraordinary ef-forts on our behalf, efforts which sometimes cost them dear. But we have our own policies which are perhaps not always the same (we have proved this) as those of the USSR." Then, blowing off steam, he exclaimed, "I refuse to dwell on this point, because asking me to say that I am not a pawn on the Soviet chessboard is something like asking a woman to shout aloud in the public square that she is not a prostitute."

Nobody at this moment could have predicted to what extent he would one day go to prove that he was not a pawn, although, had this been foreseen, it might have been predicted that without help from the United States his desperate efforts to remove himself from the Soviet chessboard would end in failure.

Later, expanding his remarks on his relations with the Soviet Union, he referred to a point Kennedy had made in his conversation with Daniel. "Why am I not Tito or Sékou Touré?" Fidel asked rhetorically. "Because the Russians have never done us any injury such as the Yugoslavians and the Guineans have complained of in the past, and because the Americans have never given us any of the benefits for which these two nations congratulate themselves today."

In mentioning Touré and Tito to Daniel, Kennedy in effect was signaling to Castro that the United States could have normal relations with a socialist Cuba and even lend it a helping hand, provided Cuba pursued a wholly independent policy vis-à-vis the USSR; but there was no necessary implication that Cuba would be expected to be hostile to the Soviet Union. On the contrary, when Kennedy received Tito in the White House, the quarrel between Yugoslavia and Russia lay in the past and their relations could be described as somewhere between good and cordial. It would seem that Castro, responding in the way he did to Kennedy's remarks, was saying that a "nonaligned" or "neutralized" Cuba, or whatever the terminology might be, would have to be achieved *with* Soviet cooperation, unlike what happened in Yugoslavia or Guinea. He did not imply that he rejected the role of a Caribbean Tito in the 1963 context of Tito's relations with Russia and the United States.

Soviet cooperation would complicate the process of negotiation, but Fidel had good reason to believe it would be forthcoming, and in any event there was no way to extricate the Russians—peacefully—without it. Dawn was approaching as the long interview drew to a close. "So far as we are concerned," said Fidel, summing up, "everything can be restored to normalcy on the basis of mutual respect of sovereignty." The word "mutual" was significant, for customarily Fidel phrased the question as a matter of American respect for Cuban sovereignty. And finally, as he was about to take leave of Daniel, Fidel said, "Since you are going to see Kennedy again, be an emissary of peace, despite everything." It was November 20, two days before Kennedy's death.

Daniel relates how a telephone call from Dorticós to Fidel in Varadero first brought the news that Kennedy had been shot and seriously wounded. "This is bad news," Fidel said as he sat down after hanging up the telephone receiver, repeating it three times. Then René Vallejo tuned in the radio on the NBC network in Miami and began to translate the flow of news for Fidel. Finally, when the announcement came that the president was dead, Fidel stood up and said to Daniel, "Everything is changed. Everything is going to change. The United States occupies such a position in world affairs that the death of a President of that country affects millions of people in every corner of the world. The cold war, relations with Russia, Latin America, Cuba, the Negro question . . . all will have to be rethought. . . . This is a serious matter, an extremely serious matter." Nevertheless, as far as Cuban-American relations were concerned, once the shock of Kennedy's death was over, he regained his hope that the dialogue between the two countries could continue —a hope that he apparently did not completely abandon until the American military intervention in the Dominican Republic at the end of April 1965.

27

■

The Logic of the "Dialogue"

The View from Washington

THERE WOULD BE NO PROFIT in speculating whether serious negotiations between the two countries might have gotten under way had President Kennedy lived, or whether they might have led to a settlement. What can be said with confidence, in the light of subsequent events, is that the stalemate to which the conflict was reduced —what in fact developed as the alternative to a return to normal relations—turned out to be of no particular benefit to the United States, nor was it by any means disastrous for the Soviet Union or Cuba. The economic and political pressures applied by the United States over more than a decade failed to isolate Cuba even from the rest of Latin America, to say nothing of bringing down the Castro regime. The heavy United States military investment required to check Cuban-linked guerrilla warfare did not prevent significant radical change, largely unrelated to the very existence of Cuba, from taking place, such as the leftist-nationalist military take overs in Peru and Bolivia and the election of a Marxist-dominated government in Chile.

As for Cuba, American policy can take little credit for contributing to Castro's colossal economic bungling after the initial impact of the trade embargo had been absorbed; but by providing a credible target for the arousal of Cuban nationalism, it can take some credit for Castro's political survival. Nor, as the record shows, do the Russians have much to complain about. For a while, trying to control Castro was like trying to hold on to a cougar by the tail. It was an expensive, nerve-wracking, and at times dangerous operation. However, from the political point of view, the worst appeared to be over by late 1968, for since then Castro has complied with Soviet policy on all major international issues. From the economic point of view, the worst was also probably over. In 1971, proclaimed as "The Year of Productivity," Fidel introduced a new Soviet-oriented drive for "rationality" and "productivity," stressing work norms, material incentives, and a novel "law on loafing," making it a crime punishable by prison for any able-bodied adult male under the age of sixty to be without regular employment.[1] In any event, with the Russians now exercising considerable supervision over the economy, the recurrence of a disaster of the magnitude of that of 1970, "The Year of the Ten Million Tons," when 8.5 million tons of sugar were produced at an incalculable cost to the rest of the economy, is unlikely.

Meanwhile, with the passage of time, the Soviet investment began to yield modest, but not negligible, dividends. It can be taken for granted that the Russians have erected a space-tracking station in Cuba whose latitude offers advantages to the Soviet Union not available elsewhere. Nor can the Russians have overlooked the fact that Cuba is conveniently situated for conducting visual reconnaissance and electronic monitoring of many kinds of activities of military interest in the Caribbean and southern Florida regions, including Cape Kennedy and the United States Atlantic Missile Range. The fishing port built by the Russians near Havana provides facilities for both the Cuban and Soviet fishing fleets, including the inquisitive trawlers that patrol the Atlantic seaboard. In July 1969 the Cuban media featured the first visit to Cuba of units of the Soviet navy and the reception given Castro aboard the commanding admiral's flagship. Subsequent visits occurred, and by early 1971 it was apparent that the Soviet Union had established a small naval base at Cienfuegos,

1. For details, see particularly Castro's speech of May 1, 1971 (*Granma Weekly Review*, May 16, 1971). During his great controversy with the Kremlin (1965–1968), he had rejected Soviet "revisionism," claiming he was moving directly into a Communist society, from which both material incentives and money would be rapidly abolished. In 1971 he returned to the general line he had sketched out in 1963, under the influence of Khrushchev, but never seriously implemented.

on Cuba's southern coast, some 350 miles northwest of Guantánamo. The Caribbean could now be added to the Mediterranean Sea and the Indian Ocean among the new zones of expanding Russian naval power. Thus, for the Soviet Union, Cuba was transformed from a liability into something of an asset.[2]

Cuba in the Context of the United States–Soviet Relations in 1963

At what point President Kennedy began to give serious thought to a settlement with Castro as an alternative to a policy designed to destroy him is not known. Nor, it appears, did he discuss his motives with his closest associates; or if he did, they prefer to remain silent. However, a brief review of the context in which he could not have failed to view the Cuban problem in the fall of 1963 should provide reasonable clues about what prompted him to enter into a dialogue with Fidel Castro. To begin with, following the missile crisis of the previous October—the "Gettysburg of the Cold War" in Theodore Sorensen's words [3]—the achievement of a détente and then something resembling peaceful coexistence with the Soviet Union had become an overriding objective of Kennedy's foreign policy. His historic speech at American University in Washington on June 10 seemed to mark the end of one period and the beginning

2. In a dispatch filed on February 19, 1971, from the United States Naval Base at Guantánamo, and published in the *New York Times* on February 27, Drew Middleton described the Russian naval base as follows: "The Cienfuegos base is much smaller than Guantánamo: barracks for 200 men, recreation grounds, a communications building, a submarine net blocking off a corner of the harbor and two . . . metal barges . . . used for storing radioactive effluent from submarine reactors." The U.S. government publicly expressed concern once the base was discovered. Drew Middleton sums it up in the same dispatch: "The Nixon administration hopes Cienfuegos will not be . . . used [by submarines armed with nuclear missiles]. Its hopes are based on an 'understanding' that the United States will not seek to overthrow . . . Castro's government and that, in return, nuclear-armed Soviet vessels will not be serviced 'in or from' Cuban ports." The Russians officially denied that nuclear-armed vessels were being serviced in Cuba. For an extensive discussion of Cuba's actual and potential strategic importance to the Soviet Union, see Hanson W. Baldwin, *Strategy for Tomorrow* (New York: Harper and Row, 1970), pp. 109–121.

3. *Kennedy* (New York: Bantam, 1965), p. 815.

of another in the search for peace. Specifically, he rejected a "Pax Americana enforced on the world by American weapons of war" and told his fellow countrymen that "we must re-examine our own attitude—as individuals and as a Nation—for our attitude is as essential as theirs [the Russians]." This speech was followed by a number of others in the same vein up to the time of his death. At the same time, words were translated into deeds, such as the hot line providing direct, instantaneous telephonic communication between the Kremlin and the White House; an authorization (in October) by the president for the sale of surplus wheat to the USSR; and most important, the signing of the Nuclear Test Ban Treaty on July 25, 1963.

Logically, the reexamination that President Kennedy called for at American University would include Cuba, the point of greatest and most dangerous friction the two great powers had thus far known. Although the resolution of their confrontation in the Caribbean had lost its extreme urgency, it was by means of a hastily improvised truce rather than a duly deliberated treaty that a measure of calm had been restored. Thus, Cuba remained a potential source of further aggravation of Soviet-American relations, but also by virtue of this fact it was an issue over which some serious bargaining and trading could be expected in the long and extended process of putting together a global settlement. However, the incorporation of Cuba in this process would not mean that Fidel Castro would be a simple spectator, as both the great powers fully realized. Thus, in terms of moving from a détente with the Russians toward a broad and stable agreement, establishing lines of communications between Washington and Havana, and searching for the basis of a modus vivendi with Fidel Castro would be clearly indicated and would not have escaped the attention of the president.

The Failure of the Economic Blockade

There were other matters that undoubtedly contributed to the president's need to reevaluate American policy toward Cuba. Quite simply, the policy was not working and prospects were not promising that eventually it would work. Ever since late February 1962, when Walt Rostrow, then head of the State Department's Policy Planning Committee, toured NATO countries in a vain effort to induce them to cut off trade with Cuba, continuing efforts to isolate Cuba from western Europe, including Spain, and also from Canada and Japan had met with failure. Thus, for example, a White House order issued on February 6, 1963, made it illegal for United States government-financed cargoes to be shipped in foreign vessels calling at Cuban ports. Nevertheless, by the following September, 181 ships of foreign registry had been placed on the American blacklist, without measurably slowing down traffic between Cuba and capitalist countries, as Senator Stennis of Mississippi, head of a subcommittee dealing with the question, reported to the Senate.[4] Apparently, the penalty for engaging in this traffic was smaller than the profit.

There were other discouraging developments, some of smaller and others of larger import; but added together they formed a consistent trend. In February 1963, for example, the United Nations approved a $3-million grant for an experimental crop diversification project to be carried out in Cuba by the Food and Agriculture Organization (FAO). It was a small amount, but the United States strenuously opposed the grant and thereby suffered a political defeat of much greater proportion. Meanwhile, although American subsidiaries and branch plants throughout the world practically without exception observed the embargo on trade with Cuba,[5] since otherwise their parent companies in the United States would be sub-

4. Report dated September 11, 1963. Among other maritime nations, France and Great Britain stated that their governments had no legal power to ban privately owned ships sailing under their flags from going where they pleased. See *Hispanic American Report* 16, no. 9 (October 1963): 867.

5. The countries whose exports were affected were undoubtedly not very happy with this arrangement. Probably some annoyance was implied when the *Economist* of London decided to publish the following letter (August 7, 1965, p. 497): "Sir: The following letter, dated June 25, 1965, from the Ford Motor Company Ltd., may be of interest: 'Thank you for your letter . . . concerning the parts you require for your 1957 Zephyr. . . . We are unable to comply with your request due to our company being American-owned and there being . . . a non-Trade Agreement [sic] in force at this time between Cuba and the USA. . . . You can no doubt appreciate that we must comply with our company's marketing policy.' I was of course aware of the 'non-Trade Agreement,' but I had assumed that a company domiciled in England would be under some obligation to respect British trade policy. Yours faithfully, Maurice Halperin, Havana, Cuba." By way of postscript, it may be noted that the parts, which cost less than $100, were subsequently purchased from a large Ford dealer in Canada by a legitimate freight forwarding agent and shipped to Havana in a perfectly normal transaction.

ject to prosecution, and although unofficial pressures brought to bear on foreign firms in one way or another dependent on American supplies or the American market achieved some success, nevertheless, as the year wore on it became evident that these efforts were only partially effective in undermining the Cuban economy and were likely to become less so as time passed. Thus, *Business Week* reported in September that equipment for a $4-million kenaf bag plant was on its way from Ireland to Santa Clara, in central Cuba, where it would be installed by Irish engineers. It also noted that the Japanese had entered into an agreement to assist Cuba with creating a modern fishing fleet and had already supplied five large tuna boats with training crews.[6]

In mid-September, in connection with a Soviet contract to purchase wheat and flour from Canada for the sum of $500 million, it was announced in Ottawa that the agreement included exports to Cuba valued at $33 million, which would be transported directly to Cuba in Soviet vessels.[7] About this time, discussions were under way in London for the Cuban purchase of Leyland buses on credit (a contract for 400 buses was signed on January 6, 1964) and in Paris for Berliet trucks on credit (a contract for 300 trucks was signed on February 7, 1964). Even more disconcerting for Washington was the fact that, despite very heavy pressure exerted on the Spanish government, it could not prevent the Franco regime from entering into an agreement with Cuba for the importation of 300,000 tons of sugar over a period of three years and the construction of up to 100 fishing and cargo vessels for the Castro government over a longer period of time. Washington went so far as to issue a formal public protest over the shipbuilding plans on December 18, 1963, but to no avail. Spain also refused to cut air and sea traffic with Cuba. With respect to the former, Iberia was the only capitalist airline to maintain a regular link between Cuba and Europe. Spain's bargaining position was strong because it supplied a base for Polaris equipped submarines at Rota.

Mutual ideological antipathy, plus Castro's expulsion of Spanish

6. Cited by *Hispanic American Report*, p. 866. Also mentioned in the same *HAR* article, but attributed to another source, was French equipment for a gas plant in a Havana suburb and a yeast plant based on sugar molasses.

7. In Cuban trade statistics, this merchandise and all other Soviet-financed goods are treated as imports from the Soviet Union.

priests (replaced by Belgian and Canadian priests), at first put a severe strain on relations between Cuba and Spain, including trade relations. However, diplomatic ties were never broken; and according to one writer, by 1961, because of an "undercurrent of hostility to the United States" of long standing, "there was considerable sympathy in Spain with the Cubans against the Bay of Pigs invaders." [8] In 1963 mutual economic benefits proved stronger than ideology, and by the end of the year all references to "fascist Spain" and unfavorable news items in general disappeared from the Cuban media. As the variety of goods exchanged expanded, trade between Cuba and Spain increased from under $11 million in 1962 to approximately $103 million in 1966, making Spain Cuba's third most important trading partner after the Soviet Union (nearly $800 million) and China ($172 million). By way of contrast, trade with Czechoslovakia, in fourth place after Spain, failed to reach $84 million.[9]

In short, the American economic blockade was considerably less than a success, mainly for the following reasons: the pressing need for the countries mentioned and others to export; with Soviet backing for Cuba firmly established, credit risks were normal, perhaps better than normal, for the record showed that while Communist regimes frequently failed to meet their commitments among themselves, they never defaulted in their payments to capitalist creditors; and the limitations of American retaliatory power. Still another reason may be added in the case of a number of countries, among them Spain and Japan: the need to guarantee supplies of sugar in the face of critical shortages on the world market in 1963 and an uncertain future thereafter.

The Shadow over the Alliance for Progress

The Alliance for Progress, proclaimed on March 13, 1961, a month before the Bay of Pigs invasion, and whose formal charter was signed at Punta del Este five months later, was the instrument with which President Kennedy proposed to meet the challenge of the Cuban Revolution in Latin America. It was to be, in the president's

8. J. W. D. Trythall, *Franco: A Biography* (London: Hart-Davis, 1970), pp. 253–254.
9. *El comercio exterior de Cuba y sus tendencias, 1966* (Havana: Ministerio de Comercio Exterior, 1967), pp. 73–75.

words addressed to the Latin American diplomatic corps on March 13, "a vast cooperative effort, unparalleled in magnitude and nobility of purpose, to satisfy the basic needs of the [Latin] American people for homes, work and land, health and schools." The alliance would aim, said the president, "to complete the revolution of the Americas" and provide "an example that liberty and progress walk hand in hand." To meet this goal, it was agreed at Punta del Este to utilize over a ten-year period $20 billion in foreign capital, of which half would be United States government funds, with $80 billion to come from domestic Latin American sources. In addition, and recognized as of prime importance, was the stipulation that the participating Latin American governments carry out various social and economic reforms considered to be prerequisites for material growth and the "peaceful revolution." "For unless social reforms, including land and tax reform, are freely made," the president had said on March 13, "—unless the great mass of [Latin] Americans share in increasing prosperity—then our alliance, our revolution and our dream will have failed."

In October 1963, when President Kennedy met with Jean Daniel, the alliance was in trouble. The most significant diagnostic indicator was the rash of military coups d'etat that began to topple Latin American governments early in 1962 and which reached epidemic levels in 1963. President Miguel Ydígoras of Guatemala was overthrown in March 1963, Carlos Arosemena of Ecuador in July, Juan Bosch of the Dominican Republic in September, and Ramón Villeda of Honduras in October. Particularly painful to the president was the ouster of Bosch, seven months after taking office in the first free elections in the Dominican Republic in thirty-eight years. Bosch, an anti-Communist like José Figueres of Costa Rica, Muñoz Marín of Puerto Rico, and Rómulo Betancourt of Venezuela, was "one of the brotherhood of the democratic left" and on his election "the Kennedy administration was determined to make the Dominican Republic a showcase of free men working through democratic institutions." [10]

A statement by Edwin A. Martin, assistant secretary of state for Latin American affairs, published in the *New York Herald Tribune*

10. Jerome Levinson and Juan de Onis, *The Alliance that Lost Its Way: A Critical Report on the Alliance for Progress* (New York: Quadrangle, 1970), p. 85.

on October 6, 1963, reflected the deep pessimism of President Kennedy and foreshadowed the gradual disintegration of the alliance in the following years. In this statement, "Martin sorrowfully observed that the basic political principle of the Alliance—'that free men working through the institutions of representative democracy can best satisfy man's aspirations'—was beyond attainment in the near future in individual Latin American countries." [11]

Under these circumstances, Latin America could be expected to remain fertile soil for Cuban propaganda and subversion. Immediately after the missile crisis, it was felt in Washington that Fidel Castro's reputation among Latin American nationalists and leftists had been dealt a mortal blow. In the fall of 1963, there was reason to doubt that this was the case. The radical middle- and upper-class youth who formed the new leadership and the shock troops of the militant left in Latin America were less concerned whether Cuba had been or still was a Soviet satellite—and for many, if not most, Fidel's recurring heretical outbursts proved that he was not—than with the fact that Cuba had successfully taken what they believed to be the indispensable first step to secure what the Alliance for Progress had promised and failed to deliver. That step was for Latin America to defy the United States and end what they perceived to be its status as an American satellite. Meanwhile, there was no com-

---

11. *Ibid.*, p. 86. Kennedy had reportedly approved the statement before it was released. What went wrong with the alliance has been a matter of debate almost since its inception. For example, in an article first published in 1964, David Horowitz stressed conflicting vested interests, American and Latin American, as the main stumbling blocks and went so far as to say that the "primary goal of the Alliance, from the very first, was not progress, but preservation—or more accurately, and with emphasis on the tactical changes introduced by Kennedy—progress only insofar as it was necessary for preservation" ("The Alliance for Progress," in *Imperialism and Underdevelopment*, edited by Robert I. Rhodes [New York: Monthly Review, 1970], p. 59). Levinson and Onis, in their book-length study, state that "our experience in the Alliance clearly demonstrates . . . how little we know about the interaction of economic, social and political conditions in developing countries" (p. 327). At the same time, they believe that the "Alliance represented innovation in both its approach to national development and its identification of the United States with concern for democracy and social justice. This innovative effort was subverted not by communism, but by two preoccupations, technocracy [that is, a narrow approach to development as economic growth] and the U.S. security interest" (p. 331).

fort in the fact that five southern republics, despite all the pressures exerted against them by Washington, still maintained normal relations with Cuba. Among them were Brazil, Mexico, and Chile, three of the four (with Argentina) most influential countries in the area.[12] In mid-July 1963 Uruguay, small but prestigious for its long-functioning parliamentary system of government, signed a new commercial agreement with Cuba.[13]

Thus, on the eve of his assassination, President Kennedy was faced with the need for a reappraisal of United States policy toward Latin America, and reappraisal logically required a review of the Cuban situation. If the problems of relations with the USSR and the limited success of the economic blockade suggested that more advantages than disadvantages could ensue from a normalization of relations with Cuba, the impact of normalization on Latin America would be more difficult to estimate. From the American point of view, there could be at least one positive result. Any kind of accommodation with Cuba would necessarily stipulate the elimination of the island as a source of propaganda and subversion directed against Latin American governments and the United States. In the climate of late 1963, with Radio Havana bombarding the region from the outside and with Cuban-assisted guerrilla movements operating on the inside, these were matters to evoke legitimate apprehension. For the rest, there would be negotiable arrangements with negative as well as positive implications to be considered. In the last analysis, normalization of relations with Cuba would have to be evaluated not only in terms of its Latin American repercussions but on the basis of global considerations.

The View from Havana

In the late fall of 1963, Fidel was eager to reach a settlement with the United States. Although in both domestic and international affairs he could play the role of Don Quixote convincingly because

12. All five countries except Mexico broke relations in August 1964. In 1970 Chile resumed relations, while Peruvian and Bolivian relations with Cuba improved considerably, although still on an informal basis.

13. With dwindling income from its traditional exports of wool and meat, Uruguay was attracted by Cuba's offer to buy rice and jerked beef in exchange for sugar. During the approximately thirteen months that the agreement was in operation, trade between the two countries amounted to $13 million. See *Cuba Socialista* 3, no. 25 (September 1963): 48 ff and *El comercio exterior de Cuba*, p. 74.

of a genuine affinity with the compulsive and impractical idealism of the embattled knight-errant of La Mancha,[14] he was not a steadfast Don Quixote as, for example, Che Guevara came to be. Whether because, unlike Che, he was only one generation removed from Sancho Panza, the down-to-earth peasant squire who accompanied Don Quixote in his adventures—Fidel's immigrant father came from Galicia, in northwest Spain, where the peasantry is reputed to be particularly shrewd—or because, again, unlike Che, he was not an "employee" but the "owner" of the enterprise that went under the name of the Cuban Revolution, the question of the survival and prosperity of the "business" could never be too far from the center of the hopes, fears, and ambitions motivating his behavior.

As we have seen, this was not the first time that Fidel held out an olive branch to the United States. He may have done so awkwardly, but each time two things were clear: he was not offering to surrender, but he did offer to bargain. What he was willing to bargain was never clarified, because his offer to begin discussions was never accepted. Presumably, effective sovereignty—Cuba's right to make its own decisions concerning domestic affairs and international relations—was something he would not bargain away. This would make his revolution pointless and would amount to surrender. Nevertheless, the exercise of sovereignty involved many considerations. Thus, it was evident that even after obtaining sovereignty, in many instances newly independent states found it practical to maintain close economic relations with the former "imperialist oppressor," and vice versa. Algerian and French cooperation, after a prolonged and bitter war, was an example that particularly impressed Fidel and he mentioned it in his conversations with Jean Daniel.[15] Cuban sovereignty, he implied, would not necessarily rule out concessions to "Yankee imperialism" in return for acceptable concessions from the latter.

14. In the Hispanic tradition, the protagonist in the classical novel by Cervantes came to symbolize the fearless and self-sacrificing champion of the poor and downtrodden rather than the eccentric visionary, the "quixotic" failure, which his name conjures up in the English-speaking world.

15. In 1971 relations between the two countries for several months were temporarily in a state of crisis as a result of a dispute over French participation in the Algerian petroleum industry, but this was nearly eight years after Daniel's visit with Castro.

Fidel had discovered that sovereignty for a small country like Cuba was easier to obtain than to keep. To remain independent of the United States, he had to accept military and economic dependency on the Soviet Union. In one sense it was an easier dependency to bear: if Soviet loans could be called investments, they were not equity investments; the rate of interest was low and in time they were expected to be liquidated. Meanwhile, in the economic exchange between the two countries, the balance of benefit to a considerable degree was in favor of Cuba. On this score, there was little to complain about. Then again, as a result of a number of circumstances already mentioned, such as Cuba's geographic location and its importance in the ideological-political confrontation between the two Communist giants, the island could enjoy a degree of freedom from political interference unknown by the client states of either the Soviet Union or the United States.

On the other hand, military and economic dependency on the USSR had its drawbacks. The missile crisis of 1962 was a striking example of what military dependency could mean. For the rest, Fidel discovered that, for all the promise held out for a diversified and industrialized economy "in the future," Cuba had no choice but to revert to the status of a sugar producer, principally for a preferential market from which it would have to obtain the bulk of its imports. If this arrangement could at first be welcomed as a guarantee of survival, it nonetheless reproduced the classic relationship whereby conceivably, basic decisions concerning the Cuban economy, political structure, and foreign policy could eventually be made in Moscow rather than Havana. Special conditions already noted provided Cuba with a larger potential for exercising its sovereignty, but this situation might not last indefinitely.

As Fidel no doubt now fully understood, the Soviet Union and all the other socialist countries were "in business," just as he was. The elimination of capitalism in the countries of the socialist camp did not eliminate the nation-state in a world organized into nation-states. The rulers of truly sovereign countries, whether Communist or capitalist and whether or not they believed their respective ideological slogans and rationalizations, were primarily and necessarily motivated in their international relations by what they conceived to be their own national interests. I tried to explain in late 1963 to my perplexed and as yet insufficiently indoctrinated students at the

University of Havana the reason for the *discrepancias* among the Communist states: "The difficulty is that in the pursuit of their professed common goals, there is no infallible and all-powerful Marxist-Leninist god to assign tasks and priorities to the peoples in his camp. If such a god existed, he could decide impartially which socialist country should sacrifice how much and for how long for the common good."

It was a moment when students at the University of Havana, many of whom held part-time jobs in the various ministries and government departments, were becoming "fed up" with the Soviet Union. To a large extent they reflected sentiment in the upper bureaucracy and, more important, some of Fidel's more intimate moods of which they had first-hand knowledge. Fidel had the habit of appearing unannounced on the campus, usually around midnight, and would be immediately surrounded by scores of students with whom he would engage in an impromptu and extended bull session under the stars. At this period, they talked mainly about economics, the cumbersome and inscrutable Soviet planning system, the inability of the Russians and other east Europeans to supply Cuba with certain essential imports, and the alacrity with which they dumped shoddy goods in Cuba for which they could find no other market (meanwhile, the Russian and other foreign technicians in Cuba were tearing their hair about the wild incompetence, profligacy, and sheer waste of the Cubans). The students complained that the Soviet economic textbooks they were required to read were long on Marxist abstractions and short on concrete economic analysis, and they cheered Fidel when he proposed to transform the Faculty of Economics from a "theological institute" (in his own words) to a modern school of practical economics incorporating the application of mathematics and cybernetics to the solution of Cuba's economic problems.

The following year, Fidel was as good as his word. "Theology" was abolished and mathematics enthroned, which had some positive results but which could not prevail against the larger irrationalities of the Fidelista system of economics. But that is another story.[16]

16. John Kenneth Galbraith is of the opinion that, "In the longer run, it is impossible to suppose that the Cuban revolution will be regarded as less to the advantage of economic development than the Mexican revolution [of 1910]" (*Economics, Peace, and Laughter* [Boston: Houghton Mifflin, 1971], p. 299). This view, expressed in his

Fidel's Goal

Toward the end of 1963 Fidel was looking for a way to maintain what he needed of the life-saving economic and military support received from the Soviet Union while at the same time to reduce his dependency on that support. From all the evidence, his aim at the time was far removed from creating the "new man" in Cuba or from sacrificing Cuba, if need be, for the sake of the "liberation" of Latin America, both of which ideas Che Guevara steadfastly continued to promote. It was more than a year later that Fidel, thoroughly frustrated by political and economic miscalculations, decided to adopt Che's program, which in turn he had to abandon after Che's military defeat in Bolivia and the economic catastrophe of the "Year of the Ten Million Tons" in Cuba. His goal at the time of his "dialogue" with Kennedy was to create in Cuba a prosperous socialist economy, relying on material rewards as incentives for increasing production and developing a more supple and sophisticated planning mechanism than the Russo-Czech system which events had forced Cuba to accept.

Politically, he could justify this goal, when the time would come to announce it, as setting up the "socialist showcase," which Che had rashly promised at Punta del Este in the summer of 1961. To achieve the goal, he could count in principle on the Soviet Union, but almost as important would be an accommodation with the United States. Meanwhile he would keep his options open.

The Sugar Paradox

Fidel's buoyant mood was shored up by a rare paradox. The Cuban sugar harvest of 1963 had dropped from 4.8 million metric tons (raw value) in 1962 to 3.8 million, a reduction of more than 20 percent and, compared with the figure of 1961, a decline of close to 45 percent. It was, moreover, the smallest amount of sugar produced in Cuba in any single year since 1945. In other words, it was something

Massey Lectures over the Canadian Broadcasting Corporation network in 1965, would seem optimistic in 1971, although in terms of "the longer run"—Castro may "settle down" and in any event he is not immortal—Galbraith may be right. Meanwhile, his prognosis has the virtue of placing the economic potentialities of the Cuban revolution in a more modest and realistic perspective than the one adopted by Fidel Castro and his followers.

of a record failure.[17] Nevertheless, in terms of sugar revenue, it was an entirely different story. The average annual price of sugar in the free-market area [18] had nearly trebled in 1963 as compared with 1962.

Prices actually began their upward trend in August 1962, when the monthly average reached 3.24 cents per pound, after a three-year period of slow decline during which monthly averages failed to reach 3 cents. By that time, it was apparent that world output would be substantially lower than the 54.7 million metric tons produced in 1961, and so in fact it was—by 3 million tons (51.6 million was the total for 1962). Cuba was responsible for two-thirds of the decline, but beet sugar production also dropped in Europe because of adverse climatic conditions, thus helping to set the stage for the unprecedented price boom of 1963, which continued well into 1964.

Despite the further decline of Cuban production in 1963—a phenomenon that could be anticipated by the astute sugar brokers in London, Hamburg, and New York before the new harvest began and confirmed early in the milling season—world production in 1963 increased by a million tons (from 51.6 to 52.6 million). However, here another factor entered the picture. While Cuba in the early 1960s was one of the world's three major sugar producers (along with the United States and the USSR), accounting for roughly 10 percent of the total prior to the 1963 decline, it was by far the largest exporter, providing about 20 percent of the sugar entering into international trade. Thus, total world exports, which declined from 22.4 million metric tons in 1961 to 21.1 in 1962, declined still further to 18.8 in 1963, causing prices to zoom upward, going above 12 cents a pound in the first week of November 1963 and resulting in the phenomenal average for that month of 11.53 cents.

Cuba was, in fact, mainly responsible for the shortage, which

17. It was partly due to a reduction in area under cane as part of a program of agricultural diversification initiated in 1961. The level of sugar production, however, was to be maintained by more intensive use of reduced acreage. There was no appreciable gain in other crops planted to replace sugar.

18. The free market is also called the world market, as distinguished from the preferential markets, such as the United States, the United Kingdom, and the USSR, where most of the sugar is imported from selected countries on the basis of special arrangements. On the average, only about one-third of total world sugar exports are sold in the free-market area, hence it is also referred to as the residual market.

in turn created the financial bonanza with which the free play of supply, demand, and speculation in the capitalist markets rewarded the gross mismanagement of a socialist economy. If Fidel had planned it this way, he could have laid claim to being one of the great financial wizards of all time. It was, however, but one more of the providential interventions that have played so conspicuous a role in the destiny of the Cuban Revolution. In any event, Cuban sugar exports fell from 5.1 million tons in 1962 to 3.5 million in 1963, the latter amount including several hundred thousand tons that normally would have been kept in reserve for domestic consumption. On the other hand, the value of Cuba's sugar exports rose. Without the availability of pertinent data concerning each transaction, it is not possible to say precisely the amount of revenue produced. However, the value of total exports in both years is known. Since it is a safe assumption that income from exports other than sugar (mainly tobacco and minerals, representing no more than 15 percent of total export value) did not increase, the rise in total value of exports can be attributed to sugar. Hence, while the quantity of sugar exported in 1963 dropped by a third compared to 1962, the increase in the price of sugar resulted in an increase of the total value of Cuban exports from $526.5 million to $544.8 million.

This was, of course, only a modest increase, although considering the disaster that had occurred in sugar production it was something of a miracle. However, the true dimension of the miracle is revealed in the data concerning exports to capitalist countries. From $95.2 million in 1962, the value rose to $178.3 million in 1963, an increase of nearly 90 percent. This was the true bonanza—the fulfillment of the dream of once more being able to acquire familiar necessities and some luxuries in the corrupt capitalist markets where goods were plentiful, quality was high, prices low, and delivery fast and dependable.

Shifting the Markets

To achieve this bonanza required the diversion of a considerable quantity of sugar from the socialist to the capitalist markets, and here Fidel must be given due credit for persuading his fraternal customers to overlook the contracts they had signed with Cuba. Principally, of course, it meant getting the cooperation of Khrushchev. In this he was eminently successful, whether by fair or foul means is not known. Cuban sugar exports to the Soviet Union were reduced from slightly over two million tons in 1962 to slightly under one million in 1963. As a result, the total value of Cuban exports to the USSR fell from something over $233 million in 1962 to $164 million in 1963, a reduction of 26 percent. Meanwhile, the value of Cuban imports from the Soviet Union rose in the same period from $411 million to $461 million. As a result, the annual Cuban trade deficit with the Soviet Union, which in 1962 amounted to $188 million, jumped to $297 million in 1963. All in all, Fidel's bonanza was a considerable burden to the Russians, as Fidel must have known, and which must have increased his confidence that Khrushchev would welcome a normalization of Cuban-American relations, which could diminish the burden.

The other contributor to Fidel's new prosperity was China, which received roughly half (500,000 tons) the amount of sugar in 1963 that it had in 1962. This, in turn, affected the balance of trade. Where Cuba's deficit with China in 1962 was $800,000, it rose to over $18 million in 1963, since the value of Cuban imports from China was substantially the same in both years. Once the Russians relinquished half of the sugar they had expected to receive, the Chinese could do no less, although almost certainly they would have been much more reluctant to do so at the end of 1963, when Fidel once more seemed to be headed for the fleshpots of revisionism, than at the beginning of the year when the sugar concessions must have been granted. Nevertheless, in mid-November 1963 a glimmer of hope—not much more—must have been raised in Peking that the sacrifice was not in vain when Florián Chomón, brother of Faure then high in the Cuban government and party bureaucracy, arrived in Tirana belatedly to set up a Cuban embassy in the Albanian capital.[19]

19. Sugar data taken from *Annual Report and Accounts for the Year 1963* (London: International Sugar Council, Annex G, p. 19; *Economic Survey of Latin America 1964*, Economic Commission for Latin America, United Nations, 1966, p. 230; *Sugar Year Book, 1967* and *Sugar Year Book, 1969* (London: International Sugar Organization [formerly International Sugar Council]), *passim*. Cuban trade figures taken from *El comercio exterior de Cuba*, pp. 73–75.

A Brilliant Outlook

"Things are moving along very well in our country, very well in-deed!" exclaimed Fidel, speaking to several thousand students at the University of Havana on November 27, 1963. He spoke of the rapid recovery of the economy from the damage inflicted by the hurricane of the previous month, of the great strides made in surmounting the shortcomings of the Revolution due to the "inexperience of us all, the irresponsibility of many of us [and] the absence of the most elementary concepts of economics, of costs" (already a familiar theme of self-criticism that he was to repeat time and again in the future). True, compared with earlier years, some semblance of order could be detected; routines had been established in the ministries; there was an enormous amount of bookeeping and of planning on paper which could create the illusion that the figures in the ledgers were sound and that plans were related to reality and were being im-plemented. Perhaps Fidel himself shared the illusion, temporarily, but what mainly motivated his optimism was sugar.

The shortage that sent prices skyrocketing he attributed, char-acteristically, to the American "imperialists who wanted to ruin us, and it cost them hundreds of millions [of dollars]. When they cut off our quota, they hoped to buy in the world market at lower prices [than they paid us]. Our sugar . . . went to other [socialist] markets; [this] produced a shortage of sugar and as a result, an ex-traordinary increase in the price of sugar." In fact, he went on to say, prices would stay high for some time: "we've sold sugar for delivery in 1965 at about 10 cents." The outlook, he declared, flushed with optimism, was for high prices to continue for "five or six years." [20]

20. Actually, by mid-1964 prices in the free-market area had dropped substantially as a result of which the average for the year came to 5.86 cents a pound, as compared with the average of 8.48 cents in 1963. In 1965 the annual average fell to 2.12 cents, below the 1962 average, and in 1966 it declined further to 1.86 cents. Nevertheless, both 1964 and 1965—but not 1966—were good years, partly because of ad-vance contracts at earlier high prices and partly because of a larger volume of sugar output and sales. Total exports by Cuba to capitalist markets in 1964 were $288 million, the high point in the boom. In 1965 they were reduced to $153 million, not far below the $178 million of 1963.

And after that, what? There will be some years of low prices, "we must expect it," he said, because of "the opportunistic policy of bourgeois sugarcane producers" who will expand production hoping to "make a profit at our expense." He was referring to the desperate race to increase output by sugar producers in Mexico, Brazil, the Dominican Republic, and elsewhere in Latin America who, in addition to being spurred on by high prices, were competing for a share of the former Cuban quota in the American preferential market. Under these circumstances, he asked, what should we do? Should we restrict our production? Should we enter into international quota agreements with the capitalist producers in order to protect the price of sugar in the capitalist markets? His answer was a categorical "No!"

Fidel Rattles His "Atomic Bomb"

Fidel then went on to explain that Cuba had the best natural conditions in the world for the production of sugar, and by modernizing its technology it could vastly increase production. "And what does this mean?" he asked. "That by 1970 we'll be producing more than 10 million tons, we'll be able to export 10 million tons; at that time there will be two possibilities: . . . either there will be a great increase in demand . . . or the bourgeois competitors of Cuban sugar will be ruined. . . . Someday these competitors will realize that they can't compete with us and that as far as sugar is concerned, we have the 'atomic bomb' in our hands."

Nothing turned out quite as Fidel had anticipated. The low prices came sooner than he expected, the recovery of Cuban sugar production was far more modest, and the total mobilization required to produce the giant harvest of 1970—8.5 instead of the projected 10 million metric tons—set back Cuban living standards and the entire economy to their lowest point since the Revolution took power. The economy held up only because of massive Russian subsidies. As for the restrictive agreements "of the bourgeoisie, of capitalism and imperialism but never of socialism," Fidel wisely decided to abandon ideology for hard currency. As a result, in October 1968 Cuba became a party to a new International Sugar Agreement designed to raise prices in the free-market area through a system

---

In 1966 at $114 million they once more approached the pre-boom figure of $95 million in 1962.

combining price control and restrictive export quotas for producing countries.[21]

Nevertheless, in the late fall of 1963, only the rare skeptic—inside or outside of Cuba—trying objectively to assess the prospects of the Cuban economy would have suspected how far Fidel would come from achieving his goals. Thus, when Fidel threatened to unleash his own counteroffensive in the economic war waged against him by the United States, when he rattled his sugar "atomic bomb," it was a credible threat. Its purpose was not difficult to surmise. It was to exert pressure on the new Johnson administration to continue the Cuban-American "dialogue" broken off by the death of John Kennedy.

21. Capitalist Cuba had been a member of the lapsed 1954 agreement, with an assigned annual export quota of 2,415,000 metric tons. Fourteen years later, socialist Cuba accepted a quota of 2,150,000 tons (subsequently raised by 10 percent). According to the 1968 agreement, the signatories pledged not to sell at less than 2.5 cents a pound. Prices immediately improved, averaging 3.37 cents in 1969 as compared with 1.98 cents in 1968. They went over 5 cents in early March 1971 for the first time since June 1964 but soon after drifted downward toward 4 cents. See *Quarterly Economic Reviews: Cuba, Dominican Republic, Haiti, Puerto Rico.* The Economist Intelligence Unit, London, no. 4, 1968 and no. 1, 1969; also, Joseph Grunwald and Philip Musgrove, *Natural Resources in Latin American Development* (Baltimore: Johns Hopkins University Press 1970), p. 350.

28

■

Cuban Subversion:

A Major Card in Fidel's Hand

The Early Motives

"OF COURSE WE ENGAGE in subversion, the training of guerrillas, propaganda! Why not? This is exactly what you are doing to us." The words were spoken to Herbert Matthews by Fidel Castro, in a moment of candor, during an interview in Havana in November 1963.[1] Fidel's justification, as far as it went, was comprehensible, but there were other considerations that Fidel did not spell out. At the moment he was convinced that Cuban-supported subversion had become a serious threat to the American-backed regime in Venezuela and that its potential threat was growing rapidly in a number of other countries. With his aim fixed on reaching an agreement with the United States, Cuban subversion in Latin America, he hoped, would give him bargaining power, along with the sugar "atom bomb." It would be another powerful element of pressure with which to exact concessions. In other words, at the time Fidel was talking with Matthews, the export of subversion was something he was prepared to give up—for a price.

The Cuban Revolution began to export subversion shortly after

1. Herbert L. Matthews, *Return to Cuba*, Bolivar House, Stanford University, 1964; cited by Tad Szulc, "Exporting the Cuban Revolution," *Cuba and the United States*, edited by John Plank (Washington, D.C.: Brookings Institution, 1967), p. 94.

taking power, but in the beginning a number of motives were involved and it would be difficult in any given instance to attribute preeminence to any single one. Tradition and temperament played a role as well as more concrete aims, not to mention the lack of firm control by any central authority over policy in such matters. In the background was the history of armed incursions on Cuban soil by Latin Americans who came to join in the struggle against Spain. More recently there was the example of the Caribbean Legion organized in Cuba after World War II. It consisted of young activists from a number of countries in the Caribbean region who proposed to eliminate by armed struggle the crude despotisms that ruled Venezuela, Nicaragua, and the Dominican Republic in particular. Havana was the headquarters of the legion and gave shelter to political exiles, including Rómulo Betancourt and Juan Bosch, until Batista's coup in 1952, when the legion moved to Costa Rica and soon faded away. It is interesting to recall that Fidel Castro's first experience in the export of revolution occurred in 1947, when he joined an expedition that was to invade the Dominican Republic. Shortly after weighing anchor, two of the three boats making up the flotilla were seized by the Cuban navy and all aboard were arrested, except Fidel who jumped overboard into the shark-infested waters of the Bay of Nipe and made his escape.[2]

The Panama Invasion

After the downfall of Batista, the first recorded involvement of Cubans in a foreign invasion occurred late in April 1959, when an expedition of some eighty or so men, armed, equipped, and organized somewhere on the island, attempted to overthrow the government of Panama. Within a few hours after the landing, the band was encircled by superior forces and, shortly thereafter, surrendered. What complicated the situation was that approximately one-half of the invaders were Cubans, including the officer in charge of the operation.

The news reached Fidel on April 27 on his way to South America from Montreal, where he had gone after his visit to the United States. As a result, his plane made an unscheduled stop in

2. The expedition left from the Cayo Confites, a tiny island in the Bay of Nipe, on the northeast coast of the island. See Luis Conte Agüero, *Fidel Castro: Vida y Obra* (Havana, 1959), pp. 22–23.

Houston where he was joined by his brother Raúl who flew in from Havana. The next day, when Fidel resumed his flight to Buenos Aires and while his plane was over Cuba, he broadcast a statement to his fellow countrymen denouncing the invasion as an act of "inconceivable irresponsibility by adventurers who possibly did nothing during the Revolution." [3] He then went on at some length to point out the harm done to the Revolution at a moment when he was abroad endeavoring to improve Cuba's international relations and ended by explaining that there was no reason for the invasion in any event, since Panama was not ruled by the kind of tyranny that prevailed in Santo Domingo or Nicaragua. Two months later forty members of the expedition returned to Havana, after negotiations between the Cuban and Panamanian governments for their release. The leader of the group explained to the press that they had expected to be met by a band of local rebels and that their landing would coincide with a general strike. Neither event materialized.[4]

With no other information to go on, it would appear that the invasion was "officially" sponsored but not at the highest levels and was largely an expression of mindless revolutionary exuberance, considerably stimulated by the scores of political exiles from Nicaragua, Guatemala, the Dominican Republic, and elsewhere who had flocked to Havana after Fidel came to power.[5] At the same time, in retrospect one can identify a permanent feature of Cuban-sponsored invasions to come, although motivated by more serious objectives and planned at the highest levels: failure to enlist reliable local support leading sooner or later to total defeat.

Santo Domingo

An event of larger repercussions was the invasion of the Dominican Republic on June 14, 1959, by a force of Havana-based Dominican exiles. Their aim was to overthrow the thirty-year Trujillo dictatorship, one of the objectives of the Caribbean Legion since its founding

3. *El Mundo*, April 29, 1959.   4. *El Mundo*, July 2, 1959.
5. Manuela Semidei, in her *Les Etats-Unis et La Révolution Cubaine, 1959–1964* (Paris: Colin, 1968, p. 62), suggests that the invasion of Panama was part of Castro's general plan to set up governments favorable to his regime in the Caribbean zone. This possibility cannot be completely discounted, in which case Fidel's broadcast in flight was an elaborate effort to disavow a bungled operation for which he was directly responsible.

and a hope shared by democrats and radicals of all persuasions throughout Latin America. However, Fidel's support of this operation was due to practical as well as revolutionary considerations. Trujillo had been a strong backer of Batista, who first sought shelter in Santo Domingo when he fled Cuba. There is also evidence that Trujillo began to plot against Castro soon after Batista's arrival.[6] Once again, however, with no support from the local population, the invasion was smashed in a few days. Unlike the Panama affair, diplomatic relations between the two countries were broken and the issue formed part of the background of the OAS consultation of foreign ministers the following August in Santiago, Chile. By a strange coincidence, while the meeting in Santiago was under way, a plane loaded with men and weapons outfitted by Batista in the Dominican Republic came down in Trinidad, on the south-central coast of Cuba. It was captured after a short, sharp struggle, with casualties on both sides.[7]

During the summer of 1959, presumably Cuban-sponsored raids by exiles against Nicaragua, Guatemala, and Haiti were attempted and repulsed. Again, the motives were as much practical as ideological. Like the Dominican Republic, these were countries whose governments would be likely to support Cuban counterrevolutionaries with arms and money and offer their territories as staging areas for invasions of the island. Later both Guatemala and Nicaragua were used as bases in the Bay of Pigs operation.

The New Phase

It was not until the following year, when relations with the United States had seriously deteriorated and the Soviet Union had begun to provide economic and other assistance to the Castro regime, that Cuba began to organize for systematic political, psychological, and paramilitary warfare and broadened the geographical scope of its targets to include points in Latin America beyond the Caribbean. In this connection, Havana was the scene of a widely attended and publicized Latin American Youth Congress that took place on July 26, 1960, the seventh anniversary of the attack on the Moncada army post. A considerable number of delegates remained in Cuba for

6. See Andrés Suárez, *Cuba: Castroism and Communism, 1959–1966* (Cambridge, Mass.: M.I.T. Press, 1969), pp. 70–71.

7. *Revolución*, August 14, 1959.

several months after the congress. There is reason to believe that some of them, picked to be the cadres of new revolutionary movements, were given professional training in the organization and operation of underground activities, including urban and rural guerrilla tactics. It may be supposed that by the end of 1963 anywhere between several score and several hundred Latin Americans—the number is a closely guarded secret—had gone through this kind of training program.

In the meantime, the Cuban military and security establishments were building up highly sophisticated intelligence services, equipped with the most modern technology in communications, logistics, and the management of the various forms of clandestine activity. It was commonly known in Havana and could easily be assumed elsewhere that, as in the case of other branches of warfare, the Soviet Union furnished the hardware and Russian experts were in charge of training. Less commonly known at the time was that all external clandestine operations were under Che Guevara's jurisdiction. And as in all cases involving military and political policy— except during the October 1962 crisis when the missiles were closely guarded by Russian troops and which no Cuban knew how to operate in any event—Cubans made the decisions. Until 1965, when the issue between Russians and Cubans over armed-struggle tactics in Latin América became acute, Moscow could tolerate this arrangement with more or less equanimity. Later, the Cuban apparatus was no doubt sufficiently developed to operate with little or no Russian assistance.

Guatemala

The case of Guatemala is an example. A guerrilla organization known as the Revolutionary Movement of November 13, or MR-13 for short, grew out of an unsuccessful nationalist-leftist military uprising on that date in 1960. One of the leaders was Captain Marco Antonio Yon Sosa, an officer in the Guatemalan army who had gone through a special course of training in counterinsurgency at Fort Gulick in the Canal Zone. Ironically, it was Yon Sosa who organized the guerrilla detachment that began operations in February 1962 in the densely wooded hills of Izábal Province, in the Atlantic coastal region.[8] A couple of months later, Yon Sosa, now highly

8. See Adolfo Gilly, "The Guerrilla Movement in Guatemala," *Monthly Review* (New York), Part I (May, 1965); Part II (June, 1965).

radicalized along Fidelista lines, and his group formed an alliance with the Guatemala Labor Party, as the Moscow-oriented Communist party was called, and established a united guerrilla organization under the name of the Rebel Armed Forces (Fuerzas Armadas Rebeldes, or FAR). As it happened, two years later Yon Sosa, in a split with the Communists, pulled out of the FAR and set up an independent operation, once more called the MR-13, thereby setting off a bitter dispute in which Fidel publicly played a prominent role.[9] In any event, when Cuba first became involved in the export of revolution to Guatemala, there could be no serious objections from the Russians since, at least in theory, the party they supported was also committed to the overthrow of the Guatemalan government by armed force.

Cuban subversion in Guatemala must have come early, probably influenced by Che Guevara's personal experience at the time of the overthrow of the Arbenz government in 1954.[10] During this period Che had formed a close friendship with a young Guatemalan Communist with whom he made his way to Mexico when Arbenz fell. In a collection of reminiscences published in Havana in 1963 under the title of *Pasajes de la Guerra Revolucionaria* ("Episodes of the revolutionary war") [11] Che gave a brief but moving account of this friendship. In the story, entitled *El Patojo* (the youth's nickname in Guatemalan slang because of his small stature), the opening sentence states, "A few days ago, a news report from Guatemala told of the death

9. In January 1966, at the founding convention of the now moribund "tri-continental" African, Asian, and Latin American Solidarity Organization in Havana, Fidel accused Yon Sosa (not invited to the conference) of being a Trotskyite (as the Russians must have seen it, it was like the kettle calling the pot black). Sosa replied from Guatemala that Castro was "at the service of the Russo-Yankee alliance" (Suárez, *Cuba*, pp. 233–234). This did not prevent them from patching up their quarrel a couple of years later when Fidel approved a reunited FAR under Yon Sosa's exclusive leadership. In 1969 the FAR split once more, and in the summer of 1970 Yon Sosa was killed on Mexican territory shortly after crossing the border, apparently having decided to abandon the struggle. See John Gerassi, editor, *The Coming of the New International* (New York: World, 1970), p. 469.

10. After the Cuban Revolution, Colonel Arbenz lived in Havana for a number of years, then moved to Mexico where he died in 1971.

11. Text quoted below from reprint in *Ernesto Che Guevara: Obra Revolucionaria*, edited by Roberto Fernández Retamar (Mexico: Ediciones Era, 1968), pp. 280–282.

of a number of patriots, among them Julio Roberto Cáceres Valle."
He had been killed, along with other guerrillas, in an encounter with
the Guatemalan army. Che explains that El Patojo came to Havana
shortly after the triumph of the Revolution, put up at Che's house,
and was given a job in the Agrarian Reform Institute. At an unspecified date, he returned to Guatemala "to do his duty." It would
be interesting to know when it was, for if Che is to be believed, and
there would be no reason not to in this instance, "El Patojo had no
knowledge of military training. He simply felt it was his duty to return to his country and fight, weapon in hand, in order somehow to
duplicate our guerrilla struggle." Clearly, Che had misgivings about
his friend's lack of preparation: "Could I tell him not to do it? By
what right? We had tried something when it was considered impossible, and now he knew that it was possible." It may be that the
fate of El Patojo was another reminder of a job to be done in
Guatemala.

There was also irony in the memorial to his friend, which Che
did not intend but which later events added to the story. In Mexico,
when Fidel accepted Che as a member of his invasion force—he
needed a physician and took on the Argentine primarily in that capacity rather than as a combatant—El Patojo also offered to enlist
but was rejected, "not on personal grounds," Che wrote; "Fidel
did not want to involve any more foreigners in this project of national liberation. . . . Fidel did not want our army to become a
mosaic of nationalities." When, in due time, internationalism became the watchword of the Cuban Revolution, Fidel's intuitive wisdom was forgotten. The guerrilla force that Fidel and Che assembled in Bolivia was truly a "mosaic of nationalities." Of its
fifty-odd starting members, slightly more than half were Bolivians.
The rest were Cubans, with a small number of Peruvians thrown in.
Serving in a liaison capacity were a Frenchman and a woman of dual
Argentine-German nationality. The commander, of course, was an
Argentine. All the evidence indicates that the presence of foreigners
aroused the suspicions of the Bolivian peasants and was one of the
factors inhibiting their cooperation with the guerrillas, a situation
that doomed the expedition from the start.

Lifting the Veil

While inferential evidence of a considerable Cuban participation in
Guatemalan guerrilla activities would crop up from time to time

during the early and mid-1960s, it was not until the end of the
decade that Cuba lifted a corner of the veil of secrecy with which it
had covered its clandestine operations. It came about in the aftermath of Che's defeat in Bolivia. The capture of Che's diaries and
other records, and the testimony of survivors, exposed the most important secrets connected with the venture.[12] In addition, Che's defeat, coming after Cuban failures elsewhere in Latin America, also
contributed to Fidel's withdrawal of his challenge to Soviet foreign
policy, and with it, the abandonment for all practical purposes of
any effective support for his henceforth muted armed-struggle thesis.

Under these circumstances, there was no longer any point in
hiding from the Cuban people and the world in general the exploits
of the exposed clandestine soldiers, particularly those who had lost
their lives. On the contrary, the time had come to rescue the soldiers
and their deeds from the wreckage of defeat and with them build a
monument that would inspire the Cuban people with pride in the
Revolution and loyalty to its leadership, during the period of grim
austerity that had set in toward the end of the 1960s. Thus, to the
vast and perpetual celebration of Che's martyrdom was added a
series of lesser eulogies for fallen heroes of lesser rank.

One of them was an army officer, a veteran of the Sierra
Maestra, memorialized in *Granma* on July 30, 1969 (*Granma
Weekly Review,* August 10), the second anniversary of his death in
action in Bolivia. "All honor and glory to the heroic internationalist
example of Captain José María Martínez Tamayo!" [13] was the concluding sentence of the tribute that recounted his outstanding exploits. Among them the following was listed: "During the October
[1962] crisis Martínez Tamayo was on an important mission in support of the revolutionary movement in Guatemala." This removes all
doubt concerning direct Cuban military intervention in Guatemala
as early as 1962. Judging from the captain's subsequent assignments,
Fidel must have considered that he did a good job in Guatemala.
And judging from the fact that Fidel, in his speech on July 26, 1963,

12. The materials have been published in a number of competing
editions. The most complete has been edited by Daniel James, *The
Complete Bolivian Diaries of Ché Guevara and Other Captured Documents* (New York: Stein and Day, 1968). The Bolivian campaign is
also dealt with extensively by the same author in *Che Guevara: A
Biography* (New York: Stein and Day, 1969).

13. Captain is the second highest rank in the Cuban army. The
highest is major, the rank held by Fidel, Che, and army commanders.

singled out the Guatemalan, along with the Venezuelan, guerrillas for special mention among all the revolutionary groups in Latin America, very likely other Cubans had accompanied Martínez and had stayed behind when the captain left sometime in 1963. In any event, at the end of 1963 Guatemala was one of the areas where Fidel could feel that his investment was sound enough to produce dividends in the form of a credible revolutionary threat. This would be a valuable asset if the conflict with the Americans continued or if negotiations to end the conflict got under way.

Peru

On May 31, 1963, *Revolución* reported the capture of Hugo Blanco, a young Peruvian intellectual turned peasant union organizer, who in late 1962 had launched a guerrilla campaign in La Convención Valley, in the highlands of central Peru. Blanco had been given a large billing in the Cuban media both at home and in dispatches distributed abroad by Prensa Latina, the Cuban wire service. A Swiss student of the Cuban Revolution, citing materials originating in Lima and Havana and published in Santiago, Chile, concluded that "*Prensa Latina* . . . did its best to present him [Blanco] as a Peruvian Fidel Castro: detailed accounts of his real or alleged successes and photographs showing him surrounded by his guerrilla fighters were furnished by the Cuban agency to the Communist press of Latin America." [14] In Peru this created complications in leftist circles since Blanco was known to be a Trotskyite. After his imprisonment, the Peruvian Communist party and other Moscow-oriented parties, in reporting on Blanco's failure, characterized it as a typical example of Trotskyite provocation playing into the hands of the class enemy, and so on. In Cuba, however, he remained a hero. When he and other political prisoners were released from jail at the end of 1970 by Peru's new leftist-nationalist military regime, *Granma* paid special tribute to him as a true revolutionary leader. [15]

Although it was a safe assumption at the time of his capture that Blanco had received more than verbal encouragement from Cuba, there was confirmation a few years later when some of the

14. Ernst Halperin, "Castroism: Challenge to the Latin American Communists," *Problems of Communism* 12, no. 5 (September–October 1963): 14.

15. *Granma Weekly Review*, January 3, 1971.

facts concerning another ill-fated adventure were made public. As Richard Gott put the story together, "In the very month that Hugo Blanco was captured . . . help was on its way. A group of young Peruvian intellectuals, returning to the country from Cuba, planned to bring him armed assistance." [16] There were thirty-five of them; in order to avoid detection they were returning to Peru overland from Bolivia. They crossed the frontier at a point close to Puerto Maldonado, a port on the Madre de Diós river deep in the eastern jungles of Peru. Here they were trapped by the police and most of them were killed, including their leader Javier Heraud, a young poet of considerable renown. Thus, the collapse of Blanco's operation was a more costly setback for Fidel than it at first appeared to be. There would be three other Cuban-supported guerrilla campaigns launched in Peru in 1965—and with equally disastrous results [17]—but in the meantime Fidel's attention was directed to Argentina, a more ambitious target which Che played a decisive role in selecting.

Argentina

Here again we meet up with Captain Martínez Tamayo, for according to the *Granma* eulogy, "In [July] 1963 he entered Bolivia to carry out preparatory work for the establishment of the guerrilla base in Salta, Argentina, under the command of Major Segundo, [pseudonym for] Jorge Ricardo Masetti . . . and participated in the founding of the People's Guerrilla Army [of Argentina]." [18] Of the "armies" created or supported by Cuba in Latin America, this was probably the puniest and most inept; and of all the disasters suffered by these "armies," the one that befell the ragtail group in northwestern Argentina was the most pathetic. Yet it was a major undertaking by the Castro regime and led to false hopes. From an account written by Ricardo Rojo,[19] an Argentine and close friend of Che who served

16. Gott, *Guerrilla Movements in Latin America* (New York: Doubleday, 1971), pp. 330–335.

17. The leader of the most important band, Luis de la Puente, was killed in late September 1965. Another group was led by Héctor Béjar, a survivor of the Puerto Maldonado encounter. Béjar was captured in early January 1966. The third group, led by Guillermo Lobatón, was wiped out at about the same time.

18. *Granma Weekly Review*, August 10, 1969.

19. Rojo, *My Friend Che* (New York: Dial, 1968), pp. 147–162. Although sympathetic toward Che, the book does not present the stereo-

as defense counsel at the trial of the captured members of the People's Guerrilla Army, and from the *Granma* story of the exploits of Captain Martínez, a fairly complete picture of the episode emerges. It is of more than passing interest, among other reasons because it touches on relations between the Cuban Revolution and Peronismo, a political phenomenon that grew out of the neo-fascist regime of General Juan Domingo Perón, who ruled Argentina from 1946 to 1955.

Jorge Masetti was a young Argentine journalist who had been a member of the Nationalist Alliance, a militant organization of Peronistas, disarmed and dismantled by the army after the fall of General Perón in 1955. When Herbert Matthews interviewed Castro in the Sierra Maestra in February 1957 and the news reached Buenos Aires that an Argentine doctor was a member of the rebel band, Masetti decided to emulate the correspondent of the *New York Times*. With the help of a note to Che Guevara from Ricardo Rojo, Masetti finally reached the rebel headquarters in March 1958. It was in this setting that the Peronista reporter first met the anti-Peronista Che, for this was Che's only clearly expressed political position from the time of his adolescence until his departure from Argentina in 1953, while Perón was still in power. The two young men, of about the same age, discovered to their mutual satisfaction that the old political labels that would have separated them a few years back no longer had the same meaning.

Peronismo and the Cuban Revolution

What had happened was that the departure of Perón for Madrid, where he was to spend many years in congenial exile under the protection of Generalissimo Francisco Franco, like himself an admirer of the Axis powers during World War II, did not end the social and political movement he had created or his continued contact with it through a series of "lieutenants" who shuttled back and forth between Buenos Aires and Madrid. The reasons can be summarized as follows: (1) the effective impact of the populist demagogy of Peronismo, principally modeled on that of Italian fascism and enhanced by the extraordinary cult of his wife Eva, a physically attrac-

---

typed image of him created in Havana and accordingly was denounced there. None of its factual material was convincingly challenged.

tive young woman who died while Perón was in office; (2) the tangible social welfare benefits that the Perón regime had provided for the underprivileged masses (Perón was overthrown before the galloping inflation he set in motion could destroy his popularity); and (3) Perón's anti-Yankee nationalism (Perón had been outspokenly pro-Nazi during World War II), which had struck deep roots in the minds of broad sectors of the Argentine population.

When the overthrow of the dictator by the conservative branch of the military establishment brought with it an attempt to return to the mixed liberal-and-conservative norms of an earlier period, Peronismo quickly revived, becoming by far the most important political movement on the left and since then the perpetual stumbling block of all efforts to form a stable civilian regime without Peronista support.[20] At the time Masetti visited Che, the Argentine Communist party was still bitterly opposed to the Peronistas, even the left wing of the movement, which was relatively untainted by the fascist complicities of earlier Peronismo and was attracting militant students and other radical youth to its banners.

Thus, Masetti was happy to conclude, as he wrote after his return from Cuba, that "the bullets fired at Batista" were not "paid in dollars or rubles or pounds sterling" and that "there had cropped up in Latin America the bewildering exception of a revolution financed by its own people," [21] while Che discovered that those of his fellow countrymen whose ideas were closest to his own were Peronistas.

This was the beginning of what developed into a series of informal contacts between the Cuban leadership and high level Peronistas. Ricardo Rojo described a meeting at which he was present in Havana in early 1961 between Che Guevara and Angel Borlenghi, the number two man in Perón's government and his minister of the interior for more than eight years. By this time, Che was able to say to Borlenghi: "There's no question about it, Perón was the most advanced embodiment of political and economic

20. C. L. Sulzberger, in a Buenos Aires dispatch published in the *New York Times* on April 7, 1971, estimated that Peronismo or neo-Peronismo, as it has come to be called, had the support of more than one-third of the population of Argentina. This was sixteen years after the coup that overthrew Perón and sent him into exile.

21. Cited by Rojo, *My Friend Che*, p. 150.

reform in Argentina." [22] Soon after, Rojo was present when Jerónimo
Remorino, a foreign minister in Perón's government, called on Che
in his office at the Ministry of Industries. Remorino was in Havana
as the representative of a French company interested in selling the
Cuban government a fertilizer plant. Rojo does not say whether Che
bought the plant, but he does explain that "Guevara and Remorino
discussed Latin American and United States politics for hours." [23]
In any event, under Che's guidance a rapport was established between the Cuban Revolution and the Peronista movement. It was a
discreet affair, in view of the unfriendly relations between Argentine
Communists and Peronistas. However, in 1966, at the meeting of
the Asian, African, and Latin American Solidarity Organization in
Havana, when Fidel's relations with the pro-Soviet Communist
parties in Latin America were less than cordial, the Peronista movement was conspicuously represented by John William Cooke, a
leader of its left wing and former high official of the Perón government.

Planning the Argentine Invasion

As for Masetti, in 1959 at Che's invitation he returned to Cuba to
head Prensa Latina, the government's newly established international
news agency and wire service. In April 1961, however, he left the
agency under pressure. "He had had all kinds of problems," Rojo
explained, "from professional rivalry with Cuban newsmen who
frowned on the editorship of an Argentine, to political differences,
especially with veteran Communists. . . . Masetti's position became
untenable. With Guevara's blessing, Masetti resigned." [24] When
Rojo next saw him in Havana in the spring of 1963, he had the impression that Masetti was spending much of his time in military
training. He did not suspect, however, that Masetti was about to
launch a guerrilla war in Argentina.

   The plan was to set up a base in Bolivia close to the Argentine
border and move men, weapons, and supplies across the border at

22. *Ibid.*, p. 104. In a conversation with Che in Havana in the
spring of 1963, Rojo relates that Che had in his possession a letter from
Perón expressing admiration for Castro and the Cuban Revolution and
that Che had raised the question of inviting Perón to settle in Havana
(p. 139).

23. *Ibid.*, p. 105.   24. *Ibid.*, p. 152.

the appropriate moment. The person assigned to make the preliminary preparations was none other than Captain Martínez, recently returned from his mission in Guatemala. Two other Cuban officers, Captains Hermés Peña and Raúl Dávila, were assigned to back him up and remain as permanent members of the guerrilla group. According to the *Granma* memorial to Martínez,

> Masetti . . . asked him to participate in the organization of *Operation Sideshow*. Without hesitation, Papi [Martínez' pseudonym; he was also known as Ricardo] accepted and asked permission from Major Ernesto Guevara to participate in the Argentine national liberation movement. He was assigned the task of preparing the necessary bases from which Masetti and his companions of the EGP [People's Guerrilla Army] would enter Salta, Argentina, from Tarija, Bolivia.

The Story of Tania

It was approximately at the same time that twenty-six-year-old Haydée Tamara Bunke Bider—better known simply as Tania—began her training as an undercover operative in the Cuban intelligence service. Born and raised in Argentina, moving to East Berlin when her refugee Communist German parents returned home after the Nazi defeat, and then in the spring of 1961 taking up residence in Cuba, she was to play an important role in setting up Che Guevara's guerrilla base in Bolivia some years later and eventually to be killed in an ambush suffered by a detachment of Che's men. Subsequently, she was to enter the pantheon of Cuba's hero-martyrs as Tania, the Unforgettable Guerrilla, the model female revolutionary just as Che became the symbol of revolutionary manhood.

From an official biography published in Havana in late 1970 under the title *Tania, the Unforgettable Guerrilla*,[25] it would appear that both the timing of her recruitment and later infiltration into Bolivia was at least in part related to Masetti's project. Her Argentine background was an asset that was recognized soon after her arrival in Cuba. She formed part of "a group to study the Argentine situation and the possibility of creating a fighting group for struggle there." [26] That was in 1961. The following year she was being con-

25. Reprinted in eight consecutive installments as supplements in the *Granma Weekly Review*, November 15, 1970 to January 3, 1971.
26. Installment no. 4, December 6, 1970, p. 38.

sidered for "a difficult task" by "the Party." [27] "One early morning in March, 1963," she began a period of intensive training as an espionage agent, from which she emerged a year later ready to be assigned to the field.[28]

> Then, in March 1964, after she had completed her training, Tania had what she at that time called the greatest thrill of her life: Major Ernesto Che Guevara received her in his offices at the Ministry of Industries to explain the work she was to do. . . . They spent several hours talking about the political and economic situation in Latin America, about the revolutionary movements that, marching in the vanguard, had already initiated armed struggle in several countries in South America.[29]

One of these movements was undoubtedly Masetti's band of guerrillas. It was a month before the debacle, which Che had no way of suspecting. As Che no doubt felt at the time, Masetti's expedition was his most important commitment.

Tania's assignment was to establish herself in Bolivia, both as a listening post for general information concerning Brazil, Argentina, and the larger Andean region and as a permanent base from which to maintain a network of subversion in neighboring countries. Tania spent six months in Europe after her meeting with Che in order to authenticate and internalize her false identity as Laura Gutiérrez Bauer. When she reached Bolivia in mid-November 1964, the Argentine movement had already been wiped out. Some two years later, after all the other movements had collapsed, including Che's fling in Africa, Bolivia itself was selected as a combat area. Finally, Tania's highly successful clandestine operation got results. She was mainly responsible for making it possible for Che to establish his guerrilla base on the lower eastern slopes of the Cordillera Oriental—where they both perished.

The Tragedy of Major Segundo

To return to Captain Martínez, the *Granma* eulogy relates how he first arrived in Bolivia in July 1963 with a false Colombian passport,

27. From a letter to her parents in Berlin, dated September 14, 1962; *ibid.*, p. 39.
28. Installment no. 5, December 13, 1970, p. 53.
29. *Ibid.*, p. 57.

and two months later obtained another passport and a voting card made out to Ricardo Morales Rodríguez, Bolivian citizen. Armed with these documents, he was able "to move freely in his work of organizing the guerrilla nucleus . . . led by Major Segundo [Masetti]. . . . Using Tarija as a base, Papi . . . traveled to different parts of the country and into Argentina, where he personally made contacts, organized communication and supply networks and carried out reconnaissance of the area where the guerrillas were to operate."

Assisted by a number of Bolivians, among them the brothers Coco and Inti Peredo, both of whom turned up in Che's campaign a few years later and died tragic deaths, Martínez appears to have done his job systematically and efficiently, in contrast to later developments. The infiltration of Masetti's "army" into Argentina began in late September 1963. When fully organized it numbered less than thirty men. The following February Martínez left for Cuba. "Once the guerrilla nucleus was established in Salta [Argentina]," *Granma* related, "Papi asked permission to become a permanent member, but this was denied." He was to return two years later, "the first Cuban to arrive in Bolivia in March 1966, where he would prepare for the arrival of Major Ernesto Guevara" and, as we know, eventually lose his life.

The debacle of the Argentine People's Guerrilla Army came quickly. "In mid-April [1964]," as Rojo tells the story, the Cuban Hermés Peña and a companion "surprised an advance guard of the gendarmery and killed one of the soldiers. It was the only real skirmish of the Argentine guerrilla war." [30] In the exchange of gunfire, the Cuban and his companion also lost their lives, bringing the score of those killed in battle to three. By then the guerrillas had executed two of their own number, for attempted desertion in one case and gross insubordination in the other. Three others died of starvation after the police had encircled the band and cut off supplies. Fourteen men were captured and "tortured . . . in a vicious manner." Masetti escaped into the jungle, "a hell of vegetation and wild animals. . . . He never returned; no one ever heard from him again. The jungle swallowed him." [31]

30. *Ibid.*, p. 161.
31. *Ibid.*, p. 161. Rojo does not account for the fate of the rest of the group.

Masetti triggered the disaster by publishing a manifesto in *Compañero*, a weekly put out in Buenos Aires by militant Peronistas. He signed it "Major Segundo," that is, "Second Major," apparently implying that there was a "First Major," presumably Che Guevara. The only significant effect of the publication was that it alerted the police who had little trouble in infiltrating two agents into the band and soon after cornering it. But this was not the worst blunder. The larger one, for which Che was equally if not more to blame—and for which ultimately Fidel could not avoid responsibility—was an extraordinary political miscalculation. In their sober moments, as they discussed their homeland, both Che and Masetti must have been aware that Argentina, because of its political traditions and geographic characteristics, offered one of the least likely prospects in Latin America for a successful rural guerrilla operation. It did not require hindsight to be able to predict that no small internationalist band, isolated in a remote and very sparsely populated corner of this vast country, 1,000 miles from its great urban and industrial concentrations, and—the height of folly—without prearranged solidly established political and logistic support by mass organizations in the large urban centers, could hope to survive for any length of time, much less ignite a great revolution. Later, some of the tactical mistakes and sheer accidents that hastened Masetti's end were repeated in Che Guevara's Bolivian adventure, which took place in a geographically similar area, some 350 miles to the north, but with very different political characteristics which Che again failed to take into account.

"The tragedy of 'Major Segundo' . . . was the quietest guerrilla defeat in Latin America," wrote Ricardo Rojo. "It received little publicity from the press, with even the leftist publications afraid to involve themselves." [32] Fairly early in the campaign the group lost contact with the outside world, including Havana, when their radio transmitter broke down. Thus it may have been weeks or months before the news of the disaster reached Cuba. Rojo suggests that Che did not learn the full story until the end of 1964.[33] Public acknowledgment of Masetti's sacrifice first came on September 7, 1968, when *Granma* prominently featured a tribute to "the Argentine newspaperman . . . who died fighting heroically for Latin

32. *Ibid.*, p. 163.   33. *Ibid.*, p. 161.

American independence." [34] Understandably, no details of the fight were given, except that "at the head of the People's Guerrilla Army he initiated the armed revolutionary struggle in the mountains of Salta, Argentina." Then, on February 16, 1970, *Granma* published a dispatch that included an "open letter" from the last two members of Masetti's group who were still in the Salta jail, serving life sentences. "Without any basis of legal evidence, valid juridical elements or any law or code," it stated, "we have been condemned because we sought freedom for our country," and so on. It was an unexpected echo of the disaster, and no less grotesque.

34. *Granma Weekly Review*, September 15, 1968.

29
∎
Intervention in Venezuela

Revolutionary Kinship

IN SHARP CONTRAST WITH THE deep secrecy maintained by the Castro regime in organizing an armed incursion into Argentina, its participation in a revolutionary movement to overthrow the government of Venezuela was, in effect, openly proclaimed. To be sure, there was the pretense that it was only lending moral support to the armed struggle against President Betancourt, but it was a transparent bit of window dressing. The difference is explained by a number of factors.

To begin with, in the case of Argentina an attempt was made to inaugurate revolutionary armed struggle where none existed. This involved transplanting an organization set up and trained in Cuba, and transporting and supplying it over great distances and, in the process, violating the laws of several states in addition to those of Argentina. Thus, discovery at any point prior to the moment when the guerrilla band was established on Argentine soil would have been fatal.

With respect to Venezuela, there was no need for Castro secretly to ignite a revolution in a country seething with its own revolutionary violence. Moreover, a similarity in primary political objectives, strengthened by geographic proximity and by sharing some common Caribbean ethnic and cultural traits, had created a feeling of close kinship over the years between Cuban and Venezuelan revolutionary movements. Thus, for example, after the fall of the ten-year dictatorship of Pérez Jiménez in January 1958, Caracas became one of the main centers of support for Fidel's insurrection. Cubans in exile and Venezuelans worked together to send money and arms to the Sierra Maestra.

It will be recalled that Castro's first effort to enlist foreign support for his new regime was directed precisely toward Venezuela. In his visit to Caracas in January 1959, his efforts to get official financial and other backing failed. The then president-elect Rómulo Betancourt was unwilling, among other reasons, to risk an alliance that he could anticipate might involve him in a confrontation with the United States.[1] On the other hand, the great multitudes that came to hear him were so familiar with his exploits and their identification with the cause of the Cuban Revolution was so close that he was received practically as if he were a native Venezuelan hero.

Given these circumstances, when the time came for Fidel to become actively involved in the movement to overthrow Betancourt, it was important for Betancourt's leftist opponents to exploit the prestige that Cuban backing could give the revolutionary undertaking. This meant that, in addition to the training of Venezuela guerrillas in Cuba and the clandestine shipment of weapons and money to Venezuela,[2] Havana openly became the center of a massive propaganda campaign, by shortwave radio and other media, in support of the armed struggle against the Venezuelan government. This campaign also involved the indoctrination of the Cuban population, both to counter Florida-based broadcasts denouncing Cuban intervention in Venezuela and, it would appear, to bolster public morale in case the intervention prompted military reprisals.

Beginning in 1961 there had been a gradual buildup in the

1. As Betancourt, who had been elected in December 1958 and formally assumed office in February 1959, told the story of his discussion with Castro: "He wanted a loan of $300 million from Venezuela to free his government from dependence on the U.S. sugar-market quota, and from the U.S. banks, and international credit agencies." Rómulo Betancourt, "The Venezuelan Miracle," *Reporter*, August 13, 1964, cited by Andrés Suárez, *Cuba: Castroism and Communism, 1959–1966* (Cambridge, Mass.: M.I.T. Press, 1969), p. 48.

2. A Venezuelan who went to Cuba in 1960, received two years of training at a guerrilla warfare and intelligence school, and later defected gave a credible account of his experience to an investigating committee of the OAS in Caracas, in June 1967. See Juan de Onis, "Former Agent Describes Havana's Guerrilla Operations in Latin America," *New York Times*, August 2, 1967.

Havana press of news featuring acts of violence directed against the Betancourt government. By 1963 scarcely a week passed without several dispatches emphasizing organized armed struggle, both urban and rural. Thus, for example, a series of illustrated articles in *Revolución*, beginning on May 10, went into considerable detail extolling the virtues of guerrillas fighting in terrain similar to the Sierra Maestra. A long theoretical article in *Cuba Socialista* was categorical in its prediction that the guerrilla war under way would shortly topple the Betancourt regime while it praised "Cuban-Venezuelan revolutionary solidarity." [3] By mid-November the theme was given maximum importance when the Cuban government decreed a special "Week of Solidarity with the Venezuelan Revolution," marked by a continuous round of meetings, speeches, television programs, and demonstrations throughout the island.[4]

The timing of the "solidarity week" was not a random decision. The Venezuelan revolutionaries had announced that they would prevent the presidential elections to choose a successor to Betancourt, scheduled for December 1, from taking place. It was to be a decisive test of strength, for which a major buildup of secretly shipped Cuban arms and munitions had been under way. Thus the "solidarity week," given maximum coverage in Venezuela by Cuban shortwave radio, was a massive propaganda effort, coordinated with the great crisis that, it was confidently anticipated, would immediately follow the sabotage of the elections.

A New Era in Venezuela

The complexities of Cuban involvement in Venezuelan affairs during the greater part of the 1960s—and its impact on Cuban-Soviet relations—can be better understood if viewed against the background of recent Venezuelan history. The contemporary period of Venezuela's political and social turmoil dates back to October 1945, when a coup d'etat by junior army officers supported by liberal and leftist civilian groups, ended nearly fifty years of crude and practically uninterrupted military rule.[5] Two years later elections were

3. "The Venezuelan People on the Road to Victory," *Cuba Socialista* 3, no. 25 (September 1963): 55–73.
4. See *Revolución*, November 16, 1963, et sequ.
5. As Edwin Lieuwen stated it, "This revolution marked the end of an era: that of the ascendancy of the army generals and the landed

held in which Acción Democrática, a party that originated as a clandestine movement in the late 1930s, won control of the new constitutional government. At the time of taking power, Acción Democrática could be described, in terms of the Venezuelan political spectrum, as being considerably left-of-center but democratic-reformist as compared with the Communist party, its most serious rival among the students and underprivileged urban population. Relations between the two parties were further embittered by the fact that Rómulo Betancourt, leader of Acción Democrática, had at one time been a prominent member of the Communist party.

After an existence of less than a year, the new government was toppled by a rightist coup d'etat. During the following ten-year military dictatorship, the quarrel between Acción Democrática and the Communist party was partly submerged and both cooperated with other outlawed parties in supporting a revolt by dissident army and navy officers which finally overthrew the dictatorship. This was in January 1958. Once more elections were held, in December 1958; and again Acción Democrática, with very strong rural support, emerged the winner. However, Acción Democrática failed to carry Caracas, the capital, stronghold of the Communist party which became a force to reckon with—in the Congress, in the university, in the teeming hillside shanty towns where most of the city's population lived, and in the streets in general.

It was under these circumstances that the government of Rómulo Betancourt, at the beginning of 1959, faced the task of grappling with the long-postponed problems of Venezuelan underdevelopment, considerably more serious than those of Cuba and further complicated by the foreign, principally American, investment in petroleum, which was far more significant both financially and strategically than the American investment in Cuba. Thus, the polarization of political forces, accompanied by violent confrontations, was rapid, notably between the government, on the one hand, and university students and faculty and the masses of unemployed, on the other. In July 1960 the left wing of Acción Democrática split off and formed a new party, El Movimiento de Izquierda Revolucionaria (Movement of the Revolutionary Left, usually referred to

---

aristocracy which had ruled the nation ever since independence [1819]."
Venezuela (2nd edition; London: Oxford University Press, 1965), p. 63.

by its acronym, MIR). It declared itself to be Marxist (eighteen months before Fidel Castro made the same claim), but was greeted with less than enthusiasm by the leadership of the Venezuelan Communist party.[6] Uninhibited by ties with the Kremlin, the MIR shortly became a consistent proponent of armed struggle. However, as tensions between the government and the left increased, the two Marxist parties drew closer together. Late in 1961, as a result of further defections from Acción Democrática, Betancourt for the first time lost his majority in Congress. This event, "coupled with increased government repression against demonstrations in October and November, 1961," according to one likely explanation, "made the drift toward open rebellion almost inevitable." [7]

Armed Struggle, the Communist Party, and the Kremlin

The main channel of Cuban intervention in Venezuelan affairs during the early efforts to overthrow the government was the Communist party of Venezuela. This situation, while it lasted, was unique in Latin America and is explained by a set of special circumstances. The party had played an active role in the overthrow of the Pérez Jiménez dictatorship, which is more than can be said of the Cuban Communist party in the case of the Batista dictatorship. The experience had created a militant section in the leadership, more easily oriented toward armed struggle and less easily "advised" by the Kremlin, than could be found in the other bona fide Communist parties of Latin America.

At the same time, party policy was subject to increasing external pressures. The intensification of disorders in the cities; the birth of independent rural guerrillas early in 1962; the spontaneous (unsuccessful) insurrections at the country's two major naval bases in May and June 1962, followed by the outlawing of the party and the MIR; the latter's growing involvement in armed struggle and the consequent possibility that the MIR would assume leadership of the revo-

6. "The majority of Communist leaders did not consider the division of Acción Democrática feasible or useful, and thus adopted a passive attitude toward the new party." Moisés Moleiro, *EL MIR de Venezuela* (Havana: Instituto del Libro, 1967), p. 146.

7. Richard Gott, *Guerrilla Movements in Latin America* (New York: Doubleday, 1971), p. 139.

lutionary movement in Venezuela—these were probably the principal factors that finally led the Communist party, in its plenum of December 1962, to commit itself to armed struggle against the government.

This decision, in turn, led to the formal organization in February 1963 of the Armed Forces of National Liberation (Fuerzas Armadas de Liberación Nacional, or FALN), a unified left-revolutionary striking force for both urban and rural operations, under a single command.[8] At the insistence of the Communist party, control of the FALN was vested in an already existing National Liberation Front (Frente de Liberación Nacional, or FLN) set up to coordinate policy and strategy between the Communist party, the MIR, and the leftist splinter of a third party. As numerically the strongest and politically the most experienced component of the FLN, the Communist party in effect took control of the FALN and the campaign to overthrow the government.

For Fidel Castro, this turn of events was obviously a source of considerable satisfaction and optimism. No doubt the example of the Cuban Revolution had exerted a broad influence in Venezuela. More directly, the creation of the MIR reflected Cuban experience and encouragement, and these in turn affected the orientation of the Communist party. All in all, this was a major conversion in a major country to the Fidelista thesis of armed struggle. In addition, the Russians put up no serious objection.

The Kremlin's acceptance of the armed struggle thesis in Venezuela needs some explanation. It was exceptional and temporary, and was the result of a complicated set of circumstances, of which Cuban involvement was only one. D. Bruce Jackson, in his monograph, *Castro, the Kremlin, and Communism in Latin America,* makes a reasonable assessment of the situation:

> paradoxically, the shift of the Venezuelan Communist Party [in December 1962] took place at almost the same time that the Soviets were retreating toward a more cautious foreign policy line as a result of the Cuban missile crisis. . . . The Soviet embarrass-

8. According to Tad Szulc, the FALN never had more than between 1,000 and 1,500 members, "but it quickly developed into a highly proficient terrorist organization" (in *Cuba and the United States,* edited by John Plank [Washington, D.C.: Brookings Institution, 1967], p. 91).

ment had produced a situation in which clever revolutionaries could demand more assistance as the price of their continued allegiance to the USSR in the Sino-Soviet dispute, and it was this tactic that the . . . Venezuelan communists began using in 1963. . . . At the East German party congress in January 1963, the Venezuelans joined the Cubans in a neutral stance on the question of condemning the Chinese Communists. . . . Russia was on the defensive against . . . Red China and could not afford to make any moves regarding existing guerrilla wars which could be portrayed as a sellout of "national liberation struggles." Furthermore, Soviet propaganada had already pictured the Venezuela government as being totally manipulated by Wall Street and the Pentagon. Moscow thus had no obvious opportunities at the Venezuelan government level which could be jeopardized by the armed struggle. Likewise, within the PCV [Venezuelan Communist party], the pro-Moscow leadership remained at least nominally in charge and committed to armed struggle tactics. Finally, of course, acceptance of violent tactics by communists in Venezuela was useful proof to ideological fence-sitters such as Castro that Soviet talk of peaceful coexistence was not equivalent to abandoning support for revolutionary struggles.[9]

Terrorism and Defeat

The exploits of the FALN during 1963 were unimpressive in the countryside, but its urban guerrilla detachments destroyed property and engaged in kidnappings and other acts of terrorism with considerable success. Early in the year the fame and prestige of the FALN was inflated by the worldwide publicity given to the seizure at sea, by FALN stowaways, of the *Anzoátegui*, a 3,000-ton Venezuelan freighter bound for New York. Eluding units of both the Venezuelan and United States navies, the ship put in at a Brazillian port where the hijackers were granted political asylum. In short, the difficulty of the authorities to control FALN sabotage and terrorism led to an overestimation by the revolutionary leadership of its capacity to topple the government. Havana, of course, shared this optimism; and perhaps even Moscow, a reluctant apologist for the armed-struggle position of the Venezuelan party, for a time wondered whether Betancourt would be able to hold out. Until the elections on December 1, possibly even Betancourt was in doubt.

    9. Baltimore: Johns Hopkins University Press, 1967, pp. 18–20.

Thus, by coincidence, it was during the Cuban "Week of Solidarity with Venezuela" that John Kennedy and Fidel Castro "conversed" through the medium of Jean Daniel, at a time when the Cuban prime minister was confident that the president of the United States would shortly be confronted with a great upheaval in Venezuela. For Fidel, there was both opportunity and danger in this eventuality. The opportunity would lie in the convincing demonstration it would present of the profound changes taking place in Latin America and of Cuba's role in promoting these changes, and consequently in the additional pressure it would exert on President Kennedy to rethink his Latin American policy and strike a bargain with Cuba. The danger would be that the fall of Betancourt would trigger military intervention by the United States, which concurrently would revive the threat of an invasion of Cuba. A few years later, however, when Che Guevara's slogan calling for "two, three, many Vietnams" in Latin America became Fidel's policy, entrapping the United States into engaging in jungle-and-mountain warfare in various parts of the southern continent would become a main objective of Cuban-backed guerrilla activities.

A very discouraging incident for Fidel was made public on November 28, 1963, when the Venezuelan government announced that it had discovered a cache of arms weighing three tons on the Paraguaná peninsula. This sparsely populated strip of land is some 250 miles northwest of Caracas as the crow flies and would be easily accessible by small fishing vessels from Cuba, approximately 600 miles to the north. The government claimed that the weapons had indeed come from Cuba, a charge later upheld by an OAS report issued on February 24, 1964. As a matter of fact, the evidence was irrefutable, making this the first instance of proven clandestine delivery of arms from Cuba anywhere in Latin America. The next day (November 29,) *Revolución* ran a front-page headline that read, "New Plot by OAS and Betancourt against Cuba. Supposed shipment of Arms." On December 2, Minister of Foreign Relations Raúl Roa issued a formal statement, which in addition to the salty invective for which he is known, included a flat assertion that "The arms that appeared on the coast of Venezuela belong to the CIA." [10]

10. *Política Internacional* 2, no. 5 (January–March 1964): 91. In a speech on July 26, 1964, Fidel for all practical purposes admitted the OAS charge but intimated that Roa's statement—without mentioning it

The loss of the weapons was more than a casual setback for Fidel but was immediately overshadowed by the much greater setback suffered on December 1. Despite the most elaborate efforts to disrupt the elections, including at the end a warning that citizens appearing at the polls would risk being shot by FALN snipers, over 90 percent of the country's three million registered voters cast their ballots. Dr. Raúl Leoni, the Acción Democrática candidate, received a comfortable plurality of the votes as a result of which he became president-elect to succeed Rómulo Betancourt. Government support came mainly from the peasantry, whose traditional backing of Acción Democrática had been reinforced by a land-reform program which, if it lacked the spectacular speed and dimensions of agrarian reform in Cuba, was nonetheless real and politically effective. At the same time, urban terrorism, however bold and disruptive, could neither paralyze the government nor gain any appreciable public support, even among the *ranchos*, the name given to the congested shanty towns that cover the hillsides surrounding Caracas.

The resounding defeat suffered by the FLN-FALN was to have serious repercussions over the next few years in Venezuela, Cuba, and the Soviet Union. The Communist party of Venezuela, supported in its decision by the Kremlin, soon withdrew from both urban and rural guerrilla activities; while the MIR, led by an expelled Communist, Douglas Bravo, and heavily backed by Castro, plunged ahead into an expanded program of rural guerrilla warfare.[11]

—was *literally* true: "bazookas and mortars made in the USA were [found] there, and they were never purchased by Cuba. So, how explain the fact that the mortars and bazookas were on the coast of Venezuela? If they say that we sent them there, they would have to begin by admitting that they sent them here first, right?" (*Política Internacional* 2, no. 7 [July–September 1964]: 164.) Very likely the weapons found in the cache (there were also Belgian and other makes) were part of the booty picked up at the Bay of Pigs, hence of CIA origin. The intention of Roa's crafty remark was, of course, to deceive.

11. However, not before Fidel broadcast unmistakable signals in a major speech on July 26, 1964, in Santiago that he was prepared to cut off all aid to revolutionary movements in Latin America, including Venezuela, in return for a normalization of relations with the United States and the other estranged republics of the western hemisphere. The offer was not accepted, no doubt in part, at least, because the serious

Nevertheless, by the end of the decade guerrilla activities in the Venezuelan countryside had dwindled to insignificance; President Leoni's elected successor, Dr. Rafael Caldera (conservative Christian Democrat), headed a stable government, despite chronic student rioting in Caracas; the Communist party was once more peddling its wares out in the open; [12] and the Soviet Union and Venezuela had established diplomatic relations. By this time, Fidel and the Venezuelan Communist party had publicly traded violent insults; Moscow had in effect been accused by Fidel of betraying the Venezuelan revolution and—the final irony—the same charge was to be made against Fidel by his erstwhile protégé Douglas Bravo after Fidel's reconciliation with the Kremlin.[13]

A Cheerful Outlook in Havana

In the early days of December 1963, no doubt Fidel was aware of the implications of the setback in Venezuela, though he could not foresee the full extent of the disaster. Coming a week after the death of President Kennedy, it added to the need he must have felt for reassessing his foreign policy. Possibly the decision to travel again to Moscow, as he did the following month, was mainly due to the importance he attached to discussing these events with Khrushchev, although the ostensible purpose was to conclude a five-year sugar agreement. Again it would seem that the chairman was to cast a spell over him: for many months after his second visit to Moscow, Fidel did not discard the possibility of reaching an agreement with President Johnson on normalizing Cuban-American relations. In any event, as 1963 drew to a close there was not the slightest hint in the propaganda that blanketed the island that Cuba had suffered a defeat in Venezuela. As if to remind Washington that Cuba had

---

depreciation of the Venezuelan "revolution" had weakened Fidel's bargaining power.

12. In January, 1971, the Communist party split in two numerically equal parts: a "conservative" wing, led by Secretary General Jesús Faría, retaining the party name, charter, and blessings of Moscow; and a "liberal" wing, led by veteran Politburo member Pompeyo Marquez, calling itself *Movimiento al Socialismo* (MAS). Neither wing was a proponent of armed struggle. (*Le Monde*, May 9–10, 1971.)

13. See *Le Monde*, January 15 and July 17, 1970, for documents and discussion.

plenty of bargaining power left, almost daily the press continued to give prominence to reports of guerrilla activities in a number of Latin American countries, including Venezuela, Guatemala, and regions hitherto less frequently heard from such as Colombia, Nicaragua, and the Dominican Republic.

Even beyond Latin America, Cuba, it was emphasized, had valiant allies fighting against imperialism on various fronts. Thus, on December 16 a whole page of *Revolución* was dedicated to "Guerrilla Centers in Asia and Africa," with stories featuring South Vietnam, Angola, Portuguese Guinea, Oman, and the Kurds in Iraq. It was all good news, and so was the news that the austerity decreed after hurricane "Flora" was lifted; that rations were back to normal; that there would be ample portions of pork, rum, wine, and sweets for the end of the year festivities; and that luxury restaurants and cabarets were again open for business. There was even an unplanned distraction to heighten the awareness of many Cubans that the times were indeed good.

30

■

Culture and the Revolution

The Battle of *La Dolce Vita*

IN HAVANA I WAS MOVED to write my impressions about a singular event that enlivened the end of the fifth year of the reign of Fidel Castro:

> *Havana, December 23, 1963.* Spirits are running high this holiday season, both figuratively and literally. The price of sugar on the world market is soaring. Capitalist traders and shippers are not averse to earning hard currency in Cuba, despite the strictures of the U.S. State Department. As a result, the harbor of Havana is jammed with boats unloading wines from Chile, brandy from Spain and toys and goodies from many parts of the world.
>
> The post-hurricane austerity has been lifted. Everywhere people are carrying huge bags of groceries, household appliances, tricycles and gaily wrapped packages of many dimensions. The big restaurants which closed down in mid-October are open again. Reservations for Christmas and New Year's Eve festivities at hotels, night clubs and out-of-town resorts were snapped up in a matter of hours. The slogan of the season is "A Merry Socialist Christmas" and the Cubans are responding with alacrity.
>
> The sense of well-being and security which pervades the atmosphere seems to have stimulated cerebral activity as well. As a matter of fact, Cuba is treating itself to what is shaping up into a first class ideological brawl that will supply plenty of spice for the traditional holiday roast pork.

What started the discussion was an article on the editorial page of the newspaper *Hoy* of December 12 about whether movies like Federico Fellini's *La Dolce Vita* (The Sweet Life), which among other things portrays the flesh-pots of contemporary Rome, and other capitalist imports currently showing in the cinema houses could be considered wholesome entertainment for the Cuban working class. *Hoy* was of the opinion that they could not be so considered.

This brought an immediate reply in the newspaper *Revolución* by ten movie directors of the official Cinema Institute in which the position of *Hoy* was likened to that of the Catholic Church and Hollywood's Hayes Code and pronounced to be a "deformation of Marxist-Leninist philosophy." The battle was joined and thereafter the fur began to fly, with Cubans scrambling to get the morning newspapers along with their special rations of Christmas cheer in the grocery shops.

Here a few words of explanation are necessary. After a year of movie drought in 1962, during which people lined up to see beat-up American films pulled out of the archives while Bulgarian, Czech, Russian and Chinese features played in empty houses, in 1963 the situation changed abruptly. Whether this was in part a reflection of "ideological" independence following the October missile crisis, or of the rising price of sugar, is difficult to say. In any event, a considerable number of Italian and French films were imported, some of them prize winners of recent vintage, as well as a sprinkling of Japanese, British, Spanish, Argentine and Mexican pictures. In addition, some lively unorthodox Polish and Russian films were added to the repertory.

Notable in the list were works by ex-patriate Spaniard Luis Buñuel (*Viridiana* and the *Exterminating Angel*), the Polish Andrei Wajda (*Ashes and Diamonds*), the Japanese Akira Kurosawa (*The Brave One*), the Soviet Mikhail Romm (*Nine Days in a Year*), the British Tony Richardson (*Thoughts of a Lonely Long Distance Runner*) and, of course, the celebrated Italian Federico Fellini. Box-office receipts skyrocketed. For the sophisticated moviegoer of any ideological persuasion, 1963 was undoubtedly a banner year in Havana.

How all of this affects the moral and ideological fibre of the Cuban spectators is the issue which has triggered off the debate. The arguments put forth are the familiar ones, and scarcely require elaboration. No one on either side questions the need for the state to control the purchase and production of films. In socialist Cuba, all cinema activities are directed by the Cinema Institute, which is a state enterprise. Films, like other goods, cost money and compete with soap and cement for a piece of the national budget.

The problem, of course, is the criteria by which the films to be bought or produced are selected and in the socialist world the value judgments can be poles apart, as in the case of China and Poland or in the different periods of Soviet cinema history. Nor is the problem in Cuba limited to the cinema. The current movie flare-up is part of a general and continuing debate on art and society in a country in which nearly all the artists and writers who embraced Fidel Castro's revolution had always had full access to the competing esthetic currents of the whole world.

What is less familiar in the Cuban film debate is the political arena in which it takes place. *Hoy* is considered to be the official organ of the United Party of the Socialist Revolution. Those whom it has attacked have struck back hard, not only in *Revolución*, but also in *Hoy* itself. The latter has thus far reprinted two long and sharp statements by Alfredo Guevara (no relative of Che and an old friend of Fidel's since student days), head of the Cinema Institute, aimed directly at Blas Roca, editor-in-chief of the paper and one of the highest ranking Party leaders.

It is now nearly two weeks since the first blow was struck and the end of the bout is not in sight. What next? The tipsters say Fidel Castro will let the boys slug it out while he takes time off to see *La Dolce Vita*. Then he'll probably have something to say about the matter. Meanwhile, one thing it clear: life is far from dull in socialist Cuba.[1]

La Dolce Vita Tolerated

Fidel's response to the "battle of *La Dolce Vita*" was quietly to put an end to it without any pronouncement, but not to remove the film or any other capitalist import from the movie circuits. However, as was later revealed, he was dismayed by the controversy, not because of the impact of the Fellini picture on the Cuban specta-

1. Most of this memoir appeared in the *National Guardian*, New York, January 9, 1964. At the time, Polish films were in the vanguard of the east European cinema, shortly to be displaced by the Czech *nouvelle vague* which was very popular in Cuba. *La Dolce Vita*, released in Rome in 1960, featured Marcello Mastroianni and Anita Ekberg. It was exhibited and praised in New York in April 1961.

tors—there was little he could do about it in any case that would not be counterproductive, because it was tremendously popular, especially among the university students to whose reactions he always attached special importance—but because it opened up the wounds of the quarrel between the "old" and the "new" Communists, and at a most inopportune time, shortly before his second visit to Moscow.

Fidel's views concerning the problem were narrowly political and wholly pragmatic rather than ideological, and they were certainly not influenced by any dogmatic approach either to the esthetics or the ethics of the film. Indeed, given his bourgeois Cuban background, his sophistication, and his high sense of humor, he must have thoroughly enjoyed the picture. However, he would have gladly sacrificed *La Dolce Vita*—and the intellectual principles that its screening in Havana upheld—as he in effect admitted three months later at the height of a much more serious rift in the party. "The truly revolutionary artist is the one for whom the socialist revolution is more important than his art," he declared, meaning, of course the "revolution" as Fidel defined it and would redefine it from time to time. He even went so far as to lay the blame for the episode not on Blas Roca but on his critics who thoughtlessly escalated an editorial into a major scandal.[2]

There was apprehension in intellectual circles, particularly when Segundo Casáliz, a popular columnist in *Revolución* writing under the name of "Siquitrilla,"[3] was singled out by Fidel as a major culprit in "heating up" passions both in the *Dolce Vita* and

2. *Revolución*, March 27, 1964, at the trial of former PSP associate Marcos Rodríguez, whose complicity with Batista's police in the killing of four students who survived the assault on the Palace in 1957 was belatedly discovered. (See reference to the trial on p. 35, above.) Fidel's dictum on the "truly revolutionary artist" carried quite different connotations from the judgment he pronounced on June 30, 1961, at the time of the *Lunes de Revolución* confrontation: "For those within the Revolution, full freedom; for those opposed to the Revolution, no freedom." See p. 252, above.

3. The Cuban peasant term for the wishbone of a chicken, hence a bone to be snapped. Camilo Cienfuegos, next to Fidel the most popular guerrilla leader in the struggle against Batista (Camilo died in an accident in October 1959), introduced the expression in reference to breaking the back of the enemies of the Revolution. This usage gave rise to the verb *siquitrillar* and the past participle *siquitrillado*.

Rodríguez affairs and was summarily fired. Paradoxically, however, the cinema continued to flourish, while the realm of the printed word gradually turned into a desert of "revolutionary" conformity and banality, inspired by whatever line Fidel was promoting at the time. Indeed, the cinema was for several years an uncommon oasis in the Marxist-Leninist world, where one could sample the best and latest products of capitalist "decadence," excluding, of course, those of the United States which, among other reasons, were not available for purchase. Conspicuous among the samplers in Havana were numerous Russians and other east Europeans who came to eat of the forbidden fruit.

Apparently Fidel, once he had weathered the crisis within the party and with domestic and foreign affairs in general moving along quite smoothly, was reluctant to crack down on his free-wheeling film people, personally loyal to him and highly talented members of a craft on which he depended for the production of newsreels, and documentary and full-length features largely saturated with his own propaganda. Besides, there was the practical matter of providing entertainment for the Cuban people, strongly addicted to the movies and brought up on American and other capitalist films.

La Dolce Vita Triumphant

Then, again, when a new rift between Cuba and the Soviet Union came to the surface in 1965 and widened in 1966, 1967, and part of 1968, nonconformity with anything smacking of "socialist realism" became a matter of practical political importance. Domestically, everything related to the Soviet cultural and ideological model was downgraded to the point of open ridicule. With respect to foreign policy, Fidel opened a systematic campaign aimed at cultivating the support of the new left, unaffiliated radical intelligentsia in western Europe and Latin America. It was thus no longer a matter of tolerating Cuban abstract painting and other cultural heresies, such as the screening of *La Dolce Vita*, but of promoting them and turning them into showpieces of Cuban independence. It was a period particularly rich in offbeat movie offerings, among them the British film *Morgan!* Superbly directed by Karel Reisz and rich in black humor, this film was mainly notable in Havana in 1967 for its irreverent spoofing of Karl Marx and the British Communist party and for a gruesome bit of pantomime depicting the cleaving of Trotsky's skull by an assassin explicitly identified as an agent carrying out Stalin's order.[4]

A high point in the campaign came in July 1967, to coincide with the convening in Havana of the Latin American Solidarity Organization (Organización Latino-Americana de Solidaridad, or OLAS), Fidel's bid (destined to be futile) to take over the revolutionary movements in Latin America from the Soviet-dominated Communist parties and the pro-Chinese splinter groups. In an elaborate deal arranged at an undisclosed cost to the Cuban economy by Carlos Franqui (little could he suspect that Fidel was later to denounce the intellectual freedom that this undertaking was designed to exalt), the Paris *Salon de Mai*, a prestigious annual exhibition of ultra-avant-garde painting and sculpture, was transported to Havana for the first time ever to the western hemisphere, along with scores of prominent artists and fellow-traveling writers. The display was the ultimate challenge to "socialist realism." It also had an original and authentic Cuban revolutionary motif: a dozen pieces of artillery and a small herd of lowing, strong-smelling cattle that had been ingeniously incorporated into the exhibit.[5]

The grand climax of the campaign came in Havana in January 1968 at an elaborate, week-long Cultural Congress—more political than cultural—attended by nearly 500 intellectuals from seventy countries, including a goodly number of those who participated in the *Salon de Mai* festivities six months earlier. On January 12 Fidel made the closing speech, by all odds the most spectacular since the one he made on December 1, 1961, when he declared that "I am a Marxist-Leninist and shall remain one until the day I die." This time

4. *Morgan!* was produced in 1965, with David Warner and Vanessa Redgrave in the leading roles. Bosley Crowther gave it a rave review in the *New York Times* of April 5, 1966.

5. See the special illustrated tabloid-size supplement of *Granma*, July 29, 1967. On the back page, under a reproduction of Pablo Picasso's *Massacre in Korea*, is a message in large type from "The European Artists to the Cuban Revolution," signed by nearly sixty of the guests in Havana. Among other things it said, "We hail its [the Cuban Revolution's] vigilance with respect to the internal dangers [dogmatism and censorship] that very frequently in the past succeeded in diverting the revolutionary élan from its true course, and which threaten every revolution." Significantly, the picture and message are framed by a red-and-black border, the colors of the Movement of July 26th.

he assumed the role of a Jeremiah among the backsliding members of the Marxist-Leninist community.

"Where did the death of Che Guevara [three months earlier] have its most profound impact?" he asked. "Precisely among the intellectual workers, . . . not organizations or parties . . . who asked why Che Guevara died, . . . who are incapable of understanding and will never understand why he died, nor will they ever be capable of dying as he did, or of being revolutionaries as he was." There was no misconstruing the "organizations or parties" he had in mind or what his target was when he declared, "Marxism must act like a revolutionary force and not a pseudo-revolutionary church. . . . We hope, of course, that for stating these things we shall not be excommunicated or turned over to the Holy Inquisition." As one writer who was present was to recall a few years later, "he came so close to an open denunciation of Soviet domestic and international policies that those of us there were worried for Cuba's economic survival." [6]

In his concluding remarks Fidel expressed his deep gratitude to the "intellectual workers" who attended the congress. "Your presence among us has been a very great honor," he said. "This great honor we shall remember forever! . . . Our Revolution will not betray the confidence and hopes which you have placed in it." That Fidel would soon repudiate everything he said here and would villify the "intellectual workers" whom he promised not to betray was unthinkable by the delegates who rose spontaneously from their seats to applaud and cheer him. [7]

6. José Yglesias, "The Case of Heberto Padilla," *New York Review of Books,* June 3, 1971.

7. A full report of the congress, including Castro's speech, can be found in *Bohemia,* January 19, 1968, pp. 40–65. According to *Bohemia,* more than 900 service personnel—stenographers, translators, guides, chauffeurs, cooks—were mobilized to attend to the delegates and representatives of the press. Most of the foreign delegates had all their expenses, including travel to and from Cuba, paid for by the Cuban government. The meals were sumptuous and especially appreciated by the Cuban delegates and other local freeloaders. Fidel never scrimped when it came to hospitality on the grand scale. The inhabitants of Havana recall that their food and beverage rations were reduced for three or four weeks before, during, and after the congress.

La Dolce Vita in Retreat

Once more the wheel turned, this time in a matter of months. When economic failure at home and revolutionary failure abroad dictated surrender to Soviet political and ideological norms, Castro lost his interest in cultivating the unaffiliated leftist intellectuals of western Europe and Latin America. And as the supply of food and other consumer goods for the population dwindled, so in direct proportion, so it seemed, did the role of the military and the security police increase. It was as if the Cuban Revolution had had its fling, with its ups and downs, for almost a decade and was now settling into a more recognizable routine of socialist governance.

An ill wind was blowing in October 1968. The legal food rations were sometimes hard to come by. During the night, long lines formed in front of the grocery shops by people hoping to obtain their rations in the morning before the supplies ran out. Prices on the black market were sky high.[8] Massive preparation for the "do or die" sugar harvest of 1970 was in full swing, directly managed by the army as if it were a military operation. Two months earlier the Russians had welcomed Fidel's statement in support of their invasion of Czechoslovakia. It was in this setting that Heberto Padilla had the bad luck of winning the annual international poetry prize awarded by the official Union of Cuban Writers and Artists (UNEAC).

His slender collection of verses entitled *Fuera del Juego* (Out

8. According to *Bohemia* (Havana, January 10, 1969, p. 16), for the year 1956 the average per capita consumption of rice, the basic staple in the diet of the great majority of Cubans, was 120 pounds, adding up to a total consumption of 345,000 metric tons. For the year 1968, no per capita figures were given, but total consumption was given as 220,000 metric tons. In that year, the population was approximately 8 million, bringing average per capita consumption down to 60 pounds, or one-half of the 1956 figure. According to *Bohemia*, close to 61 percent of 1956 consumption, or some 210,000 tons, were produced in Cuba. In 1966, the last year for which a figure is available, rice production had dropped to 66,400 tons. (*Cuba 1968: Supplement to the Statistical Abstract of Latin America*, Latin American Center, University of California, Los Angeles, 1970, p. 137.) René Dumont (*Cuba est-il socialiste?* [Paris: Seuil, 1970], p. 242) states that the Havana black market price of rice from January–July 1969 fluctuated between 2 and 2.5 pesos per pound, or 10 to 12 times higher than rice obtained on ration books in government stores.

of the Game) was the unanimous choice of a five-man jury of repu-
table literary figures of the left, from as many countries. An uproar
by the directors of UNEAC greeted the award: Padilla's poetry was
counterrevolutionary. However, in the face of sharp protests by the
jury and others, a compromise was reached. *Fuera del Juego* was published, according to the rules of the contest; but in addition to the
customary foreword by the jury,[9] the book also carried a blistering
attack on the poet and his work—an attack that, of course, he could
not answer. Meanwhile, the army weekly *Verde Oliva* opened a slashing campaign against ideological and political heresy among the intellectuals.[10] This pinpointed the source of the trouble. Raúl Castro,
minister of the armed forces, determined the editorial policy of
Verde Oliva. And on any issue as important as the Padilla controversy, editorial policy, if it were not directly dictated by Fidel, would
faithfully reflect his views.

What came to be known as the "Padilla affair" (as it turned out,
only the first installment of the affair) also included that of the Cuban Antón Arrufat, winner of the drama prize with his *Los Siete
Contra Tebas* (The Seven Against Thebes) and victim of the same
treatment, but he quickly vanished into the shadows. Padilla, on the
other hand, was a poet of some stature and a target of the "old"
Communist literary bureaucrats since the time he was one of the
editors of *Lunes de Revolución*, which Fidel sacrificed in the cultural
crisis of June 1961. Thus *Fuera del Juego* was also published in
French translation in Paris, and the circumstances of its original publication received considerable attention in literary circles outside of

9. The jury pointed out that the "objectionable poems . . . four or
five at the most" had previously been published in the leading Cuban
literary magazines. "The strength and what gives revolutionary meaning
to this book," it went on to say, "is precisely the fact that it is not
apologetic, but critical, polemical. . . . It supports the Revolution . . .
and adopts the attitude that is essential for the poet and the revolutionary." It must be acknowledged, however, that Padilla's criticism, as
truthful as it was wholesome, was nevertheless as painful as a dentist's
drill, as for example in a very short poem entitled "Instructions for
Joining a New Society": "First: optimistic./ Second . . . obedient./
. . . And finally to take/ as every member does:/ one step forward, and/
two or three backward:/ but always applauding." Citations from the
Buenos Aires edition, Aditor, 1969.

10. *New York Times*, November 17, 1968.

Cuba. Among the celebrities who commented on the affair was the Argentine novelist Julio Cortázar, a long-time sympathizer with the Cuban Revolution, who argued that although Padilla believes in the Revolution, as a critic and poet he cannot submerge himself blindly in it. "Like myself and so many others," he wrote, "Padilla is condemned to remain in part 'out of the game.' He has the courage to say so while so many others remain silent. His sadness, but also his hope in the future man, are expressed in these verses. . . . They are not counterrevolutionary." [11] As it turned out, Padilla's courage was later to be put to a more severe test, which it failed to survive.

It is possible that there would have been no second installment of the Padilla affair if the planned ten-million-ton sugar harvest of 1970 had been a resounding success; if instead of an unmitigated economic disaster it would have brought even a slight upturn and a ray of hope for the future; if because of mounting absenteeism in factories and on state farms it had not become necessary to create the "new socialist man" by making "loafing" a crime punishable by prison; [12] if the survival of the Castro regime had not become more dependent on the Soviet Union than ever; if Fidel's exercise of arbitrary and absolute power for more than twelve years had not warped his judgment and crippled his sensibility.

La Dolce Vita Defeated

Heberto Padilla was arrested on March 20, 1971. Some five weeks later he was released, after having written a 4,000-word statement repudiating his work and confessing that he was guilty of moral and cultural turpitude, thereby "committing serious transgressions . . . against the Revolution itself." [13] It was a document in the classical style, except that Padilla did not claim to be an agent of the CIA. In this department he merely stated that two eminent French intellectuals, the writer K. S. Karol and the agronomist René Dumont, were "beyond any doubt" CIA agents. Each had been a guest of

11. *Marcha*, Montevideo, April 29, 1969; cited by Yulan M. Washburn, *Hispania* 52, no. 4 (December 1969): 943–944.

12. Law no. 1231, on loafing, enacted March 16, 1971; text of the law in *Granma Weekly Review*, March 28, 1971.

13. *Le Monde*, April 29, 1971. Excerpts published in the *New York Times*, May 26, 1971.

Castro several times and had written about him and the Cuban Revolution sympathetically, but in a speech a year earlier—foreshadowing things to come—the prime minister had mercilessly raked them over the coals, objecting to their criticism of him in their latest books.[14]

Shortly after the publication of Padilla's recantation, Juan Arcocha, for many years an intimate friend of the poet, contributed a moving article in *Le Monde* of April 29, entitled "Le Poète et le Commissaire." "I tremble when I think of the future of the Cuban Revolution," he wrote. "We have already seen in other parts where such practices may lead." It was precisely during the month of April eight years earlier that his glowing dispatches in *Revolución* on Fidel's tour of the Soviet Union had angered the Kremlin, which led to Fidel's unprecedented public reprimand of *Revolución* and eventually to Carlos Franqui's and his own separation from the newspaper.

Professor Charles Bettleheim of the University of Paris, an eminent Marxist who served as a consultant to Castro's government on several occasions, was more explicit than Arcocha. In an article in *Le Monde* of May 12, entitled "La Révolution Cubaine sur la 'Voie Soviétique'" (The Cuban Revolution Takes the Soviet Road), he blamed Soviet influence for "favoring the antidemocratic tendencies [in Cuba] and a policy that blocked Cuba's road toward economic independence." In a situation "of arbitrary decisions and growing social inequalities," where "criticism from below . . . cannot be tolerated

14. René Dumont's *Cuba est-elle socialiste?* is a well-documented and insightful monograph. K. S. Karol's book, *Les guérilleros au pouvoir* (Paris: Robert Laffont, 1970), is one of the better books written about the Cuban Revolution. Without mentioning their names, it was clear he was referring to them, among others, as "leftists hacks, . . . superrevolutionary theoreticians . . . who haven't the slightest notion of reality, . . . a bunch of disgusting liberaloids, . . . charlatans. . . . Sitting in Rome and Paris, . . . many of them are outright CIA agents and others are idiots. . . . In case there are some who still do not understand: we are not bourgeois liberals. We are Marxist-Leninists and we are antiliberal." Fidel also took pains to link up his antiliberalism with a ringing defense of the Soviet Union, whose existence he described as "one of the most extraordinary privileges enjoyed by the revolutionary movement," and an attack on those who criticize it "from leftist positions" with "an absolute lack of honesty." Speech by Fidel Castro, April 22, 1970. *Granma Weekly Review*, May 3, 1970.

by a political leadership" (he was referring to the visible emergence of a highly privileged class of top army, party, and government functionaries), he declared, "there is no other course for it to take but to impose discipline from above. This orientation is supported by their Soviet friends. . . . It is thus the process of the degeneration of the Cuban Revolution that explains the absurd and disgraceful accusations against René Dumont and K. S. Karol whose books circulate under cover in Cuba and are read . . . by revolutionary youth and students worried about their country's grave difficulties."

Two open letters addressed to Fidel Castro by his most prominent western European and Latin American supporters, among them some who participated in the *Salon de Mai* and the cultural congress, had more serious and much wider repercussions. The first, appearing in *Le Monde* on April 9, over some thirty signatures including those of Jean-Paul Sartre, Simone de Beauvoir, Alberto Moravia, and four major Latin American novelists, Julio Cortázar, Carlos Fuentes, Gabriel García Marquez, and Mario Vargas Llosa—as well as Carlos Franqui, the only Cuban and at the time in Rome—expressed bewilderment and dismay over the news of the arrest of Padilla. It was the first time that any of them had publicly expressed any doubt about the integrity of Fidel Castro.

The second letter (*Le Monde* and *New York Times*, May 22) came after Fidel had greeted their first with scorn and derision, as I shall presently explain. This time it carried sixty signatures, again including Sartre, Moravia, Franqui, and most of the original thirty and among the new names, Susan Sontag. "We hold that it is our duty to inform you of our shame and our anger," the letter declared. "The contents of this confession, with its absurd accusations and delirious assertions . . . recall the most sordid moments of the era of Stalinism, with its prefabricated verdicts and its witch-hunts. . . . The contempt for human dignity implied in the act of forcing a man into ludicrously accusing himself of the worst treasons and indignities does not alarm us because it concerns a writer but because any Cuban . . . can also become the victim of similar violence and humiliation."

The break between the renowned intellectuals of the left and Fidel Castro was complete. As for Carlos Franqui, veteran of the Sierra Maestra and many battles of the Cuban Revolution thereafter, ideologically speaking it could be said that he did not defect from Castro but that Castro defected from Franqui.

The timing of Padilla's arrest and extortion of his *mea culpa* (apparently Fidel, personally involved in this shady business, correctly estimated that the confession would be easy to come by) was not accidental. It set the stage for the First National Congress on Education and Culture, held in Havana from April 23 to April 30, 1971. On the final day, a 12,000-word declaration was adopted, which was published in *Granma* the next day and in the *Weekly Review* on May 9. It covered a wide range of problems in the school system, despite the large investment no less vexing than those in other sectors of the Revolution.[15] However, it was chiefly significant because of the large portion devoted to what were essentially the issues involved in the "battle of *La Dolce Vita*" which had perturbed Havana more than seven years earlier.

This time, however, the decision was clear and unequivocal: "every form of expression of bourgeois ideology" is to be condemned. "In the field of ideological struggle," the document continued, with specific reference to the mass media, including the cinema, as well as the arts and letters,

> there is no room for palliatives or half measures. . . . There is room only for ideological coexistence with the spiritual creation of the revolutionary peoples, with socialist culture, with the forms of expression of Marxist-Leninist ideology. . . . Thus all trends are condemnable and inadmissible that are based on apparent ideas of freedom as a disguise for the counterrevolutionary poison of works that conspire against the revolutionary ideology on which the construction of socialism and communism is based.

15. Fidel had already said in a speech in Matanzas (*Granma Weekly Review*, May 2, 1971) that "there is a contradiction between our country's available economic resources and our educational services. Our educational and medical services are way above what our material economic base allows us; . . . our expenses in education and public health are above our resources and our possibilities." School attendance was another serious problem, particularly in view of the extraordinary investment in education. At a trade union meeting in Havana on December 31, 1970, Raúl Castro spoke of "300,000 to 400,000 children and adolescents between the ages of 6 and 16 who drop out of school for one reason or another" (*Granma Weekly Review*, January 10, 1971). According to the census of September 1970 (same issue of *Weekly Review*), individuals in that age group numbered slightly over 2 million (out of a total population of 8.5 million). The dropout rate was thus between 15 and 20 percent.

So much for doctrine, fundamentally indistinguishable from the neo-Stalinist obscurantism that still guided official cultural policy in Moscow or the cruder version that prevailed in Peking. The congress, however, did not neglect specifics:

> We reject the claims of the Mafia of pseudoleftist bourgeois intellectuals to become the critical conscience of society. They are the bearers of a new colonization, . . . agents of the metropolitan imperialist culture who have found a small group of mentally colonized people in our country who have echoed their ideas. . . . Many pseudorevolutionary writers . . . who play at Marxism, but are against the socialist countries; those who claim to be in solidarity with the liberation struggles but support the Israeli aggression . . . perpetrated against the Arab peoples with the aid of U.S. imperialism; and those who in the final analysis turned leftism into merchandise will be unmasked.

It was the official reply to Jean-Paul Sartre, Julio Cortázar, and company and unrepenting "mentally colonized" Cubans such as Carlos Franqui and Juan Arcocha. Along with it went a recommendation that the "rules governing the national and international literary contests sponsored by our cultural institutions must be revised" and that it is "necessary to establish a strict system for inviting foreign writers and intellectuals, to avoid the presence of persons whose works or ideology are opposed to the interests of the Revolution."

Finally, on April 30 in a speech at the closing session of the congress, Fidel revealed by the bitterness and violence of his invective another facet of the enlarged Padilla affair: his deep personal resentment against those whom he had invited to Cuba at considerable expense to praise him, but who finding less and less to praise over the years instead criticized him, however gently and considerately in most cases. "They are at war against us," he exclaimed, "brazen pseudoleftists, . . . shameless Latin Americans," and at another point, "fakers" and "intellectual rats," who have used Cuba by pretending to defend her. "Now you know it," he went on, "bourgeois intellectuals and bourgeois libelants, agents of the CIA and intelligence services of imperialism, you will not be allowed to come to Cuba! . . . Our doors will remain closed indefinitely." [16]

Such was his personal message to Sartre, Cortázar, Dumont,

16. *Granma Weekly Review*, May 9, 1971.

Karol, and company. Whether it was by coincidence or consciously to emphasize respect for the true Marxist-Leninists and revolutionaries, later in his speech he mentioned "the cooperation of the socialist countries and their support, . . . especially of the Soviet Union." When the applause died down, he introduced "a Soviet delegation here with us today, headed by Comrade Baibakov, president of the GOSPLAN and deputy prime minister of the Soviet Union."

Among the dignitaries on the platform the day Fidel made his speech was Blas Roca. A large photo in the *Granma Weekly Review* of May 9 shows him standing next to Raúl Roa, his old ex-enemy about to complete his twelfth year as Fidel's foreign minister. One who knew Roa, and perhaps with the help of only a slight bit of imagination, could read into the minister's barely perceptible smile, and the hint of amusement in his eyes, the bored acquiescence of the one-time outspokenly libertarian intellectual, who had tasted the hardships of exile and was now mired in the comforts and perquisites of a top-ranking bureaucrat.[17] In sharp contrast was the expression on Blas Roca's face, his broad features wreathed in an ear-to-ear grin, looking very much like the Cheshire cat which—to mix the metaphor—had swallowed the canary. Blas Roca had had rough sledding after losing the first round of the battle of *La Dolce Vita*. When *Hoy* was abolished in the fall of 1965 to make way for *Granma*, he slipped into virtual obscurity (although nominally a member of the secretariat of the party), where he remained during the three years of Fidel's great controversy with the Kremlin. After the turn in Cuban-Soviet relations in August 1968, he began to emerge from the shadows. With the Padilla affair, his hour of vindication and triumph had come.[18]

17. On June 11 he was to make his first official visit to Moscow, "in response to an invitation issued by the Soviet government" (*Granma Weekly Review*, June 20, 1971). The twelve years that had elapsed between his appointment as Cuban foreign minister and the Kremlin's willingness to receive him was something of a record, but understandable. Among Fidel's cabinet officers, he had been the sharpest and most prominent critic of the Soviet Union prior to assuming office.

18. Less than a month later, very appropriately and to nobody's surprise, he headed the Cuban delegation to the fourteenth Congress of the purged Communist party of Czechoslovakia, his first political assignment abroad in many years. The full text of his speech on May 27 was published in *Granma Weekly Review*, June 6, 1971.

31

■

The Fifth Anniversary

The Setting

"NEVER BEFORE HAS CUBA celebrated with greater joy" read the banner headline of a full page of *Revolución* on January 2, 1964, describing the festivities of New Year's eve. In Havana alone there had been 10,000 reservations for the traditional supper—a record, the paper said, and it could have added truthfully that food and service were as good as they had been under capitalism. All fifty of Havana's cabarets had been jam-packed and, the paper reported, not a single "artist" failed to appear at the scheduled "shows" (a term incorporated in Cuban Spanish but restricted to designating nightclub performances). Pictures of the young ladies once more proved that Cuban socialism was unique: it was socialism with cheesecake.

There were also pages of the customary congratulatory messages on the occasion of an anniversary of the revolutionary government. They came as usual from the state and party leaders of the "fraternal" countries, as well as from the Communist parties of a score of capitalist countries. This year being the fifth anniversary, they tended to be longer and more profuse in their praise and more ardent in their predictions of the radiant future to come.

The most prominently displayed, as well as the longest, were the messages from the Soviet Union and China. Each took up nearly a double column in larger than ordinary type, on the right- and left-hand sides of the same page, and were headed by goodly sized photos of Nikita Khrushchev and Mao Tse-tung. There was a marked difference in what each chose to stress. For the Russian leader, it was the peaceful building of socialism: "We are convinced that the

Cuban people will strengthen the cause of socialism even more with their self-sacrificing labor." For the Chinese, it was revolutionary fervor: "Cuba is a brilliant example of revolutionary struggle for the peoples of Latin America." Mao was not yet ready to concede that Castro was irrevocably committed to Soviet "revisionism" and the corollary doctrine of peaceful coexistence, and in this he turned out to be right. Precisely two years later Fidel would convene his ultrarevolutionary "tricontinental" congress; but by a strange irony, it was also the precise moment that he would launch a bitter attack on China, and Mao in particular, for cutting down shipments of rice to Cuba and political meddling in Cuban internal affairs. Relations with China would not get back to normal, a cool normal at that, until after Mao's "great cultural revolution" in 1970. At this time, by another twist of fate, Cuba was once more back in the Soviet fold.

The military parade that preceded Fidel's speech in the Plaza on the morning of January 2 could only be described as astonishing, especially if compared with the parade of the previous year. It was not only the equipment on the ground that inspired respect—tanks of formidable appearance, self-propelled artillery of various calibers, heavy mortars, surface-to-air missiles, naval rockets, and armored amphibious troop carriers as well as the MIG-15 and MIG-21 fighters, and the giant helicopters over head—but also the precision of the formations and marching order of the military and naval personnel, the parachutists, and the contingents of male and female militia. The equipment was Russian, of recent vintage and donated, not purchased, as Fidel would explain some years later (see p. 198, n. 13, above). The men and women, however, were Cuban, the same Cubans who in the factories, fields, and offices were disorganized, undisciplined, careless about their equipment, loath to learn from foreign technical advisers, inefficient. For a foreigner who dealt with the Cubans every day and observed the parade, it was an absorbing and puzzling phenomenon.

There were perhaps as many as a half million persons in the Plaza when the parade began. Another two or three million over the length and breadth of the island must have been listening and watching over radio and television. On the platform behind Fidel were his brother Raúl, Che Guevara (the last time he would be present on the anniversary of the Revolution), Dorticós, the various ministers and vice-ministers, the accredited foreign ambassadors from socialist and capitalist countries, the fraternal delegations from all the continents, and a number of distinguished guests from abroad. The most important of the official visiting dignitaries was Nicolai Podgorni, near the very top of the Soviet Communist party leadership. The most prominent among the unaffiliated guests was the former Dean of Canterbury, the "Red Dean," Hewlett Johnson.

Fidel Speaks

When the parade ended, Fidel began to speak in a quiet, measured voice. After welcoming the assembled foreign delegations and guests, he addressed himself to the people of Cuba: "Five years have gone by since the triumph of the Revolution. Have we a right to feel proud of these five years?" And he paused while a great roar of "Sí" arose from the multitude below him. Pride was to be the principal theme of his two-and-a-half-hour speech, and it was understandable. Five and its multiples are magic numbers; and here at the end of the first *lustro* (half-decade), the Revolution had not only survived but it was strong and prosperous. Consider, for example, the weapons that have passed in parade, he said. They are not the "old junk the imperialists gave their lackeys in order to oppress the workers . . . but the most modern combat equipment our Revolution has received in order to resist the imperialists." With these weapons, "not only can we defend ourselves against attacks by mercenaries, by puppets of imperialism, . . . but we can fight against the best and most fully equipped units of the imperialist army of the United States."

The fact of the matter was that a Bay of Pigs type of invasion was now unthinkable, and an attack by the United States, even if it were politically feasible, would be considerably more costly than at the time of the October missile crisis when Cuba's military capability was already a restraining factor while the pros and cons of an assault on the island were debated in Washington. In this respect, Fidel could justifiably speak on the fifth anniversary from a position of strength. And it could be foreseen that in the coming years Cuba's military establishment would grow in might and effectiveness. What could not easily have been foreseen is that it would make incomparably greater progress than any other branch of activity on the island.

An Assessment by the *New York Times*

The *New York Times* did not refer directly to the question of military strength, but it probably entered into its assessment of the Cuban Revolution published as an editorial on December 31, 1963. Entitled "Five Years of Revolution," it came to the conclusion that the "Castro regime is certainly strong and possibly stronger than ever." It attributed this as much to the regime's social reforms— "new in the history of Cuba" [1]—as to "Soviet bloc help." It was a fair assessment at the time, as was the opinion that there was "no apparent weakening of Premier Castro's appeal inside Cuba or of his stature as a world figure." It would be only later that it would be possible to see that "Soviet bloc help" was decisive in the survival of the Revolution, not only from a military standpoint, but also in making possible by its massive subsidies the costly social overhead that the overburdened and stubbornly unproductive Cuban economy could in no way maintain.

Fidel quoted extensively from the *New York Times* editorial, not omitting its critical comments, and altogether with enormous satisfaction. At the same time, he found one important consideration missing. Comparing Cuba with any other Latin American country, he stated that "there is no other country in [Latin America], burdened by the economic blockade, . . . obstruction against trade, . . . sabotage, . . . subversive activities . . . to which we have been subjected by the United States. . . . Nevertheless in no other country has there been the change, the rapid and extraordinary advance that has taken place in Cuba." It was a convincing argument at the time.

The Role of the Soviet Union

It was not unexpected that Fidel would pay his respects to the Soviet Union. This he did fully and warmly (it was a well-kept secret that in less than two weeks he would be in Moscow), and not merely to butter up his benefactors. Having full confidence in the security of his regime and in the verdict of history concerning its achievements, he could speak with a fair amount of objectivity without fear of diminishing the importance of his own exploits:

> In the midst of our legitimate pride as revolutionaries, we must bear in mind that the Cuban Revolution was only possible under the new conditions that exist in the world; that the Cuban Revolu-

1. "All children are getting some education; the great bulk are being well fed and taken care of, however poor their parents. The Negro and mulatto population—a third to a quarter—is getting genuine equality. The Government leaders are untainted by any fiscal scandals."

tion forms part of that very powerful movement . . . of liberation . . . by exploited and colonialized peoples. . . . Part of that
powerful revolutionary movement which began with the historic
revolution of the workers and peasants of the Soviet Union . . .
[and which is] today the power behind all the countries of the
socialist camp and all the countries that are struggling on all continents against colonialism and imperialism.

Fidel did not always choose to stress the idea that the survival
of the Cuban Revolution was due to "the new conditions," but he
never denied it. As for the Soviet Union being the bulwark of socialism and revolution "on all continents," this notion he would vociferously reject at a later period and then once again assert at a still
later time. Meanwhile, this part of Fidel's speech must have been
an altogether depressing experience for the Chinese delegation seated
behind him, all the more so in view of the glowing tribute sent by
Chairman Mao two days earlier. Nor was Fidel to make a single
reference to China during the course of his long address.

The Economy

His review of the economy was less than complete or systematic.
There was not a single production figure, with one exception, and
this was a prediction. "As we have already announced, by 1970 we
shall produce ten million tons of sugar," he declared and went on to
rattle anew his "sugar atom bomb." He promised other great deeds
in the future, and although he had already accumulated a sizable
record of unfulfilled promises, there was an infectuous quality—
much more than usual—in his optimism on this anniversary: "today
the Revolution no longer has to rely on words and promises: the
Revolution gives you deeds. We declared at the time of the hurricane
that caused so much damage to the country, that on the 15th of
December, distribution of consumer goods would be back to normal;
and so it was. And for the holidays at the end of the year, there were
incomparably more goods available for the people than in previous
years."

This was obviously true. There were other deeds, equally impressive:

Our economic situation is improving fantastically. Let me give you
a few figures, just a few, and you'll understand: when the Revolu-

tion took power, our reserves totaled less than seventy million
[dollars]; at this moment our foreign exchange reserves are above
one hundred million. . . .[2] So you can see how much better everything was in 1963 than in 1962, . . . in spite of the hurricane.
. . . How much better our situation will be in the future when
all this skill in organization, all this experience we are acquiring,
is put to use, when we improve the quality of our work, as we
keep on learning to apply technology in our production.

Few of those who were listening to him were in a position to understand that the relative affluence of 1963 was due almost entirely, if
not exclusively, to one single factor: the phenomenal increase in
the price of sugar in the free-world market.[3] Even the author of the

2. According to what Castro said in a television appearance on April
22, 1960, reserves at that time were $142 million, which was understand-
ably inconvenient to recall. He also said that in January 1959, reserves
were $78 million (*El Mundo*, April 23, 1960).

3. I have already commented on this situation and the related drop
in Cuban sugar output. Production in 1962 in nearly all other sectors of
the economy for which comparative data exist had notably fallen in
volume below that of 1961. In 1963, only in exceptional cases was there
improvement over 1962, as for example, maize (up 10 percent although
in 1964 it was to drop to less than half of 1962) and nickel ore (up 14
percent), due to rise modestly but steadily for a number of years. However, in the case of the two basic food staples, rice declined by 1.2 percent (and would further decline by 34 percent in 1964) and beans
declined by 40 percent (and in 1964 would be half of 1962). Tobacco
was down by 7 percent and coffee by 33 percent. Other mainly less
important agricultural products for which statistics are available show
gains in some cases and losses in others. With respect to most industrial
production, no figures are available for 1962, making comparison with
1963 impossible. Despite improvement in eggs, poultry, and beef (sustained only in eggs), in the aggregate, and taking into account the low
reliability of most statistics, excepting foreign trade, the best that can
be said for 1963 is that nonsugar output stagnated. At the same time, the
annual foreign trade deficit increased from $238.6 million in 1962 (it
was only $14 million in 1961) to $323.5 million in 1963. By the end
of 1967, the cumulative trade deficit since the beginning of 1962 would
amount to approximately $1,710 million. The above data are calculated
from figures in *Cuba 1968: Supplement to the Statistical Abstract of
Latin America*. For a critical evaluation of Cuban statistics, see Carmelo
Mesa-Lago, "Availability and Reliability of Statistics in Socialist Cuba,"
Latin American Research Review, Part I, vol. 4, no. 1 (spring 1969), pp.
53–91; Part II, vol. 4, no. 2 (summer 1969), pp. 47–81.

editorial in the *New York Times* did not appear to be aware of the relationship between the material and social progress which he credited to the Castro regime and the price of sugar. It was another case of a beneficent accident occurring at a most propitious moment —that is, on the fifth anniversary when Fidel and all the world would be taking stock of the Cuban Revolution.

Nor could anyone of goodwill on this happy day of reckoning imagine that the "quality of work," of which Fidel spoke so hopefully and confidently, would fail to improve and would even decline in the following years, so that again and again Fidel would return to this theme, each time more desperately, as, for example, in his May Day speech in 1971: "in this flood of bad habits, irrational use of human resources, irresponsibility, in short, of lack of awareness of this important problem of productivity—lack of awareness in the party, and among the administrators and workers . . . work productivity must from now on be the number one objective of the labor movement." [4]

Signals to President Johnson

Fidel devoted the last part of his speech to foreign policy, which boiled down to the question of relations with the United States. It was approximately six weeks since his conversation with Jean Daniel at Varadero was interrupted by the news of the assassination of President Kennedy. During this period he had come to the conclusion that the chances of a settlement with the United States were as good, and possibly even better, under President Johnson than under Kennedy. He read to his audience several passages from the exchange

4. *Granma Weekly Review*, May 16, 1971. The year 1964 was designated as "The Year of the Economy," the third in a row focused on essentially the same and progressively more acute problem. Then in 1965, came the "Year of Agriculture," actually an extension of the same theme, with a sectoral emphasis. This was followed by three "political years" during the great dispute with the Soviet Union: in 1966, "The Year of Solidarity" (meaning with the revolutionary movements of the Third World); in 1967, "The Year of Heroic Vietnam"; and in 1968, "The Year of the Heroic Guerrilla Warrior" (that is, the example of Che Guevara). The next two years were again "economic," but aiming at the single task of the enormous sugar harvest: 1969, "The Year of the Decisive Endeavor," and 1970, "The Year of the Ten Million." In 1971 Fidel was back once more to the basic, unsolved, and neglected elementary task: it was "The Year of Productivity."

of New Year messages between Johnson and Brezhnev (at the time titular head of the Soviet state). Concerning Johnson's statement he said, "Certainly this is a declaration of peace, . . . a promising declaration of peace." Fidel explained, however, that he had his "reservations," and reminded Johnson that only a week earlier a bomb, which he claimed was planted by the CIA, went off alongside a Cuban naval vessel, killing three and wounding seventeen sailors.

It was unusual, to say the least, for Castro, after expressing his proper indignation over this "criminal attack," to speak of peace and coexistence with the government he declared was responsible for the atrocity, but this is what he proceeded to do. Prefaced by a long discourse mainly intended to show that he was speaking from a position of strength, he made his proposal to President Johnson: "We have no right to intervene in the internal affairs of Venezuela, but neither do the imperialists . . . [and this includes] Vietnam. . . . On the basis of a policy of norms [accepted standards of international behavior], of fullest respect for the sovereignty of all countries, we can live in perfect and absolute peace with any country and any government of Latin America, and with the United States, independently of the social regime in these countries."

The explanation for Fidel's hope and optimism—and he was not alone in misreading the style and temperament of Lyndon B. Johnson—lay in his belief in the new president's vision, in his belief that Cuba had a stake in the presidential elections of the following November in which Johnson was the candidate of peace and coexistence and Goldwater the proponent of war and direct aggression against Cuba,[5] and in his understanding that Johnson's freedom of action—including the curbing of the CIA—was limited by the requirements of his electoral campaign.

There was even the prospect that Johnson would push ahead before the elections. Fidel quoted from a Washington dispatch: "Persons close to the president pointed out that Johnson believes that the United States cannot wait a whole year, until the next elec-

5. It was reported that on September 20, 1963, Barry Goldwater proposed in the United States Senate that "the U.S. establish a Cuban government-in-exile at the Guantánamo naval base and that Washington equip, train and supply a Cuban army-in-exile on American soil." *Hispanic American Report* 16 no. 9 (October 1963): 864.

tions, before exerting the greatest pressure in favor of peace. Johnson and Prime Minister Nikita Khrushchev today exchanged mutual promises that they would make every effort to improve relations in 1964." [6]

National Pride

Fidel began his speech with an appeal to the pride of the Cuban people. In his peroration, he gave expression to the deepest feeling that can move a whole people—national pride:

> The Cuban Revolution marches forward. The Revolution gave our country a name; it made our country known in every nook and corner of the world, where they thought it was an extension of Florida, another tiny cay in the chain of tiny cays that lies south of the United States. The Revolution has given hope and courage to millions of oppressed and has given us friends everywhere in the world. . . . This is our Revolution . . . which is five years old today and which in time will celebrate its fiftieth and hundredth anniversaries!

A tremendous and prolonged ovation followed his final words. It was obviously genuine and spontaneous. None of those present, or watching over television and listening to the radio, could remotely imagine the disappointments and failures that lay ahead, and that on the tenth anniversary of the Revolution, there would be only bitter austerity and hard work—and the tarnished but unflinching charisma of Fidel—to arouse their enthusiasm.

6. Retranslated from the Spanish.

Index